The Human Condition in Latin America

The Human Condition in Latin America

ERIC R. WOLF
EDWARD C. HANSEN

NEW YORK
OXFORD UNIVERSITY PRESS
LONDON 1972 TORONTO

Ninth printing, 1979

Copyright © 1972 by Oxford University Press, Inc.
Library of Congress Catalogue Card Number: 77-177997
Printed in the United States of America

Preface

Our work is an introduction to Latin American society which aims at defining the existential conditions under which most Latin Americans live. To this end we have compiled documents and primary sources from both analysts of and participants in the Latin American drama. We have attempted to present materials which would serve as diagnostic portraits of various facets of contemporary Latin American societies. From these portraits we have inductively woven our own analyses of the broader social phenomena which the portraits exemplify. The forms of analysis are as varied as the portraits themselves by deliberate design; we have tried to expose the reader to the richer traditions of societal analysis. These forms include ethnographic description, history, kinship and network analysis, investigation of social stratification (along the classic lines of class, status, and power), and finally, a description of culture, here viewed as particular sets of symbolic representations. We have also tried to give our work something of a narrative flow, both in choice of materials and also by cutting out footnotes except where absolutely necessary.

One of the reasons that we wrote this book grows out of the traditional anthropological concern for what happens at the grass-roots level of society. Latin American history is no longer being made by bureaucrats and oligarchs alone, but by popular social groupings hitherto unrepresented in the council of state. It is astonishing to us that, for example, the Cuban *guajiro* has become the prototype for the *Hombre Neuvo* when only a few years ago he was merely a prototype for esoteric field studies by anthropologists and folklorists. In a way, then, our work is a quiet celebration of the re-entry of the masses into Latin American history.

In this respect, our approach is different than those found in many other general works on Latin American society. Specifically, it stands in opposition to those works which attempt to reconcile social phenomena with modernization theory. We do not share the optimism of these theorists who seem to believe that Latin America is on the same uni-linear track toward economic development that developed Western nations rode to prosperity some time ago. We can not find a happy home-grown capitalist class patiently developing national resources for national ends, while simultaneously offering education, remunerative employment, and cultural uplift to grateful masses, who are in their turn clamoring for parliamentary democracy.

Rather, what we see is a growing polarization between rich and poor, caused in great part by the growing irrelevance of the masses to the increasingly concentrated forms of production generated by overseas metropolises. As the economic separation between elites and masses increases, so does the tension between them. Under such circumstances, power becomes the most salient aspect of the relationship between the two groups, and part of analysis must necessarily encompass the conflicts inherent in such a relationship. In one way, our account of Latin American society is concerned with the many different arenas in which this conflict is enacted.

This polarization and the changes which it portends make it impossible to keep politics out of an analysis of the human condition in Latin America. By politics we do not mean tugs of war between national parties of international interest groups, although these have importance in their own right. We are more interested in politics in its wider sense: the analysis of the shifting nature of the relationships between definable social groupings, with an emphasis on the power incumbent in such relationships. This aspect of social relationships is one which too many of our fellow social scientists seem prone to neglect. By doing so, they forfeit the opportunity of examining one of the crucial ways in which complex societies are integrated.

In light of the preceding remarks, a few words on the organization of the book may help to further orient the reader. Chapter 1, "Briefing on Latin America," is designed to locate Latin America in an international context. While the emphasis is on the varied forms of economy found in city and countryside, we have attempted to give the chapter unity by stressing that Latin American development has always occurred under the aegis of overseas methopolises. The demands of these metropolises have led to regional development and underdevelopment, rather than to integrated national economies. Chapter 2, "Indians and Europeans," is concerned with conflict between colonizers and colonized in the early colonial period. Chapter 3, "Communities," describes the way in which some of these populations became transformed as they were harnessed to the needs of the colonizers. Chapter 4, "The Role of Religion," is devoted to a description of religion as one of the earliest social and ideological integrative devices of Latin American society. Chapter 5, "The Human Side of the Enclave Economy," is concerned with the conditions of life of the popular classes under modern imperialism and internal colonialism.

Chapter 6, "Politics," deserves a special note. Here we are trying to trace the evolution of political life in Latin America, from colonial times to the present, with special reference to the different ways in which power has been wielded. We argue that the poor have been progressively divorced from access to power since the wars of independence in the early nineteenth century, on the one hand, and that the elites have had their power progressively circumscribed by metropolitan intervention, on the other. One somewhat surprising conclusion is that apparently the metropolitan interests increasingly view the Latin American elites as incompetent to govern in their own countries, and seem much more prone to interventionism than in the days of "gun-boat" diplomacy.

This book has had a long odyssey from conception to publication. It was originally conceived for the Anthropology Curriculum Project some years ago. That august body found this work incommensurate with its educational mission. It then wended its way to various reviewers, most of whom were both uncomprehending of its substance and dismayed by its style. After many revisions, we were fortunate to have Oxford University Press offer us the opportunity to see our work in print. We wish to thank in particular Oxford editor James Raimes for his encouragement and editorial assistance.

Many other people also made it possible for this work to exist. Specifically we owe thanks to Anthony Leeds, whose detailed criticism improved the book greatly; to Marshall Sahlins, for his customary gentle kindness and encouragement when the days were the darkest; to Barbara Bleiweis and Marilyn Sherman for research legwork; to Mollie Lamster and Dorothy Reisman for typing parts of the manuscript; to Cecelia La-Ferrara for heroic general assistance in overhauling the work; and to Elizabeth de G. R. Hansen, for general collaboration and bibliographic work.

ERIC R. WOLF
EDWARD C. HANSEN
June 1971

Contents

The Human Condition
in Latin America

1

Briefing on Latin America

FIRST WORDS

In everyday speech we speak casually of "America" and mean by this the United States. Sometimes—if we take a little thought—we include Canada, and thus use the term to mean North America. But we rarely extend the term to cover that other America south of the border, Latin America, just as American as ourselves.

America, as you probably know, is named after the Italian merchant and explorer Amerigo or Americus Vespucci who lived between 1451 and 1512 and was responsible for some of the first published maps of the newly discovered hemisphere. But why Latin America? "Latin," because the European colonists who in the course of the sixteenth century invaded, conquered, and settled the lands to the south spoke languages which ultimately derive from Latin, the language of administration, warfare, literature, and trade of the Roman Empire. One of these daughter languages spoken by the new colonists was Portuguese; the other was Spanish. In the course of their overseas expansion, the Portuguese reached Brazil; and Portuguese has to this day remained the language of Brazil, spoken today by close to 50 million people. The Spaniards who fanned out in all directions from their initial beachhead in the Caribbean occupied the remainder of Latin America; and Spanish has thus come to be the dominant language in all the former Spanish colonial possessions.

But, of course, the Spaniards and Portuguese were not the first discoverers of America; America had been discovered some 35,000 years before by populations coming across the Bering Straits from Asia. When the Iberians landed, they found the New World already inhabited by the descendants of these people. Thinking that in their westward travel they had reached India, they called these first settlers of the land *indios* or

Indians. But these Indians differed greatly among themselves in ways of life, and spoke quite distinct—often unrelated and mutually unintelligible—languages. Some of these languages are still spoken in areas where large concentrations of the original population remain. Such languages are Quechua (spoken by close to 2 million) and Aymara (800,000 speakers), spoken largely in the Andes of Peru and Bolivia: Maya (1,700,-000 speakers), spoken in southeastern Mexico, Guatemala, and Yucatán; and Nahuatl, spoken largely in Central Mexico (800,000 speakers). All of these languages possessed a rich literature in the days before the Spanish conquest; but today they are spoken only by poor rural people. Spanish has replaced the "Indian" languages as the language of command, trade, and literature, and is slowly replacing the Indian languages, even in their remaining strongholds.

But the distinction between Latin America and what (forgetting for a moment the French settlers of Canada) we might call Anglo-America is not merely one of language; it is also a distinction in the accustomed ways in which people deal with the problems of life. These customary ways of meeting the problems of life anthropologists call *culture;* and the distinctions between Latin America and Anglo-America are not merely linguistic but also cultural. But more than that: Anglo-America and Latin-America differ not only in the ways people deal with the problems of life. These problems are themselves different. We want to explore these differences and their implications. When members of a bombing crew go on a mission, they attend a "briefing" to give them a concise overview of the problems they will meet in the course of their flight. When the President or a member of his cabinet is asked to define the reaction of the United States to a particular problem in some part of the world, he asks for a briefing on the background of the problem. Similarly, let us try to define the major problems of Latin America in such an initial briefing, so that we can better understand the ways Latin Americans have worked out to confront these problems.

THE EXPORT ECONOMY

One of the most important things to realize about Latin America is that it is heavily dependent upon exports. Each country produces one or more major products which it must sell abroad. These products are strategic. If the markets for them dry up or decline, or if prices fall, the effects on the country producing them are disastrous. The following table brings together in readily available form some of the basic information about the export products of Latin America and their importance to each of the constituent countries.

TABLE 1
Export products of Latin America

	Exports as % of gross national product 1966	% of exports to the U.S. 1968	Leading two exports as % of total exports 1968	Leading two exports 1968
Bolivia	45.4	39.5	59	tin; silver
Venezuela	39.5	31.3	95	oil; iron ore
Dominican R.	25.0	86.9	65.2	sugar; coffee
El Salvador	34.1	25.9	51	coffee; cotton
Costa Rica	29.7	41.2	58.5	coffee; banana
Chile	19.9	24.9	77	copper; nitrates
Honduras	40.3	56.3	58.6	banana; coffee
Nicaragua	18.9	21.9	52.3	cotton; coffee
Peru	18.5	42.4	45	copper; fishmeal
Guatemala	23.7	30.9	85	coffee; banana
Ecuador	17.1	56.1	75	banana; coffee
Paraguay	14.5	24.5	45.2	timber; meat
Uruguay	13.3	12.4	77.2	wool; meat
Colombia	13.1	43.1	69.4	coffee; oil
Haiti	11.1	42.1	49.7	coffee; bauxite
Panama	10.3	67.2	77.7	banana; refined oil
Argentina	9.5	7.7	44.7	meat; wheat & corn
Mexico	10.2	62.6	19.8	cotton; coffee
Brazil	5.8	33.4	48.1	coffee; cotton

SOURCE: Compiled from UCLA Latin America Center, *Handbook for Latin America*, 1968, pp. 263, 258 (Los Angeles: UCLA, 1969).

But the economies of Latin America are not merely "export" economies. They also export products of a particular kind. If you look in the last column of the table, you will see there that the commodities exported are primarily raw materials or extractive commodities, principally derived from the mining of ores and oil, or from agriculture. Reliance on one or two extractive commodities, however, has serious consequences for the economy of a country.

Here is what the economist Robert Heilbroner has to say about this:*

This means that they [such countries] are dependent for their foreign earnings on goods whose prices are notoriously unstable. Hence rather than being able to plan ahead for a fairly steady and reliable flow of earnings, they find their export receipts subject to wild and sometimes disastrous changes. The price of copper, for instance, rose by 42 percent from 1954 to 1955, then plunged 34 percent from 1953 to 1954, fell by 27 percent the next year and by 33 percent in 1958. Wool fell by over 50 percent from 1952 to 1958; cocoa by as much in the single year 1956. Such fluctuations can deal staggering blows. It has been estimated, for instance, that for every penny by which copper falls on the New York market, the Chilean treasury loses four million dollars, and that each penny drop in the price of green coffee costs Latin America fifty million dollars. To be sure, as our instances show, these fluctuations can also give rise to tremendous windfalls. No small part of the over-all growth of the underdeveloped world during the first postwar decade was attributable to a commodity boom—a fact which may hardly be reassuring for the long run but which must be given its due.

But there is yet another complication. Whereas raw commodities fluctuate both upward and downward in price, in recent years the manufactured wares for which they are exchanged have tended to fluctuate in only one direction—up. Thus the "terms of trade"—the actual *quid pro quo* of goods received against goods offered—have moved against the interests of the commodity exporter: he has given more and more raw material for less and less machinery. The drop in coffee prices alone in the last ten years had cost the Latin American countries over ten billion dollars. In 1957 and 1958 this adverse tendency assumed grotesque proportions when commodity prices fell badly, following a United States recession, and manufactured goods prices remained steady to higher. The result was that the poorer nations receive some two billion dollars less in actual purchasing power, *which was more than all the "aid" they received that year.* In effect the underdeveloped nations involuntarily subsidized the developed world.

* From Robert L. Heilbroner, *The Great Ascent,* copyright © 1962 by Robert L. Heilbroner. Reprinted by permission of Harper & Row, Publishers, Inc., and the William Morris Agency, Inc.

This Aztec speech scroll is used to indicate the beginning of passages quoted from essays and documents that were not written by the authors.

It is also important to realize that many of the products produced for export in Latin America must meet the competition of other foreign producers. Coffee is not only produced in Brazil, or Colombia, but also in East Africa and Southeast Asia. Rubber is produced not only in Brazil but also in Southeast Asia. Even so precious a commodity as oil must compete in a world market already glutted with oil. The Soviet Union, for instance, has in recent years sharply stepped up its oil exports. Thus, for example, Venezuela exported 30 million more barrels of oil in 1960 than in 1959, but received 56 million bolivares less for its product.

ECONOMIC ENCLAVES

But the economies of Latin America are not merely export economies, relying on one or two economically weak products to underwrite their livelihood. They are also "enclave" economies. By this we mean that the strategic products on which each country must rely tend to be produced in relatively restricted areas, by relatively few enterprises, often surrounded by a vast hinterland which participates but little in the strategic processes of production and distribution. Thus, for instance, all the oil produced by Venezuela (and accounting for most of its exports) comes from the hot and humid lowlands surrounding Lake Maracaibo. This oil is produced on fields requiring great outlays of capital and equipment. Yet the oil fields employ less than 2 per cent of the total number of persons listed as gainfully employed in the country as a whole. The highly capitalized oil industry exists next door to a very obsolete agricultural sector. Forty per cent of the population lives off the land; but the agriculture produces only 7 per cent of the gross national product, and the country cannot feed itself without substantial food imports. Four thousand landowners—less than 2 per cent of all farm owners —hold four-fifths of all the cultivated land in the country. Two-thirds of all farms are smaller than 13 acres, and 14 per cent are less than 3 acres in size. Some 350,000 farm families, nearly a third of the total population, own no land at all. Venezuela produces only half the corn, half the meat, one-third of the green vegetables and grains, and half the milk it consumes.

The lopsidedness of this economic picture is increased still further when it is realized that most of the oil is owned by foreign companies. About 54 per cent comes from the Creole Petroleum Company (Standard Oil of New Jersey); 25 per cent from wells of the Royal Dutch Shell; a little over 15 per cent from the Mene Grande Oil Corporation (Gulf).

Less than 5 per cent of the total production came from Venezuelan-owned wells. During the period 1953-57, the foreign companies operating in Venezuela were responsible for approximately 23 per cent of total Latin American exports.

A similar picture exists in Chile where enormous modern industrial complexes have been built by North American firms, since nationalized, as, for example, at Chuquicamata or El Teniente, near Rancagua. However, even these large mines and others, producing 77 per cent of Chile's exports, employ only some 80,000 of a total population of nearly six million.

Oil fields, mines, plantations thus produce the wealth which Latin America must have in order to live. Yet all too often they are mere islands or "enclaves" in a countryside which participates but little in this economic effort. This contrast between the enclave and its surroundings has many facets. To create and sustain such an enclave, first of all, requires great masses of capital. To render such economic effort possible the enclave enterprise must be large and efficient. It takes money to buy the land, the oil-rigs, the drilling equipment, the cultivating and processing machinery that will produce the strategic wealth-making product in sufficient quantity to satisfy the needs of the international market. This is a task quite beyond the capacity of the wildcat oil strike, the small strip mine, or the small local farm where sugar cane is still ground by oxen, patiently turning around the pivot that moves the grinding stones.

There must be capital, further, to set up the social organization adequate to the running of the enterprise. For such a highly productive unit needs both a staff of trained technicians to guide production, and a force of laborers able and willing to drill for oil, to scrape ore from the heart of a mountain, to cut cane, to pick the ripe coffee berries from the branches of the bearing tree. Accustomed as we are in this country to enterprises which closely mesh the tasks of a technical staff with those of the labor force, we may forget all too easily that other world areas lack the conditions for this kind of organization. There may not be enough schools to train the technicians to run the plants or plantations; and there may not be laborers willing and able to fit the rhythm of their lives to the demands of such exacting work. The plantation or mine is single-minded. It needs men only for their labor. It pays them wages for their work, but otherwise cares little for their needs. Thus it may not always be easy to find workers willing to relinquish the slower and more leisurely pace of other pursuits and to accept the discipline and mute

The enclave economy moves into the hinterland: petroleum plant near Santo Tomé de Guayana, Venezuela. Note that this is a port facility with no surrounding settlement. Oil is simply piped to the facility without reference to the human development of the area. (Courtesy United Nations)

obedience of labor of such a concentrated labor process. The laborers for such a plant are therefore always obtained by a process of selection in which many more are called than are finally chosen. In special circumstances it is even more practicable to import laborers from somewhere else, to obtain a labor force cut off from local social ties and obligations and forced to devote their energies entirely to the work required of them. Thus, for example, East Indians have been introduced into many of the sugar-growing areas of the Caribbean during the last fifty years.

The productive enterprises of the enclave economy stand in striking contrast to the area that surrounds them. The enclave and its setting or matrix differ in capitalization, in organization, in rhythm of life, in the purposes to which life is devoted. Hence the contrasts which visitors to Latin America from other parts of the world find so striking. The tin mine in the Bolivian Andes, with its lights blazing and its high-powered conveyors, contrasted with the silent age-old life in the Indian villages of the high country. The oil fields of Mexico along the Gulf, illuminated by great flares of natural gas, contrasted with the reed-covered huts of the Totonac Indians hidden away in the surrounding tropical forest. The sugar plantations on the southern side of Puerto Rico, with their sprinkler systems and motorized field machinery, contrasted with the small farms of the hill people barely scraping a meager living from diminishing soils. The contrast between enclave and matrix thus gives rise to other contrasts, to gaps in the economic and social order which create problems and strains for the countries of the continent.

UPS AND DOWNS OF THE ECONOMY

These contrasts, moreover, are not new, but old. We have already seen how much the export economies of Latin America are dependent upon the fluctuations of outside markets. Frequently, in the past, a crop or product has experienced a boom, only to suffer afterward the consequences of a sudden slump. For a time sugar might be king, and sugar cane would expand everywhere, even into landscapes unsuited to its production. Then sugar prices would collapse, spreading misery wherever people had been rash enough to put all their economic eggs into one basket. Latin America has a long-standing history of such boom-and-bust cycles. During the sixteenth century, for example, when the people of the Iberian peninsula first occupied the continent, there was much new economic activity and much commercial going and coming across the ocean. But in the seventeenth century, suddenly, commerce dried up,

In the foreground, a statue of the Virgin guards the recreation area of a miners' compound (background) located north of Copiapó, Chile. The recreation area is part of the El Salvador copper mining complex. (Sergio Larrain, Magnum)

and in that time only two fleets crossed the Atlantic from Seville, the Spanish trading center, to Vera Cruz, the place of landing in Mexico. The eighteenth century again witnessed an intensification of trade and a widening of hopes and horizons. But the early nineteenth century brought on political chaos and disorder, to make men despair of orderly economic and political progress. Brazil, for example, first put its hope on sugar cane production in its humid northeast, until a decline set in around the beginning of the eighteenth century. Then thousands began to migrate into the interior in search of gold and diamonds. The gold fever lasted about a century, ending about 1830. Instead, rubber tapping gained in ascendancy, until the rubber boom collapsed around the 1900's. Instead, cacao became economically significant after 1875, and coffee began to boom after 1885. Similarly, Chile has alternately exploited nitrates, guano (bird dung), and copper. We must thus realize that much of the export economy of Latin America is fraught with uncertainties. It should not surprise us, therefore, that everywhere on the continent—alongside the highly capitalized and productive enclaves tied to the export markets of the world—we find more traditional, less capitalized, enterprises of smaller scale—farms, artisan shops, stores—which people are unwilling to relinquish. This is due in large part to the incapacity of the enclave sector to absorb all the people who might wish to work in it; but it is also due, in part, to the desire of people to maintain a source of livelihood not completely dependent upon the vagaries of stock markets located thousands of miles away.

ENCLAVE ECONOMIES AND SIPHON ECONOMIES

Yet, while the people in the hinterland live on the fringes of the enclave economy, they are affected by it. They do not possess the capital, the technical skills and labor force, the command over resources and organizations, which are in the hands of those who control the plantations or mines. But they, too, must sell and buy. Wholly self-subsistent areas are rare, if they exist at all. Everywhere there are stores which bring to the countryside goods like machetes, kerosene, soap, dried codfish, pots and pans, cloth, salt. Everywhere, therefore, the rural population must have something to sell in order to purchase these commodities, and they produce such salable goods in the form of cash crops—sugar cane, coffee, tobacco, livestock, cacao, sisal. To make a crop, moreover, they must often borrow money, seed, tools, insecticides; and they thus come to live in a web of commercial transactions which reaches far into the backwoods and mountain fastnesses. There exist, therefore, well-established channels through which goods travel to and from the hinterland to the more advanced sectors and beyond, and it is through these channels that much of the produce and money of the hinterland is siphoned off to the cities and beyond, to the markets of the world. Latin America is therefore characterized by a duality of economies: enclave economies in which the very processes of production are transformed by the controllers and raised to new high levels of productivity; and siphon economies in which the traditional manner of working the land and producing goods remains the same, but in which the fruits of such labor are tapped through the processes of distribution. The enclave economies set much of the economic pace of a country; but the siphon economy distributes the effects of development through the backward countryside.

THE LATIN AMERICAN TRAFFIC PATTERN

The export economy of Latin America has had a direct bearing on the transportation and traffic patterns of the continent. Before the advent of the Spaniards and Portuguese, the lines of political consolidation connected the coasts with the highlands. Thus, the Inca rulers of Peru ruled the Andes from a highland center at Cuzco; the Aztec rulers of Mexico dominated the Mexican triangle from their capital at Tenochtitlán, located at an altitude close to 7000 feet in the midst of a landbound lake. The new conquerors, however, sought to break open these continental polities, and to drain off their wealth across the oceans to Spain or Portugal. They might use the traditional Indian capitals as centers of government, but the strategic lifelines for their new colonial empires were the traffic lanes connecting the interior with the sea, and across the sea with their European home ports. Hence Mexico City, built upon the ruins of Tenochtitlán, was connected with Vera Cruz on the Gulf Coast, and—through Vera Cruz—with the Iberian peninsula. Cuzco remained a center of administration; but on the coast arose Lima, to act as the drain cock regulating the seaward flow of goods. Thus also Quito in Ecuador acquired Guayaquíl, its port; Bogotá in Colombia acquired Cartagena; Santiago in Chile, Valparaíso. Thus also, Bolivia in the highlands was connected via a long overland route with Buenos Aires in Argentina, a connection later severed by political developments. Where there were no strongly organized Indian states with centers located in the interior, the new colonists from the beginning planted ports along the seacoast. Thus arose Bahía, Rio de Janeiro, and São Paulo in Brazil; Asunción and Montevideo in southeastern South America; Panamá and Portobello on the Panamanian Isthmus.

This orientation toward the sea has fragmented Latin America into a large number of centrifugal units, each pulling seaward and away from the continental heartland. This maritime pull has been strengthened by the formidable physical barriers of mountains, tropical rivers, and fierce steppes which block easy access into the interior.

OBSTACLES: ANDES AND AMAZON

One such enormous barrier to traffic and contact is the mountain wall of the Andes, running north to south along the western side of the continent. It is difficult to obtain a realistic picture of the size and volume of this obstacle. With related ranges, it covers 5500 miles from Cape Horn to the Peninsula of Paria in the northeast. Placed across the United States, the Andes would dip into the Pacific Ocean one thousand miles beyond San Francisco, another thousand miles east of New York into the middle of the Atlantic. It varies in breadth from a few miles near the extremities to 400 miles in Bolivia and Colombia. The Himalayas may be higher than the Andes, but the total volume of the Andean chain is vastly greater. The Andes of Peru alone are nearly equal to the Himalayas' total base area. In height they dwarf anything on the North American continent. North Americans have had the good fortune of occupying a continent with mountain ranges that can be bypassed or crossed with relative ease. Its passes can be crossed at a height of only 6000 to 7500 feet. Suppose instead, that the Andes divided the north from the south of the United States. Every railway would have to climb to passes located at 12,000 to 15,000 feet. To date only one road and one railroad cross the Andes, from Santiago, Chile, to Mendoza, Argentina, leading over Uspallata pass. The motor road crosses at 12,795 feet, while the railroad traverses a tunnel two miles long hewn from the solid rock, at 10,486 feet. Five other railroads penetrate into the Andes, but do not cross them. One of them, running from Lima to Oroyo in Peru, is the highest standard-gage railroad in the world, reaching 15,806 feet.

If the Andes would effectively wall off the north from the south if placed across the United States, the Amazon would convert the United States into a vast network of uncontrolled water. The Amazon Basin as a whole is as large as the United States, comprising more than 2 million square miles. Through it runs one-fifth of all the river water on earth,

The Andes interpose a formidable barrier to communication between eastern and western South America. Highway and railroad bridges over the Rimac River in Peru. The highest point on the Ferrocarril Central (center bridge) reaches more than 15,000 feet. (Courtesy Standard Oil Co.)

The huge Amazon River system carries four times as much water as the Mississippi; it is both barrier and channel for human communication. (Courtesy United Nations)

while the river itself spews forth into the ocean twelve times as much water as the Mississippi.

"When New York City is imagined at the mouth of the Amazon, instead of the Hudson," writes Roland H. Sharp,* correspondent for the Christian Science Monitor,

a resident of the United States has a basis of comparison for realizing what Brazil has to contend with in Amazonia. As far inland as Chicago, the central maze of waters would then constitute a barrier that splits the country. This barrier would be due to the attempt of nearly the whole United States to disgorge the Mississippi, Colorado, Columbia, and all its other rivers from one mouth at New York, and to do so after tropical rains have swollen floods beyond the imagination even of levee tenders at Cairo or New Orleans. Building levees along the Amazon would be as though children scooped banks of sand against the sea. Floods are not controlled. They spread over both banks and often range so far they meet other flooded areas. Such conditions prevail during three to six months over large segments of the basin. If the first thousand miles of the central Amazon were serpentined between New York and Chicago instead of Belém and Manaos, the upper river with its flood area would extend nearly to California.

THE GREAT PLAINS

To the south of Amazonia, running down all the way into Tierra del Fuego (Fireland) we encounter great plains. Sometimes this is desert, covered with the hardy brush of arid zones; sometimes it is short grass steppe. Along rivers, it becomes savanna, interspersed with small trees. Toward the humid zone of the southeast, it becomes tall grass prairie or *pampa*, extending without breaks to the limits of the horizon. This has been the home of the South American cowboy, the *gaucho*, who led his life from the back of his horse. Here "everything lives in the distance— and from the distance," said the Spanish writer Ortega y Gasset. The landscape facilitated movement. Riding his *tropilla* of anywhere from six to thirty geldings—for the gaucho scorned to ride a mare—a man could move great distances. By changing horses every ten miles and riding at a gallop, with the *tropilla* following, a man could cover 125 miles be-

* From Roland H. Sharp, *South America Uncensored*, New York, Longmans, Green and Co., 1945.

tween sunup and sundown. Yet this reliance on men on horseback also meant that the port cities had little direct political influence over their hinterland. Power was held by troops of cowboys, under the leadership of local lords. As the Argentine Juan Bautista Alberdi rightly saw in 1853,

only the railroad offers the means of righting the topsy-turvy order that Spain established on this continent. She placed the heads of our states where the feet should be. For her ends of isolation and monopoly this was a wise system; for our aims of commercial expansion and freedom it is disastrous. We must bring our capitals to the coast, or rather bring the coast into the interior of the continent. The railroad and the electric telegraph, the conquerors of space, work this wonder better than all the potentates on earth. The railroad changes, reforms, and solves all the most difficult problems without decrees or mob violence.

Do you want the government, the legislators, the courts of the coastal capital to legislate and judge concerning the affairs of the provinces of San Juan and Mendoza, for example? Bring the coast to those regions with the railroad, or vice versa; place those widely separated points within three days' travel of each other, at least. But to have the metropolis or capital a twenty days' journey away is little better than having it in Spain, as it was under the old system, which we overthrew for presenting precisely this absurdity. Political unity, then, should begin with territorial unity, and only the railroad can make a single region of two regions separated by five hundred leagues.[1] [trans. ECH]

The first Argentine railroad started operating in 1857, and today Argentina leads other Latin American countries in railroad mileage. But due to the coastal position of Buenos Aires, the railroad network is oriented primarily to the coast and its function is largely to facilitate the overseas shipments of Argentine beef and wheat. Built largely by British capital, it uses British rolling stock and burns British coal.

UNEVEN DISTRIBUTION OF TRAFFIC LANES

Thus we see how Latin America is riven by contrasts between economic

1. Juan Bautista Alberdi, *Las Bases*, Librería la Facultad, Buenos Aires, 1915, pp. 88-89.

enclaves and matrix, and how the magnet of overseas trade has forced the meager lines of transportation toward the sea, pulling the Latin American countries centrifugally from each other. Thus, as a result of past history, the Latin American countries have their face turned toward the oceans rather than toward the interior of the continent. This is true even of Bolivia, the one completely landlocked nation of the area. Once possessed of an outlet to the west coast in the port of Antofagasta, it lost this outlet to Chile in the War of the Pacific (1879-1883) and sought in vain to obtain an outlet to the sea in a bloody war with Paraguay (1932-1935). Rather than being effectively locked together on the same land mass, the countries of Latin America are, in effect, islands connected by coastwise shipping.

At the same time, and for the same reasons, the export economy and the export-oriented transportation grids leave uncovered and unattended a wider hinterland. The political map of Latin America shows twenty independent nations, each represented as a coherent unit with a well-defined frontier. Together, they form a jigsaw puzzle without missing pieces. But when we keep in mind the spotty distribution of the export-oriented enclaves, the meagerness and scatter of internal transportation lines, the enormous physical barriers separating one part of the continent from another, we realize that we must redraw this map and substitute another in which economically strategic areas, colored red, would be shown connected with their ports by transportation lines colored black, yet both set in vast blank spaces inhabited by populations only secondarily connected with the economy and society of the nations that lay claims to them.

UNEVEN DISTRIBUTION OF PEOPLE

This picture of discontinuous distribution of strategic economic enterprises and transportation facilities is also matched by a discontinuous distribution of people. There are 185 million people in Latin America in all, with an average density per square mile of ten persons. In comparison Africa has 345 million, Asia (without the USSR) 1999 million, and Europe (again without the USSR) 459 million. The land surface extending from the southern border of the United States to the tip of South America covers 19 per cent of the total area of the world's inhabited continents; but the population which lives there numbers less than 7 per cent of the world's population. Yet such absolute figures tend to misrepresent the real situation. A more accurate picture could be obtained if we had a measure of relative concentration or dispersion of the population in different parts of the continent. Existing census figures are not adequate to the task, but a report of the United Nations has attempted an approximate estimate. This report proceeds by listing the administrative divisions of each country in order of population densities. It then compares the average density of the divisions inhabited by one-half of the national population (a figure called A) with the average density of the divisions most thinly occupied yet making up one-half of the national area (a figure called B). The comparison of A with B can be expressed in the form of a ratio. The lower the ratio, the more even the distribution of population. The higher the ratio, the more uneven the distribution of population. This is represented in Table 2. This would make

TABLE 2

	Year of census or estimate	Average density of administrative units comprising half of the national population at highest densities	Average density of administrative units combining half of the national territory at lowest densities	Ratio of A to B
Argentina	1960	49.0	1.1	45.0
Bolivia	1950	7.4	0.7	11.0
Brazil	1960	43.7	0.7	66.0
Chile	1960	120.7	1.0	120.0
Colombia	1960	75.4	0.3	200.0
Costa Rica	1960	66.4	9.8	6.8
Cuba	1953	86.2	30.7	2.8
Dominican R.	1960	120.2	31.0	3.9
Ecuador	1950	33.1	0.4	80.0
El Salvador	1961	179.3	78.8	2.3
Guatemala	1950	87.1	5.1	17.0
Haiti	1950	129.0	96.0	1.3
Honduras	1961	31.4	1.9	17.0
Mexico	1960	64.0	5.0	13.0
Nicaragua	1950	32.5	1.0	34.0
Panama	1960	55.8	2.6	22.0
Paraguay	1960	61.8	0.3	200.0
Peru	1961	34.7	1.3	26.0
Uruguay	1958	197.1	5.4	36.0
Venezuela	1961	63.0	0.5	120.0

SOURCE: Compiled from U.N. *Demographic Yearbook*, 1963, Table 27, and *Statistical Abstract of Latin America*, 1967, pp. 68, 60-61.

Chile, Colombia, Ecuador, Paraguay, and Venezuela the five countries characterized by the most uneven distribution of population, while Cuba, Costa Rica, Dominican Republic, El Salvador, and Haiti would be the five countries of greatest evenness in distribution. The over-all conclusion of the report is that one-half of the population of Latin America lives in administrative units inhabited at an average density of sixty or more to the square kilometer, while one-half of the territory is inhabited at a density of only two persons to the square kilometer or less.

CITY VS. COUNTRYSIDE

Enclave economies, uneven transportation grids, spotty distribution of population—Latin America is thus much less a homogeneous unit than a set of export-oriented economic islands, of disconnected traffic patterns, of population clusters. Let us complicate the picture still further by introducing the very real distinction between cities and countryside, between the quickened life of fast-growing metropolitan centers and the isolated and sleepy existence of villages in the hinterland. We have already spoken of cities built by the Spaniards and Portuguese upon the ruins of Indian towns or constructed along the seashores to serve as relay stations in the commercial traffic connecting their American colonies with the Iberian peninsula. Here we encounter still a further paradox, that of a self-conscious, sophisticated urban life set in a wider hinterland barely able to sustain itself economically and more often than not only poorly controlled from the urban citadels of power. The Iberians came not merely to plant cash crops and dig for gold and silver; they were also "planters" of cities, often where there had been but bare rock or jungle before.

To understand this trait we must remember that Latin America was settled by men of the Mediterranean, an area where living in urban centers was old and valued. The ancient cities of the Levant, of the Aegean Sea, of Greece, of Rome, of Spain and North Africa had all been cut upon the same basic model. From early times on towns in the Mediterranean had been built around a central square. The Greek city or *polis* had its *agora;* the Roman towns its *forum.* Around the central square lived the people of consequence, controllers of wealth and power, the elite. The houses of the poor clustered around this inner ring occupied by the powerful. The settlement was surrounded by a wall, dominating the countryside around it. The pattern was copied also in the smaller towns and villages. The Spanish village to this day has its *plaza*, the Italian village its *piazza*, the Greek village its *agora*. The plaza is the focus of public activity. Here stand the public buildings, the seat of government and the church; here one shows one's public face. One sleeps and eats at home, but one "lives" in the plaza. These residential and social patterns were also taken to the New World and planted there together with the new settlements. Here, too, every village longs to have its well-lit central square, surrounded by plants and trees carefully set in concrete containers, equipped with a central fountain, even though the surrounding streets remain unlit, unpaved, and ill-equipped with water mains. For the plaza in Latin America, as in Mediterranean Europe, is the public face of the community.

But it is not merely that the invading Europeans from the Mediterranean area brought with them the custom of living in towns. Like other Mediterraneans, they value life in town and look down upon life in the countryside. Again this is based on the millennial experience of living in towns in an area where civility was identified with civic life, i.e. life in cities; polite forms and polish could be acquired only in a *polis*. The Mediterranean is not an area where living on the soil and gaining one's livelihood with the sweat of one's brow yield social honor. It is rather an area where land has been bought and sold for millenia, where the tie to the land has become impersonal, based upon calculations of yield and profit. The elite that controls the land and its yields has its face set toward the plaza, not toward the surrounding countryside. And people in the countryside attempt to emulate this elite. The Mediterranean is an area inhabited by people who, in the words of the English anthropologist Julian Pitt-Rivers, "dwell in towns from which they go out to cultivate the earth, but who do not love it."[2]

This polarization of town and country, and the social magnetism exercised by the town upon the surrounding countryside, enshrined another hidden opposition, the contradiction between the growing and grasping city and a rural area strained to the limits in its capacity to support its metropolis. We have an example of this in the rise and decline of the Roman Empire. The growth and success of this political unit was based in large part upon the creation of a super-urban complex in the Mediterranean, linking many smaller provincial cities to the great metropolis on the banks of the Tiber. But the resources of the empire were totally inadequate to support and maintain this urban network. What is commonly described as the decline of the Roman Empire is better under-

2. J. Pitt-Rivers, *The People of the Sierra*, University of Chicago Press, 1961, p. 47.

stood as the processes involved in the slow decline of the large city and the return to a more even relation between town and countryside in the various parts of the empire previously dominated by Rome.

This tendency of cities to hypertrophy is important to remember in trying to understand Latin America. For here, too, an urban complex was introduced ready-made and set down in a countryside which frequently lacked the necessary prerequisites for its support in capital formation, labor, and channels of trade and transport. And when we examine the growth rates of Latin American cities today, we often witness an astonishingly rapid expansion of population, out of proportion to the supportive capacity of the existing economic base.

THE AGRICULTURAL POPULATION

This contrast between city and rural hinterland entails some other, more hidden, discontinuities between people in the city and people in the countryside. Here we must remember that much of Latin America's population is still dependent upon employment in agriculture. To understand this fully, we need some historical perspective. When we look at the cumulative development of human society the world over, we discern two great jumps forward. The first of these was a consequence of the agricultural revolution of the eighth millennium B.C., which allowed men to live off a controlled supply of energy produced by cultivated plants and domesticated animals. The second jump was brought on by the industrial revolution which harnessed the energy of fuels to allow machines to carry out the tasks of men. Until the onset of the industrial

TABLE 3

World Area	Estimated percentage of active population engaged in agriculture (1965)
Central America	53
South America	46
North America	6
U.S.S.R.	32
Europe	23
Asia (excluding mainland China)	65
Africa	74

SOURCE: F.A.O. *Production Yearbook,* 1969, p. 24.

revolution, it took nine farming families to feed one family not engaged in agriculture. At the moment, in the United States of America, it is possible for one family on the land to feed nine families carrying on occupations other than those connected with agriculture. Thus, a rough measure of where a population stands in transforming its society from one based primarily on agriculture to one based primarily on industry is the percentage of active population employed in agriculture. Table 3 compares these percentages for major world areas, including Central and South America.

BIG LANDOWNERS AND MANAGERS

But this population engaged in agriculture is itself differentiated into those with greater command over resources in land and labor and those

TABLE 4

Country	Percentage of active population engaged in agriculture (1965)	Estimates of the percentage of the population in the middle and upper rural strata
Argentina	18	8
Bolivia	65	1
Brazil	48	2
Colombia	47	10
Costa Rica	48	8
Cuba	35	1
Chile	26	1
Equador	52	0
El Salvador	59	1
Guatemala	64	2
Haiti	79	1
Honduras	65	0
Mexico	52	no estimate
Nicaragua	59	no estimate
Panama	43	0
Paraguay	51	2
Peru	47	no estimate
Dominican Republic	57	no estimate
Uruguay	17	no estimate
Venezuela	29	2

SOURCE: F.A.O. *Production Yearbook,* 1969, pp. 21-22.

with less command over these factors of production. It is therefore useful to set these figures on the total population engaged in agriculture alongside estimates on the size of the middle and upper strata in the countryside. By inference the remaining percentage of the population would belong to the category of small farmers or agricultural workers. From these figures (see Table 4) emerges the important conclusion that while large percentages of the working population live in the countryside, those who manage or own the resources of the country, or assist in their management and ownership, live not in the countryside but in the city. It is in the cities that the commanding heights of wealth and power are located. It is in the cities that we find the elites that control the fate of the countryside, although the span of this control should not be overestimated. Where a country is primarily dependent for its wealth upon exports, and where the export market is either controlled outright by firms that do not make their home in the countries they control or at least strongly influenced by such firms, the economic wealth that is available to sustain power is also dependent upon such outsiders. Such is the case, for example, in Venezuela, where the government receives a percentage of all revenues drawn from the oil fields as a payment into its governmental funds; or in Guatemala, where the United Fruit Company contributes heavily to the government's budget. Irrespective of the economic merits of such an arrangement, it means that such a government, too, must rely more strongly on the enclave and export economy of the country than on its rural hinterland. Add to this the difficulty of reaching the interior by effective means of transportation, and we discover that what political scientists call the funds of power are equally skewed and restricted, a phenomenon of very considerable importance to political developments on the continent.

PEOPLE OF THE HINTERLAND

It is in the Latin American countryside that dwell the people variously labeled *caboclos* (Brazil), *cholos* (Peru), *rancheros* (Mexico), *jíbaros* (Puerto Rico), *guajiros* (Cuba)—rural folk with little access to the channels of schooling and literacy, polish and sophistication, power and wealth. The terms carry a negative meaning, something like our "hillbilly" or "red-neck." They reveal the superior attitude of city people, living near the fleshpots of command and wealth, around a plaza, where public life counts, against the population of a hinterland isolated not merely geographically but also economically, socially, and politically.

This attitude is strengthened still further in countries with sizable Indian populations. For in such countries there exists still a further distinction among the people of the countryside—that between Indians and non-Indians. Where the non-Indians live on the fringes of the nation but still in some connection with it, the Indians live encysted in the traditional settlements to which they either withdrew or into which they were pushed by others. The countries with such sizable Indian minorities are Bolivia (51 per cent of the total population), Guatemala (55 per cent), Peru (40 per cent), Ecuador (55 per cent), and Mexico (33 per cent). These minorities, speaking languages of their own and often unable to communicate in Spanish, live their lives in villages run according to their own cultural patterns, doubly isolated from the flow of strategic goods, services, and skills.

UNEVEN INVOLVEMENT IN NATIONAL LIFE

We could thus draw some diagrams, maps depicting not isolation in physical space but isolation in social space, which would show something of the tissue of social connections in Latin America.

The first of these applies to countries without important Indian minorities.

The two diagrams would depict the concentration of resources at the center, and the diminishing control over resources as one travels outward from the commanding cities. The further you travel from the center, the greater the barriers not only in physical communication but to common understandings. The world of city people still has many more understandings in common than the world of country people with the city. At the same time the city has its outposts in the small towns of the hinterland, and we have already spoken of the urban pull exercised by cities in Latin America on their hinterland. There is thus often an urban pull, even where the hinterland lacks the requisites for participation in the power and skill system located in cities. But in countries with a sizable Indian minority we note still further the existence of communities quite outside the mainstream, communities speaking their own languages and operating their own social and political order, often in competition with the national order which emanates from the central city and weakens as it reaches the Indian fringe.

The anthropologist speaks of such relatively self-contained patterns of life as *culture*. The culture of the countryside is still a subculture of the total cultural network that emanates from the city; but all too often—

in Peru, Bolivia, Ecuador, Mexico, Guatemala—the culture of the Indian village is an autonomous and separate entity, existing in the larger stream of power, wealth, skills and communications but not *of* it. Much of the recent events in the countries of Latin America can be understood as efforts to move the countryside *nearer* to the center, to tighten the connecting links between them. In countries with Indian minorities, this has meant increased efforts to end the autonomy of the Indian villages and attempts at incorporating the Indians into the flow of national events.

SUMMARY

Our briefing has shown us that Latin America is a world of great contrasts, contrasts between enclaves and hinterland, zones geared to export into a world market and zones organized to sustain local life on the narrow edge of subsistence, zones of dense transportation facilities and zones barely held together by footpaths, zones of concentrated populations and those of great population scarcity, burgeoning cities and impoverished countryside, poor people in the country and managers in towns, people who live close to the centers of wealth and power and communication and those who live far away from them. How are we to explain these contrasts and differences? One way is to ask how they came to be, to inquire into their history. In Mexico City there is a tavern called "The Memories of the Future." At first this title seems nonsensical; but when we think about it a bit we come to realize that the future always has "memories" because it is built upon the past. That past is inescapable; what will happen in the future is to some extent determined by what has happened in the past. Let us therefore explore for a moment the Latin American past, especially that point in time when the Europeans reached the New World and encountered the Indians. For that encounter was fraught with significance because it laid the basis for the future which we are trying to understand.

2

Indians and Europeans

THE EXPANSION OF EUROPE

The voyages of Columbus into the Caribbean Sea opened up a new world for discovery and plunder. Looked at in isolation, it seems like the act of a single man engaged in a mad and unlikely task; but this Spanish foray across the Atlantic Ocean was but one move in the explosive expansion of European peoples across stable frontiers and traditional physical barriers. From A.D. 1000 on, there had been a steady movement of soldiers, traders, and missionaries from Italian bases eastward into the Levant. From the northern fringes of the Spanish peninsula, the Spaniards advanced southward to push back the Arabs who had conquered all but the northernmost part of Spain. This reconquest ended with the conquest of Granada in 1492. In that year the Spaniards began their overseas expansion. In the north, the English began to advance on the Welsh and Irish, a frontier operation often fought with the same ferocity as the Indian wars of the United States. In the European northeast the Knights of the Teutonic Order and the Order of Livonia pressed upon the Slav and Baltic peoples, and initiated a century-long process of forced culture change which has only been reversed since the end of World War II.

These early movements on the continent of Europe set off a second set of movements, pressing overseas into new and unexplored territory. In the northeast, in 1552, the Russians began their century-long march eastward to the Pacific Ocean. The Spanish, the Portuguese, the Dutch, the British, the French, in quick succession, established footholds on all the major continents outside Europe. In this great overseas movement the Spanish expansion is but one episode, an episode governed by the longing to discover new worlds, to tap new sources of wealth, to rule hitherto unknown populations. The three motives went hand in hand. Discovery revealed opportunities for the accumulation of wealth. The extraction of wealth and its transfer to Europe required the exercise of power over people. Thus this great expansion of the Europeans across the oceans was but a prelude to a vast transfer of overseas wealth into European coffers.

INDIANS WITH STATES AND WITHOUT

To discover new worlds, to find gold, to rule over people—these were also the motives of the Spanish and Portuguese conquerors who came to America. In a brief twenty-five years they established their sway over most of the key areas of the continent. But in attempting to impose their power over the newly conquered populations, they discovered one important distinction between them. On the one hand there were people long accustomed to political control from above, living in clustered settlements, with complex skills of craftsmanship, exchanging their goods in market places, with carefully worked-out systems of tribute and labor payments, with armies and courts. Here rulers gave orders and were obeyed by a peasant population. Outstanding among people like these were the Inca of the High Andes and the Aztecs of Middle America. On the other hand there were people living in small groups in scattered hamlets or camps, led by chiefs whose leadership was based on personal renown and skill but whose authority was neither hereditary nor binding. The newcomers discovered that the Indians organized into great states were easily subdued; the Spanish conquerors could merely kill or displace the rulers, put themselves in their place, and rule an organized populace according to already established rules. The other Indians, without states, could not be so controlled. Each group acted on its own, and very often individual members or a group could adopt a course of action in opposition to the larger whole. In relation to the Iberians this meant that any small group could at any time engage in warfare with the new invaders, and any subgroup could raid and pillage on its own. At the present time we are rediscovering something the Spaniards and the Portuguese found out during the conquest of Latin America: it is very much easier and less costly in human energy to engage well-organized enemy armies in a great battle than it is to hunt down countless small guerrilla units. Thus the Spaniards took over densely settled Mexico without much difficulty; but the pacification of the northern frontier where they encountered many small warlike tribes, each acting on its own—very much like the Indians of the Great Plains of the United States—took a great deal of both time and money.

THE INCA

What the great organized states were like is best described in the words of some of the Spaniards who conquered them. One of these was Pedro de Cieza de León, born in 1520 in Extremadura, Spain. Fifteen years old, he sailed for the New World where he fought in campaigns, as he himself says, "from Uraba in Colombia to Potosí [in Bolivia] . . . a distance which I estimate at a good 1200 leagues." Twelve hundred leagues are the equivalent of 3000 miles. Wherever he went he kept a diary, because, he says, "there came over me a great desire to relate the admirable things that have existed and much of what I have written I have seen with my own eyes." You must imagine this man setting down his impressions each night as he camped with the intrepid band of horsemen engaged in the task of seizing control of an entire continent. "It seems temerity," he says, "on the part of a man of so few letters to attempt what others more learned have not undertaken, especially being so occupied in matters of war; for often when the other soldiers were resting, I wearied myself in writing. But neither this, nor the difficulties of land, mountains, and rivers of which I have spoken, intolerable hungers and trials have ever stood in the way of my two callings, those of writing and following my standard and my captain without abate." In 1540 he returned to Spain and died shortly afterward. But in his diary he has left us a vivid account of the Inca and their social and political order:*

CHAPTER XVII

Which treats of the order maintained by the Incas, and how in many places they made the waste places fertile, by the arrangements they made for that purpose.

One of the things for which one feels envious of these lords is their knowledge of the way to conquer the wild lands and to bring them, by

---

* From Pedro de Cieza de León, "The Travels of Pedro de Cieza de León A.D. 1532-50," contained in the second part of his *Chronicle of Peru*, translated and edited with notes and introduction by Clements R. Markham. Hakluyt Society, Second Series, No. 68, London, 1864.

good management, into the condition in which they were found by the Spaniards when they discovered this new kingdom. I often remember, when in some wild and barren province outside these kingdoms, hearing the Spaniards themselves say, "I am certain that if the Incas had been here the state of things would be different." So that the advantage they were to us was well known. For under their rule the people lived and multiplied, and barren lands were made fertile and abundant, in such manner and by such admirable means as I will describe.

They always arranged matters, in the commencement of their negotiations, so that things should be pleasantly and not harshly ordered. Afterwards, some Incas inflicted severe punishments in many parts; but formerly, it is asserted on all sides, that they induced people to submit by great benevolence and friendliness. They marched from Cuzco with their army and warlike materials, until they were near the region they intended to conquer. Then they collected very complete information touching the power of the enemy, and whence help was likely to reach them, and by what road. This being known, the most effective steps were taken to prevent the succour from arriving, either by large bribes given to the allies, or by forcible resistance. At the same time forts were ordered to be constructed on heights or ridges, consisting of circles with high walls, one inside the other and each with a door. Thus if the outer one was lost, the defenders could retire into the next, and the next, until refuge was taken in the highest. They sent chosen men to examine the land, to see the roads, and learn by what means they were defended, as well as the places whence the enemy received supplies. When the road that should be taken and the necessary measures were decided upon, the Inca sent special messengers to the enemy to say that he desired to have them as allies and relations, so that, with joyful hearts and willing minds they ought to come forth to receive him in their province, and give him obedience as in the other provinces; and that they might do this of their own accord he sent presents to the native chiefs.

By this wise policy he entered into the possession of many lands without war. In that case, he gave orders to his soldiers that they should do no harm or injury, nor commit any robbery or act of violence; and if there were not sufficient provisions in the province, he ordered that it should be sent from other parts. For he desired that his sway should not appear heavy to those who had newly come under it, so as to know and hate him at the same time. If any newly conquered province had no flocks, he ordered that so many thousand heads should be sent there, to be well looked after, so as to multiply and supply wool to clothe the people; and none were to be killed for eating until the lapse of a certain number of years. If, on the other hand, they had flocks, but needed some other thing, a similar course was pursued to supply the want. If the people lived in caves or thickets, they were led, by kind words, to build houses and towns on the more level parts of the mountains; and when they were ignorant as regards the tilling of their land, they were instructed, and the method of making channels to irrigate their fields was taught to them.

In all things the system was so well regulated that when one of the Incas entered into a new province by friendly agreement, in a very short time it looked like another place, the natives yielding obedience and consenting that the royal governors and *mitimaes*[1] should remain with them. In many others, which were conquered by force of arms, the order was that little harm should be done to the property and houses of the vanquished; for the lord said, "These will soon be our people, as much as the others." For this reason the war was made with as little injury as possible, although great battles were often fought, where the inhabitants desired to retain their ancient liberty and their religion and customs, and not to adopt new ways. But during such wars the Incas always had the mastery, and when the enemies were vanquished, they were not destroyed; on the contrary, orders were given to release the captives and restore the spoils, and allow them to retain their estates. For the Inca desired to show them that they should not be so mad as to revolt against his royal person and reject his friendship; rather they should wish to be his friends, as were those in the other provinces. In saying this to them, he gave them beautiful women, pieces of rich cloth, and some gold.

With these gifts and kind words, he secured the good-will of all, in such sort that those who had fled into the wildernesses returned, without fear, to their houses, and all cast aside their weapons; while those who saw the Inca most frequently, looked upon themselves as most fortunate.

All were ordered to worship the Sun as their god. Their own customs and religious usages were not prohibited, but they were enjoined to conform to the laws and customs that were in force at Cuzco, and all were required to use the general language of the empire.

Having established a governor, with garrisons of soldiers, the army then advanced, and if the new provinces were large, it was presently ordered that a temple of the Sun should be built, and women collected for its service, and that a palace should be erected for the lord. Tribute

1. A term referring to peoples forcibly relocated by the Incas. Incas generally relocated peoples who threatened to revolt against the empire. [Ed.]

was collected, care being taken that too much was not exacted, and that no injustice was done in anything; but that the new subjects were made acquainted with the imperial policy, with the art of building, of clothing themselves, and of living together in towns. And if they needed anything, care was taken to supply it, and to teach them how to sow and to cultivate their lands. So thoroughly was this policy carried into effect, that we know of many places where there were no flocks originally, but where there has been abundance since they were subjugated by the Incas; and others where formerly there was no maize, but where now they have large crops. In many provinces they went about like savages, badly clothed, and barefooted, until they came under the sway of the Incas; and from that time they have worn shirts and mantles, both men and women, so that they always hold the change in their memories. In the Collao, and in other parts, the lord gave orders that *mitimaes* should go to the mountains of the Andes to sow maize and coca, fruits and edible roots, for each town the quantity that was required. These colonists, with their wives, always lived in the places where the crops were sown and harvested, and the produce was brought from those parts, so that the want of it was never felt. And no town, however small, was without these *mitimaes* in the valleys. Further on we shall treat of the lot of these *mitimaes,* and what they did, as well as how they fared.

CHAPTER XVIII

Which treats of the order they adopted in the payments of tribute by the provinces to the Kings, and of the system by which the tribute was regulated.

As in the last chapter I wrote of the method adopted by the Incas in their conquests, it will be well in this one to relate how they levied tribute from so many nations. It is a thing very well understood that there was no village, either in the mountains or in the valleys of the coast, which did not pay such tribute as was imposed by those who were in charge. It is said that when, in one province, the people represented that they had nothing wherewith to pay the tribute, the king ordered that each inhabitant should be obliged, every four months, to give a rather large cane full of live lice, which was a sign of the care taken by the Inca to make every subject contribute something. Thus we know that they paid their tribute of lice until such time as, having been supplied with flocks, they had been industrious enough to multiply them, and to make cloth wherewith to pay more suitable tribute in the time to come.

The system which the Orejones of Cuzco and the other native lords of the land say that the Incas adopted in imposing tribute was as follows: He who reigned in Cuzco, sent some of his principal officers to visit the empire, one by each of the four royal roads of which I have already written. One was called Chincha Suyo, which included all the provinces as far as Quito, with all the valleys of Chincha towards the north. The second was Conde Suyo, which includes the provinces on the sea coast, and many in the mountains. The third was called Colla Suyo, including all the provinces to the south as far as Chile. The last road led to Ande Suyo, which included the lands covered with forests at the foot of mountains of the Andes.

So it was that when the lord desired to know what tribute would be due from all the provinces between Cuzco and Chile, along a road of such great length, as I have often explained, he ordered faithful persons whom he could trust, to go from village to village, examining the condition of the people and their capacity for payment. They also took note of the productiveness of the land, the quantity of flocks, the yield of metals, and of other things which they required and valued. Having performed this service with great diligence they returned to the lord to submit their reports. He then ordered a general assembly of the principal persons of the kingdom to meet. The lords of the provinces which had to pay the tribute being present, he addressed them lovingly, saying that as they received him as their sole lord and monarch of so many and such vast districts, they should take it in good part, without feeling it burdensome, to give the tribute that was due to the royal person, who would take care that it was moderate, and so light that they could easily pay it. Having been answered in conformity with his wishes, the lords of provinces returned to their homes, accompanied by certain Orejones who fixed the tribute. In some parts it was higher than is paid to the Spaniards at present. But, seeing that the system of the Incas was so perfect, the people did not feel the burden, rather increasing and multiplying in numbers and well being. On the other hand, the disorder introduced by the Spaniards, and their extreme covetousness, have caused the prosperity of the country to decrease in such sort that a great part of the population has disappeared. Their greed and avarice will destroy the remainder, unless the mercy of God should grant a remedy by causing the wars[2] to cease. Those wars have certainly been permitted as a just

2. The "wars" were, of course, the civil wars which began in 1536 between those partners in the conquest of Peru, Almagro the Blinkard and Francisco Pizarro. Almagro was defeated at the battle of Salinas in 1537 and was garroted by the vic-

scourge. The country can only be saved by the taxation being fixed by moderate rules, so that the Indians may enjoy liberty and be masters of their own persons and estates, without other duty than the payment by each village of what has been fixed by rule. I shall treat of this subject a little more fully further on.

When the officers sent by the Incas made their inspection, they entered a province and ascertained, by means of the *quipus*,[3] the number of men and women, of old and young. Then they took account of the mines of gold and silver, and, with so many thousand Indians at work, the quantity that should be extracted was fixed. An order was given that such quantity should be delivered to the overseers. As those who were employed to work at the extraction of silver could not attend to the cultivation of their fields, the Inca imposed the duty upon the neighbouring province to find labour for the sowing and reaping of the crops of the miners. If the mining province was large, its own inhabitants were able both to carry on the mining works and to cultivate the ground. In case one of the miners fell ill, it was arranged that he should return to his home, and that another should take his place. No one was employed in the mines who was not married, because the wives had to supply their food and liquor; besides which, arrangements were made to send sufficient provisions to the mines. In this manner, although men might be at the mines all their lives, they were not overworked. Besides, there was provision to rest for certain days in each month, for their festivals and for pleasure. But in fact the same Indians did not always remain at the mines; for there were periodical reliefs.

The Incas so arranged the mining industry, that they extracted great abundance of gold and silver throughout the empire, and there must

---

torious Pizarros. ("He died," wrote Cieza, "at the age of sixty-three . . . a man of short stature with ugly features but of great courage . . . he was of such humble origin that it may be said of him that his lineage began and ended with himself.") Francisco Pizarro was in turn assassinated by Almagro's men in 1541, and this brought on further anarchy, which distant Spain tried to quiet by sending out a representative of the Crown with the "New Laws": these favoring the Indians brought on a complete revolt by Gonzalo Pizarro, brother of the conquistador, who was urged by some to marry an Inca *coya* (queen) and proclaim himself "king of Peru." The battles, which were many and sanguinary, did not end until the final defeat of Pizarro at Xaquixahuana in 1548. These civil wars killed more Indians and Spaniards and destroyed more of the evidences of Inca culture than the years of the conquest. Cieza relates it all in his books: *The War of Quito, The War of Salinas, The War of Chupas,* and the lost manuscript, *The War of Huarina.* (See the Hakluyt Society publications, Vols. LVI, SLII, and XXXI.) [Ed.]

3. String-knot mnemonic devices. [Ed.]

have been years when more than fifty thousand *arrobas* of silver and fifteen thousand of gold were produced. It was always used for the royal service. The metal was brought to the principal place of the province, and in the manner that the mines were worked in one district in the same way were they ordered in all the others throughout the empire. If there were provinces where no metal could be extracted as a tribute, the people paid taxes in smaller things, and in women and boys, who were taken from the villages without causing any discontent. For if a man had an only child it was not taken, but if he had three or four children, one was required in payment of his dues.

Other provinces made their contributions in the form of so many thousand loads of maize, at each harvest. Others provided, on the same scale, a certain number of loads of dried *chuñus*,[4] in the same way as the maize, and others again paid in *quinua*, or other products. In other provinces the tribute consisted of so many cloth mantles, and in others of shirts, according to the number of inhabitants. Another form of tribute was the supply of so many thousand loads of lances, another of slings and *ayllos*,[5] and all other kinds of weapons that they used. Other provinces were required to send so many thousand labourers to Cuzco, to be employed on the public edifices of the city and of the kings, with supplies of their needful provisions. Other provinces contributed cables to move the great stones, while others paid tribute in coca. The system was so arranged that all the provinces of Peru paid something to the Incas in tribute, from the smallest to the most important. Such perfect regularity was maintained that while the people did not fail to provide what was required, those who made the collections never took even a grain of maize too much. All the provision and warlike stores that were contributed, were served out to the soldiers, or supplied to the garrisons which were formed in different parts, for the defence of the empire.

4. Essentially, dehydrated potatoes. To prepare it, the Indians used their worst agricultural enemy, frost. *Chuño* properly made cannot be injured by either frost or damp. Potatoes are spread out, allowed to freeze, then trod upon to squeeze out all moisture; the process is repeated day upon day until the *chuño* is white and dry. It is of two kinds, *tunta* and *moray*. *Chuño* was used for thickening of soups. No precise period can be ascribed to its "invention," but it pre-dates the Incas by at least two thousand years. (See Redcliffe E. Salaman, *The History and Social Influence of the Potato*, Cambridge, Mass.: Cambridge Univ. Press, 1970.) [Ed.]

5. *Ayllos*, which the Spaniards called *bola(s)*, is a sling, used to entangle the feet of warriors or animals. It consisted of two weights of stone varying in size from that of a pullet's egg to that of an orange. The weights were wrapped in rawhide and attached to the sling. It was used (and still is in Argentina by Gauchos) with extreme accuracy. [Ed.]

When there was no war, a large proportion was eaten and used by the poor; for when the kings were at Cuzco they were served by the *anaconas*, which is the name for perpetual servants who sufficed to till the royal fields, and do service in the palaces. Besides which, there was always brought for the royal table, from the provinces, many lambs and birds, fish, maize, coca, edible roots, and all kinds of fruits.

Such order was maintained in the tribute paid by the Indians that the Incas became very powerful, and never entered upon any war which did not extend their dominions.

To understand how, and in what manner, the tributes were paid, and the other taxes were collected, it must be known that in each *huata*, which is the name for a year, certain Orejones were sent as judges, but only with powers to inspect the provinces, and give notice to the inhabitants that if any felt aggrieved he was to state his complaints, in order that the officer who had done him the injury might be punished. Having received the complaints, and also ascertained whether any tribute had not been paid, the judges returned to Cuzco; whence others set out with power to inflict punishment on those who were in fault. Besides this, it was the rule that, from time to time, the principal men of the provinces should be permitted to appear before the lord, and report upon the condition of the provinces, on their needs, and on the incidence of taxation. Their representations then received attention, the Lords Incas being certain that they did not lie, but spoke the truth; for any deceit was severely punished, and in that case the tribute was increased. The women contributed by the provinces were divided between the service of the kings, and that of the temples of the Sun.

CHAPTER XX

How Governors were appointed to the provinces, and of the manner in which the Kings visited their dominions, and how they bore, for their arms, certain waving serpents with sticks.

It is well known that the lords of this kingdom had their lieutenants or representatives in the principal places, in the time of their sovereign power; such as Vilcas, Xauxa, Bombon, Caxamalca, Guancabamba, Tomebamba, Latacunga, Quito, Coranqui, and on the other side of Cuzco towards the south, in Hatuncana, Hatuncolla, Ayavire, Chuquiabo, Chucuito, Paria, and others as far as Chile.

In these places there were larger houses and more resources than in many of the other towns of this great empire, so that they were the central positions or capitals of the provinces; for the tribute was brought into these centres from certain distant places at so many leagues distance to one, and at so many to another. The rules were so clear that every village knew to which centre it had to send its tribute. In all these capitals the kings had temples of the Sun, and houses with great store of plate, with people whose only duty it was to work at making rich pieces of gold and great vases of silver. There were also many soldiers as a garrison, and also a principal agent or lieutenant who was over all, and to whom an account had to be rendered of all that came in, while he was expected to keep the account of all expenditure. These governors were not allowed to interfere in the administration of any neighbouring province; but within his own jurisdiction, if there was any disturbance or uproar, he had the power of inflicting punishment, much more if there was any treasonable movement or rebellion of one denying allegiance to the king. For it is certain that full powers were entrusted to these governors.

If the Incas did not make these appointments and establish colonists, the natives would often rise and assume the royal power for one of themselves. But with so many soldiers, and such resources, it was not easy to set any treason or insurrection on foot. For the governors had the full confidence of their sovereign and all were Orejones, generally with *chacaras* or estates in the Cuzco district, with their houses and families. If one proved to be incompetent as a ruler with an important charge, another was presently appointed in his place.

If the governors, at certain times, came to Cuzco on private business or to consult with the king, they left lieutenants in their place, not men selected by favour, but those who knew their duties and would perform them with greatest fidelity, and with most care for the service of the Incas. If one of the governors or lieutenants died at his post, the natives quickly sent a report of the cause of the death, with proofs, to the lord; and even the bodies of the dead were sent by the post road when it was considered desirable.

The tribute which was paid to the central station by the natives, as well gold and silver as weapons, clothes and all other things, was delivered to the *camayos* who had charge of the *quipos*, that an account might be taken. These officers kept the records with reference to the issue of stores to the armies, or to others, respecting whom they might receive orders, or to be sent to Cuzco. When overseers came from the city of Cuzco to examine the accounts, or the officers went there to submit their *quipus* for inspection, it was necessary that there should be no mistake, but that the accounts should be balanced. And few years were allowed to pass without these examinations of the accounts being made.

These governors had full authority to assemble soldiers and organize an army if any disturbance or rising should make it necessary to meet a sudden emergency, either to put down an insurrection or to oppose an invasion. The governors were honoured and favored by the lords, and many of them continued in perpetual command in the provinces when the Spaniards came. I know some of them who are now in office, and the sons of others who have inherited their posts.

When the Incas visited the provinces of their empire in time of peace, they travelled in great majesty, seated in rich litters fitted with loose poles of excellent wood, long and enriched with gold and silver work. Over the litter there were two high arches of gold set with precious stones, and long mantles fell round all sides of the litter so as to cover it completely. If the inmate did not wish to be seen, the mantles remained down, but they were raised when he got in or came out. In order that he might see the road, and have fresh air, holes were made in the curtains. Over all parts of these mantles or curtains there was rich ornamentation. On some were embroidered the sun and the moon, on others great curving serpents, and what appeared to be sticks passing across them. These were borne as insignia or arms. The litters were raised on the shoulders of the greatest and most important lords of the kingdom, and he who was employed most frequently on this duty, was held to be most honoured and in highest favour.

Round the litter marched the king's guard with the archers and halberdiers, and in front went five thousand slingers, while in rear there were lancers with their captains. On the flanks of the road, and on the road itself, there were faithful runners who kept a lookout and announced the approach of the lord. So many people came out to see him pass, that the hill sides were covered, and they all blessed their sovereign, raising a great cry and shouting their accustomed saying, which was:—"*Ancha hatun apu intip churi, canqui zapalla apu tucuy pacha ccampa uyay sullull.*" This means, "Very great and powerful lord, son of the Sun, thou only art lord, all the world hears thee in truth." Besides this they said other things in a loud voice, insomuch that they went little short of worshipping their king as a god.

Along the whole road Indians went in front, cleaning it in such a way that neither weed nor loose stone could be seen, but all was made smooth and clean. The Inca travelled as far as he chose each day, but generally about four leagues. He stopped at certain places where he could examine into the state of the country; hearing cheerfully those who came with complaints, punishing those who had been unjust, and doing justice to those who had suffered. Those who came with him, did not demand anything, neither did they go a single pace off the road. The natives supplied what was necessary, besides which there was more than enough of all provisions in the storehouses, so that nothing was wanting. By the way, many men and women and lads came to do personal service if it was needed. The lords were thus carried from one village to another, where they were taken up by those of the next village, and as it was only one day, or at most two, they did not feel this service to be any hardship. Travelling in this way, the lord went over his dominions for as long a time as pleased him, seeing what was going on with his own eyes, and giving necessary instruction on great and important matters. He then returned to Cuzco, the principal city of the whole empire.

THE AZTECS

Alonso de Zorita, author of our second report, was quite a different person from Cieza de León. Born a member of the lower nobility around 1511 or 1512, he studied law at the University of Salamanca—one of the great law schools of the period—and entered upon a public career as a lawyer. In 1547, he left for the Indies where he held a number of responsible public positions concerned with controlling the unruly Spanish conquerors in their relations with the new subject populations and with each other. In 1556 he was appointed judge of the highest court of appeals in the Viceroyalty of Mexico. There, for a decade, he used his great legal skills to defend the Indians against oppression. In 1556 he developed a project to pacify the Indians without states of the uncontrolled north by peaceful persuasion rather than by extermination; but the project failed and Zorita asked to be relieved of his duties. Upon his return to Spain he wrote his *Brief and Summary Report on the Lords of New Spain*, cast in the form of answers to a royal questionnaire sent out in 1553 to collect information on the nature of Indian tributes before the conquest. The report was finished in 1585, apparently not long before Zorita's death. In this report he describes the social and political conditions of Mexico before the conquest, as follows: *

* From Alonso de Zorita, *Life and Labor in Ancient Mexico: The Brief and Summary Relations of the Lords of New Spain,* translated and with an introduction by Benjamin Keen, Rutgers University Press, 1963. Reprinted by permission.

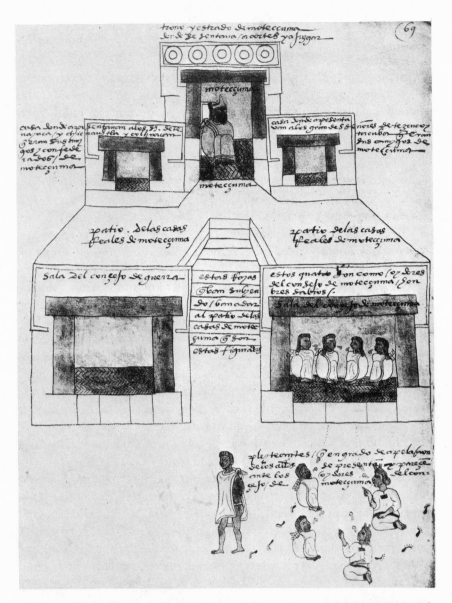

Moctezuma's palace, center of the Aztec polity at the time of the arrival of the Spaniards. This picture, taken from the Codex Mendoza, shows the throne room (center), the chambers where the king met the lords of the realm (upper right), the military council chamber (lower left), and the civil council chamber (lower right). (Courtesy American Museum of Natural History)

The supreme lords the Indians called *tlatoques,* from the verb *tlatoa,* which means to speak, because they, as supreme lords, had civil and criminal jurisdiction, and the government and command of all their provinces and people whose lords they were. They had subject to themselves two other kinds of lords.

If, at the death of a ruler, the son, grandson, or whoever was to succeed was still a youth, it was customary for some old kinsman to govern in his place according to the rule whereby the closest relative who was qualified was chosen to act as regent. If there was no suitable relative, they chose some other principal, who was elected for this purpose and confirmed by another ruler. For Texcoco and Tacuba the confirmation was made by the ruler of Mexico, and for Mexico, by the rulers of Texcoco and Tacuba. The regent was, as it were, a tutor or guardian for the youthful new ruler. On the regent's death (for he held power during life) the successor named by the deceased ruler took office. This arrangement prevailed not only in regard to the supreme lord but in regard to the inferior lords of provinces in which they were supreme. Some maintain that if the guardian or assistant was a relative, he lost his post when the young ruler came of age, but that the latter continued to consult the former guardian in all the work of government. They also say that if the regent was not a relative, his power expired when the lord came of age. I found this was the case in a large town near Guatemala City. The age of majority for the ruler was thirty and over.

From the above it is evident that, aside from the ceremonies, almost all they did in the matter of succession and election of their rulers conformed to Natural Law, and in some degree to the Divine Law, and even to Civil and Canon Law, although they were ignorant of this. I could cite other things to show that these people are not so devoid of intelligence as some people assert. The same conclusion flows from many other things to be told of in this book and in my treatise on tributes. As occasion offers, I shall single out and call attention to these things.

Lords of the second kind were called *tectecutzin* or *teules.* They were of many sorts and were named after their dignities and pre-eminencies, which, being very long and not to the point, I omit. They were like the *comendadores* of Spain, who hold *encomiendas,* [royal grants of tribute in labor or kind; eds.] some being of greater value and income than others.

It may be of interest to note that in naming dignities and offices, and also towns, mountains, forests, and the like, the Indians assigned names that indicated the quality or property of each place, its fertility or infertility, or the things in which it abounded. Thus they gave Michoacán its name because it was a land of many fish, and Tehuantepec was so named because it was a land of vipers, and so on.

The lords who were called tectecutzin, or teules, in the plural, held office for life, because the rulers promoted them to these dignities for their exploits in war or in the service of the state or the supreme lords. The rulers rewarded these lords with these dignities, just as Your Majesty grants an encomienda for life. Some of these dignities were high, others of an inferior kind.

The houses of these lords were named *teccalli*, which means the place of such a lord (from *teccutli*, "lord," and *calli*, "house"). This teccutli or lord had command and dominion over certain people attached to that teccalli, and some had command over more people than others.

The benefits these lords received were these: Their people gave them personal service in their households and brought them fuel and water, the assignment of tasks being made by the lord. Their people also worked certain fields for the lords, the size of the fields depending upon the number of people. Because of this they were exempt from service to the ruler and from working his fields, and their only other obligation to the ruler was to serve in time of war, from which none was excused. In addition, the ruler furnished them with wages, meals, and lodging, for they served as gentlemen in waiting in his palace.

These lords were responsible for the working of the fields, both for themselves and for their people, and they had overseers who saw to this. The lords also had the duty of looking after the people in their charge, of defending and protecting them. Thus these lords were appointed and intended to serve the general as well as their private good.

When one of these lords died, the ruler granted his dignity to one who merited it by his services, and a son did not succeed his father unless the ruler promoted him to this dignity. The rulers always inclined, however, to give preference to sons over others, if they deserved it. Otherwise they remained *pilles*, which means *principales* or *hidalgos* [petty nobles; eds.].

Lords of the third kind are called *calpullec*, or *chinancallec*, in the plural. This word means heads or elders of very ancient ancestry, and comes from *calpulli*, or *chinancalli* (both mean the same). A calpulli or chinancalli is a barrio of known people or an ancient lineage which holds its lands and boundaries from a time of great antiquity. These lands belong to the said kindred, *barrio,* [neighborhood; eds.] or lineage, and they call such lands calpulli, meaning the lands of that barrio or lineage.

There are many such calpullec or lineages or barrios in each province. The barrios assigned for life to lords of the second class had their heads or calpulli. The lands these barrios possess they obtained in the distribution made when these people first came to this land. At that time each lineage or group obtained its shares or lots of land with their bounds, which were assigned to them and their descendants. These lands, which they call calpulli, they still possess today. They do not hold them individually but communally. Individuals cannot alienate their lots, but can enjoy their use for life and leave them to their sons and heirs.

Calpulli is the singular, calpullec the plural form of the word. Some of these calpullec or barrios or lineages are larger than others, and some possess more land than others, depending on the manner in which the ancient conquerors and settlers apportioned the lands among the various lineages. If a certain family dies out, the lands remain in the common ownership of the calpulli, and the head or chief elder assigns them to some other member of the same barrio who has need of them.

Thus the Indians never give these lands to a person who is not a member of the calpulli or barrio, just as the Israelites were not permitted to alienate their tribal lands and possessions. This, by the way, is one reason why some are disposed to believe that the natives of these regions descend from the people of Israel, since many of their ceremonies, practices, and customs conform with those of that people. Thus it is said that the language of Michoacan, which once was a great kingdom, has many Hebrew words; and this and almost all other Indian languages resemble Hebrew in their pronunciation. Men who have traveled in the provinces of Peru and other parts of the Indies make the same point about the rites and ceremonies of those regions. The calpullec of New Spain are what the Israelites called "tribes."

A barrio or calpulli might rent land to another barrio in order to meet the public and communal needs of the renting calpulli. Only for this reason, and no other, could land be rented. If it can be helped, the Indians never allow people of one calpulli to work the lands of another, that there may be no mixing of the two groups and that none may leave his lineage.

One reason why the Indians rented these lands, instead of allowing another calpulli to have them for nothing, was that sometimes the land they gave had already been cultivated. The rent was small or simply a part of the harvest, depending on the terms of the agreement. Members of one calpulli would rent from another because the land was better than that which they had or received from their calpulli or because their calpulli had no more land to distribute, or because they could work both their own and the rented fields.

If a member of one calpulli or barrio went to live in another, he lost the lands that had been assigned to him for cultivation. This is a most ancient custom among them, and one that is never broken or contravened in any way. The vacated fields remain the common property of the calpulli; and the chief elder distributes them among landless members of the barrio.

If some land is left vacant or becomes uncultivated in a calpulli, the Indians take great care lest the member of another calpulli encroach upon it. They engage in great litigation over this, each calpulli hotly defending its lands.

If a member of a calpulli has no land, the chief elder, in consultation with the other elders, gives him land in accordance with his needs, condition, and capacity to work it, and he can pass on this land to his heirs. The chief elder does nothing without consulting the other elders of the calpulli or barrio.

If a member of a calpulli held land and cultivated it, no one could intrude on this land, nor could the chief elder take it away and give it to someone else. If the land was not good, he could leave it and look for other land that was better and apply to the chief elder for such land. If this land was vacant and could be given without prejudice to another, it was given to him in the manner aforesaid.

A person who held land from his calpulli and did not work it for two years running through his own fault and negligence, or without such just cause, such as the condition of being a minor, an orphan, very old, or too ill to work, received warning that he must work it the next year or lose it to another. And so it was done.

Inasmuch as this land is the communal property of the calpullec or barrios, there has been much impropriety in allotting it to Spaniards. Let some Spaniard observe or learn that some of this land is not being cultivated, and he will apply to the governor for it. As a rule the individual who is appointed to look into the matter has little interest in the Indians' welfare. If by some chance a good Christian is appointed, the petitioner usually finds ways and means of having him replaced by another more satisfactory to himself, especially if there is some possibility of collusion or bribery, which is ever present. As a result, the examiner invariably submits the opinion that the land can be given to the petitioner without prejudice to another, because it is lying idle. It does no good for the people of the barrio or calpulli to contradict him, to offer proofs that the land has been cultivated, and to affirm that the land is being held in reserve for landless members or those who marry. The officials reply that it is all a clever ruse. Incorrect information of this kind was given to Your Majesty by some persons who seem to have had a personal interest in the question, as appears from a section of a letter that Your Majesty sent to the Audiencia [Viceregal Court; eds.] of Mexico City in September 1556.

To give a field or other land to a Spaniard is to cause great injury to the Indians. The Spaniards have taken their lands, pushed back their boundaries, and put them to an endless labor of guarding their fields against the Spaniards' cattle, yet those cattle continue to eat and destroy the Indians' crops. Sometimes an official will give away Indian land that is under cultivation or sowed, claiming that cultivation is a mere ruse designed to keep the land out of Spanish hands. That is why some Indian towns already are so diminished and encircled by Spanish farms that the natives have no space in which to plant. Elsewhere their fields are surrounded by cattle ranches from which they receive great injury, for their small plantings are destroyed or eaten by the cattle, which wander about without restraint. In vain do the Indians keep watch day and night over their fields. As a result they suffer need and hunger throughout the year. There are still other impediments to their sowing and enjoying the fruits of what they sow, as will presently be told.

Failure to comprehend that the calpullec or barrios hold their lands in common has been the cause of the Indians' having been left without enough land for their needs. This is especially true of towns that are situated near the Spanish towns or that have good land. Great mischief has been done by taking the land from the Indians. Great harm has also been done by herds belonging to the encomenderos, who always keep their cattle in the towns they hold in encomienda.

The commoners of these barrios or calpullec always have a head, and cannot conceive of being without such a head or elder. He must be one of them and not of another calpulli, nor a foreigner, for they would not suffer such a thing. He must be a principal, and capable of defending and protecting them. They choose him from among themselves and hold him for their lord; he is like the *pariente mayor* in Biscay or the Montana. He does not hold office by right of succession, for on the death of an elder they choose another, an old man whom they regard as best qualified because he is the wisest, most honorable, and ablest of all. If the deceased elder left an eligible son, they elect him, always choosing a relative of the deceased if suitable for the post.

This principal is responsible for guarding and defending the calpulli lands. He has pictures on which are shown all the parcels, and the boundaries, and where and with whose fields the lots meet, and who cultivates what field, and what land each one has. The paintings also show which lands are vacant, and which have been given to Spaniards, and by and to whom and when they were given. The Indians continually alter these pictures according to the changes worked by time, and they understand perfectly what these pictures show. It is also the business of the elder to give land to one who needs it; or, if his family has outgrown his parcel of land, to give him more. The elder is also responsible for protecting the people of the calpulli and for representing them before the Spanish judge and governors. The members of the calpulli also meet in the principal's house to deliberate concerning the group's needs and the payment of tribute, and to plan their festivals. This is very expensive for the elder, for to keep his guests happy and peaceful he must provide them with food and drink at these meetings, which are held frequently throughout the year.

I shall tell of the revenue that these lords receive, and how they defray the cost of entertaining the commoners, in my reply to the fourth article of the royal cédula [decree; eds.].

One must understand the concord and unity that once prevailed in these calpulli if one would treat them justly and put an end to the confusion that now prevails in almost all of them. Today they are so divided that they can never return to the peace and order they once enjoyed. Because Spanish officials have made no effort to understand this communal system, they have adjudged to many Indians as private property lands which they held from their calpulli, simply because these persons could prove that they and their forebears had possessed and worked such land. These Indians have been cajoled into doing this by Spaniards and mulattoes and mestizos who exploit and profit by their folly. In vain do the principales contradict what these Indians say and explain with loud remonstrance that the land belongs to the calpulli. They are not heard, and this is a great injury to the other members of the calpulli, for the individuals to whom the land is adjudged as private property sell and alienate it to the prejudice of the calpulli.

Lords of the fourth class were such by virtue not of dominion or command, but of lineage. These lords were called *pipiltzin*, which is a general term denoting nobles, or as we would say in Castile, caballeros. This category included all the sons of the supreme lords or rulers, who were called *tlacopipiltzin* ("sons of rulers"), and all their grandsons and great-grandsons, whom they called *pipiltzintl*. This class included other persons called *tecquiuac*, who were hidalgos, sons of nobles holding important charges. All these and their successors were free of tribute because they were hidalgos and warriors. A certain number of them were always in attendance in the ruler's palace as ambassadors to various regions, and were reassigned by his order; they also served as his ministers and executors of justice. In addition to being free from tribute they had many other privileges, and the ruler provided them with wages and board. Now, however, they are reduced to tribute-payers, and are abased, miserable, and poor.

The second part of this article asks about the power and jurisdiction that these caciques and lords exercised in the time of their heathendom. I reply that the supreme lords had civil and criminal jurisdiction, and appointed governors and officials and ministers for the administration and execution of justice. My replies to the questions that follow, being the third and fourth parts of this article, will throw more light on the matter.

In order to reply to the third part of this article, which asks what power these lords exercise at present, I must first explain their mode of government before and immediately after the land was conquered by the Spaniards. For a better understanding of this, it should be noted that the Mexican kings and their allies, the kings of Texcoco and Tacuba, left the natural lords of these provinces in command of all the land they conquered and acquired. This was true of the lesser as well as the supreme lords. They also allowed all the commoners to keep their land and property, and permitted them to retain their customs and practices and mode of government. The kings of Mexico, Texcoco, and Tacuba reserved for themselves certain lands which were cultivated for them by all the commoners. On these lands were grown the things that each region yielded. The conquered people did this by way of tribute and in acknowledgment of vassalship. The commoners brought the produce to the majordomos whom the native ruler appointed for the collection of tribute, and these majordomos in turn took it to the persons sent thither for the purpose by the ruler of Mexico, or Texcoco, or Tacuba. Each person thus paid tribute to the ruler whose subject he had become and to whom he owed the duty of obedience and service in war. This was the general rule in all the provinces subject to the Confederacy. The former rulers preserved all their former authority and governmental power, with civil and criminal jurisdiction.

In the provinces not subject to the Confederacy, such as Michoacan, Metztitlan, Tlaxcala, Tepeaca, Cholula, Huexotcingo, and Yopitzinco, Acapulco, Acatepec, and others, government was in the hands of native rulers. The people brought them tribute consisting of the things they grew. The common and general mode of paying tribute consisted in the payment in kind of the things that were grown or made in the land, each man paying in the products of his craft or trade. The whole of what each man gave was small, representing little value and less labor. But since the number of people was very great, a large quantity of tribute was collected.

When New Spain was conquered by the Spaniards, this mode of government of the natives was retained and continued for some years. Moctezuma alone lost his kingdom and dominion, which were vested in the royal Crown of Castile. Some of his towns were given in encomienda to Spaniards. All the other lords of provinces, both those who were subject to him and those who were independent, including the rulers of Texcoco and Tacuba, possessed, ruled, and governed their lands, but they did this as representatives of Your Majesty or of encomenderos. These lords did not have as much land or as many vassals as they had once had, but the people brought them tribute of produce and other things as before the Conquest, and they were obeyed, feared, and respected. The towns that they retained also brought them tribute to give to Your Majesty and the encomenderos. Each ruler appointed persons to collect this tribute; and Your Majesty's officials in the Crown towns and the encomenderos in their towns received the tribute from the ruler.

Thus the ancient dignity and authority of the rulers were preserved, and they were well obeyed by their subjects, who served them in their ancient way by giving them tribute and service. Even today, in both Crown and encomienda towns, the Spaniards make the lords responsible for the collection of tribute. The Spaniards even harass the lords about this, although they are ruined and abased and are no longer obeyed by their subjects.

At that time the alcalde's rod of justice was unknown, and there were no *gobernadores* or *alguaciles* [bailiffs; eds.], those agents of abuse and ruination of the lords. One cause of their downfall has been the arbitrary action of the encomenderos, who stripped the lords of their authority if they would not do the Spaniards' will in regard to tribute and personal service. In the lord's place they would set up some macehual who would do all that was demanded of him. The example of the encomenderos was followed by the *calpisques*, persons appointed by the encomenderos to compel the people in their towns to give personal service daily, and to rent out their service to others, to send people to the mines, to compel payment of tribute, and to harass the lords and all the commoners in every way they could think of. These calpisques also removed and set up lords at their will and pleasure.

The result of having appointed all the alcaldes, *regidores*, alguaciles, and fiscales, of whom there are now a great many, is that many of them rob the common people, and do so brazenly, with no one to say them nay. The *escribano de gobernación* draws in a pile of money at the beginning of every year, for all these officials run to the governor for confirmation of their posts. Some or most of them fall ill or even die by the wayside, for they come from different climates and great distances (some journey 100 leagues and more). In this business they fritter away what little money they have or assess the people of their towns to defray the cost. It is most necessary that a stop be put to this going away for confirmation of office and that these Indian officials simply be chosen in their own towns. It would be still better, however, to do away with the alcaldes and alguaciles for the present, because they are good for nothing but to rob and harass the commoners, and make idlers instead of tribute-payers of them. Besides, today there are everywhere Spanish *alcaldes mayores, corregidores, tenientes,* and alguaciles who have civil and military jurisdiction over the Indians and Spaniards of their towns, but it would be very prudent to keep them out of the Indian towns, as will be explained below.

When the natural lords governed, then, they kept their people in peace and subjection. These lords sent for the tribute their subjects were to give, and took care that the communal fields and those of individuals were cultivated, and saw to it that each town provided the people needed for personal service to the Spaniards. They took into account the capacity of each town to do or give what was expected of it, they gave each man his due, and to them everyone applied for everything. That is the reason why today the lords are still troubled with such matters. All the towns were peaceful then, without intrigues and lawsuits. The lords possessed their remaining lands, tenants, lessees, and patrimonies in peace; they received their tribute according to ancient custom, as the lords they were, and in the manner they used to receive it through inheritance from their forebears or other just cause before they gave obedience to Your Majesty.

The land being well governed, then, and most conveniently for both the lords and their subjects, certain religious began urging with saintly zeal a certain course of action upon the caciques and lords who came to confess to them, to discuss with them matters of Christian doctrine or conscience, and to give account of their rule and tributes. They urged these lords to reduce the tribute they collected from their subjects because the latter were also paying tribute to Your Majesty and to his encomenderos in his royal name to compensate them for providing the Indians with religious instruction and priests, with ministers of justice, and with an Audiencia to favor and protect them. The lords agreed to do what these servants of God advised them, for they were ever obedient to the friars and held them in great respect. What they agreed upon was put down in writing, and the lords signed it, that there might be a record of their undertaking. This arrangement appeared very good to certain lawyers and other learned persons, and they gave it their approval. The viceroy who governed New Spain at that time also thought so well of it that he determined to make a similar agreement with the other lords of the land, and began to take steps to this end.

Yet this move, which was inspired by saintly zeal to help the *macehuales* (who are the commoners and peasants), has been the cause of their present turbulence and of the total ruin and abasement of the natural lords. For subjects and vassals had a pretext for complaining of their lords, saying that they did not do what they had agreed and had been ordered to do. Moreover, Spaniards, mestizos, and mulattoes now began to appear among the Indians and incite them against their lords, fishing in troubled waters. As a result, lords and commoners alike have been ruined spiritually and temporally, while the men who threw them into turmoil prosper on their misery.

Under the old system of government, then, the whole land was at peace. Spaniards and Indians alike were content, and more tribute was paid, and with less hardship, because government was in the hands of the natural lords. This state of things continued until some of their subjects began to persecute the lords in the manner aforesaid. These ambitious, cunning troublemakers were egged on by Spaniards, mestizos, and mulattoes who know the native language and go among the Indians in order to rob them. Learning that the officials who had jurisdiction over them would attend to their complaints if they were paid for it, the Indians sought to rob and ruin their natural lords. In this manner began the plague of lawsuits that they bring against each other in their towns, subjects against lords throughout New Spain, towns against towns, and provincial towns against provincial capitals. This has given rise to much expense, the death of great numbers along the roads, comings and goings to hear suits; and all the while the Indians do not know what they are litigating about, what they want, or why they carry their cases to the Audiencia. They succeed only in throwing away their money and their lives, being egged on by men whose only interest is in squandering the Indians' estates.

Lords and principales, and many commoners, together with their wives and children, who always go with them to carry provisions, have lost their lives. Many lords and principales and macehuales have been sentenced to labor in the mines and on public works, where they are left to die, lost and forgotten by their wives and children.

Great turmoil in the provinces and towns and very great confusion in everything have resulted from this. Lords and commoners alike have been impoverished and ruined; all have suffered great spiritual and temporal decline.

No harmony remains among the Indians of New Spain because the commoners have lost all feeling of shame as concerns their lords and principales, because they have risen up against their lords and lost the respect they once had for them. Withal, it is most necessary for the spiritual and temporal welfare of these people that they be well governed; and the lords used to make them do what was needful and proper for both. For the common people are like children, and having lost their fear and sense of shame, they lose all the good that was implanted in them. Only those whom they fear and respect will they obey and only for them will they do what they must do. This is why the lords and principales are so necessary, for they alone understand and know how to deal with the Indian commoners.

This state of affairs has led to other evil consequences, easily divined from what was said above, and all because there is so little understanding of these people, of their character and condition. As for the outsiders who pretend affection for and interest in these people, their only real interest is in fomenting the present disorder and confusion.

Had these people not been allowed to engage in their senseless lawsuits, they would not have ruined each other, the deaths of many would have been avoided, and they would not find themselves in their present sorry state. Far better had it been to make them go to their caciques and lords, who know the truth of what each man claims, than to listen to troublemakers who were incited by others. This would have avoided many offenses to Our Lord: false swearing, hatreds, enmities, ruin of towns and provinces, and great wickedness on the part of those who urge them on in order to rob them, all leading to confusion so great that a solution now appears hopeless.

All this could have been avoided had there been observance of what

Your Majesty provides in one of the New Laws, namely, that common law proceedings should not be allowed in suits between or with Indians, that such cases should not be drawn out but should be summarily determined, and that their customs should be observed when they are not clearly unjust. In addition, attorneys, lawyers, and solicitors should not be allowed to take part in the proceedings, for the facts in such cases are easily ascertained if they are not confused and muddied by lawyers and others of that breed. In dealing with Indians, it is easy to learn where the truth lies, for the lords and principales will state the truth with all candor. The very parties to a suit will speak the truth if they are not induced to act to the contrary by outsiders among them, by lawyers, or by others of that kind. Even if some do not tell the truth, there always are present many others who know and are willing to tell the facts of the case.

When these commoners rose up against their lords, they justified their ambition to destroy them and usurp their places by displaying a seeming zeal to aid the common people, for they stirred up the multitude by declaring their aim was to defend the commoners and free them from their lords. To this end they called upon the commoners to disobey their lords. Thus factions arose among the Indians, and since the lords had no means of defending themselves, they were quickly overthrown. The rebels and their corrupters always begin by making the vassals rise against their lords and stop giving the service and tribute they formerly gave. Thereby the lords are reduced to great poverty, abasement, and misery; they become stupefied, as it were, not daring to speak, not knowing what to say or to whom to complain or how to complain.

All men are against them, for all have been poisoned with false information to the effect that the lords rob and harass their subjects. As for the encomenderos, they care little, for they do not lose their tribute; indeed, the encomendero's tribute is paid better than before that he may keep silent and side with the rebels who hold the commoners in the hollow of their hands. In a single moment, then, the rebels tear down and ruin their lords, for all their wealth and sustenance consists in the service their vassals give them, and if this be withheld for even one day, the lords lack food and all the other necessities of life. Meantime their enemies, who are numerous, and who rob the people for themselves and for the benefit of their hangers-on who incite and assist them, never lack for anything, because they receive and enjoy what formerly was given to the lords, on top of all they can steal. In this way they go on ruining and annihilating the lords.

Another cause of the ruin of the lords has been the practice of naming them gobernadores of the provinces and towns of which they are the natural lords. Now their numerous rivals among their own people, aided by Spanish and mestizo allies, commenced suits against the lords, charging them with misgovernment, and were able to prove whatever served their ends. As a result the Audiencia deprived the lords of their offices, which meant the end of their authority, and appointed their subjects and rivals to these offices, thus making the lords subjects of subjects. These evils continue, and all is topsy-turvy, with the lords ruined and abased and commoners raised to high estate.

Many of the lords, seeing the power and swift rise of the rebels, followed their example and rose up with a part of their towns, allowing the rebels to do what they pleased in the others. Here lords and commoners alike rob and connive to be appointed governors, alcaldes, and regidores to help them in their robbery. These lords cater to the wishes of the multitude and the rebels and the Spaniards and mestizos who egg them on, and all steal and live by the sweat of the poor macehuales. And since all is turned topsy-turvy, these wretches soon achieve all their ends.

As a result the land has lost the splendor and majesty and good government it once enjoyed under its lords, without benefit of alcaldes, regidores, alguaciles, or gobernadores; for the lords were well obeyed and all did what was ordered and each did his duty. To this end the lords appointed persons who maintained order, causing less affliction than the Indians now suffer from all the ministers and rods of justice; the provinces and towns were united and peaceful, the lords were obeyed and esteemed. Now all has come to ruin because the lords are ruined and abased, and their authority, dominion, and system of government done away with.

— Some Spaniards assert that the lords rob their subjects, and say that that is why certain persons have incited the macehuales against them and why the lords' dominion, vassals, tribute, tenants, and *mayeques* have been taken from them. (These mayeques are people who live on the lords' lands, and some have risen up and seized the land for themselves, while others give the lords only what they please, the lords meanwhile not daring to say a word for fear that these people will sue them and rise up against them.) There is no truth, however, in the unqualified statement that the lords rob their subjects. This is true only of the lords who have joined with the rebels to be able to live as they do, and of the commoners who have risen up and made themselves lords in the ways described above. These last are public and most harmful robbers, for they have usurped what is not theirs through inheritance. And because they fear that some day others will revolt against them and lay them low as they did their natural lords, they steal all they can as long as they remain in power; for when they fall, they will return to what they were at first. This conduct is the mark of the tyrant. And these people, who are improperly called caciques, lords, and principales, being naught but intruders, have caused the Spaniards to say that the lords are robbers.

The natural lords cherish and support their vassals, for they love them as their own, as their inheritance from their forebears. They fear to lose them and strive not to offend them lest they rise up against them, as have other vassals against their lords. Therefore the natural lords seek to ease their vassals' burdens, treat them like their own children, defend and protect them. Of such lords but a very few remain.

The lords who act in a contrary manner are the ones who have taken the way of the rebels, who do the will of agitators who steal and eat at the expense of poor folk who know not how to resist, do not understand what is in their interest, or believe those who say they are acting in their interest. The commoners have suffered great injury, yet never seek revenge or reprisal, and they do what they do because they are blinded by the desire of being without lords who correct them and compel them to live virtuously.

It was necessary for me to speak at such length about the lords and principales, indicating the difference among them, with their names and mode of succession, in order to comply with Your Majesty's order. Besides, when Your Majesty wrote to the Audiencias of those lands for information on the topics cited in the royal cédula, it was generally believed that the inquiry was being made for the purpose of ordering the reinstatement of the Indian lords in their dominion. If this were to be done (and it is proper and necessary that it should be done), it were useful to have set down here in such detail the dignities, lords, lordships, and their mode of succession. It were also well to know how they have been ruined and destroyed, and which lords ought to be restored to their former estate, and which should not be restored. This can easily be determined on the basis of the information given above.

In the Andes and in Middle America the Spaniards seized control of the Indian states. In the villages, a humble way of life continued; but in the capitals of these states—in Cuzco and in Mexico-Tenochtitlán—the former rulers sorrowed over their defeat. Some of these songs of sorrow

This illustration, taken from the post-Hispanic Codex Osuna, written partly in Nahuatl, partly in Spanish, shows Indians laboring on a Spanish estate. (Courtesy American Museum of Natural History)

have come down to us in the original Quechua or Nahuatl. Here is an example of a Mexican dirge, bemoaning the fate of the former proud rulers of the Aztec state.

good poetry

FLOWERS AND SONGS OF SORROW*

Nothing but flowers and songs of sorrow
are left in Mexico and Tlatelolco,
where once we saw warriors and wise men.

We know it is true
that we must perish,
for we are mortal men.
You, the Giver of Life,
you have ordained it.

We wander here and there
in our desolate poverty.
We are mortal men.
We have seen bloodshed and pain
where once we saw beauty and valor.

We are crushed to the ground;
we lie in ruins.
There is nothing but grief and suffering
in Mexico and Tatelolco,
where once we saw beauty and valor.

Have you grown weary of your servants?
Are you angry with your servants,
O Giver of Life?

"POLITICAL" INDIANS AND SAVAGES

In the Andes, then, as in Middle America the Spaniards were confronted with orderly societies, already possessed of a machinery for the wielding of power, a machinery which the Spanish conquerors could take over and wield for their own benefit. The Spaniards called the Indians living in such systems *Indios de policía*. Here the word *policía* means not only

* From Miguel León-Portilla, *The Broken Spears: The Aztec Account of the Conquest of Mexico*, © 1962 by the Beacon Press. Originally published in Spanish under the title *Visión de los Vencidos*, © 1959 by Universidad Nacional Autónoma de México. Reprinted by permission of the Beacon Press.

policed Indians but political Indians, Indians with political systems. The Spaniards contrasted this with *Indios salvajes,* savage Indians, Indians organized not into large and complex societies but into small groups, captained not by hereditary rulers but by chiefs whose power was exercised not through courts and armies but through the consent of their fellowmen. This contrast between populations already organized into states and stateless populations has been one of the most important determining factors in governing the kind of expansion open to the Europeans. Where states existed, they could be taken over and bent to the purposes of the new rulers. Where these did not exist, the conquerors could not gain a grip on their new subjects. Unused to internal control as well as to control from the outside, such stateless populations rose in continuous rebellion against attempts to impose such controls on them. This has been characteristic of the Indians of the North American continent, where finally the only good Indian came to be a dead Indian, because the Indians would not be "good" and submit to the demands of the new claimants to power. This also confronted the Spaniards as soon as they ventured from the Andean redoubts into the Chilean plains and forests; in their attempt to penetrate the open steppe country of the South American continent, the *pampa;* and in their conquest of northern Mexico, the Gran Chichimeca, the land inhabited by unruly and indomitable tribes. In all three areas, moreover, a phenomenon very like that with which we are familiar from countless movies occurred. The savage Indian tribes acquired horses from the Spaniards and, mounted, presented a threat that was only finally eliminated with the advent of the repeating rifle, the telegraph, and barbed wire. In South America the campaigns against the mounted tribesmen ended only with the conquest of the desert in Argentina in 1878-79, about the same time as the Indians were finally subdued in North America west of the Mississippi.

THE TUPINAMBA

In the tropical steppe and forests of Brazil, the Portuguese encountered similar groups. Here the tropical environment inhibited the adoption of the horse, and the Indians continued to fight on foot and in small bands, as they had done before the advent of the Europeans. One of the earliest reports of such a group is of the Tupinamba of Brazil. They are first described in *The True History and Description of a Country of Savages, a Naked and Terrible People of Cannibals in the New World*

Called America, which appeared in Marburg, Germany, in 1557. The author was one Hans Staden. Born in Hesse in Germany, and evidently possessed of some measure of education, Hans Staden had, in 1547, found employment on a ship carrying convicts from Lisbon in Portugal to Pernambuco in Brazil. The year 1547-48 found him engaged in defending the newly won Portuguese footholds in the New World against the original Indian inhabitants. Having been put in charge of a new Portuguese stronghold, he was captured by the Tupinamba. They threatened to eat him, but a combination of circumstances conspired to save him. He pretended to be a curer and prophet—a role also played with success among the Indians by Cabeza de Vaca on his long journey back to Florida through what is now the southeastern United States—and a set of accidental illnesses and cures among his captors gave him an opportunity to play his part to the hilt. Perhaps he was also helped by his extraordinary appearance—he had a fiery red beard. At any rate he lived, and in 1555 returned to Europe, where he wrote a most matter-of-fact account of his adventures among his cannibal friends. His book is quite free of the fanciful exaggerations characteristic of so many other writers of this period; near the end he cites the names and occupations of individuals who could testify to the truth of his story. From this account we have taken passages which illustrate clearly the nature of Tupinamba patterns.*

Concerning the dwellings of the Tuppin Inba, whose prisoner I was.

These people have their dwellings close by the sea, in front of the range of mountains of which I have spoken. Their dwellings extend also some sixty miles inland behind the mountains, and a river flows down from the hills to the sea, on the banks of which they also have a settlement called Paraeibe. They have settlements as well for some twenty-eight miles along the sea shore, and on all sides they are encompassed by their enemies. To the north they are bounded by a nation of savages called Weittaka who are their enemies. On the south are the Tuppin Ikin. On the land side their enemies are called Karaya, while the Wayganna inhabit the mountains, and between these two are the savages called Markaya. These tribes harass them greatly and make war also

* From Hans Staden, *The True History and Description of a Country of Savages*, G. Routledge and Sons, Ltd., 1928.

among themselves, and when they capture one of the others they eat them.

They prefer to set up their dwellings in places where they have wood, water, and game and fish close at hand. When they have exhausted one place they move to another, and their manner of settling is this. A chief among them collects a party of forty men and women, as many as he can get, and these are usually friends and relations. They set up their huts, which are about fourteen feet wide and quite 150 feet long, according to the number of those who are to inhabit them. These huts are about twelve feet (2 fathoms) high and are round at the top and vaulted like a cellar. They roof them closely with the branches of palms to keep out the rain. Inside, the huts are all one: no one has a separate chamber to himself. Each couple, man and wife, has a space in the hut on one side, the space measuring about twelve feet, and on the other side lives another couple, and so the hut is filled, each couple having its own fire. The chief of the huts has his dwelling in the center. The huts have generally three doors, one at each end, and the other in the middle, and the doors are so low that the people have to stoop to get in or out. Few of the villages have more than seven huts. Between the huts is a space where they knock their prisoners on the head.

The savages fortify their huts as follows. They make a stockade of palm trees, which they first split and then set up to a height of about nine feet (1½ fathoms). This they build so thickly that no arrow can pierce it, but they leave little holes here and there through which they can shoot. Outside this stockade they build another of high stakes, which they set up close together, but so that the space between them is not sufficient for a man to creep through. Among certain of the savages it is the custom to set up the heads of the men they have eaten on the stockade at the entrance to the huts.

In what manner they make fire

The savages have a kind of wood called Urakueiba which they dry. They then take two sticks of this wood, about the thickness of a finger, which they rub.

Concerning their government by chiefs, and their laws

The savages have no special form of government or law. Each hut has its chief or king, and all their chiefs belong to one family with one common authority and control. Beyond this a man can do what he will. It may happen that one by experience in war has more authority than another, and when they make war, greater respect is shown to him, as in the case of Konyan Bebe whom I have mentioned. Otherwise I have seen no particular authority among them except that by custom the young defer to their elders.

If a man slay or shoot another his friends are ready to take vengeance and to kill the slayer, but this seldom happens. They obey the orders of the chief of the hut: this they do without compulsion or fear, but of their own free will.

CHAPTER XXI

What is their greatest honor

Their greatest honor is to capture their enemies and to slay them; for such is their custom. And for every foe a man kills he takes a new name. The most famous among them is he that has the most names.

Why one enemy eats another

This they do, not from hunger, but from great hate and jealousy, and when they are fighting with each other one, filled with hate, will call out to his opponent: *Dete Immeraya, Schermiuramme, heiwoe*:—"Cursed be you my meat": *De kange Fueve eypota kurine*:—"To-day will I cut off your head": *Sche Innamme pepicke Reseagu*:—"Now am I come to take vengeance on you for the death of my friends": *Yande soo, sche mocken Sera Quora Ossorime Rire* etc.:—"This day before sunset your flesh shall be my roast meat." All this they do from their great hatred.

Of their plan of campaign when they set out to invade their enemy's country

When they desire to make war in an enemy's country the chiefs gather together and take counsel how best to achieve their purpose, all which they make known in the huts, so that the men may arm themselves. They name the time of the ripening of a certain fruit as the date of their departure, for they have not the art to reckon by the day or year. They also fix their expeditions by the time of the spawning time they call Pirakaen. Then they equip themselves with canoes and arrows, and lay in stores of dried root-meal called Vy-than. After this they enquire of the Pagy, their wise men, whether they shall return victorious. These will say "Yes," but will warn the enquirers to note well their dreams when they dream of their foes. If many dream that they are roasting their enemy's flesh that signifies victory. But if it is their own flesh which they see in the pot, that is an evil omen and they had better stay at home. If their dreams are propitious they arm themselves and prepare much drink in the huts after which they dance and drink with their idols, the Tammaraka, each one beseeching his idol to assist him in catching an enemy. Then they set out, and when they draw near to the enemy's country, on the night before the attack, the chiefs once more direct their men to remember their dreams.

I accompanied them in one of their expeditions and on the night before they intended to attack, when we were close to the enemy's country, the chief went up and down in the camp, telling the men to note well their dreams that night, and ordering the young men to set off at daybreak to hunt for game and catch fish, which was done, and the food was cooked. Then the chief summoned the other chiefs to his hut and when they were all seated upon the ground in a circle he gave them to eat, after which they all told their dreams, that is, such dreams as were favorable, and then they danced and made merry with the Tammaraka. They spy out the enemy's huts at night and attack at dawn. If they take a prisoner who is badly wounded they kill him at once and carry home the meat roasted. Those that are unwounded they take back alive and kill them in the huts. They attack with loud yells, stamping on the ground, and blowing blasts upon trumpets made of gourds. They all carry cords bound about their bodies to make fast their prisoners, and adorn themselves with red feathers so that they may distinguish their friends from their foes. They shoot very rapidly and send fire-arrows into the enemy's huts to set them alight. And if they are wounded they have their special herbs with them to heal their wounds.

Of their manner of killing and eating their enemies
Of the instrument with which they kill them,
and the rites which follow

When they first bring home a captive the women and children set upon him and beat him. Then they decorate him with grey feathers and shave off his eyebrows, and dance around him, having first bound him securely so that he cannot escape. They give him a woman who attends to him and has intercourse with him. If the woman conceives, the child is maintained until it is fully grown. Then, when the mood seizes them, they kill and eat it.

They feed the prisoner well and keep him for a time while they prepare the pots which are to contain their drink. They bake also special pots in which to prepare the mixture wherewith they paint him, and they make tassels to tie to the club with which he is to be killed, as well as a long cord, called Mussurana, to bind him when the time comes. When all is ready they fix the day of his death and invite the savages from the neighboring villages to be present. The drinking vessels are filled a few days in advance, and before the women make the drink, they bring forth the prisoner once or twice to the place where he is to die and dance round him.

When the guests have assembled, the chief of the huts bids them welcome and desires that they shall help them to eat their enemy. The day before they commence to drink, the cord Mussurana is tied about the victim's neck and on this day also they paint the club called Iwera Pemme with which they intend to kill him. This is of the shape depicted here.

It is about 6 feet (a fathom) long, and they cover it with a sticky mess, after which they take the eggs of a bird called Mackukawa, which they break up to powder and spread upon the club. Then a woman sits down and scratches figures in the powder, while the other women dance and sing around her. When the club Iwera Pemme is ready decked with tassels and other things, they hang it in an empty hut upon a pole, and sing in front of it all night.

In the same manner they paint the face of the victim, the women singing while another woman paints, and when they begin to drink they take their captive with them and talk to him while he drinks with them. After the drinking bout is over they rest the next day and build a hut on the place of execution, in which the prisoner spends the night under close guard. Then, a good while before daybreak on the day following, they commence to dance and sing before the club, and so they continue until day breaks. After this they take the prisoner from his hut, which they break to pieces and clear away. Then they remove the Mussurana from the prisoner's neck, and tying it round his body they draw it tight on either side so that he stands there bound in the midst of them, while numbers of them hold the two ends of the cord. So they leave him for a time, but they place stones beside him which he throws at the women, who run about mocking him and boasting that they will eat him. These women are painted, and are ready to take his four quarters when he is cut up, and run with them round the huts, a proceeding which causes great amusement to the others.

Then they make a fire about two paces from the prisoner which he has to tend. After this a woman brings the club Iwera Pemme, waving the tassels in the air, shrieking with joy, and running to and fro before the prisoner so that he may see it. Then a man takes the club and standing before the prisoner he shows it to him. Meanwhile he who is going to do the deed withdraws with fourteen or fifteen others, and they all paint their bodies grey with ashes. Then the slayer returns with his companions, and the man who holds the club before the prisoner hands it to the slayer. At this stage the king of the huts approaches, and taking the club he thrusts it once between the slayer's legs which is a sign of great honor. Then the slayer seizes it and thus addresses the victim: "I am he that will kill you, since you and yours have slain and eaten many of my friends." To which the prisoner replies: "When I am dead I shall still have many to avenge my death." Then the slayer strikes from behind and beats out his brains.

The women seize the body at once and carry it to the fire where they scrape off the skin, making the flesh quite white, and stopping up the fundament with a piece of wood so that nothing may be lost. Then a man cuts up the body, removing the legs above the knee and the arms at the trunk, whereupon the four women seize the four limbs and run with them round the huts, making a joyful cry. After this they divide the trunk among themselves, and devour everything that can be eaten.

When this is finished they all depart, each one carrying a piece with him. The slayer takes a fresh name, and the king of the huts scratches him in the upper part of the arm with the tooth of a wild beast. When the wound is healed the scar remains visible, which is a great honor. He must lie all that day in his hammock, but they give him a small bow and an arrow, so that he can amuse himself by shooting into wax, lest his arm should become feeble from the shock of the death-blow. I was present and have seen all this with my own eyes.

The savages have not the art of counting beyond five. If they have to count more they make use of their fingers and toes. Beyond that they point to four or five persons and reckon up the number of fingers and toes which they have between them.

We see here that Hans Staden encountered Indians with a vastly simpler culture than that possessed by such peoples as the Inca or the Aztec. They lived in temporary settlements of kinsfolk, forty strong, as opposed to permanent village sites, populated by hundreds of men, in huts rather than in houses made of sun-dried brick. The settlements were surrounded by a wooden palisade, where the Inca built elaborate fortresses and the Aztec fortified their elaborate temples. Each hut had a headman or chief, but chiefly authority was based on personal qualifications, not on inherited office. There were no courts, no police, no jails; the chiefs persuaded, they did not rule. "Beyond this," says Staden, "a man can do what he will." They engaged in continuous warfare, but it was warfare for reasons of prestige, not for reasons of conquest and political and economic domination. Warfare was carried on to acquire new names, and to obtain victims for a cannibal feast. Cannibalism had magic properties; eating a man one incorporated his virtue and strength. Warfare was a form of raiding rather than true war by large organized bodies of men. The art of counting was in its infancy, unlike the elaborate systems whereby the Inca and the Aztec kept account of tribute and labor services. The community was self-sufficient, taking no tribute and attending no markets.

Slowly, over time, these peoples too were pushed back into the fastnesses of the tropical forest and gradually decimated by incoming colonists and rubber gatherers. Yet here, too, there still remain—scattered outside the area of effective political control—tribelets warring against each other and against the encroaching outsider. Thus, Napoleon Chagnon,* who is investigating one of these remnant groups living around the headwaters of the Orinoco River in Venezuela, writes in his letters:

Mouth of the Mavaca River
Amazonas, Venezuela
January 22nd, 1965

I am up to my eyeballs in Indians; they appear in larger numbers at the crack of dawn and make it difficult for me to get anything done. I suspect that the recent surge of comradeship is a result of the fact that about ninety percent of the men are inland trading with the Shamataris. There go all my axes and machetes! The only inhabitants of the village are the women and children and about 6 or 7 men. They normally disperse into the jungle when the men are away, but since I have a shotgun they feel safe as long as they can stay in my hut—the entire population. They are all afraid that the next village down the Orinoco will raid them and steal some women since the men are gone; so am I. The other night a few men from the next village were seen nearby, and some men stood guard all night, without my knowledge. I can't leave the house for

* Professor Chagnon's letters are reprinted by permission.

a minute unless I kick out all my guests. The moment I turn my back anything edible or easily concealed disappears and my questions fall on a host of innocent faces.

There is an immense trading network here, which also involves the Maquiritari Indians. Within the Yanomama language family things like cotton, hammocks, ebene (their hallucinatory drug), aluminum pots, machetes, dogs, bows, axes, fishhooks, and so forth are exchanged at a fairly high velocity. Some villages specialize in making one or another object; others who have special sources of access purvey axes or machetes and pots to the rest. The Catholic missionary at the mouth of the Ocamo has given his village of about 100 people over 3000 machetes during the last eight years alone and there are probably no more than 30 in the village at the present time. The Mariquitaris manufacture dugout canoes for the entire population of the Orinoco, including the Venezuelans. The Waicas get canoes from them, too, and give glass beads in return. They get the glass beads from the missionaries, in exchange for native foods and physical labor.

The Catholic missionary has just dropped in on me unexpectedly to warn me that he has received a radio communication from the Catholic mission at Platanal to the effect that all the men from that village are heading this way, allegedly on a raid. He must have taken it seriously, since he came up the Orinoco three hours in the dark, which is quite dangerous at this time of the year. I'll have to warn the villagers. They are pretty jumpy as it is, since the men have been gone about two weeks. That's what I call a hot bulletin on the current state of warfare on the Upper Orinoco!

The day before yesterday six men from upriver came through my village. I gave them a ride across the river and treated them for malaria and colds, then arranged to visit their village. They must have cased the joint and reported back that the women at the Macava River were poorly guarded—just one puny anthropologist. They were quite aggressive in my house—which is unusual—they are usually timid when outside their own village. They must be a riot in their own stomping grounds. The same goes for the village downstream. I was almost completely derobed by them when I visited them; they pulled a lot of hair out of my chest. I must spend a few days with them to get their genealogies and watch them make clay pots—they specialize in that. I can hardly wait.

All in all, things are going well . . . There is green mold over everything, including my hammock, and the rats are eating large quantities of my food. I have not yet gotten malaria. I haven't seen any jaguars or boa constrictors, but I killed a coral snake in my hut yesterday, and nearly stepped on a Bothrop atox on a visit I made to the temporary village inland a few days back. I haven't had dysentery yet.

On Visit to Caracas
February 25th, 1965

The village I'm living in really thinks I am the be-all and end-all. I broke the final ice with them by participating in their dancing and singing one night. That really impressed them. They want to take me all over Waicaland to show me off. Their whole attitude toward me changed dramatically. Unfortunately, they want me to dance all the time now. You should have seen me in my feathers and loincloth! They were so anxious to show me off that they arranged to take me to the first Shamatari village so that I could dance with them.

I had an exciting evening the other day. There was a feast and three villages were visiting mine to participate. Some of the visitors were clandestinely stealing plantains from their hosts' gardens at night, so the hosts challenged the visitors to a duel of chest-pounding. They pounded each other on the chest for three hours—I still can hardly believe it— getting angrier and angrier. Then one of them got hurt and the whole mass of warriors, about 25-30 from each side, armed to the teeth with axes, machetes, and bows, began drawing back from each other and, after tipping their arrows with curare [poison] points, began to draw beads on each other. It came very close to erupting into an all-out war . . . The visitors charged the group I was standing with and began to club them. But it ended at that. Next day they were friends again, but still quite sore from the chest-pounding. Some of them were even coughing up blood.

This is their mildest form of violence. Next come duels in which they club each other over the head with 15 inch poles. There was one of these shortly after I got here, but I missed it; they held it at the crack of dawn. After club fights comes shooting bows and arrows. It is quite remarkable how rapidly they can get into a rage and then snap out of it and forget all about it. One has to be cautious with them at all times for this reason; when they're in a bad mood they'll do anything. I've learned to avoid some of them when they take their drug, as I've had a few unpleasant experiences . . . Even Pablo, my most trusted informant and friend, "almost" got angry with me one day—which means that he "almost" got violent with me; they use the term for "almost" in just this way—it literally means just that—because I told him to stop chopping up the poles I had paid him to collect for my house. On another occasion Pablo got angry because he stubbed his toe while we were carrying a log. He threw the log down, squashing my finger between it and another log. Fortunately, I just lost a finger-nail, but I suspect that I cracked a bone, because my finger is still about a third as large as it should be. Pablo lives with me most of the time, and usually goes with me when I travel. He is a Shamatari, and a sort of permanent outsider in the village where I am living. Since he is an outsider, I can get all sorts of information from him that one of the local "insiders" wouldn't tell me. As I am a permanent visitor also, he regards me as an ally.

Crazy as it seems, I am looking forward to going back in. I'm already pleased that I have an opportunity to do field work among a truly primitive people. But it affects you. My wife told me that for the first few days I was home I kept making a funny "clicking" noise and was sort of off on cloud nine. The Waicas make this noise all the time, but I wasn't aware that I had picked it up. As to being on cloud nine, I guess I was just suffering from culture shock—civilization looks different on re-entry. I hadn't spoken English for two months, and it was a little strange to carry on a conversation in a language that I know intimately.

Boca Mavaca
Amazonas
Venezuela
April 17, 1965

Still haven't caught malaria or dysentery, but I have a beaut of a cold. I went monkey hunting with the gang this week in preparation for a big feast. It takes a pretty good sprinter to chase down a pack of monkeys. I was so sweated up that I jumped in the river to cool off—now I have a cold.

The feast is in honor of the slain headman of the next village up. This particular war got started the day I arrived in the field (cause: woman stealing), and it is getting hotter and hotter. About a month or so ago the village which lost the woman attacked Monou-tedi, the next village up, and killed the headman. They are going to eat his remains this week, and perhaps have a little reprisal raid afterwards. Monou-tedi has since moved in with my group for self-defense, and will probably be here for some time to come. There was even some hanky-panky with the women of their new group-mates, and it ended in a club fight. Got some pretty good photos of this. I feel a little better, as I missed the last club fight by an hour or so.

I was happy to hear that the clay pots reached the museum in one piece; the arrows weren't the best that the Waicas have to offer, but I have since collected about forty, much more representative of their technology. I also have a few ebene tubes and some pack baskets. I'll send them on when I come out in June or July. What kind of shape were the first one's in? I also found a rather large archaeological site just littered with potsherds. About ninety percent of them were as crude or cruder than the Waica's present pots, but a few were quite delicate. I also found a stone ax on the ground with the sherds. The Waicas have repeatedly told me that they find them in this manner, but seeing is believing.

Silver was the motor of the Spanish economy in the New World. This picture shows the interior of the Rayas mine of Guanajato, Mexico. The average burden of carriers was between 225 and 250 pounds, hauled over exceedingly steep ascents. (From D. T. Egerton, *Egerton's Views of Mexico*, London, 1840)

3

Communities

INDIANS AND CREOLES

We can draw a lesson from these sharp contrasts between the various aboriginal populations in Latin America. Here the past truly determined the course of the future. Where states existed, the Spaniards could lay hold of the machinery of government and continue to rule peoples already accustomed to the ordering of society from the top. Here efforts were made to maintain the Indian communities—under Spanish aegis, to be sure—but as viable and integral units of the new social order. This pattern of preserving the life-ways of populations under outside political control has been called the pattern of *indirect rule*. Where the Indians had no states, and where indirect rule was therefore impossible, the new conquerors adopted the other alternative, that of pushing back and eliminating the aboriginal population and replacing it with newcomers more suited to the task of connecting the newly won colonies with the mother country back home. In the areas of pre-conquest Indian states, therefore, we continue to find Indians living in Indian communities. In the areas inhabited by Indians without states, in contrast, we find today largely new populations whose life-ways did not develop primarily in the traditional setting of Indian society. These people might intermarry with Indians, and their descendants therefore carry some of the genetic equipment of Indian ancestors. But their way of life was no longer characteristically Indian. These new people are Creoles, *criollos*, or Iberians born in the New World.

This contrast between Indian and Creole areas of Latin America goes a long way toward explaining the patterns of life lived in Latin American communities today. For the maintenance of Indian life-ways in some areas and the replacement of Indian life-ways in others caused the two

Peasant plowman with oxen in Chambí, Bolivia. (Courtesy United Nations)

areas to develop quite differently. Maintenance of Indian communities not only allowed the conquerors to establish indirect rule over large populations, it also gave the Indians an organized way of keeping their life patterns going against encroachment by outsiders and innovators. The Indian communities in areas of indirect rule are so many little cultural islands, each a stronghold of a traditional way of life. Economically, they favor the growing of traditional Indian subsistence crops like maize (Indian corn), squash and beans in Middle America, potatoes and quinoa (a seed-bearing plant related to pigweed) in the Andes. They strive to keep land in the hands of their members by forbidding sales to outsiders, or even using plot of land as pawns to obtain credit outside the community. They insist strongly that community members marry others like themselves, also members of the community, and they thus prevent the entry of strangers into their little world. Moreover, each community worships its own body of Catholic saints, often regarding them as quite different from the saints of neighboring communities. In the course of this worship, they lavish great quantities of wealth on feasting, fireworks, and on the maintenance and improvement of churches, chapels and of the cult objects stored in them. The men who contribute to these celebrations are accorded prestige, and gain the right to have a say in community affairs. This means that only men who are members of the community and who have contributed to its most important purposes have a right to administer the affairs of the community. This has two effects. First, a man can acquire authority only by submitting to the ways of the community. His authority derives from participation in communal ritual, and he can exercise it only through the community as a whole. Second, outsiders are barred from taking part and therefore cannot gain a political foothold in communal affairs. Each community thus has its own economic, social, political and religious order, striving to keep outside interference at bay, and to maintain its independence of it.

In contrast to these are the communities of people formed either in *tierras de salvajes* or outside the reach of closed communities of the described type. Here too people live their lives within the relatively narrow confines of their villages or neighborhood, but these lives are strongly connected to the happenings of the outside world. The community, as such, lacks strong organization. Rather, the individual can reach out beyond the community to enter whatever advantageous relationship is open to him. In contrast to the closed communities of the highlands, these communities are "open" to the world. Economically, the production and sale of cash products—growing coffee or tobacco, pping, logging, mining, wage labor—is valued above the grow-ing of subsistence crops and brings outside money through outside con-nections. Marriage may be contracted with insiders and outsiders. There are local cults and celebrations in the honor of local saints, but participa-tion in the ceremonial system is not tied so intimately to political affairs. Men gain authority over others through their own political activities, not through the workings of a communal religious cult. Politics is power politics—the attraction and control of individual adherents by individ-ual leaders. Since individuals in such communities rarely possess the wherewithal necessary for independent economic or political activity, they seek to ally themselves with individuals more powerful than them-selves who are often outsiders. Anthropologists speak of such relations as relations between patrons and clients. The term patron means "boss" or chief or superior person; it derives from the Latin word *pater* for father. The client promises loyal support; the leader pledges supplies and help. More important than the genetic makeup of a population is whether or not they are willing to become followers or clients in rela-tion to an outside leader or patron. This the Indians are unwilling or un-able to do; their closed communities keep potential patrons at bay. But the Creole is willing to reach out beyond the confines of the local com-munity in which he lives to establish ties with dominant outsiders, to be-come a client to outside patrons, or—if fortune smile upon him—a patron of clients himself. Economically this means that he is willing to deal with outside merchants to sell his produce, to accept credit from them and, through their credit, also their influence over much of his economic life. Politically it means that he will support the political aspirations of a patron against other potential patrons, each surrounded by his own fol-lowing of clients. At the same time, these connections with patrons also constitute potential roads of occupation and political mobility. If he has skill and luck, he may add to his economic wherewithal and rise in the economic scale, or he may add to his political assets and rise in the politi-cal scale. Where the Indian, therefore, is oriented toward the community and sets his face against the outside world, the creole is oriented toward the outside—the city, the region, the nation—and toward the holders of power positions who operate at these levels. He may often himself be poor and powerless, but he *participates* in the economic and political processes of the nation to which he belongs. He is a citizen of the state to which he belongs, not merely in name but in aspiration and participa-tion. Where the closed community of the *tierra de policía* strives to elim-inate patron-client relations and to keep them at bay, the members of

Members of a farmers' co-op in the Cauca region of Colombia clearing a field before planting potatoes. (Courtesy United Nations)

the open Creole communities welcome them and link themselves in manifold commitments to the outer world which they represent.

A CLOSED COMMUNITY: HUALCÁN IN PERU

We have seen that the pivot of such a closed community is the politico-religious system in which men gain merit by sponsoring a series of religious festivities and acquire authority in the community only after they have gone through these economic and ritual obligations. Let us look at how such a system operates in one such community, the settlement of Hualcán, located in the cool and dry uplands of Ancash at between 9000 and 10,000 feet. An American anthropologist, William W. Stein, did field work in this community of 740 Quechua-speaking Indians for a period of seven months in 1951-52.* He revisited the community briefly during its main religious festivity in October of 1959. Anthropological field work means that you do not merely study a people as an outsider. You go to live with them for a prolonged period of time. You act as a "participant observer"—participating in their activities as well as observing. On particular questions you also interview individuals who are knowledgeable about them; but you do not come to the community with a set of queries prepared beforehand. You must formulate questions as they arise in the context of people's lives. It has been the experience of anthropologists that you cannot ask reasonable questions before you know something of the shape and texture of this strange and unfamiliar life; the ability to find such questions comes only after protracted contact with the people you wish to study.

The Hualcainos are all farmers. Some of them are, in addition, also part-time potters, weavers, tailors, traders, and curers. Many of them also work three or four days out of every week on nearby estates, *haciendas*, where they are paid in kind, receiving a plot of land to farm or to pasture sheep on, free firewood, and *coca* to chew. Most of the people were born in the community, though some are outsiders. In 1951 the parents of two-thirds of the children born had both been born in Hualcán itself; one-third had one parent who came from outside. Life is hard. "The economy," says Stein, "is marked by scarcity and inadequate production."

* The quotations on the following pages are from William W. Stein, *Life in the Highlands of Peru*, © 1961 by Cornell University. Reprinted by permission of Cornell University Press.

Yet in sharp contrast to this scarcity is the comparative richness of the religious organization. There are six types of major festive occasions: the important week-long October festival, held in honor of the communal patron saint, St. Ursula, who looks after the health and harvests of the Hualcainos; Carnival; Lent; Easter; Corpus Christi; and the rogation masses. In addition, there are many minor festivities. Each is carried out by an organization of men consisting of a leader and his assistants. These are the *mayordomos* or stewards of the festivity. The festivity of the patron saint, St. Ursula, for example, involves the services of a chief steward, five minor stewards, together with numerous contributions by dancers, banner-bearers, and minor participants. To become chief steward, one must first have worked up the ladder of positions, starting from the position of dancer or banner-bearer. Ultimately every man is expected to act as chief steward for St. Ursula. It is "a post which every man is expected to take. In a broad sense, this confirms his status as an adult male member of the community." One may not refuse. Nicacio Mateo of Hualcán says:

One has to accept the post of mayordomo at all cost. One has to do it in any way that is possible for fear of the punishment that the Virgin Ursula would inflict on one. One just has to do it. One's family could get sick or die, or one could die oneself, or one's animals could die, if he did not serve the Virgin. Because of that fear, one has to do it in the best way one is able.

The expenditures for the festivity of San Ursula are large, amounting to roughly $750. A considerable part of this comes from the store of wealth of the chief steward, the rest from miscellaneous contributions.

When a man has been chief steward for St. Ursula, he becomes eligible for political office in the community, the position of *Varayok*. *Varayok* means person of the *vara* (Spanish for staff), signifying the staff of office, a staff about one yard long and carved with the symbols of that office. Men look forward to becoming *Varayok*. Thus Feliciano Berrospi says:

I have been mayordomo of Santa Ursula Capitana. I have not been a *Varayok*. I would like to be one. I would like it, but it has not come to me. I would like to take it soon. When one does not take it, people do not have dealings with one. They say: "You are worthless. You are not a man." This is why I am going to enter to be *Varayok,* so that people will not say anything to me. It is the custom that everybody does the *Varayok* offices.

There are six *varayok,* headed by a commissar or *comisario.* They direct the labor of the community toward the repair of paths, bridges, and irrigation ditches, as well as toward fulfillment of public works projects in the larger district of which Hualcán forms a part. They collect contributions for the festivity of St. Ursula, and also the water tax to be paid to the provincial government. They settle disputes within the community, and they represent the community as a whole to the beings of the local religious pantheon, to the saints, and, ultimately, to God. Their turn of office is one year. Each year, the outgoing commissar and his assistants select the new commissar in consultation with the other distinguished men of Hualcán, that is, with those who have been stewards in the service of the saints and have expended their substance in that service. The new commissar in turn picks his own assistants. Only a wealthy man can hold the position of commissar, since the incumbent is required to give a series of relatively large fiestas throughout the year. Stein quotes Miguel Chuecas on this point:

When their turn has come, people . . . have to occupy the offices. If they can, they do it by selling their cattle or mortgaging their *chacras* [small holdings]. Or they get it in loans from some other person. One time, Alejandro Armey entered the office of *comisario.* Since he did not have anything for his expenses, he mortgaged his chacra to me, the property and the harvest. There was another, a Mayor Kampu, who entered and sold his young bull to make the expenses for his fiesta. Some also sell their sheep because they need the money to make the expenses for their guests. When I passed comisario, I worked every Sunday, sewing clothes. And that is how I earned the wherewithal for my fiesta. People mortgage their chacras among themselves here in Hualcán. They get their mortgaged chacras out of debt when they get the money.

These *varayok* are the real, de facto government of the community, although they are not officially recognized by the Peruvian government. The Peruvian government maintains its own official in the community, a *teniente* or lieutenant, who passes on information to the officials in town, represents the police power of the state to the peasantry, and also captures men for army service when they are needed. For this he is cordially disliked by the villagers; and to maintain order in the countryside the provincial authorities must in fact rely on the *varayok* whose authority it does not officially recognize.

There are other religious stewardships, in addition to the ones centered upon the "official" cult of the patron saint of Hualcán. Most of these are taken up only after men have risen to prominence in the *varayok* organization. Thus, says Stein,

At an advanced age one can still keep one's hand in the fiesta system and attract even greater respect from the rest of the community. The *devotos* of the other saints are, consequently, for the most part old men or men who have made some special vow.

Having served as stewards and *varayok*, men achieve the honored position of *Yaya*, "fathers of fathers." Miguel Chuecas defines a *yaya* as follows:

Yaya is someone who knows a lot. He is the oldest. He knows how to talk. Children learn from him. There are twenty or twenty-five persons in Hualcán who are yaya. They are men who own property and who work hard. They pass alcalde and make fiestas in the village and in town. They pass *mayordomo* [ritual sponsor; eds.]. They are good farmers. They have *compadres* [baptismal sponsor; eds.]. They are very good men, and they bother themselves about the rest of us.

A child, in Hualcán, is described as *llullu*—unripe. A man who participates in the obligations of stewardship and *varayok* grows in ripeness. A *yaya* is *alli nuna*, a complete person. Thus we see how strongly this little community has geared the motivations of its inhabitants to the operation of its social system, and how strongly this social system operates to channel these motivations to the maintenance of communal solidarity. Prestige goes to the person who achieves ceremonial standing. Ceremonial participation subjugates wealth, diverting it to non-economic purposes. Ceremonial participation also subjugates individual power, in that authority in the community can only be had as a result of ceremonial advancement and that only for a limited span of time. The *varayok* lay down the staff of office to return to a renewed cycle of stewardship and religious participation.

This religious and political system is the hub of the community: like the central part of a wheel into which the spokes are inserted, it connects the separate and quite autonomous households of which Hualcán is composed. "In many activities," William Stein says, "Hualcán seems not to be a community at all, with the expected mutual interests and ties. It consists, rather, of social clusters of households, each insulated, if not isolated, from other clusters."

Each household is a little world of its own. Let us look at them a little more closely. Households are usually larger than the basic husband-wife team that is formed at marriage. When a couple marries, they usually go to live with either the groom's or the bride's parents—that is, they join another couple already in existence. Only where such a new husband-wife has an abundance of land and stock can they afford to set up a separate household of their own when the first child is born. More usually they stay with their parents. When the parents die, similarly, families of brothers or sisters may stay together; and often a household also contains people who are not relatives, such as an orphan or a widow who came to live within its confines. Each household is a working unit, its members laboring together in cultivation or herding, contributing their outside earnings, and drawing on the common stock of produce for their sustenance. The person in charge is the senior male. In consultation with others, he makes plans for

planting a field, preparing for a fiesta, going to town for trading, or buying something new for household use. The senior male member also serves as an adviser to others, often chewing coca in order to divine the outcome of a proposed venture by one of the junior members. The senior male member also represents his household in the community, and intercedes for the other members if they get into any trouble. He guarantees *enganchos* [labor contracts] with his property and pays fines and bribes, if he has the money, to keep junior members out of jail or out of the army.

The household is also a working unit in sponsoring fiestas, working on public works projects, and in dealing with the owner of the nearby hacienda. If the head of the household has pledged himself to work on the hacienda, in return for land or pasture rights, his entire household contributes its labor to make good the contract.

Thus each household has considerable internal unity, because it operates as a working unit under central direction. In contrast, relations *between* households tend to be cool, unless the households are related. "There is no regular visiting back and forth outside kinship relationships, and no one could conceive of entering a neighbor's house freely and easily simply on the basis of neighborliness." One does not rely on neighbors; one relies on relatives by blood or marriage. You can count on relatives; you cannot count on "outsiders." This social gap between a relatively narrow personal orbit of relatives who promise aid and support and the wider orbit of people on whom one cannot count is very important, and we will meet it again in many guises in our discussions of Latin America. In Hualcán, this gap is bridged by the system of stewardship and *varayok*. We have compared it to the hub of a wheel which moves the spokes inserted in it. The hub is the system of ritual and authority; the spokes are the separate clusters of households. Through its operations, the central system imparts a common motion to the households that are connected with it. Were it not for this system, Hualcán would not be "a community at all." It is the organization of fiestas and authority that makes Hualcán a working social unit.

AN OPEN COMMUNITY: SAUCÍO IN COLOMBIA

We have looked at a closed community. Now let us see how one investigator characterizes an open community in Latin America. From 1949 to 1951, Orlando Fals-Borda of Colombia studied the neighborhood of Saucío near the town of Chocontá in the province of Cundinamarca.*

Saucío is the name not of a clustered, concentrated settlement, but of a neighborhood, a *vereda*. *Vereda* originally meant a path, from the Latin *veredus*, a horse used for the distribution of mail. Here it designates a neighborhood comprising an area of some five square miles, enclosed by surrounding hills and held together by paths which travel along the foot of these hills. Within this neighborhood live 356 persons, organized in 77 households. Most are small farmers, farming holdings of four or five acres in size; these holdings lie within the confines of the neighborhood.

The neighborhood is not a legal unit, but a social unit defined by the relationships of people within it. Roughly two-thirds of the heads of households were born in Saucío or its vicinity; one-third of the heads of

* The passages on the following pages are from Orlando Fals-Borda, *Peasant Society in the Colombian Andes: A Sociological Study of Saucío*, University of Florida Press, 1955. Reprinted by permission.

households come from elsewhere in Cundinamarca province. Men marry "the girl next door"; most marriages take place within the neighborhood. When asked where they come from, people say they are "from Saucío." This name

also carries certain connotations, especially to informed outsiders. For instance, by hearing that A is from Saucío, other Chocontanos immediately know that A is a Liberal in politics, that he lives one mile south of Chocontá, that he frequents certain stores, and who his friends are. Likewise, when a family name is connected with the name of a vereda, the identification becomes easy. Thus the "Torres of Saucío" can be readily identified from the "Torres of Puebloviejo." The use of a toponym—a name handed down in this locality from generation to generation—thus is very helpful in the determination of who really belongs in the vereda.

But the people in Saucío also participate in a common economic network, in a common educational system, in common religious activities, and in common politics. Farmers all, they deal with stores and markets. The neighborhood contains two stores, centrally located. These

attract an almost daily flow of local folks, a flow which increases considerably on Saturdays and Sundays. Although individuals from other veredas stop here to rest and to drink while walking or horseback-riding home, the main purpose of these stores is to provide recreational facilities to the local farmers.

Fals-Borda describes the rich life that centers upon these stores as follows:

The two hamlet shops serve as local "country clubs," where farmers find a room dedicated to the sale of beverages and food. This area, which is not very large, is a part of the house where the owner family lives. While interior apartments are partly independent, this social room is open either to a yard or directly to the highway. A big wooden counter separates the clients from the manager; shelves occupy the whole wall behind the counter at one side.

The two owner families indulge in a division of labor for the management of their respective stores. The male head is the supervisor, who transports beer and foodstuff from Chocontá and who sees that there are no fights in the store; the adult females of the house are placed behind the counter, and they serve the customers, keep track of accounts, and receive the cash. (There is a folk-saying which forbids having male bartenders: "Ventera, que no ventero, porque ventero es la ruina—onde's ventero el que vende, ni siquer'el diablo arrima." That is, not even the Devil would be a customer if there were a male attendant in the store.) Besides beer and cigarettes, which are the main trade articles, the stores sell bread, *panela*, candy, candles, and sundry items.

The stores also furnish tables and benches for the clients. Most farmers, however, prefer to stand by the counter for hours, exchanging information, joking, and gossiping. Otherwise, they organize a match of *tejo* for which the store supplies the necessary metal discs, and sometimes the gunpowder bags.[1] It is also the responsibility of the store to keep

1. Tejo, also called *turmeque,* is a game played only by males, organized in two teams of from one to six members each. Metal discs of variable weight, worked into truncated conical shape and small enough to fit between the outstretched thumb and index finger, are thrown from one end to another of a court about 20 yards (18 meters) long. The purpose is to hit small, flat paper bags filled with gunpowder, usually four in number, placed on the rim of an iron ring about four inches in diameter. There are two such rings, one sunk into a clay incline located at each end of the court. The discs are thrown by swinging the arm forward from below, bowling style. When properly thrown, the disc soars gracefully and falls near or on the iron ring with the powder bags. It takes considerable skill and practice to throw these discs with style and accuracy.

Three points are given a team for each bag exploded. In case no bag is exploded, one point is awarded to the team whose disc falls closest to the ring. The first team to score nine points wins a game, and another game starts immediately. Bets are made on the number of games won rather than on individual points accumulated.

Some special rules of the sport offer shortcuts to the winning of games. When a disc lands inside the iron ring without moving it (*embocinada,* roughly, a "spare"), six points are earned. When a disc not only falls inside the ring but causes the explosion of one or more bags (*monona,* or "strike"), nine points are earned, that is, a full game. If the score is eight to zero and the team with no score performs a monona, that team is awarded three complete games (*viudo*). But when a game ends nine to nothing, the winning team earns two complete games instead of one (*doble*). And when three partners of one team throw their discs closer to the ring than any of their opponents, the game is immediately granted to the former (*chipolo*). These special rules serve to keep the players in constant excitement and earnestness.

The cost of the beer and gunpowder is prorated according to the number of games played. Each team pays for the games it lost. For example, if the final score is five games to three and there is an expense of eight pesos, each game will cost one peso; the winners pay three pesos and the losers pay five. Then these costs are, of course, distributed among the members of each team.

Market woman arranging a geometric display of ripe bananas in the Cuernavaca, Mexico, market. (Courtesy Susan Porter)

these courts in good shape, to even the clay at both ends, and to moisten it in order to achieve the proper consistency. These courts are adjacent to the beer establishments—this is important because drinking is a part of the game.

It is the custom of the peasants to arrive on Saturdays and Sundays at about two o'clock in the afternoon. The climax of activity is four hours later, when tejo players come back into the *tiendas* [stores; eds.] to settle their accounts. Then, slightly inebriated, they start new and endless rounds of beer drinking.

The formality demanded in these beer bouts is as strict as that for the presentation of credentials by an ambassador. It follows the general pattern found in many areas of the Western World. When a person walks into a store and is acknowledged, those already in it will offer him a bottle of beer. After the newcomer gulps his first bottle, if he is a gentleman he is expected to offer a round of beer to all those in his conversation group. If this group is composed of six persons, the other five then feel the same obligation to reciprocate for the group. It is easy to calculate the number of bottles of beer a man may drink in one night simply by counting the number of men in his conversation group. If more newcomers join, this geometric progression of beer buying and drinking becomes staggering. Needless to say, the men invariably return to their homes drunk and without much money left. Women also drink, but they do not frequent the stores with the assiduousness displayed by the men. But drinking is not looked upon as a vice. It is the normal outlet of sociability; it is expected of all adults. As declared by a peasant: "No person can have friends if he does not drink." It is natural for a farmer to go to a tienda to drink, if for no other reason than that the store is the only organized institution in which he can have a "clean, good time." The only sport indulged in with interest is tejo, but this is never played without a bottle of beer close at hand.

Abstention from drinking is actually a deviation or a sign of aloofness or separation from the local culture. The nonacceptance of alcoholic drinks means, in general terms, one of two things—either the abstainer considers himself superior and is thus insulting his fellows (who think they know him better), or, perhaps worse, he may be suspected of saving his money for some purpose other than drinking. In the first case, social isolation of the snob is the result. In the second case, the miser is pointedly reminded with a common phrase: "En asuntos de tomata no se pierde la plata" (When it comes to drinking, money is not wasted).

Those conversation groups which form have, as a rule, three main topics: personal problems which include farm activities; the exchange of labor and the loaning and borrowing of money; and gossiping (often about women), in about that order of importance. Occasional family visitors from Bogotá and elsewhere fill the evening hours by answering questions; they relate their experiences while the peasants listen with deep interest, and, it should be added, with respect and admiration. It is also at the stores that the latest political events are commented upon, and that informal agreements on action are made among the people. The role of the store owner in these cases is often to serve as a witness, a role which indirectly gives him a sort of superiority or leadership. This does not mean, however, that the store owners are *gamonales,* that is, individuals who coerce voting for certain candidates. They seem to be, rather, political symbols, or political high priests officiating at a semi-secret ritual ceremony.

By eight o'clock many farmers are out of hand. By nine, if perchance an outsider walks into the store, he will find a disagreeable atmosphere, somewhat antagonistic toward him; it would have been, indeed, an unfortunate mistake or an act of daring, if such an outsider were a member of the Conservative party, for example. Conflicts usually start at that hour. If there is no fight, the anticlimax is shortly after nine, when farmers have their last beer (*la de p'irnos*). If a few stalwarts stay, the stores do not close their doors; however, the establishments are seldom open after eleven o'clock.

During the other days of the week, the shops sell sundry articles and foodstuffs to nearby homes. Then the stores are open at some time between four and six o'clock every afternoon. But hardly any peasant arrives with the purpose of drinking. During week days there are certain pastimes such as a game with coins, called *pite,* or a hand of cards in which young farmers can engage. Otherwise, few other activities in the tiendas are worth noting. Their owners continue to work in the field, and the women keep themselves to their domestic affairs. Marketing, however, has to be carried on in Chocontá.

The economic activity of the Saucites is oriented toward the markets which have their locus in the main square at the town of Chocontá. Until about forty years ago these markets were held on Sunday, but when the county became a full-fledged parish, the Dominican fathers transferred the former practice to Saturday.

Even though the general appearance of the market is one of disorder and chaos, there are well-established procedures and customs designed to smooth operations. Potatoes, for instance, are one of the first articles brought to the plaza; sometimes, if there is no danger of rain, farmers unload their *cargas* in the open space the previous night, leaving a small boy to sleep beside them. Potatoes are also among the first articles to be sold; they are sold mostly to middlemen who walk up and down the square with fat rolls of bills. Prices paid depend on the amount of produce which is present at the square at about eight o'clock in the morning; after this hour, they have inconsistent fluctuations. Prices usually tend to decrease toward noon, when farmers want to get rid, at practically any cost, of the produce which they have transported from their homes with the greatest of difficulties.

Tents belonging to merchants and others who arrive from Bogotá and from other *municipios* [municipality; eds.] are always installed on the southern portion of the plaza. These tents harbor a wide variety of articles, such as cheap jewelry, *ruanas* (ponchos), clothing, shoes, *alpargatas* (sandals), plateware, and china. The sale of meat is always on the east side. Pottery is found on the north side, where peasant women are the sole vendors. Men, on the other hand, engage in major transactions, such as the sale of potatoes, wheat, and other wholesale articles. Each vendor brings his own table, tent, and stool, which he takes back at the end of the market day. A small tax is paid the municipio for the privilege of installing such tents and tables.

When there is a disagreement as to the weight of some agricultural produce (and such disagreements are frequent), the parties summon a county employee who brings the "official" *romana* scale. This scale, of course, is supposed to be exact, and its readings are final. This service costs fifty centavos ($0.20) per carga weighed.

Much activity is displayed during the market. Because this is the day of concentration of the larger community, the parish house, the church, the cemetery, the *Caja Agraria* [Rural Credit Bank; eds.], local government offices, stores, and, of course, the jail, are open for business. The major uses such days for the promulgation of orders and government decrees; he announces these through loud-speakers installed in the courthouse. On certain Saturdays, local police surround the square in order to catch the men of military age who have not served in the army. There are the usual sights of men loaded with sacks of farm produce pushing their way into the crowd, women loudly advertising their articles, clients calmly strolling by, oxcarts squeaking their way down the streets, trucks impatiently honking their horns, beggars wailing for alms, thieves shuffling away from pursuers, dogs fighting, and humans wrangling.

The square begins to be vacated at about noon, when most of the best

Arrival at dawn for the weekly Saturday market, Otovalo, Ecuador. (Courtesy United Nations)

articles have been sold. From twelve o'clock to about four the farmers engage in a number of *tronches*,[2] depending on the business transacted. Then, when they are able to tear themselves away from the store counters and their conversation groups, the peasants return home after a full day of financial activity and social intercourse.

Marketers leave truckloads of litter on the square. The cleaning of this (mostly leaves and dry vegetation which farmers use to pack the harvests) is the responsibility of the municipio government. Inmates in the town jail do that cleaning at night or early in the morning before Mass starts at seven o'clock.

A second and minor market is held on Tuesday morning, but very few people attend it. Those who have something to sell, mostly women who seem to specialize in petty transactions, simply place the salable articles on the western side of the plaza, close to the main street, sit next to them, and wait until a customer arrives. It should be noted that much of what outsiders regard as bickering over prices or the bargaining process at this or at the main market, actually is no more than an impulse of gregariousness on the part of the women vendors. They are ignorant of the costs; they do not know if the prices they ask cover all the expenses incurred; they do not seem to care if they win or lose in the long run. Thus bargaining appears to be done more in a spirit of sociability than in bad faith. As a rule, the women break down and sell at any price, but only after they and the clients debate the price and other questions at some length.

Cattle transactions are held five blocks north of the main square in a fenced-in field, called a *plazoleta*. Much speculation is entered into by the farmers and *hacendados* at this fair. Heads purchased early in the day sometimes increase their price after a few hours. If they can, many peasants buy and sell cattle in the same day at this unusual "stock exchange." Otherwise, those animals which the farmers wish to keep are herded along the main street and the highway toward Saucío. This is done at about noon after the traditional tronche is enjoyed.

While Saturday brings the Saucites to town for business reasons, Sunday sees them there in church. Saucío itself has no church or chapel, and no resident priest; the devout must hear services in Chocontá. A neigh-

2. *Tronche* is an institution set up to show mutual appreciation and friendship after business deals are completed; it implies reciprocation of beer and liquor to celebrate the agreements. This is done in a *tienda* with the usual protocol.

borhood committee gathers alms which go to decorate the church and outside alters, to pay musicians, and to buy fireworks, "for no holy day is complete without colorful and noisy displays of fireworks which are set off in the square immediately after the Mass and during the evenings." The main reasons for regular attendance at church are "the bargaining for favors from the saints, the avoidance of the accumulation of penalties when confession time comes, and the fear of incurring God's displeasure and going to hell." As among peasant peoples the world over, religion is matter-of-fact and down-to-earth, rather than concerned with complex thoughts which seek for deeper meanings behind the visible symbol and rituals.

Lacking a church, Saucío yet bears witness to its religious involvements.

Practically the only decorations and pictures found in these homes are images of saints, sacred cards, and religious calendars purchased during festivities. These objects literally cover whole walls of interior rooms. If it were not because clothing was perched near such pictures, and hoes and sickles reclined against the walls, the general appearance of living rooms and bedrooms would approach that of a Russian iconic shelter. Sacred images are the first objects peasants look at when they wake up in the morning, and the last objects which they see at night while praying before going to bed. Farmers live surrounded by saints, immersed in a sacred world of their own, in an atmosphere of piety which is quite emotional. Peasants even carry the saints with them in the form of scapularies, pocket and chain crosses, small cards for pocketbooks, and in other forms.

They cling, Fals-Borda says, "to His material presence."

Linked by ties of common origin and marriage, by a life organized around common stores and school, involved in common institutions of marketing and church, the Saucites also feel a common political bond. Within the community, each head of a household must stand up for himself, each be a defendant of his own self-respect:

No campesino suffers an insult idly. He first attacks his insulter with fists. If the brawl develops well, he resorts to such other weapons as a beer bottle, a knife, a machete, a heavy stick, or a revolver if available. These brawls seem to have an aspect of prestige-restitution: farmers often fight in an attempt to prove that they are *machos* [masculine], and that they can uphold the self-respect of the family. Peasants find it easy, and even pleasurable, to insult those individuals whom they do not like, it does not matter whether they are new or old acquaintances. . . . They are proficient in the use of cutting, double-meaning remarks; these are employed especially in stores, where this sort of social exchange is bound to cause friction. . . . Because no one knows just what to expect when he goes into a tienda, many peasants carry a knife hidden under their belt or between their trousers and underwear. The *ruana* and the coat conceal these weapons. No mental, religious, or social reservations or inhibitions seem to be felt when brandishing a weapon. There is little feeling of guilt in *medir el aceite* (literally, to measure the oil level in a car motor) with a knife into the stomach of an opponent who, in the mind of the peasant, deserves to be punished. This becomes especially prominent in those times and areas in which the police are unable or unwilling to do justice. If the guilty one is pursued by the police, he migrates for a few months, not returning until the storm has passed. If the police do not forget quickly, he lives in hiding—his friends never turn him in. His action is justified as a natural response to a challenge against his personal security, self-respect, and social standing.

Killings or beatings may in turn unleash blood feuds, in which the family members of the victim seek revenge. "Then the pride of the whole family group and its prestige are considered challenged, and drastic action is expected. But the peasants do not seek their revenge in haste. They patiently, laboriously, work toward vengeance."

As a whole, however, Saucío is Liberal in politics. This identification of party affiliation with politics is widespread in Colombia. "Neighborhoods with a balanced number of Conservatives and Liberals are hard to find. When rural families migrate, they tend to move to veredas of the same political affiliation, where they will not be harassed, and where they can count on the solidarity of the whole group in case of emergencies." Saucío became Liberal in the 1860's under the influence of influential men in the countryside who became foremen and overseers for nearby estates, owned by men who had strong affiliations with the Liberal cause. In contrast, other nearby veredas sided with the Conservatives, since influential patrons there supported the Conservative cause.

Political rivalry has unleashed a series of violent incidents which have led to further violence in turn. Politics

has become almost a struggle for existence. When all these big and little conflicts reflect upon families, the result is obviously a concatenation of vengeances performed by its various members. Then vendettas and other expressions of group action cause the Saucite to be born into a party. The family is the best transmitter of political ideology and the most effective preserver of party allegiance. Party allegiance runs in the 'blood,' and one who changes party in his adulthood is looked upon as a despicable traitor. This can hardly be otherwise. When blood is spilled, the memory of relatives is infused with a desire for revenge, and preparedness for retaliation is a factor *sine qua non* for family survival. Hereditary political cohesion is, therefore, indispensable, compelling beyond the power of any one given individual.

In Fals-Borda's words, "politics is the Achilles' heel of peasant society."

Here we note again a theme which has become familiar to us from the preceding analysis of Hualcán. In Saucío, as in Hualcán, the basic social units are families, clusters of relatives. In Saucío, too, we find households larger than the husband-wife team that contracted the original marriage; but close to three-fourths of all households here do not have any relative residing with the family. Moreover, unrelated persons living in Saucío households are very few in number. As in Hualcán, authority in the household is vested in the senior male; but since the senior male is almost always the father of the family, it is he who makes the relevant decisions for his wife and children. There is less giving and granting of advice; the word of the father is much more stringent and binding. Men

are knights in their castles, entitled to all prerogatives; they are at the same time responsible for discipline, domestic respect, and the upholding of family pride. He makes all the decisions which affect his conjugal family. He works hard in the field and, in recompense, has a right to become noted for his tienda demeanor and ensuing prestige. Women, on the other hand, are mainly to serve their husbands, to give them children, to wash and cook for the family, to help in certain farming chores, to haul water from the springs, and to spin wool.

Men strongly emphasize their rights; and we can see that these rights have a double aspect. A man's show of dominance is closely linked to his prestige among his fellow men: only a man who can keep his women folk submissive is accorded standing in the community of males. Similarly, a woman's behavior reflects directly on her husband. A show of independence, either in her domestic life or in flirting with other men or in taking lovers, immediately calls into question a man's "honor," and leads to serious trouble. This stress on masculinity, on being a *macho* or male is very characteristic of Creole Latin America. It always wears a double face. The woman's activities in the household, in the domestic sphere, have a bearing on the man's standing in the world outside the household, in the public sphere. This is important to remember, because —as we shall see later—it has repercussions in the ways in which public life is conducted.

As in Hualcán, so in Saucío it is among relatives that one seeks aid and comfort. These relatives include relatives by blood and marriage, and also *compadres*, "relatives" one acquires by baptizing a child. As we shall see later, the godparents of a child also become co-parents of the child's parents. While not related at the outset, they are thought to be related as a result of the ritual performed. This is an instance of what anthropologists call "ritual kinship." Such ritual kin are also thought of as part of the operating circle of relatives. Since one turns to relatives for aid and support, one also owes one's primary loyalties to relatives, loyalties which emerge most clearly in the fights and quests for vengeance connected with defending family honor and standing in the community. As in Hualcán, then, there is here, too, an inner circle of kin and friends; people or institutions who do not belong to this inner circle, are "outsiders," and thought of as more distant, more unpredictable, more dangerous, more unreliable than those inside. But—unlike Hualcán—Saucío does not have a religious and political system which serves as a hub through which the households are connected to each other, above and beyond ties of kinship. Rather, social relations in Saucío resemble a loose net. The knots in the net are the households, the string between them the social ties that connect them. But the net is irregular, and there are many loose threads in the total fabric. In Hualcán people are contained within the community by a firm boundary; in Saucío the boundary is weak and changing. The size of the network is a function of the moment: at any time, new threads can be spun between any household in Saucío and the outside, without taking account of a central religious and political system which intervenes between the community and the greater outside.

CONFLICT AND ITS SETTLEMENT IN
HUALCÁN AND SAUCÍO

In comparing Hualcán in highland Peru and Saucío in highland Colombia we have compared a closed community—organized around the hub of the religious and authority system—and an open community—in which social ties form a loose net. We have seen that in Hualcán households are not free and easy with one another, but that they are all subordinate to a common authority, held by the *varayok*. In Saucío there is no common authority, and households regulate their own relations with one another. From this we can predict something about the way in which conflicts between households will be handled in the two communities. In Saucío we have already seen that there are many occasions on which men can come into conflict with another, over who pays first for a round of beer at a store, over insults, over politics; and we have seen that men are quite touchy about their honor and ready to defend it, weapon in hand. There is a court in town, in Chocontá, but it is far away; and men often take the law into their own hands. If there are killings, there are also attempts at vengeance. This is what happened between the Hatfields and the McCoys of West Virginia, and this is what happens here: "feuding and fighting" are likely to become continuous. But in Hualcán there are local authorities, the *varayok*. They settle disputes within the community, because the operations of the central religious and political system requires that men cooperate, and they strive to prevent killings, because they know that a killing will involve the community with Peruvian law. They strive to prevent the interference of outsiders in the affairs of the community, and the Hualcainos cooperate in trying to settle disputes within the community in order to avoid such interference. Therefore we might predict that there will be in communities like Hualcán more reliance on controls by the community as a whole. People will stop a fight where possible. But this does not abolish the source of conflict. People will still dislike and hate each other. One of the ways in which hatred can be shown, without directly injuring your opponent, is through witchcraft. When people in Hualcán are involved in conflict—especially when they are not relatives—both partners to the conflict will fear that the other is bewitching him and both may ask a wizard to protect him against witchcraft, to "fend off" witchcraft. When a person falls ill for any reason, the suspicion of witchcraft will be uppermost in his mind. You might say that witchcraft is a way of carrying on the conflict by other indirect means when community opinion tends to stop a direct fight.

We might diagram the contrast between Saucío and Hualcán somewhat as follows:

Saucío

conflict of interest→hatred→insults→fighting →
→ possible killing→vengeance between A and B

Hualcán

conflict of interest →hatred→insults and fighting
\   stopped
\
↘ witchcraft

ONCE AGAIN:
CLOSED AND OPEN COMMUNITIES IN MEXICO

This contrast between closed and open communities comes out especially clearly in a comparison of two communities in Mexico, Eloxochitlán and Tajín. They were studied by Carmen Viqueira, a psychologist, and Angel Palerm, an anthropologist. Both communities are inhabited by Indians whose mother tongue is a language called Totonac. But there the resemblance ends. Eloxochitlán is a tightly clustered settlement, lying in the cool mountains of the eastern Sierra Madre, near the town of Zacatlán. Its inhabitants farm and act as middlemen in the trade between highlands and lowlands. Land is scarce in relation to population; Eloxochitlán feels the pinch of insufficient resources. In contrast, Tajín lies in the tropical lowlands. Its population lives in scattered hamlets. People grow maize (our "Indian" corn) on fields carved out of the jungle, planted for two years, and then abandoned for another similar field somewhere else. But they also have a commercial crop to sell, vanilla. Land is readily available, and the economic horizon of the people appears to be widening.

In both communities the basic social unit is the household. In Tajín it usually consists of a senior male head, his wives (multiple marriage is permitted and practiced), his single and married sons, his daughters-in-law, his unmarried daughters, and his grandchildren. The household operates as an economic unit, under the authority of the senior male,

Market, Silvia, Cauca Region, Colombia. (Courtesy United Nations)

cultivating and processing maize and vanilla as a household enterprise. These households vie with one another for prestige, and they do so by showing off their wealth in houses, in number of wives, in clothing—especially in the costly embroidered dresses of the women—and in occasional fiestas offered to neighbors which require dancing, music, and abundant food and drink. But households do this voluntarily; there are no ways—outside the force of public opinion—of making them conform to this pattern. Some men are charged with authority; but they can only advise, they cannot force anyone. They do not have the considerable powers of the *varayok* of Hualcán. Instead, they persuade; they do not rule. If there is a serious case of conflict, they may appeal to the Mexican authorities at Papantlá, much as the people in Saucío could go to Chocontá. But the world of Tajín and the world of Papantlá are distinct social orbits, and a Totonac from Tajín will but rarely get involved with the seat of power in the nearby town.

In Eloxochitlán the household tends to be small, accommodating only the husband and wife pair with their children. But there we find—as in Hualcán—a complex ceremonial and political system. Men strive to occupy the positions of stewardship and to rise to positions of authority. In both positions they must organize fiestas—at great cost to themselves—and there are severe penalties if they do not. Frequently a family in Eloxochitlán will sell a portion of its land or livestock or go heavily into debt as a result of trying to meet its ceremonial-political obligations. At the same time, the community acquires a body of men who are capable of exercising real authority through fines, forced labor, and jail sentences. In Eloxochitlán—in contrast to Tajín—the authorities rule, they do not persuade. In Tajín there are no ways the authorities can force men to settle their conflicts peaceably; but in Eloxochitlán the authorities interfere readily and frequently in relations between community members, and strive to restrict and reduce the show of violence in order to maintain the internal cohesion of the community around the ceremonial-political system.

From this we might predict—as we have done above—that in Tajín the show of violence will tend to be direct; in Eloxochitlán, indirect. Let us see whether our prediction is correct, and what forms conflict assumes in the two communities.*

---

* The quotations on the following pages are from Angel Palerm and Carmen Viqueira, "Alcoholismo, brujería y homicidio en dos communidades rurales de México," in *América Indígena*, Vol. XIV, No. 1, January 1954, pp. 7-36. (Trans. eds.) Reprinted by permission.

First, our authors observed that in Eloxochitlán drunkenness

is normal, systematic, continuously sought after, and readily accepted. The frequent public and semi-public meetings in the homes of the authorities and in the square, and also at reunions of family and friends; religious and civil celebrations; births and deaths; marriages; house-warmings; magical rites, and so forth take place accompanied by an enormous ritual consumption of alcohol and end in collective drunks. An ordinary week, involving no special fiestas or celebrations, implies, at any rate, at least two or three days of routine drunkenness for most of the men, especially for those who occupy public posts.

Unmarried men drink less; unmarried girls may not drink; but adult women do. Despite this great intake of alcohol, nobody becomes aggressive. "We have not observed serious fights between drunks, and if there is some quarrel, it remains restricted to shoving and insults. People become alternatively talkative and silent, excited and morose; but 'a drunk in Eloxochitlán cannot be considered dangerous.'"

In Tajín, in sharp contrast, social drinking is rare and measured. Drinking in connection with religious or magical ritual is important—as in offerings to the deities—but people rarely get drunk. When this occurs, however, the Totonac of Tajín exhibit a degree of violence which is in marked contrast to their everyday behavior. The Tajín drunk is dangerous; he may attack suddenly and unpredictably with machete or fire arms. To avoid such behavior, men are made to yield up their arms on public occasions, and aggressive drunks are tied up and jailed. Yet hostility breaks out in still another way, in personal vengeance and resultant homicide. Homicide is frequent; in two years more than 10 per cent of the local male population has been assassinated. Assassination is done from ambush; sometimes the assassin waits for his victim for days and even weeks. The victim's body is disfigured beyond recognition. The motives for homicide are threefold: theft, especially of vanilla pods; infidelity of women; and vengeance for past killings. Thus, as in Saucío, we find that in Tajín men take the law into their own hands. Household deals with household; the relation is direct and not mediated through superior authorities. Direct also is the expression of conflict between households. As we might expect, there is little witchcraft in Tajín.

In Eloxochitlán, however, the direct expression of conflict is inhibited by its own system of organized authority. There is much drunkenness, perhaps as an escape from problems and anxieties; but the drunk does not turn violent. At the same time, in Eloxochitlán, witchcraft

is used constantly to harm enemies and to free oneself of [spells] sent by one's adversaries. The people live in permanent fear of witches, and of the illwill of supernatural beings. But, in turn, they look to wizards to bring illness, ruin, or death upon their enemies. The procedures are innumerable, knowledge of them widespread, and the wizards numerous and resourceful. Dead chickens and wooden dolls are buried in the land of the enemy; the dead are sent to visit him (which is always harmful); magical animals (nahuales) are sent forth to cause illness; animals, water, tools are bewitched; women are rendered sterile and children are killed. Those affected by witchcraft—and in fact this applies, in one way or another, to everyone—appeal to countermagic and to other more powerful wizards to heap evil upon the head of the presumed guilty party. The war is silent but pitiless, and no one will avoid reference to one or more enemies to explain his difficulties and misfortunes as the result of witchcraft.

In sharp contrast to Tajín, Eloxochitlán has witnessed but one homicide in twelve years. The victim was an outsider who sold alcohol and was accused of mistreating members of the community. He was killed by the men of Eloxochitlán as a body, and the community as a whole assumed responsibility for his death.

Thus we note again that the two communities are divided by a consistent set of features. In Tajín, it is the household which forms the axis of social organization. Relations between households are direct, without the intervention of superior third parties. Relations of conflict are also direct; conflict is settled by outright killing. In contrast, we see that Eloxochitlán—like Hualcán—organizes its household around a common hub, the religious and political system. Relations between households are interfered with by superior authorities, representing the unity of the community as a whole. The direct expression of conflict is inhibited; only indirect expression is permitted. In Eloxochitlán, say Viqueira and Palerm, "the individual must identify himself with the group."

4

The Role of Religion

RELIGION IN CLOSED AND OPEN COMMUNITIES

We have passed in review closed and open communities in Latin America and examined their several characteristics. Among these, religious activities and religious involvement are ever-recurrent themes. In the closed communities we have found that participation in religious activities is closely geared in with the search for prestige and the attainment of authority in the community. The right to participate in the religious affairs of the community defines who is a member of it and who is not. Those who are included in the circle of participation are members; those who are outside it are not members. Religious participation thus defines the boundary between the community and the outside. Those who participate belong; those who do not participate remain strangers. But religious participation also dovetails with many other activities. Some are economic, because wealth is needed to sustain the religious system. Some are social, involving the striving for social merit, the gaining of prestige. And still other aspects are political, in that prior religious participation is a prerequisite to the holding of political authority. That authority is in turn temporary. A man who has held it returns once more to religious participation after he has given up his political post. Religion as a set of activities is thus of central importance to the life of the closed community. It constitutes the pivot around which the life of the community turns.

In the open communities we have noticed a contrasting situation. Here, too, religion is of importance, but it does not form the hub of life. It is rather one set of activities among other sets of activities; one dimension of life among other dimensions. In Saucío the use of amulets and sacred images in the home enables the peasants to gain reassurance;

Church and market at Santo Tomás Chichicastenango, Guatemala. The worshipers burn copal-gum incense on the church steps before entering. (Courtesy United Nations)

Fals-Borda says "they cling to His material presence; they strive to make Him their constant helper and servant."

Latin America is Roman Catholic, and thus shares the belief, the ceremonial, the organization of Catholicism elsewhere in the world. Yet there are also subtle differences which distinguish Catholicism in Latin America from Catholicism, say, in Ireland or Poland. We have already discovered one source of these differences, when we noted how religion works in different communities. In Hualcán and Eloxochitlán it formed the pivot of communal life; in Saucío it imparted a greater feeling of security to the individual. Thus one source of such differences seems quite clear: Catholicism in any area of the world must be anchored in the customs of particular local groups. Let us add still one more example to clarify this point. In 1948, anthropologist Charles Wagley studied life in Itá, a small town situated on the lower Amazon River in the state of Pará, Brazil. Itá is inhabited by merchants and officials, farmers and rubber gatherers. In describing the cult of Itá's favorite saint, St. Benedict, Wagley also shows us how responsive Catholicism has been to the demands and interests of a local population.*

The patron saint of Itá is St. Anthony, the patron saint of Portugal. But the saint who is most loved, most famous, and most worshiped is St. Benedict, known in Brazil as the "black saint." The image of St. Benedict in Itá is famous throughout the Lower Amazon. He is known as a special protector of rubber gatherers. In Itá St. Benedict is considered "the people's saint," while St. Anthony is the saint of the First Class and the "whites." The latter, selected by the Iberian founders of Itá, did not find favor with the people who came to make up the bulk of the population— the Indians, the mestizos, and the Negroes. Yet, since St. Anthony is the official patron of the town, the Catholic priest encourages his devotion; and with the full support of the padre St. Anthony's day in June is one of the major festivals of the town. The festival of St. Benedict, however, celebrated in December, is by far the most important and the best attended festival in Itá. It is a festival famous throughout the entire region.

About a generation ago, the festivals in honor of these two saints were organized by brotherhoods similar to those which exist today in the rural neighborhoods. The brotherhoods of the town were richer and larger in membership than those in the rural districts of today. Both the Irman-

* From Charles Wagley, *Amazon Town.* Copyright 1953 by Charles Wagley. Reprinted by permission of The Macmillan Company, New York.

dade de São Benedito and the Irmandade do São Antonio maintained cemeteries in which the members were buried. These are still in existence. In keeping with the social position of the people devoted to each saint, the Brotherhood of St. Anthony was made up of "whites" and First Class, while the Brotherhood of St. Benedict consisted of the "people"— the town Second Class, the farmers, and the rubber collectors. Especially were *Os velhos pretos* (the old Negroes) devoted to St. Benedict, and they are said to have been the leaders in the brotherhood. Today both brotherhoods exist in name only. Each year before the festivals of St. Anthony and St. Benedict, an announcement is printed listing the officers of the brotherhood sponsoring the festival and the names of the judges and the major-domos. The Catholic priest is always listed as attorney for the saint for both brotherhoods. The other officers are always people of some official position, such as the mayor, the schoolteacher, or the federal tax collector, or important merchants. The judges and the major-domos are always the same each year, and all are of the upper strata of Itá society. The festivals are actually organized by Dona Branquinha, the devoted schoolteachers, with the help of a few other upper-class ladies. The cost of the festivals is met to a great extent by a collection made among the townspeople. Substantial donations are expected from the merchants of the town, who stand to profit by them. The names of those who contribute most are listed as major-domos of the brotherhood. Actually, however, these associations have ceased to exist; there is no membership body, and the directorate consists only of the upper-class sponsors listed on the printed announcement.

Of a once strong brotherhood, only the *folia* group of St. Benedict remains as an organized body. The *folia* is composed mainly of lower-class mulattoes and Negroes, descendants of the "Old Negroes" once so devoted to St. Benedict. There is a master of ceremonies, an official in charge of saint's errands, and musicians (drummers, a rattle player, and a scraper), all of whom learned their duties and the traditional verses and songs from men who held the positions when the brotherhood was an organized association. These members of the *folia* of St. Benedict feel that the image of the saint belongs to them: "It has been taken away from us by Dona Branquinha and the padre." Nowadays, the padre no longer allows the *folia* group of St. Benedict to take the image out of the church. The long journeys throughout the Lower Amazon on which they once took their saint, singing his praises and collecting contributions, are now reduced to a short procession through the town, supervised by the padre and Dona Branquinha. Only on the actual saint's day is the *folia* group allowed to follow behind their saint's image in the procession. The *folia* may not nowadays go from house to house carrying the image and asking for donations, nor may they play and sing inside the church as they once did. The festival of St. Benedict, once directed and organized by the brotherhood, has now been expropriated by the official Church.

The festival of St. Anthony is rather a formal affair. The Catholic padre, who comes to Itá for the occasion, does not believe in mixing religion with pleasure: thus the recreational aspects of the celebration are minimal. In form the festival follows the pattern described for rural festivals. In the past there was the day of raising of the mast followed by a novena for the saint ending on the saint's day. A mast is seldom raised now, but the upper-class devotees still celebrate a novena. On St. Anthony's Day, there is a Mass and a procession. Numerous baptisms and marriages are performed, for this is one of the two days of the year when a Catholic priest is certain to be present in the town. Several hundred people are generally attracted to Itá for the occasion. Business is brisk in the town stores, and the merchants put up a few stands to sell soft drinks and sweets. Sometimes a dance is furtively organized, against the wishes of the priest, by some of the townspeople. There is generally an auction where the few gifts offered to the saint are sold. According to Dona Branquinha, the festival of St. Anthony "does not pay the expenses of decorating the church."

On the other hand, the festival of St. Benedict not only pays for the decoration of the church for both festivals but also provides the cash to pay for repairs on the church throughout the year. Since St. Benedict is the special protector of rubber gatherers, most collectors donate the first day's harvest of each season to their saint. In a normal year this amounts to more than one thousand pounds of crude rubber. Boats passing by Itá fire off rockets in honor of St. Benedict and frequently stop to offer a donation to the saint. Both the townspeople and the rural dwellers of the Itá community present gifts to their favorite saint during the year in return for his favors. As St. Benedict's festival approaches, the voluntary offerings increase. They consist of rubber, a calf, manioc flour, chickens, pigs, and almost any salable produce. Dona Branquinha receives the offerings and lists them in a book with the name of the donor and later, the amount they bring when they are sold at auction on St. Benedict's day. In two years Dona Branquinha was able to pay the expenses of decorating the church for the festivals and to accumulate approximately $2000 (cr. $40,000) used for repairing the church. "St.

Anthony lives in St. Benedict's house and at St. Benedict's expense," people complain. Dona Branquinha considers that these funds "belong to the Church," and she makes an accounting of them to the padre, but the people feel that the money belongs to their saint.

In the past, St. Benedict received even more donations than he does now. During the years of the rubber boom, the saint's annual income was fabulous in terms of Itá's economy. In those days the brotherhood sent the *folia* group with the saint's image on two long trips to collect contributions and offerings. The saint's image was placed on a temporary altar in a large sailing vessel manned by members of the brotherhood. They sailed almost 125 miles upriver, stopping at each settlement or trading post, singing and praying to their saint, and collecting offerings. Returning to Itá, the group unloaded their cargo of rubber, cattle, pigs, manioc flour, and other gifts and then proceeded downriver, returning only on the eve of the raising of the mast to inaugurate the festivities. The return of the *folia* was always anxiously expected, and the stories of the miracles performed by St. Benedict on these expeditions are told with pride by older men. Nowadays, "because the padre no longer allows the image to go out of the church with the *folia*," one devotee explained, "St. Benedict is poor."

In the past the celebrations for St. Benedict, like those for St. Anthony, followed the traditional pattern of the raising of the mast, the evening prayers during a novena, the social dancing, a Half-Moon nautical procession, the *folia* group playing in front of each residence, and the cutting of the votive mast and the sweeping of the houses. St. Benedict's festival differed from those held today in the rural zones only in that it was more elaborate and attended by many more people. Today many phases of the saint's festival are abbreviated, even omitted, because of the greater controls of the Catholic Church. As before, however, people begin to gather by December 1st, and the crowd increases each day until December 8th, when the mast is raised. At least one thousand visitors from the rural districts and from neighboring municipalities attend the inauguration of the festival. By December 25th and 26th, during the climax of the festivities, there are generally more than two thousand people in Itá—almost four times the normal population of the town. To feed the many visitors, there are stands in the streets serving foods, assai juice, sweets, and soft drinks. In every Itá household there are guests and even paying boarders. Other people sleep in the boats that bring them, and still others, braving the possibility of rain, hang their hammocks outdoors under the trees.

Celebration of Spanish saint as seen in procession at Cuzco, Peru. (Cornell Capa, Magnum)

Each night there are dances. Admission to these dances is five cruzeiros for men. Ladies enter free of charge. The music is furnished by an orchestra consisting of a flute, a guitar, a ukulele, and a scraper. And every night and all day long during the last days of the festivities, there is samba dancing in the pavilion to the beat of drums. The samba, as danced on this occasion and at the rural festivals, differs from the characteristic Brazilian samba of the city, both in tempo and in the movements of the dance itself. The old-style samba of Itá is danced by couples, but the partners dance apart without touching each other. Their steps are short and shuffling; their bodies are stiff with only the arms swinging for balance. The tempo is fast, and the drummers are replaced at intervals; the dancing is almost continuous. Samba dancing in the pavilion is traditional during St. Benedict's festival, and people gather to "dance a hand" and to watch the better dancers. Order is kept by the folia group, the remnant of the brotherhood, who do not allow men to dance with their hats on and forbid drinking in the vicinity. The pavilion is a central attraction of the festival, but nowadays people are beginning to prefer the baile pegado (joined dancing), as modern social dancing is called, and these commercial dances attract many visitors away from the pavilion.

Under the direction of the master of ceremonies, Benedito Torres, a descendant of one of the "old Negroes," the folia of St. Benedict still meets to practice in the evenings for several weeks before the festival. There are several good drummers as well as players of the scraper and of the rattle. All of them know the versinhos (quatrains)[1] to be sung on each specific occasion during the festival. They still hold forth in front of the church on the occasion of the raising of the mast, and from time to time during the festival they sing an alvorada (morning serenade) at the break of day, and at sunset an Ave Maria. Only on the vespers of St. Benedict's day, however, do they sing in front of people's homes asking for donations. The padre allows them to carry only the esplendor (the saint's crown) as a substitute for the image itself. On December 24th the folia sings for the Half-Moon procession, occupying the first canoe with their saint and accompanying the image back to the church. Afterward they sing its praises from the church doorway.

In Itá Christmas is hardly celebrated at all, except for a midnight Mass. It is overshadowed by the climax of the festivities for St. Benedict, which continue from December 24th through the 28th. On the 24th

---

1. These quatrains are introduced by the leader, the master of ceremonies, who is known for his good voice. The instrumentalists join him in the refrain.

there are the processions and the singing of the *folia* group, and on the 25th there is samba dancing. The activities of the *folia* group are nowadays suspended on Christmas day at the request of the padre. Early on the 26th there is an early Mass for St. Benedict, and in the afternoon the traditional auction of the donations to the saint begins. This generally continues well into the next day. Samba dancing and social dancing are continuous on the 26th and 27th. On December 28th the mast is cut down as the *folia* group sings again. The leaves used to decorate the mast are much sought after by townspeople and visitors alike as medicine. A large crowd rushes to gather them as the votive pole falls. The custom of sweeping out the houses of the judges and the major-domos at the end of a festival is still maintained in the town of Itá, although these people are sponsors in name only. On New Year's Eve, after the influx of visitors is over, the merchants offer the townspeople a dance "because they have made a great deal of money." Coming just before the heavy rains of "winter" begin, St. Benedict's day is the climax of the year.

LATIN AMERICAN CATHOLICISM

Catholic belief and practice will differ necessarily, as it is fitted into various local situations, each marked by its particular history and problems. But there is still another source of difference, more subtle and also more difficult to explain. Anthropologists have long realized that people in different parts of the world imagine supernatural beings differently. In trying to understand these differences they have discovered that everywhere men use the familiar to understand the unfamiliar. They fall back on their relationships with other human beings to imagine and speak about their relations with the supernatural. Thus, for example, Catholics speak of God the Father, because they have grown up in a culture which links fatherhood with authority and power. God the Father is not like any human father, nor are his power and authority like those of any father on earth. Nevertheless, in order to think about an all-powerful and just supernatural entity, Christian believers are led to cast their thoughts in terms of a relation that is familiar to them, that of a father and his children. Let us put this in another way. Men strive to come to grips with the supernatural, and they do so in terms which they draw from their habitual dealings with other people. The habitual relations of people toward each other offer possible ways of thinking about the supernatural and dealing with it: they are *models* for the supernatural. A model is a construction which stands for something. A model of a jet airplane which you build up from a modeling kit is not the same thing as a jet airplane; it is a picture of it. Such a model is a tangible, visible thing—but there are also models which you can shape in your head. When you think of such things as a "county fair," or "a date," you do not think of a particular county fair or date, but of a construction which you have made in your head, a mental picture or model. Thoughts about the supernatural —about gods, spirits, demons, ghosts—are also models, and the experiences which go into the construction of such models are derived from experiences with other people which have become habitual in your group. But groups differ, and so also differ their experiences with people and the particular problems of life to which people address themselves. Let us return to Latin America. What is there about the habitual dealings of people with each other in Latin America which serves as a model for coping with the supernatural? What is there about social relationships in Latin America which would explain why Catholicism in Latin America possesses a different cast from Catholicism in Ireland or Poland, or from Buddhism in Burma or Ceylon, or from the belief in spirits in New Guinea?

Let us remember what we have said of the way social relations are patterned in Latin America, especially of the contrast between the intimate personal orbit and the larger world beyond the personal circle. Relations within the personal circle are relations of trust, of primary loyalty, of warmth. But relations beyond the personal circle are relations of distrust, of diminishing loyalties, of conflict both potential and actual. Let us also remember that a division of labor exists in the family. Within the family, it is the mother who ministers to the needs of husband and children; it is her pre-eminent domain. Outside the family it is the man of the house who represents the family. He looks for a job, he administers the resources of the family to public ends, he deals with other heads of households in the various operations of life. He acts for the family in the public sphere. That public sphere implies the competition of personal circle with personal circle, and the opposition of personal circles to the larger institutions of the society. Hence the men are involved pre-eminently in that social arena characterized by distrust, by conflict, by competition, sometimes by violence.

Are there parallels to this contrast in social relationships in the sphere of religious beliefs? In that sphere, too, there are supernaturals who are thought of as being further removed from mortals, others who are in closer relations to them. God is "far away." "For most Latin Americans," say anthropologists William W. Whyte and Allan R. Holmberg, "God is a kind of vague entity like a corporation. He is a hazy and inaccessible power with whom it is impossible to deal directly. Consequently, He gets little attention in religious life."[2] Again, "God exists, no doubt," says Tomás Fillol, an Argentine economist discussing the social factors relevant to economic development in Argentina, "and one should pay Him respect. But God is not easily accessible despite man's good intentions. God is like luck, since an individual's efforts, ability, and initiative count little if He does not help."[3] Let us note that God is similar to the larger society in this respect: powerful, dominant, important, but at the same time unpredictable.

In everyday social life one influences that larger society through intermediaries—kin, friends, patrons. Similarly, therefore, there should be supernatural beings to whom men can turn in dealing with that ultimate unapproachable and unpredictable power. These intermediaries are the Virgin Mary and the saints. The saints say Whyte and Holmberg, "act as intermediaries between God and man and are viewed as real people with whom it is possible to personalize relations . . . in religious life one frequently identifies his fortunes in life with a particular saint, just as in politics one may do so with a particular political leader." In Catholic belief the saints receive the prayers of the faithful and present these petitions before the throne of God. Similarly, the Mother of God is thought to be able to intercede for men with her son, Jesus Christ, God the Son. Men therefore turn to these supernatural intermediaries when they seek to connect their personal lives with the greater power beyond. They approach the saints and the Virgin as friends and patrons, just as in real life they seek both friends and patrons. There are many such supernatural patrons. There are saints who are patrons of particular activities, like Saint Anthony who in popular thought is "good for" finding a house, St. John who helps unmarried girls find husbands, St. Christopher who aids wayfarers. There are patron saints of households and of entire communities, as St. Ursula was in Hualcán, or Our Lady of Health who is the patron saint of Chocontá, the larger community of which Saucío forms a part. There are patrons of entire regions, as the Virgin of Zapopán in Mexico who has predominant influence in the west-central highlands, or the Lord of Zacapulas in Honduras who attracts pilgrims from a number of adjacent countries. There is, finally, the patroness of

2. William F. Whyte and Allan R. Holmberg, "Human Problems of U.S. Enterprise in Latin America," *Human Organization,* Fall 1956, p. 3.
3. Tomás Roberto Fillol, *Social Factors in Economic Development: The Argentine Case,* MIT Press, 1961, p. 11.

Remembrance of pre-Columbian colonial times: procession to a festival in Andean Peru. (Sergio Larrain, Magnum)

the Americas, the Virgin of Guadalupe whose church stands in Mexico City. There are thus many supernatural patrons who connect ever widening circles of social life with the greater power of the ultimate deity.

It is these multiple intercessors who are important in the everyday existence of people. In closed communities, such as Hualcán, the entire religious life is built around the cult of the saints. The saints are served by the numerous stewards and their helpers, and the cult of the saints is pivotal to the entire organization of the community. Each cult is sponsored by a steward and his helpers who in turn take charge of the necessary festivities until the end of the calendric round. Merit gained in such religious good works then becomes the springboard to authority; the *mayordomia* or stewardship leads to the position of communal *varayok*. Through its own religious organization Hualcán as a whole maintains good relations with its particular supernaturals, and as a whole asks for their protection and blessing. At the same time it also declares its autonomy from the wider world. Stein says, "Hualcainos themselves organize and direct the activities of the community, and outsiders such as priests and *patrones* play only minor roles. Religious organization belongs to Hualcán and the Hualcainos."[4]

In open communities we find no such tight organization of the community as such. There, individual households are free to form their own relations of kinship, friendship, and patron-clientage with other households. Thus we would expect that relations with the supernatural intermediaries would also be more individualized, that each household would have some choice in selecting and dealing with its own supernatural go-between. Individuals have a wider choice of personal attachment to particular saints. Moreover, we see that the relation between the supernaturals and people parallels the relations of men among themselves. Just as men make contracts in real life, to further their common interests, so men make compacts with the saints. Fals-Borda tells us that people in Saucío approach the supernatural in a spirit of bargaining. People will pledge pilgrimages or masses to their favorite saints in return for help in problems of money, health, or love. "Saucites supposedly go to the confessional with the desire of atoning to God for moral transgressions committed up to that time (especially when mass confessions are held twice a year) and to avoid their continued accumulation. If the things the priest tells them to do are done it then becomes the responsibility of the Church to see to it that God keeps His side of the bargain by pro-

4. Stein, *Life in the Highlands of Peru*, p. 236.

tecting the believer from damnation." Similarly, Eric R. Wolf* says of the highlands of Puerto Rico that

the household offers the saint certain goods and devotions at regular intervals, and the saint is expected to reciprocate with gifts of good fortune for members of the household. These reciprocal relations between people and their saints are conceived as a series of payments, just as in real life people regard exchanges with their neighbors as reciprocal payments. When people plan to hold a sung devotion in honor of the Virgin, they say they are going to "pay" (*pagar*) the Virgin. When people plan to hold a devotion to Saint Anthony, they are "paying" (*pagando*) the saint. If the payments are made properly and at regular intervals, the saints are bound to produce good results. Payments at the right time ensure good harvests and keep misfortune away from the family.

Among these intercessors the Virgin Mary plays a special role. The special adoration of the Virgin is old in Spain, but in Latin America it is especially deep and passionate. In contrast, Christ is a more problematical figure in Latin America than elsewhere. It is notable that in religious painting and sculpture he very rarely appears in the form in which he is most familiar to North Americans, as a teacher at the height of his mature judgment and wisdom. Nor are there many representations of Christ Victorious, risen from the dead, whose resurrection has guaranteed the salvation of the world. Instead, he is depicted either as a babe in the arms of his mother—little Jesus, but not yet Christ (from the Greek *Christos*, the anointed one)— or as the suffering Christ who has taken the suffering of the world upon his shoulders but is not yet certain of resurrection. It is the broken man who thinks himself foresaken by God who is depicted here. What is there in the world of Latin American social relations which would explain this special attachment to the ministering supernatural Mother and the predilection for the suffering and unredeemed Christ?

Let us return to our contrast between the two spheres of social relations. The personal and intimate circle centers upon the family; the family is in turn the domain of the ministering mother. Motherhood involves suffering, but that suffering contributes to the atmosphere of trust

* From Eric R. Wolf, "San José: Sub Cultures of a 'Traditional' Coffee Municipality," in Julian H. Steward, *et al.* (eds.), *The People of Puerto Rico,* University of Illinois Press, 1956. Reprinted by permission.

Feasting at graveside in a cemetery in Bolivia. (Cornell Capa, Magnum)

and warmth that characterizes the circle. Within the circle, morality is strong and certain. In contrast, it is the men who represent their households in the public sphere, the sphere of distrust, questionable loyalties, conflict and violence. They also suffer; but their suffering is connected with the sphere in which morality is weak and uncertain. Does this have a parallel in the religious imagery? Just as the Mother of Christ represents the sphere of warmth and moral certainty, so the suffering Christ represents the moral uncertainty, the potential violence and brutality of that other, public, sphere. This is the sphere of men. They must operate in that sphere in which, as the peasants of Saucío say, all too often "Christ turns his back." There is thus a parallel between the suffering Christ and men who suffer on earth. As Christ bears his cross, so they must bear theirs. Fals-Borda says of the peasants of Saucío that they "have accepted almost cheerfully their obvious earthly suffering. This is their cross; it is part of the bargain of life. Suffering is life, and life is suffering." Hence also not many "fully conceive of the redemptive role of Christ, who has been pictured to them mainly as the long-suffering, thorn-crowned Son of God, nailed to a cross and resigned to His death— an example of impotence."[5] Once more we can recognize in the arrangement of ideas about the supernatural the arrangement of relations between men in the society in which they make their lives. Yet there is still another way in which religion functions in Latin American life, and that is as an art form. The richly laden churches, the solemn processions, song and music, the splendor of fireworks—all these impart to religious activities a dimension of festiveness, of extraordinary events, out of the ordinary because they contrast so sharply with everyday existence. During such days, writes the perceptive Mexican poet Octavio Paz,*

the silent Mexican whistles, shouts, sings, shoots off fireworks, discharges his pistol into the air. He discharges his soul. And his shout, like the rockets we love so much, ascends to the heavens, explodes into green, red, blue, and white lights, and falls dizzily to earth with a trail of golden sparks. This is the night when friends who have not exchanged more than the prescribed courtesies for months get drunk together, trade confidences, weep over the same troubles, discover that they are broth-

5. Fals-Borda, *Peasant Society in the Columbian Andes,* p. 227.
* From Octavio Paz, *The Labyrinth of Solitude: Life and Thought in Mexico,* translated by Lysander Kemp. Copyright © 1961 by Grove Press, Inc. Reprinted by permission.

ers, and sometimes, to prove it, kill each other. The night is full of songs and loud cries. The lover wakes up his sweetheart with an orchestra. There are jokes and conversations from balcony to balcony, sidewalk to sidewalk. Nobody talks quietly. Hats fly in the air. Laughter and curses ring like silver pesos. Guitars are brought out. Now and then, it is true, the happiness ends badly, in quarrels, insults, pistol shots, stabbings. But these too are part of the fiesta, for the Mexican does not seek amusement: he seeks to escape from himself, to leap over the wall of solitude that confines him during the rest of the year. All are possessed by violence and frenzy. Their souls explode like the colors and voices and emotions. Do they forget themselves and show their true faces? Nobody knows. The important thing is to go out, open a way, get drunk on noise, people, colors. Mexico is celebrating a fiesta. And this fiesta, shot through with lightning and delirium, is the brilliant reverse to our silence and apathy, our reticence and gloom.

Now we understand better, perhaps, what is meant when people say that "Latin America is Catholic." We have seen how much religion is a part of people's lives: as an element in local organization, as a set of models for their thought and behavior, and as experience, ranging from the solemnity of a procession to the festive noise and color of a fiesta. But it is also important to note that religion on this plane of local or personal experience is not identical with the Church. The Church is a large-scale, complex, international organization of men and materials, dedicated to certain beliefs and practices. The religious beliefs and activities of communities like Hualcán or Saucío or Itá may fit into this large scale and complex scheme, but the fit is loose and elastic. Local beliefs and practices may correspond to those of the larger organization, but they are likely to undergo many changes in the hands of the local practitioners. Like players in a theater who improvise from a basic script, they change it and adapt it to local needs. They add new elements, they neglect old ones. The result is that the Catholicism of the people, popular Catholicism, is never the same as formal sophisticated Catholicism. Religion as practiced in the countryside is not the same as the religion envisioned by the leaders of the Church. Sometimes it is even possible for people to engage themselves wholeheartedly in local religious experience but to be indifferent or even hostile to the Church at large.

This gap between popular and formal religion constitutes a great challenge to the Church in Latin America. It means that the great mass of

Catholics only come into contact with the Church on certain rare occasions, notably when they apply to the priest for the sacraments of baptism, confirmation, matrimony, extreme unction, communion, or penance. But while the Latin American priest has been a dispenser of these sacraments, he has not been greatly concerned with the social life of his parishioners. In the words of Father Roger Vekemans, a Belgian Jesuit who directs Centro Vellarmino, a center for social studies in Santiago, Chile,

Spanish Catholicism has never been incarnational, meaning that it has never been concerned with man's life in this world. An overly spiritualized religion can exist without challenge in a static society, which Latin America was for several centuries. But when it comes in contact with the harsh realities of a headlong society, a conflict arises. People see that the Church has been here for four centuries and does not seem able to make for them a life they can be satisfied with in the face of modern advances.[6]

This means, says Leonard Gross, a senior editor of *Look*, that the Latin American Church

in being passive about responsibility in the social sphere, has failed to present an image the individual Catholic could duplicate. Lacking an example to follow, the individual did not develop the missing concept. Such an omission is particularly crucial in Latin America, critics charge further, because it lacks other inspirational forces existing in a well-organized, industrialized and heterogeneous society.[7]

6. Cited in L. Gross, "The Catholic Church in Latin America," *Look*, Vol. 26, No. 21, October 9, 1962, p. 31.
7. *Ibid.*

5

The Human Side of the Enclave Economy

So far, we have spoken of communities of small farmers who may raise some small amount of cash crop or work as laborers on nearby estates but whose life is centered mainly on provisioning their own households. While these small farmers are numerically important—they make up the bulk of Latin America's population—their role is secondary when we look at Latin America from the economic point of view. Then the small farmers recede into the background, and what we see rather are the enterprises of the enclave economy—the commercial, agricultural, and industrial complexes which link the hinterland to the city, and the economy of each Latin American country to the greater economy of the world. There is a lot an economist could tell us about these complexes and their external economic relations: about capital and capital investment, or about prices and price fluctuations, or about productivity per unit of capital invested or per worker.

But the anthropologist is less concerned with these technical aspects involved in the operation of an economy; his primary interest lies in the people who make it function. An industrial plant or an estate is not merely a combine of capital, tools, and skills—it is also a human organization of people working together, synchronizing their actions for certain purposes. Certainly the primary function of plants and agricultural estates is to produce goods—it is specially important to keep this in mind in Latin America where plants and estates were called into being to produce goods for sale, to produce commodities as the economist says. But production and distribution also involve men and their motives. To produce, men must be organized and motivated. It is not self-evident to a small farmer with his banana patch why he should labor endless hours in the sun, in carefully synchronized action with other men, under the command of an overseer, to cut a quantity of sugar cane that belongs to someone else. Nor is it self-evident why in exchange for work on the estate he should accept little metal pieces which he cannot eat himself but which he must take to a store to obtain the bananas that he could, under other circumstances, grow himself on his own land. Nor is it self-evident that after ten hours of labor in the field the cane which he has cut does not belong to him but to a landowner who has spent the day far away sitting on the cool porch of his house or in an office surrounded by typewriters and secretaries.

Production and distribution on a large estate or in a factory therefore involve human beings who have to learn new skills, new forms of social organization, and new understandings—new solutions to life problems, in other words—the development of a new culture. This then is one of the tasks of the anthropologist, to understand that human aspect of commercial production, to throw light on the social relations involved in the running of an enterprise. We shall examine these relations as they obtain in a number of different enterprises: stores, rubber lanes, large agricultural estates, cattle ranches, and industrial plants. In some cases these enterprises still exist today. Such are the enterprises of the rubber trade in Brazil, the large estate or hacienda of the Andean highlands. Some are relatively new, like the factories in Argentina. Some existed in the past, like the Brazilian *fazenda* worked by slave labor and the traditional cattle ranch of Argentina. These have disappeared: slavery was abolished in Brazil in 1888 and the traditional cattle ranch in Argentina has given way to a more modern kind of enterprise, especially after the introduction of electric refrigeration.

Nevertheless they were once so important in the life of people that their influence endures to this day. Specifically, it is the way in which they organized people in relationship to each other which exerts a continuing influence. Put in another way, the particular habits built up then to solve life's problems have persisted and affect the ways people go about solving the new problems of a new day. As we describe and analyze each of these major ways of producing and distributing goods, therefore, we are also describing major ways of life characteristic of large areas of Latin America and of prolonged periods of Latin American history. Each of these major ways of life represents a response to certain particular problems; but in the end we shall also try to see if there are things they all have in common. Specifically, look at the social relationships characteristic of each, and compare them to the others to see if they have a common denominator. Such a common denominator anthropologists call a *pattern*. We will be interested in the distinctive characteristics of each of these ways of life, but we shall also seek the common pattern uniting them all.

STORES

In our initial briefing, we spoke of the great cleavage which exists between the highly capitalized enclave economy and the poorly capitalized hinterland. We must keep this contrast firmly in mind if we are to understand many of the *social relations* which we find in Latin America. On the basis of our previous analysis we can predict that there will be not only the networks of social relations which bind people within the great enclave enterprises and the social ties which bind the inhabitants of hinterland villages and hamlets to others of their own kind. There must also be social relations uniting enclave and matrix, the capitalized sector and its relatively more poverty-stricken hinterland. We have already followed some of these social strands when we listened to Fals-Borda describing the operation of stores in the open neighborhood of Saucío in Colombia. We saw there that the stores are not merely entities in the chain of distribution, but that they function as "country clubs," centers of amusement and social interchange, as well as sales organization in the countryside. At this point let us take a closer look at the economic functions of such stores, and see what we can learn from a more general analysis of their operation.

One of the most interesting aspects of stores is that they frequently serve as rural credit institutions. While there are few formal credit institutions in the countryside, there are a wide variety of informal credit mechanisms. The rural storekeeper often functions in this capacity. Thus there are as many credit institutions as there are storekeepers. This proliferation of credit mechanisms has not gone unnoticed by economists, some of whom argue that this unregulated credit system is harmful for economic development. Where the economy suffers from a *lack of funds* readily available, people pin their hopes on their ability to pay in the future, and there arises an army of credit merchants ready to extend goods, in return for promises to pay in the future, usually at very high rates of interest.

The picture is complicated further by the fact that people must eat and consume goods throughout the year, even though their ability to pay for the goods they consume varies with the seasons. A cultivator must await the harvest to obtain goods he can sell for money. During

Purchase at a jewelry store in Peru. (Cornell Capa, Magnum)

Market lady, Cuernavaca, Mexico. (Courtesy Susan Porter)

the rest of the year he must live on credit in the hope of repaying it after the crops are in. Similarly, a cane cutter may work only two or three months out of the year, during the peak harvest period; but he must feed himself and his family and buy goods at stores for the remaining nine or ten months, though wages for cutting cane are only forthcoming during two months. Thus the store owner must often give credit, merely to tide over his clientele until harvest time returns again. The store owner's dilemma is well described by George M. Foster for the Mexican community of Tzintzuntzan:

In order to keep one's customers one must continue to extend credit; if credit is stopped, they simply switch their patronage to another store and the entire amount on the books is irrevocably lost. On the other hand, the debtor knows that if he doesn't pay a little on account from time to time, he can no longer buy, and his bad reputation will spread to other stores. So a delicate game ensues; the buyer tries to get as much as possible on credit, to pay as little as possible, while the storekeeper tries to determine how far he can push his customer without losing him entirely, what is the minimum credit he must continue to extend to keep him.[1]

Storekeeper and buyer thus find themselves in a situation in which each must pursue an interest hostile to the other, and where they must yet reach some balance in order to continue the relationship over time. The storekeeper may wish to maximize his returns of cold cash, but he must both scale down his prices to the level of the buyer's power to purchase, and he must lend on account because the buyer may not have enough money at any given time. On the other hand, the buyer may wish to pay as little as possible, and is yet forced to go into debt, and to accept the higher prices charged as interest in order to obtain the goods which he desires. The result is a "delicate game" between the two partners to the exchange, a game which involves them strongly with one another on the personal level. The storekeeper strives to maintain *his* clientele; in turn, each purchaser of his wares strives to maintain an even relation with *his* storekeeper. As a result, storekeeping is not the impersonal operation characteristic of an American supermarket, but more akin to the personal give-and-take of the traditional backcountry store.

1. G. M. Foster, *Empire's Children: The People of Tzintzuntzan,* Institute of Social Anthropology Publication No. 6, Smithsonian Institution, 1948, p. 141.

RUBBER TAPPING

Let us look at another analysis of relations between enclave economy and hinterland, this time a case study of the relations between rubber tappers and rubber traders in the Amazon. The author of this case study is Robert F. Murphy who spent a year in 1952-53 among the Mundurucú Indians of the Upper Xingú River. Former headhunters, the Mundurucú are giving up a culture basically akin to that of the Tupinamba described by Hans Staden to become rubber-tappers, dependent upon an outside economic system interested in acquiring quantities of rubber for commercial sale. Such a process of culture change in which a group strives to fit its own culture patterns to the demands of another culture is called "acculturation" by anthropologists. Murphy discusses the implications of one such case of acculturation:*

In many of the so-called "under-developed" areas of the world, we find in operation a very simple system of exchange, related to the modern Western economy through external market connections, but not partaking of many of its principal characteristics. This mode of exchange, which I shall call "barter-credit," is characterized by an almost complete absence of the use of cash in economic transactions, although monetary units are used as referents in bookkeeping procedure. Payment is made, instead, in the form of credit. But, lacking modern exchange and banking facilities, this credit is not easily transferable or negotiable. Also, since the enterprises associated with such a system of exchange are invariably lightly capitalized, debt positions are supported by little security. A debt is not a promise of money, but rather a commitment to future delivery of a marketable commodity. Business relations are personal and monistic, that is, primary producers and middlemen usually sell to and buy from only one correspondent.

Little systematic work has been done on the analysis of barter-credit as a distinctive type of total economy nor on its role within the world economy. This article will not deal with this very complex and extensive subject. It will attempt, rather, to show the differences and the mutual incompatibilities between the two by the study of one case of sharp and clearly defined conflict between them in a local situation.

* From Robert Murphy, "Credit Versus Cash: A Case Study," in *Human Organization*, Vol. 14, No. 3, Fall 1955, pp. 26-28. Reprinted by permission of the Society for Applied Anthropology, Washington, D.C.

Rubber tapper, filling gourd with latex from rubber tree, Belém, Brazil. (Courtesy United Nations)

In 1952-53, my wife and I were engaged in an ethnological study of an Indian group whose lands lie near one of the large southern tributaries of the Amazon. Travel was slow and difficult, and we passed considerable time with the rubber-tapping neo-Brazilian population of this river. Although we did not attempt exhaustive research among the latter people, we did try to acquaint ourselves with them in order to better understand the nature of the acculturative influences affecting our Indian population.

Upon our departure from the field, the exigencies of travel forced us to stay at the camp of a labor force engaged in building an emergency landing field on the banks of the river. While there, we had the opportunity to listen at length to the arguments of both sides of a controversy raging over the labor policies of the airfield. This argument crystallized the differences between the barter-credit economy of rubber gathering and the cash economy introduced by the airfield from urban Brazil.

Some background information on the economy of rubber gathering is necessary. Essentially, the socio-economic structure prevailing on this river is the same described by Wagley for a town on the Amazon River.[2] The actual exploitation of the wild rubber trees is carried on by individual collectors, each of whom gathers crude latex from the trees of one to four rubber "avenues" or paths leading through the forests. The gatherer's house is located near his avenues, and due to the large area exploited by each individual, houses are scattered along the river banks at some distance from one another.

The rubber tapper does not own his rubber avenue, however. Title to rubber-bearing regions is held by *seringalistas*, who may be individual traders, or the directors of large companies with offices in Belem. Where the *seringais*, or rubber districts, are held by companies controlling extensive regions, the company installs traders at scattered points in its holdings. These traders operate on a percentage of net receipts and have no rights to the lands.

The trader, whether independent or a company representative, controls a rubber district and its gathering population, which may include from fifteen to fifty rubber tappers. The latter come every week or two to the trading post to deliver their production. The collector is not a wage laborer, but sells his rubber to the trader for 50 to 60 percent of the price prevailing in Belém. He is credited at that rate on the trader's books. While there, he also makes purchases, for which he is accordingly debited. Money rarely passes hands.

2. Charles Wagley, *Amazon Town*, The Macmillan Co., 1953.

This is much more than a simple accounting procedure. The trader advances credit to new rubber tappers so that they may buy household utensils, the tools of their work, and food. The family of the rubber tapper also lives on credit during the rainy season, when collecting is impossible. The trader also finances various other activities: the *festa* that accompanies a wedding; a trip to the hospital on the Amazon; or a new dress for the tapper's wife. All such costs are duly entered on the books against the tapper's future production. Under such circumstances, the trader must be able to rely upon future delivery.

Most rubber tappers are in debt. Wagley notes that the trader makes more money on the resales of the rubber bought from the tapper than on the prices of the goods sold to him, exorbitant though they may be.[3] The trader then attempts to exact as much production from the individual as possible. His demands make it difficult for the worker to devote time to agriculture, and he is forced to buy most of his food. Also, the trader does not hesitate to sell to the tapper beyond the latter's immediate ability to repay. The chief means of holding a worker, and thus of maintaining production, is by keeping him in debt.

The tapper cannot easily flee from his indebtedness. It is understood in the Amazon that if a worker changes his locale and trader, his new trader must repay the former one and transfer the tapper's debt to his own books.

The Brazilian government had long planned the emergency airfield on the banks of our river, and, after considerable delay, work commenced in earnest in 1953. It was to be a large installation, capable of accommodating four-motored passenger airliners, and a 4000-meter landing strip had to be cut out of high virgin forest. Heavy construction equipment could not be freighted through the rapids of the river and certainly could not be carried by air; the forest had to be felled and the ground levelled by manual labor. The man in charge of construction began forthwith to recruit labor in the region.

The chief of the airport project, whom I shall call by the fictitious but typically Iberian name of Sr. Ribeiro, was a well-educated and progressive young man from São Paulo. His background was urban, and although he had spent some time on the Brazilian frontier, this was his first experience in a rubber region. He was sympathetic towards the impoverished population of the river and wished sincerely to improve their condition. Thirty-five cruzeiros a day plus room and board was offered to single laborers; those with families received the additional privilege

3. *Ibid.*, p. 99.

of buying their food at the airfield store at low city prices. All goods were freighted in by airplane and sold at cost. The workers received the additional benefit of free medication, albeit from a first-aid man.

The response was gratifying to Sr. Ribeiro. Laborers drifted in from their rubber avenues slowly but steadily, and few returned at the beginning of the collecting season. Reasonably comfortable barracks were erected to house the workers and their families.

The local traders soon grew irate. One, whom I shall call Sr. Galvão, had traded at a locale near the airport for some forty years and was especially hard-hit by the emigration of rubber tappers to the airport. I did not record verbatim the conversations I held with him on this subject, but the following is a faithful reproduction of the content.

When we first came out of the Indian country and arrived at the trading post of Sr. Galvão, he told us of the "terrible" things that had happened on the river. He exclaimed that he had lost one-third of his rubber tappers and, thus, of his year's production to the airfield. Furthermore, many of these workers had owed him money. He had, of course, he said, gone to Sr. Ribeiro and requested payment of the back accounts of those rubber tappers who left him while still in debt. And Sr. Ribeiro had refused to remunerate him! Sr. Galvão told me that such practices were unheard of on the river. It was a dereliction of responsibility on the part of the employer and contrary to custom. Moreover, many of these ingrates who had deserted him for the airfield were his *compadres;* he had sponsored their children at baptism. What was this world coming to if such things were allowed to continue, averred Sr. Galvão?

Sr. Galvão had a strong case in his favor. As he said, the airfield was detrimental to rubber production and, therefore, to the region. And what will happen to its workers after heavy construction ceases and maintenance is assumed by skilled technicians, he asked? Sr. Galvão felt that he could not cooperate with the airport management because of the antipathy of their respective interests, and he would deal no longer with his debtors because of their breach of faith. But despite his indignation he quietly bought cigarettes and other articles at city prices in the airport commissary. Bad though it might prove in the long run, the airfield offered temporary advantages, even to the trader.

Sr. Ribeiro, the airfield superintendent, was no less righteous in presenting his side of the story. He was indulgent, for these were "only backwoodsmen," but he explained carefully that he could under no circumstances cooperate with the traders. He was especially confused by the attitude of Sr. Galvão. The latter, he said, had come to him demanding liquidation of the debts of his laborers. "Why should I pay you," asked Sr. Ribeiro. "Why, of course, because these people traded with me and now they work for you," answered Galvão. The city man responded that, if these people owed money to the trader, he should seek payment from *them*. His position was simply that he was hiring labor at thirty-five cruzeiros a day, and if an able-bodied man presented himself he would employ him. He suggested non-committally that Sr. Galvão should see the debtors on payday. Sr. Galvão was shocked at the attitude of the airfield manager. He was further concerned that his former customers might accrue a cash balance, draw it, and summarily depart on a passage-free government airplane. His worries were justified, for several workers did just that. Hard cash gave a mobility and freedom that was unsuitable to the labor requirements of rubber gathering. Both sides to this dispute were acting justly and properly in terms of the economic understandings of their respective sub-cultures. Both sincerely felt that the other was guilty of unethical practice. Sr. Ribeiro pointed to the high prices charged by Sr. Galvão as the reason why most of the trader's former customers were in debt. But he ignored the fact that the Amazon trader has to charge high prices in order to make even a slight margin of profit. The small volume of sales, high cost of transportation, and the service charge upon the debt in a capital-short area necessitate price markups that would seem fantastic to an urban American.

Sr. Ribeiro was even more indignant about another aspect of the disagreement. He could in no way see that he was responsible for the debts of his employees—he was neither their owner nor their keeper. Such an implication appeared to him an infringement upon the liberty and dignity of the employee and an unjust burden upon the employer.

As of the time we departed from the airfield, the situation had not been resolved, nor was there much possibility that it would be. This was much more than a conflict of economic interests; it was also a clash of values. Not only did each think the behavior of the other unethical, but neither had any clear understanding of the implicit basic premises by which the other operated. Sr. Galvão could have gone to court, perhaps, and had the salaries of the debtors attached, but resort to formal legal mechanisms is expensive and contrary to custom in the Amazon region. Economic relations are personalized, and most disputes are settled informally. Moreover, this would not have resolved the trader's problem satisfactorily, for he would still lose the resale profit on the rubber the work would have produced.

Economic exchange, even in the United States, is conducted chiefly through credit mechanisms. Farmers borrow from banks against the next season's crops; the office worker buys a television set with his future salary as security. There is, however, a difference between the use of credit in a cash-based system and in the situation we have outlined. The bank does not require the farmer to buy seeds, food, and tools from it, nor does it expect to receive the farmer's grain in payment. It wants no more than the repayment of the loan, plus interest, within a certain period. Also, the borrower must post security against the loan. Any single borrower-lender relationship has a limited frame of reference in the United States; each such relationship impinges upon only the economic life of the parties. Moreover, each affects only a limited sector of the principals' economies. The individual debtor or creditor probably has a number of such relationships, none of which structures a large sphere of interpersonal behavior. In brief, a cash system is depersonalized.

A highly developed barter-credit system, such as we find in the Amazon, implies a whole range of phenomena which make for significant sub-cultural differences. It carries a different ethic and a different view of human relations. It is a complex of values, social structure, and economic practices which has much broader ramifications than what is usually inferred by the word "economic."

A credit system can be effectively carried out only through a web of interpersonal relations and not through impersonal market mechanisms. The trader must feel personally confident that his customer will make delivery to him. His advances are based on no other security than this. The rubber tapper, in turn, has no other economic security than the goods advanced to him by the trader. He prefers this to wage labor, for his family will continue to eat if he falls ill, and he is not faced with the semi-starvation that low-salaried workers experience immediately before payday. If an emergency of any sort occurs, he can depend upon his trader to aid him. Much as the rubber tapper may complain of the exactions and high prices of the trader, he needs him in this depressed economy. The high wages (for the Amazon), low prices, and free medication offered by the airport came as a rare, and temporary, form of security.

The trader's customers depend upon him not only for their total economic life, but socially and politically, as well. He serves as godfather to their children, he is the arbiter of all disputes, and his wife is the social and often religious leader of the little community which he and his customers constitute. His customers are not merely pages in his ledger book. He feels responsible for them, although he may, paradoxically, exploit and defraud them at the same time. On the other hand, the ru____ tapper must recognize the authority of the trader and must not shirk his obligation to produce for him and to deal with him alone.

The trader in such a system is indeed his customer's keeper. Mobility, freedom of choice, and impersonality are essential to the assemblage and direction of a wage-labor force for work on such a highly capitalized operation as the airport. They are disastrous to the rubber trade. Only in this light can the irreconcilability of the conflict between Srs. Galvão and Ribeiro be understood.

The implications of this case for applied anthropology are obvious. This situation is not peculiar to the Amazon. Barter-credit economies are of such wide distribution that they may be said to constitute a sector of the core or primary patterns of a cross-culturally identifiable type. It is to be hoped, therefore, that the experience of action anthropology in one area will have predictive value for others.

In his account, Murphy speaks of *compadres,* men linked by their common involvement in the baptism of a child. We are acquainted with the institution of godparenthood from our own cultural background. Among Catholics and some Protestant sects in our country a friend of the family usually acts as the sponsor of a child at baptism, and becomes his godparent. But where in our country the main emphasis is placed on the relation between the sponsor and the child, in Latin America it is the tie between the parents of the child and the sponsor which is most important; not godparenthood but co-parenthood of the same child is what is significant. Let us diagram the contrast. In making our diagram we use the standard anthropological notations of △ for a man, ◯ for a woman, a vertical line to indicate descent (i.e. that a person is another person's son or daughter, and thus descended from him or her), and two horizontal lines (=) to show marriage. Thus the godparenthood relation could be diagrammed as follows:

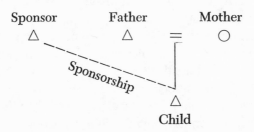

Sponsor   Father   Mother

Child

But the co-parenthood tie operates in addition to the tie of sponsorship. It links the parental couple and the sponsoring couple on the same generation level, as follows:

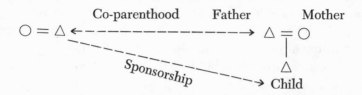

Such a tie of co-parenthood does not end with the baptism of the child; it is a pact for mutual support between the two *compadres,* co-parents, involved. Such a pact can be entered into between two *compadres who are each other's equals* in social and economic standing. Very often, however, it is formed between people, of whom one is wealthier, of higher social standing and more powerful politically than the other. Here the tie is not horizontal, between equals, but vertical, between individuals occupying different positions in the social and economic order. To see how this vertical *compadre* tie can operate in an economic context, let us look briefly at another study concerned with the rubber economy of Amazon. Murphy saw the operations of the rubber business upriver in the hinterland. Charles Wagley, who has spent years studying Indians in Guatemala and Brazil, reported on its operations in Itá, the town at the mouth of the Amazon River which we have already observed in its worship of St. Benedict, its patron saint. In Itá the most frequent type of *compadrazgo* is vertical, and of the vertical forms the most significant is that between store owner and client.

That vertical *compadrazgo* should occur in Itá between store owner and customer may at first seem surprising since almost everyone in Itá is involved in production for the world rubber market. The town grew up during the boom days of the rubber industry in the second half of the nineteenth century. Rubber collecting still remains the most important economic activity; all men in Itá have worked at one time or another as collectors. Perhaps the most typical pursuits of lower-class men involve spending the rubber season as collectors, and the rest of the year raising a manioc garden from which salable manioc is produced in addition to manioc grown for subsistence.

The instability of the rubber market, which is quite beyond the control of the people of Itá, appears to be responsible for the instability of the town's society; community membership fluctuates constantly. It also seems responsible for the partial commitment of many people to rubber collecting, and to subsistence and cash cropping agriculture. In short, few collector-peasants in Itá have real roots in the community; if debt or other adverse fortune is their lot, they can, and do, move to another spot further down the Amazon River.

Storekeepers, on the other hand, depend upon receiving raw materials, primarily rubber, from the various extractive industries practiced by the collector-peasants. These goods are shipped up the river to larger towns, and finally reach the export-import houses of the larger cities. In exchange for these raw materials, the store owners receive stock for their stores. Some of this is exchanged with the lower-class people for goods. These storekeepers do not receive cash from their suppliers in the larger towns; if their books show a profit, their suppliers simply advance them more credit. This means that transactions at the level of Itá are carried on in a virtual absence of capital, in spite of the fact that the community's economic activities are integrated into the national and world economies, which are based on money.

The chains of credit and production can be diagrammed schematically as follows:

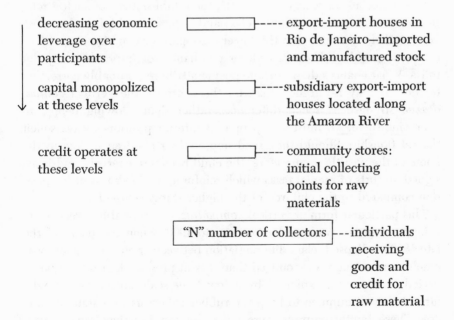

Absence of capital means that a storekeeper is deprived of a powerful weapon to use against his clientele—that of economic leverage derived from the social inequalities which capital creates. For where money, in the sense of capital, is in use, it is a vital resource, just like the land a man lives on. Those who have it are imbued with power; those who do not, with weakness. This lack of money, coupled with a lack of force and a highly mobile clientele, poses great problems for a storekeeper who wants to remain in business.

The success or failure of these store owners depends on their personal characteristics, which must be such that the gatherers of raw material will seek them out as *compadres*. Only through such a relationship can the storekeeper exert moral leverage over his rubber-producing counterpart to induce the latter to honor his end of the bargain. Only with a number of good *compadres* can a storekeeper in Itá turn a profit. At the same time, a poor man who becomes *compadre* to a storekeeper need not worry about his credit being cut off.

It is not surprising to learn that person's prestige in Itá is directly proportional to the number of *compadres* that he has; one storekeeper, for example, has nearly three hundred *compadres*. This man is considered to be the leading citizen of the whole town, as well as its wealthiest man.

It is important to realize that, in Itá, the establishment of such a relation between a person of lower class and a person of higher class does not entail the promise that the lower-class partner can rise in social or economic position. There is little or no chance for improving one's lot in Itá. What chances do occur, the people attribute (probably correctly) to luck. It may be argued that, on the contrary, the vertical *compadrazgo* strengthens social differences rather than allowing people to overcome them. To illustrate: people of inferior position always solicit the relationship. Should they send one of their children to live in the home of the wealthier *compadre,* the child becomes a servant and is assigned all sorts of menial tasks which reinforce the lowliness of his position compared to the children of the higher status *compadre.*

This particular form of vertical *compadrazgo* is probably a recent development in the Amazon basin. Prior to 1900, when the boom of the late 1800's collapsed, class differentiation between "rich" and "poor" was much more strongly pronounced than it is at present. During the boom period, rubber was exploited by a few large-scale entrepreneurs who hired bands of gunmen to keep the rubber collectors in a state of slavery. These family empires were aided by the Brazilian government, whose police force also helped control the rubber collectors. With the collapse of the boom in the first decade of the twentieth century, these large family empires folded, and the patterns of rubber collecting presently practiced began. In light of these developments, the particular trader-collector *compadrazgo* relationship represents one possible solution to the problem of control over the peripatetic rubber gatherers, once naked force was no longer used.

We thus see complex economic relations mediated through the social tie of *compadrazgo*. In *compadrazgo*—especially of the vertical kind—the two partners, storekeeper and client, rubber collector and rubber trader, maintain their divergent interests. Yet they are linked in a personal tie, surrounded by a quasi-familial aura. This personal, quasi-familial tie makes possible the continued interchanges between the two persons involved. If a client at a store or a rubber-tapper closes his account and takes his business elsewhere, the result is not only the breaking of an economic bond, it is a clear case of personal disloyalty. Because *compadrazgo* is a quasi-kinship relation, it guarantees reciprocity between parties; where one might cheat a stranger, he does not cheat his brother, uncle, or son. The storekeeper will not refuse credit to a rubber-gathering *compadre;* the rubber gatherer will consistently provide rubber for his storekeeping *compadre*. Not because they are storekeeper and gatherer; rather, in spite of it. They reciprocate because they are *compadres*. At the same time these personal, quasi-familial bonds serve as a social bridge between two very distinctive economic sectors, between the highly capitalized enclave economy, oriented toward the markets of the world, and the economy of the hinterland, oriented toward covering the subsistence needs of poor people struggling to remain alive by farming a small impoverished piece of land and/or collecting rubber from rubber avenues deep in the interiors of a vast continent.

LARGE ESTATES: THE SLAVE-OWNING *FAZENDA*

But Latin Americans live not only in closed or open communities of cultivators, or in camps of rubber gatherers. One enduring feature of Latin American economic, social, and political organization has been the large estate, or *latifundium*. In most countries of Latin America, a relatively small number of men own most of the fertile land on which can be grown the commercially viable export crops, such as coffee, cocoa, sugar cane, bananas, or the crops which feed the large cities and centers of population. These large estates came into being shortly after the European conquest. They took two essential forms. In the areas of Indians without organized states, such as Brazil, the dominant form was the

Bundling sisal, Bendouro, San Francisco River basin, Brazil. (Courtesy United Nations)

fazenda, largely operated with the labor of slaves imported from Africa. In the areas populated by Indians with states, the dominant form was the *hacienda,* which drew its labor from the local population. For a long time, the sugar-growing *fazendas* of the Brazilian northeast were the wealthiest and most powerful institutions of their kind. They are long gone now, but—as in our own south—their past still has power over the present. Let us listen to the Brazilian sociologist Gilberto Freyre, as he describes these massive organizations of people: *

In Brazil the relations between the white and colored races from the first half of the sixteenth century were conditioned on the one hand by the system of economic production—monoculture and latifundia—and on the other hand by the scarcity of white women among the conquerors. Sugar-raising not only stifled the democratic industries represented by the trade in brazilwood and hides; it sterilized the land for the forces of diversified farming and herding for a broad expanse around the plantations. It called for an enormous number of slaves. Cattle-raising, meanwhile, with the possibilities it afforded for a democratic way of life, was relegated to the backlands. In the agrarian zone, along with monoculture that absorbed other forms of production, there developed a semi-feudal society, with a minority of whites and light-skinned mulattoes dominating, patriarchally and polygamously, from their Big Houses of stone and mortar, not only the slaves that were bred so prolifically in the *senzalas,* but the sharecroppers as well, the tenants or retainers, those who dwelt in the huts of mud and straw, vassals of the Big House in the strictest meaning of the word.

The plantation Big House that the colonizer began erecting in Brazil in the sixteenth century—thick walls of mud or stone or lime, covered with straw or with tile, with a veranda in front and on the sides and with sloping roofs to give the maximum of protection against the strong sun and tropical rains—was by no means a reproduction of Portuguese houses, but a new expression, corresponding to the new physical environment and to a surprising, unlooked-for phase of Portuguese imperialism: its agrarian and sedentary activity in the tropics, its rural, slave-holding patriarchalism. From the moment the Portuguese, while

* From Gilberto Freyre, *The Masters and the Slaves* (*Casa-Grande and Senzala*): A *Study in the Development of Brazilian Civilization,* translated by Samuel Putnam. Copyright 1946 by Alfred A. Knopf, Inc. All rights reserved. Reprinted by permission.

still longing nostalgically for his native realm, a sentiment to which Capistrano de Abreu has given the name of "transoceanism"—from that moment he was a Luso-Brazilian, the founder of a new economic and social order, the creator of a new type of habitation. . . .

The system necessitated slave labor and was inimical to a varied-crop system. It demanded slaves to be "the hands and feet of the plantation-owner," as Antonil puts it. And this was true not only of the Portuguese planters, already vitiated by the institution of slavery, but of the Dutch as well. The latter, when they installed themselves on the sugar-cane plantations of Pernambuco, realized that it was necessary for them to rely upon the Negro, for without slaves they could not produce sugar. And a large number of slaves, at that: to plant the cane; to cut it; to bring it to the mills run by a water-wheel—the *engenhos d'agua*, as these mills were called—or to those that were turned by oxen or other animals; the so-called *almanjarras* or *trapiches;* and afterwards there was the sap to be purified in the kettles; and the heated sugar had to be congealed and then refined and whitened in clay forms and the *aguardente,* or sugar-brandy, drained off.

The Big House completed by the slave shed represented an entire economic, social, and political system: a system of production (a latifundary monoculture); a system of labor (slavery); a system of transport (the ox-cart, the *bangue* [a litter with leather top and curtains], the hammock, the horse); a system of religion (a family Catholicism, with the chaplain subordinate to the paterfamilias, with a cult of the dead, etc.); a system of sexual and family life (polygamous patriarchalism); a system of bodily and household hygiene (the "tiger" [a chamberpot], the banana stalk, the river bath, the tub bath, the sitting-bath, the footbath); and a system of politics (*compadrismo* [reliance on *compadres—* sponsors in religious ceremonies, i.e. a system of nepotism and patronage]). The Big House was thus at one and the same time a fortress, a bank, a cemetery, a hospital, a school, and a house of charity giving shelter to the aged, the widow, and the orphan. The Big House of the Noruega plantation in Pernambuco, with its many rooms, drawing-rooms, and corridors, its two convent kitchens, its dispensary, its chapel, and its annexes, impresses me as being the sincere and complete expression of the absorptive patriarchalism of colonial times. An expression of the gentle and subdued patriarchalism of the eighteenth century, without the air of a fortress that characterized the first Big Houses of the sixteenth century. "On the plantations it was like being on a field of battle," writes Theodoro Sampaio, with reference to the first century of colonization. "The rich were in the habit of protecting their dwellings and manor

houses by a double and powerful row of stakes, in the manner of the natives; and these stockades were manned by domestics, retainers, and Indian slaves and served also as a refuge for the neighbors when they were
unexpectedly attacked by savages."

The plantations at the end of the seventeenth century and those of the
eighteenth century, on the other hand, more nearly resembled a Portuguese convent—a huge estate with the functions of a hospital and house
of charity. The indescribable air of aloofness that characterized the
houses at the beginning of the seventeenth century, with their verandas
that appear to have been erected on wooden stilts, was no longer to be
met within these end-of-the century dwellings and those of the eighteenth and the first half of the nineteenth century; the latter were houses
that had been almost wholly demilitarized and, accentuatedly rustic in
appearance, offered to strangers an easygoing and expansive hospitality.

It was the slaves who literally became their master's feet, running errands for their owners and carrying them about in hammock or palan-
quin. They also became their master's hands—at least, their right hands;
for they it was who dressed them, drew on their trousers and their boots
for them, bathed and brushed them, and hunted over their persons for
fleas. There is a tradition to the effect that one Pernambucan planter
even employed the Negro's hand for the most intimate details of his
toilet; and von den Steinen tells us that a distinguished nobleman of the
Empire was in the habit of having a slave girl light his cigars for him
and then pass them to the old fellow's mouth. Every white of the Big
House had two left hands, every Negro two right hands. The master's
hands served only for telling the beads of Our Lady's rosary, for playing
cards, for taking snuff from snuffboxes, or *corriboques,* and for playing
with the breasts of young Negro and mulatto girls, the pretty slaves of
his harem.

Conquerors, in the military and technical sense, of the indigenous
populations, the absolute rulers of the Negroes imported from Africa for
the hard labor of the *bagaceira* [where the *bagasse* or pressed sugar
cane is stored], the Europeans and their descendants meanwhile had to
compromise with the Indians and the Africans in the matter of genetic
and social relations. The scarcity of white women created zones of frat-
ernization between conquerors and conquered, between masters and
slaves. While these relations between white men and colored women did
not cease to be those of "superiors" with "inferiors," and in the majority
of cases those of disillusioned and sadistic gentlemen with passive slave
girls, they were mitigated by the need that was felt by many colonists of
founding a family under such circumstances and upon such a basis as

this. A widely practiced miscegenation here tended to modify the enormous social distance that otherwise would have been preserved between Big House and tropical forest, between Big House and slave hut. What a latifundary monoculture based upon slavery accomplished in the way of creating an aristocracy, by dividing Brazilian society into two extremes, of gentry and slaves, with a thin and insignificant remnant of free men sandwiched in between, was in good part offset by the social effects of miscegenation. The Indian woman and the *mina* [name given to the light-skinned Negro women of Bahia who became companions and housewives of their masters. After Forte de el Mina, one of the slave ports in West Africa] or Negro woman, in the beginning, and later the mulatto, the *cabrocha* [a dark-skinned mestiza], the quadroon, and the octoroon, becoming domestics, concubines, and even the lawful wives of their white masters, exerted a powerful influence for social democracy in Brazil. A considerable portion of the big landed estates was divided among the mestizo sons, legitimate or illegitimate, procreated by these white fathers, and this tended to break up the feudal allotments and latifundia that were small kingdoms in themselves.

There is no slavery without sexual depravity. Depravity is the essence of such a regime. In the first place, economic interests favor it, by creating in the owners of men an immoderate desire to possess the greatest possible number of *crias* [young Negroes born and reared—*criado*—in the Big House]. From a manifesto issued by slave-holding planters Nabuco quotes the following words, so rich in significance: "The most productive feature of slave property is the generative belly."

Their wives, on the other hand, were all of them married prematurely young, some of them having been physically incapable of becoming mothers in the full sense of the word. Once married, one pregnancy succeeded another; one child came after another. It was a grievous and continuous effort to multiply the species. Many infants were born dead—"angels" who were promptly interred in sky-blue caskets. Others were saved from death only by a miracle. But in each case the mother was left a mere shred of a human being.

Our patriarchal grandsires were nearly always great procreators, and sometimes terrible satyrs, with a scapular of Our Lady dangling over their hairy bosoms; and these insatiable males, who got a weird sexual thrill from marrying small girls, rarely had the pleasure of the same wife's company until they reached old age; for the wives, despite the fact that they were much younger than their husbands, soon died, and the widower would then marry his first wife's younger sister or one of her cousins. These grandfathers and great-grandfathers of ours were, in a manner of speaking, Blue Beards. There were many cases in the old days of planters, captain-major of the province, big estate-owners, barons and viscounts under the Empire, who were married three or four times and who had a numerous progeny. These are the facts that are pointed to with something like pride in their wills and testaments and on the tombs and gravestones of the old burying-grounds and plantation chapels. This multiplication of the species was accomplished at the cost of a great sacrifice on the part of the womenfolk, who were true martyrs in the cause of generation, consuming in the effort first their youth and, before long, life itself.

Coreal in Bahia was impressed by the voluptuousness of the colonists. They were a lot of big loafers, always lying stretched out in their hammocks. (This was, however, a voluptuousness and an indolence broken in upon by the spirit of religious devotion, which only in the nineteenth century began to diminish in the menfolk, to find a refuge with women, children, and slaves.) In the seventeenth and even in the eighteenth century there was not a white gentleman, however indolent, who would avoid the effort involved in the sacred duty of kneeling before the niches of the saints in prayer—prayers that were sometimes endlessly drawn out by Negroes and mulattoes. The rosary, the chaplet of Our Lord, the litanies. They would leap from the hammocks to go and pray in the oratories; for this was an obligation that must be fulfilled. They would go, rosary in hand, and with holy medals, reliquaries, scapulars, St. Anthony hung about their necks, everything that was needed for their prayers and devotions. Maria Graham speaks of hearing litanies sung at nightfall in the streets of Bahia, with whites, Negroes, mulattoes, all praying to the same God and the same Our Lady. Some of the more devout women would accompany the sacrament to the homes of the dying. Within the house they prayed in the morning, at mealtimes, at midday; and at night they prayed in the room set aside for the saints, slaves accompanying the whites in the rosary and the Salve Regina. If there was a chaplain, he would intone the *Mater purissima, ora pro nobis.* In Cantagalo, in the Big House of the *fazendeiro* Joaquim das Lavrinhas, Mathison was charmed with the patriarchal character of the master of the house kneeling in front of all those on the plantation—relatives, tenants, slaves—to ask God's blessing and the protection of the Virgin Mary. It seemed to the Englishman that there was nothing more praiseworthy in the colonial Brazilian than the fact that in his house he always set aside a place for divine worship. The sign of a "respect for religion," the visitor concluded. And he does not forget to stress the observance of the rites of the Church by the Negroes. One chronicler tells us that at dinner the patriarch would bless the table and each would put his food on his plate in the form of a cross. Others would bless the water or the wine, first making in the air the sign of the cross with the goblet. Finally, they would say grace in Latin:

> Per haec dona et coetera data
> Sit Sancta Trinitas semper laudata.

Upon going to bed, the whites in the Big House and, in the slave huts, the older Negroes would pray:

> With God I lay me down, with God I rise,
> with the Grace of God and of the Holy Spirit.
>   May Thine eyes
> watch over me as I sleep this night;
> and if I should die, then wilt Thou light
> me with the tapers of Thy Trinity
> into the mansion of Eternity.

And in the morning, when they rose, it was also with the name of Our Lord in their mouths: "My God, it is thanks to Thy goodness that I again see the light of day. Wilt Thou see that I walk safely, guided by Thy unfailing providence!" When anyone sneezed, he was greeted with a "God save you!" Negroes would receive a blessing from their master, saying: "Praised by the name of Our Lord Jesus Christ!" And the master would reply: "Forever!" or "Praised be!"

When it thundered loudly, whites and blacks would gather in the chapel or the sanctuary to sing the Benedicite, intone the Magnificat, and recite the prayers of St. Braz, St. Jerome, and St. Barbara. They would light candles, burn holy boughs, and recite the Credo. Certain ailments were treated with prayers and anointings with oil as in apostolic times—erysipelas, for example:

> Peter and Paul went to Rome
> and met Jesus Christ on the way,
> who to them did say:
> "Well, and what brings you here?"
> " 'Tis the erysipelas, Lord, we fear."
> "Bless it with olive oil
> And it will disappear."

They would tack up prayer-papers to the windows and doors of houses to protect the family from thieves, assassins, lightning-bolts, and tempests. Prayers to Jesus, Mary, and Joseph. And on the old patriarchal plantations they would sing hymns to the Holy Family. . . .

On the day on which they began grinding the cane, the priest never failed to be there to bless the sugar-mill, and the labor was undertaken with the Church's benediction. Mass was first said, and then they all made their way to the mill, the white males in their sun-hats, slow-paced and solemn, and the fat *senhoras* in their mantillas. The Negroes were happy, thinking of the *batuques*, or dances, they would have that night. The young Negro lads shouted *vivas* and set off fireworks. The priest made the sign of the cross in the air with the hyssop and sprin-kled the mill with holy water, many of the slaves taking good care to be sprinkled also. There followed other slow gestures on the part of the priest. Latin sentences. At times a sermon. It was not until all this ceremonial had been completed that the first of the ripened cane was placed in the mill, in bundles tied with green, red, or blue ribbons. Only then did the labor begin on these patriarchal plantations. That was the way it had been ever since the sixteenth century. As far back as Father Cardim's day that priest, speaking of the plantation-owners, had ob-served: "They are accustomed, the first time they go to grind, to have the mills blessed, and on that day they make a great feast, inviting those from round about. The priest, upon being requested to do so, blesses some of those present, a thing that is very much esteemed." The blessing of the mill was followed by a banquet in the Big House, with revelry and dancing by the slaves on the terrace, and the merrymaking would last until dawn. At the banquet they would serve young calves, pigs, hens, turkeys. All of this with the blessing of the Church, which, how-ever, did not officially number "among its rites an ecclesiastical cere-mony vulgarly known as the Litanies of May, which are nothing more than prayers to God for a prosperous harvest."

Finally, Freyre compares the slave plantations of Brazil with those of the south of the United States. In the south, too,

there evolved, from the seventeenth to the eighteenth century, an aristo-cratic type of rural family that bore a greater resemblance to the type of family in northern Brazil before abolition than it did to the Puritan bourgeoisie of another part of North America, which was similarly of Anglo-Saxon origin, but which had been influenced by a different kind of economic regime. There were almost the same country gentlemen—chivalrous after their fashion; proud of their slaves and lands, with sons and Negroes multiplying about them; regaling themselves with the love of mulattoes; playing cards and amusing themselves with cock-fights; marrying girls of sixteen; engaging in feuds over questions of land; dying in duels for the sake of a woman; and getting drunk at great family feasts—huge turkeys with rice, roasted by "old mammies" skilled in the art of the oven, jellies, puddings, dressing, preserved pears, corn-cakes.

In Brazil slavery was formally abolished in 1888; but social relations of dominance and dependence did not give way and have continued into the present time. The American anthropologist, Harry W. Hutchinson, who studied this plantation belt in 1950-51 has described this pattern of relation as follows:*

everyone has his *patrão* (Protector) in the person of the owner, and in case of an emergency, accident or sickness, he expects help from him. This personal element is very important on most plantations in the vicinity of Vila Recôncavo; as a rule, the owner knows all the workers by name, knows their families and their family troubles and problems. He is aware of their love affairs and up-to-date on the health of newborn children and their mothers. Nearly all cases of sickness, from common colds and rheumatism to more serious ailments, are brought directly to the attention of the *patrão* or his wife. The owner, returning from a prolonged stay in the city, receives visits from the workers or from their wives, during which all the personal gossip is exchanged. The workers inquire about the owner's family and more extended family, for they generally know them all. Engagements, weddings, births, deaths and illnesses are reported on both sides. Complaints or requests are also made to the owner. The relationships are highly personal, intimate, gentle and frank.

Increasingly, however, these relations have proved insufficient to cope with the changing problems of scale and organization. Today, this area is one of the great areas of agrarian unrest in Brazil. The arid hinterland

* From "Race Relations in a Rural Community of the Bahian Recôncavo," in Charles Wagley (ed.), *Race and Class in Rural Brazil*, UNESCO, Paris, 1952. Reprinted by permission of UNESCO.

of this lush coast has always been an area in which men have rebelled against the central government. Sometimes they have done so in the name of some overwhelming religious vision, as in the uprising led by Antonio Conselheiro (the Counselor) whose rise and fall are the subject of *Os sertoes,* a famous Brazilian epic written by Euclides da Cunha in 1902. Sometimes the uprising took the form of a *cangazo,* a bandit revolt, as that of Lampeaõ, the best known of the northeastern bandit chiefs who dominated much of the area in the first part of this century. Since 1925, however, the year of the first sedition with an outspokenly political program, the rebellions have increasingly taken on *political* flavor. In that year Luis Prestes, a rebellious army captain who later became Brazil's leading Communist, began a march across country in which he successfully eluded army attack while preaching a new gospel of justice for the poor and punishment for the rich. With this movement rebellion moved out of the arid hinterland into the tropical coast. More recently, in 1955, peasants in the state of Pernambuco refused rent payments and successfully resisted expulsion from the lands they occupied through the forming of a league. Since then peasant leagues have sprung up all over the area. Since 1960 they have found an important spokesman in the state deputy Francisco Juliaõ. Juliaõ has organized a movement of peasants, landless laborers, and urban poor to exert pressure for change in the economic and political organization of the zone.

LARGE ESTATES: HACIENDAS AND PEONAGE

In Brazil the major form of commercial enterprise in agriculture was the estate worked by slaves. There, as to the southern United States, men and women were brought in large numbers from Africa to replace the intractable aboriginal population, to furnish a stable and dependable labor supply. But in areas where large aboriginal populations had existed before the conquest, and where these populations had been accustomed to accept orders from their own rulers, the same need for an imported labor supply did not exist. The labor supply was at hand in the Indian villages. The result was the institution of the *hacienda,* a large estate worked not by slaves but by laborers attracted in another manner. One way of getting people to work for you was to extend credit to them—credit they needed to pay taxes or to buy at stores—force them into debt, and then allow them to work off that debt by laboring on the estate. Over time, this arrangement could be made hereditary,

Mexican landowners in the early nineteenth century. (From Carlos Nebel, *Viaje pintoresco y arqueológico sobre la parte de la República Mexicana en los años transcurridos desde 1829 hasta 1834*, Paris, 1839)

with sons working off the debts of their fathers. A day laborer was called a *peón*, and such a system has been called *debt peonage*. Also, an estate owner could attract poor or landless men from neighboring Indian villages. He would allow them use of a piece of land on his estate, and in turn exact a pledge of so many work-days a week for his own commercial crop. We have seen this system in operation in the Peruvian community of Hualcán. Sometimes the haciendas bought the land of entire Indian communities—or occupied that land by force and trickery—thus forcing them to work on the lands of the estate. Through such means hacienda owners also forced their laborers to recognize no other lords than themselves. The hacienda owner adopted the role of the dominant father, prepared to guide the steps of his worker-children:*

As long as the worker remained dependent and submissive, he received his just reward: a sum of money, a draft of pulque [century-plant beer], a plot for growing corn. When he rebelled against authority, or provoked its anger, he was tied to the whipping post, possessed by every hacienda, and cruelly lashed. . . . Deprived of their ability to rule their own lives, the workers in turn invested the relation of owner and worker with the elements of personalization. The owner's person became the governor of their lives, their relation with this person the major guaranty of the security and stability on which depended their daily bread and a roof over their heads. Only the owner could materially raise a man's prospects in life, only he could reduce the risks to which the worker was subject. This person, clad in authority and living a life far beyond the reach of his laborers, had to be won over, placated into benevolence, by a show of humility, a pantomime of servitude. The worker not only put his labor time at his owner's disposal; he also offered himself and his family, to secure perhaps yet another advantage in the struggle for support.

To produce its cash crop, the hacienda usually farms only a small portion of its total lands, usually its best land. But it does so with an

* Eric R. Wolf, *Sons of the Shaking Earth.* © 1959 by the University of Chicago. All rights reserved. Published 1959. First Phoenix edition 1962. Sixth impression 1967. Printed in the United States of America. Reprinted by permission of the University of Chicago Press.

unchanging and outmoded technology, based on the use of the ox-drawn wooden plow in field operations and on the water-powered wheel in processing. Production involves the use of many men, each contributing his own meager output to make a big aggregate product. In the technical language of the economist, the hacienda is labor-intensive. It relies on massing land and men, it stints on capital; it is capital-extensive.

Where the hacienda persists—and it continues to be especially strong in the Andes and in Central America—it thus tends to tie up land and men in the operation of a relatively unproductive kind of agriculture. At the same time, the owners of the haciendas are lords of great estates and masses of men—they hold power, and they use this power to maintain their own sway. But they also face a rising double challenge. First, there is everywhere in Latin America a growing demand for a more equitable distribution of land. Second, there is a rising tide of dissatisfaction with a system in which the owners of great estates are able to strangle innovations and changes which would undermine their hold over their dominions.

Table 5 illustrates the uneven distribution of land in Latin America.

TABLE 5

*Estimated percentage distribution of land holdings
in Latin America, 18 countries, 1960-65*

Size of farms in hectares	Percentage of farms	Percentage of total land area
0-20	75.6	6.6
20-100	16.8	9.5
100-1000	6.6	24.1
over 1000	1.0	59.8
Total	100	100

SOURCE: Compiled from *Statistical Abstract of Latin America,* 1967, pp. 190-91.

This much of recent Latin American history can be read as a prolonged and recurrent struggle to rectify a situation in which less than 8 per cent of all farms control more than three fourths of all the land, while more than 90 per cent of all farms occupy less than 16 per cent of the land. The first great uprising against such an uneven distribution of land occurred in Mexico. When the Mexican revolution broke out in 1910, more than 90 per cent of the heads of rural households were propertyless.

Since that time more than half of the available crop land has been distributed to small cultivators, principally by granting title to land to towns or villages for distribution among their members. This is the so-called *ejido*. Under ejido tenure, a household has the right to use land as long as the land is worked, but ejido lands cannot be sold or mortgaged. The next country to effect a major land reform was Bolivia where, before the reform decree of 1953, 92 per cent of the land was held by 6.4 per cent of all farms. There land reform was begun in direct response to a peasant uprising in the area of Cochabamba in which cultivators drove the landowners off their estates. The Bolivian reform law granted the cultivators outright title to the land. The most recent attempt at land reform is that of Venezuela where 74 per cent of the land was held by 1.7 per cent of all farms, all above 1000 hectares. In 1960 the Venezuelan government began redistribution of the land. Its announced purpose is to benefit all the landless families of the country, while at the same time compensating the landlords who will lose their land and furnishing technical assistance to the new farmers.

But land reform creates as many problems as it solves. We have already seen that it strikes at the traditional sources of power. By depriving the owners of haciendas of both land and men, land distribution also strikes at their "fund of power," at the resources which have given these men power over others. Says economist Robert L. Heilbroner: *

. . . we tend to forget how profoundly dislocating, how *revolutionary*, such changes are. To take but one instance, when we approach the question of the rationalization of agriculture, we tend to slough off the problem as one which can be solved by "land reform." But we forget that land reform, for nations in which landownership is the central pillar of the structure of social privilege, is not a small concession to be wrung from landlording groups, but a profound and wrenching alteration of the very basis of wealth and power. We can better imagine the ease with which it may be accomplished by supposing that *we* were an underdeveloped country and that some superior power offered us aid on the condition that we would undertake "share reform"—that is, the redistribution (or even the abolition) of our present concentrated ownership of corporate securities. How rapidly would our own powers-that-be acquiesce in such a proposal?

* From Robert L. Heilbroner, *The Great Ascent,* Copyright © 1962 by Robert L. Heilbroner. Reprinted by permission of Harper & Row, Publishers, Inc., and the William Morris Agency, Inc.

Tearing down the great estates is but one side of a process which inevitably results in the creation of many small farms. They must become economically viable, through the extension of credit facilities and the introduction of new agricultural techniques, or fail in providing sufficient food for an ever-growing population. A plot of six acres may be enough to feed one household. But in the next generation the father who received the grant of land may be faced with dividing his piece of land between two sons, both of whom then have to live off three acres each. In a short period of time, land units will again be too small to provide adequate sustenance to its occupants. Land reform therefore must go hand in hand with a program of technical improvement on the land and—even more importantly—with the creation of alternative jobs to which people can turn to relieve the growing pressure on the land. What we are really saying is that a whole new social and economic order has to come into being to give the new cultivators a secure grasp on life. Thus land reform is not merely a matter of social justice. In destroying the hacienda you also destroy a framework of economic, social, and political ties within which people have grown up and within which they have learned to cope with life's problems. A new economic, social, and political framework has to be devised, and people have to learn the know-how and the social relations necessary to make the new institutions work. This is not a matter of this or that minor change or innovation, of introducing hybrid seed corn into communities that lacked such productive seed before or of curing yaws with penicillin. It involves the learning of new habits of action and thought, of adapting old habits to new demands, and of dealing with people in new ways, all steps as necessary as they are painful. Thus we see again how the past determines the future. We inherit the problems of the past and the solutions devised over time to cope with these problems, and this inheritance is the basic equipment with which we confront the new day. Men never start completely anew; their point of departure is already determined for them by what has happened centuries of millennia before their time.

THE CATTLE RANCH

The characteristic enterprise in the populated highlands was the hacienda; in the Brazilian lowlands, the slave estate. In the great open spaces of the Pampa to the south of the tropical forest, however, the great enclave enterprise came to be not a large farm, but the cattle ranch or *estancia*. Let us hear a description of life on Argentine cattle farms written by an English writer of the late nineteenth century eager to acquaint his fellow countrymen with the economic opportunities of a new frontier.*

Gauchos is the general appellation of the country-folks of South America. From the rich *estanciero*, the owner of uncounted acres and almost countless herds, to the purchased slave, they are all called *gaucho*, and are nearly the same in dress and habits. In summer, a cotton shirt, a light pair of drawers, a *cheropa* (cloth petticoat), a small jacket, a pair of boots stripped from a foal's hind legs, and a straw hat, complete their usual dress, the materials of which are fine or coarse, according to the means of the wearer. The higher classes are further distinguished by accoutrements of silver—such as the knife, spurs, stirrups, head-piece of the bridle, etc.; but their manner of feeding is very little different from that of their laborers, the *peons*. Some of the principal farmers, however, have houses in the towns, as well as on their *estancias*; many of these are dandies in their way—they drop the gaucho dress, and are Creole gentlemen. The *gauchos*, of low as well as of high degree, are, perhaps, the most independent creatures in the universe. Their wants are so few and so easily supplied—their pursuits in life are so free from care—and their habits from expense, ostentation, or rivalry, that if it were not for the purpose of gambling, a vice which overruns the country, they would not know what to do with the little money they receive.

In some places they are clouded with superstition, and sunk in idleness; but more generally, they live too remote from the priesthood to have been much influenced by them. Their frank independent carriage renders them more acceptable to the English traveller than the more polished inhabitants of the great towns. Their hospitality is very great; and a traveller passing through the country, may step into any *estancia* in his way, and take a hearty meal with the family with as little ceremony, or expectation of his paying for it, as if he were taking a draught of water from a pump on the road side in England. This hospitality, however, is beginning to subside as travelling increases.

* From J. A. B. Beaumont, Esq., *Travels in Buenos Ayres and The Adjacent Provinces of The Rio de La Plata with Observations, Intended for The Use of Persons Who Contemplate Emigrating to that Country; or, Embarking Capital in Its Affairs,* London, James Ridgway, 1882.

Play at duelling at a gaucho fair, Argentina. (Rene Burri, Magnum)

If a traveller require concealment, they will enter into his case with zeal, and encounter danger to themselves sooner than betray him, or give him up; but in the exercise of this virtue they are not very discriminating—they do not inquire into particulars—it is enough that a man crave their protection. Hence, it often happens that a robber or murderer is shielded from the pursuit of justice as effectually as the fugitive prisoner of war, or the object of a rabble's violence.

The *peon* is a hired laborer; his business is to tend the flocks, to prevent their straying, or to do any other laboring work about the farm which may be required, provided always it can be done on horseback. In the towns, *peons* on foot ply at the corners of the streets as porters; they carry very heavy loads. Their dress consists of a long white cotton frock, a shirt, and a pair of drawers of the same material. . . .

Cattle farms (*estancias*)—the breeding and disposal of cattle is the staple business of the country. It is the most profitable employment, and is managed with the least difficulty. A cattle farm is, by law, of the extent of one square league and a half, but these farms frequently extend to ten or twenty square leagues. In some convenient part of this domain is the homestead; this generally consists of a large shed-looking building, with mud walls and floors, covered with a thatched roof; this is divided into three or four apartments—a sitting room, a bed room for the family, another for strangers, with a spacious room or rooms, proportioned to the estate, for the deposit of jerked beef, hides, tallow, and other goods; the kitchen is generally a detached building in the rear of the house, and connected therewith is frequently a *rancho,* or lodging house for the *peons*; there are never less than these two buildings at an *estancia*; but sometimes there are three, four, or more, for store rooms or lodging rooms, when the estate is large and well stocked. Formerly, every considerable estate had its chapel; these buildings are now, for the most part, converted into store rooms, or *pulperías* (public houses).

If the *estancia* be a rich one, the owner's principal residence is in the city, or chief town of the province; but he must still pass a considerable part of his time on his estate, to superintend personally the operations of buying and selling; for as those transactions take place generally between persons who know nothing of the arts of writing and account keeping, unless the payments come direct into the hands of the principal himself, sad mistakes are too likely to occur, or, even if they do not, to be suspected. The well-educated European, therefore, if he become a cattle owner, and would escape pillage, must become a *gaucho* in his own person; and it is curious to see with what facility a polished Eng-

lishman mixes in the almost savage state of society of the native herdsmen, and adopts their manners. One of the most expert horsemen and
efficient herdsmen whom I met with in the country was a Mr. MacCart-
ney, who had an *estancia* near Villa de la Concepción, in the province of
Entre Ríos; on his estate he was a complete *gaucho,* and he was equally
at home as a well bred gentleman in the best society at Buenos Ayres.

Every *estancia* has a master herdsman (*capataz*), who has under him
a *peón,* for every thousand head of cattle, or thereabouts. The business
of the farm consists in riding round the herds occasionally, followed by
dogs, and gathering them into one spot (*rodeo*), where they are kept
some time, and then allowed to disperse. This is done to accustom the
cattle to keep together, and to discipline them from straying. At other
times they are employed in marking the cattle with the stamp of the
estate, in cutting young steers and foals, in breaking in young horses,
and, in the winter and spring, in killing cattle, for their hides, tallow
and jerked beef (*cherca*).

The *capataz,* and the *peons* who are married, have generally separate
huts. The furniture of these huts usually consists of a barrel to hold
water, a small copper pot to boil the water for *máte* (an herb tea), a
few gourds used as *máte* cups, a large iron pot to boil meat in, a bull's
horn to drink from, and some sticks or wooden spits for roasting the
meat. Ox skulls generally serve to sit on, but some have a few manufactured stools, or a bench, and a bed to sleep on. This last consists of a
frame, on which a hide is stretched, and which is raised on four legs,
about a foot from the floor. The *peons* more generally sleep on the
ground, and on their horses' furniture (*recado*). This consists of one
or two coarse cloths, of about two yards by one, which are folded and
laid on the horses' backs, to receive the saddle; a piece of hide, nearly
five feet by two, is laid over the cloths, then comes the saddle, a wooden
tree with a high pummel and crupper, stuffed with straw and covered
with leather; this at night, forms the pillow. The saddle, is indeed, of
very general use to the herdsman; it not only furnishes his bed room,
but his cuisine, for when other means are not at hand for dressing his
meat while travelling, he puts it between the saddle and the horse's
back, and after a good gallop, it is turned out very tender, well soaked
in gravy and enough done. This is frequently described, but I never
saw it. Another use of the saddle is to secure their clothes against a
storm. When they are out on the plains, and a heavy rain is about to
descend, they take off their clothes (an operation, which, without some
pressing occasion, they do not take the trouble to do sometimes for

weeks together), and place them under the saddle; they then ride about stark naked, under a plentiful shower bath, and after this is exhausted, they resume their dry clothes. This, too, is as the story goes, I never saw it.

In this zone of replacement, then, there arose a frontier culture very much like that of our Wild West. Its heroes were the owners of huge herds, the cattle bosses, and the cowboys who worked for them, the *gauchos*. You may read of this life in the famous novel by the Argentine writer Ricardo Guiraldes, *Don Segundo Sombra*, which describes the transformation of an orphan boy into a full-fledged cowboy. It was a life in which the prizes went to the strong, the aggressive, the hardy, the courageous. Leadership necessarily went to the person capable of enforcing his command. In a situation where families lived miles apart, says the Argentine writer Domingo Sarmiento,

all government becomes impossible; municipal rule does not exist, orderly government cannot function and civil justice has no way of catching up with the delinquents.[4]

Once again we find that direct relationships between persons take the place of more formal institutions of law and order. The ranch owner needed a foreman who could enforce his will over a group of unruly cowboys. To become boss of a wagon train, says Sarmiento, one needed "a will of iron, a personality fearless to the point of recklessness, in order to control the audacity and turbulence of the bandits of this land whom he has to govern and dominate by himself alone in the unprotected desert." The country judge "needs courage above all other things; the terror his name inspires is more powerful than the punishments which he inflicts. The judge is naturally someone grown famous in the past whom age and family have called to an orderly life. Certainly, the justice he administers is wholly arbitrary; his conscience or his passions are his guide, and his sentences are without appeal. . . . The judge makes himself obeyed by his reputation of fear-inspiring courage, his authority, his formless justice, his sentences, his 'it is I that orders it,' and his self-invented punishments." Often the government sought out such

4. D. F. Sarmiento, *Life in the Argentine Republic in the Days of the Tyrants: or Civilization and Barbarism*, translated by Mrs. Horace Mann, New York, 1868, p. 16.

self-made bosses and gave them the title of *comandante,* commander, but, says Sarmiento

since the city is weak in the countryside, without influence or followers, the government makes use of the men whom it fears most, to give them this task in order to control them; a very well known method used by all weak governments, and one which staves off the evil of the moment in order to let it grow to enormous proportions later on.[5]

Such leaders who could play the part of a gaucho among gauchos could thus concentrate upon their persons the loyalty of these cowboys, and thus come into possession of redoubtable forces of armed cavalrymen. We shall see later how important this relation between leaders and followers came to be for the development of Latin American politics. Here let us note merely that the cattle ranch, too, involves the creation of two quite distinct social positions, that of superior boss and of dependent cowhand. We have encountered such contrasts between superior or dominant positions and inferior or subordinate positions in each of the economic activities we have discussed. To the series of positions exemplified by

1. storekeeper—customer
2. rubber trader—rubber tapper
3. fazenda owner—slave
4. hacienda owner—peon

we can now add a fifth:

5. rancher or cattle boss—cowboy.

In each of these pairs, the first denotes the boss, the second the person who takes orders from him. The first positions are positions of wealth or power, the second those who lack these attributes—they are filled by men who must work for others. But with wealth and power also go obligations. In Latin America the *patrón* or *patrão* is expected to protect his dependent; the servant, in turn, owes personal loyalty and support to his patron. Relationships based on economic transactions— buying and selling, or employment—are strongly personalized.

We said at the outset of this chapter that we would look at several ways of life, each with its own problems and particular solutions. But we also hoped to find some common denominators or *patterns* which

5. *Ibid.,* p. 53.

would unite them all. In the patron-dependent relationship we have defined such a pattern, a pattern of continuing and enduring importance in Latin America.

INDUSTRY

This patron-dependent relation appears again, in modern guise, in the organization of modern industry and business in Latin America. An economist, Thomas C. Cochran, and an anthropologist, Reuben Reina, both of the University of Pennsylvania, joined hands to study the development and operation of one great industrial-commercial complex in Argentina, called S.I.A.M. S.I.A.M. was the product of one man, Torcuato Di Tella; his enterprise can be considered characteristic of the organization of a Latin American business enterprise. Let us see what our two investigators can tell us of this organization.*

Up to his death, Di Tella kept a tight personal hold on the company. He drew his top administrators from *hombres de confianza*

whose devotion to Di Tella and his enterprises was beyond doubt. These men formed the nucleus of the "S.I.A.M. family," a term that should not be confused with the North American cliché of the business family. In S.I.A.M., the relationship on the middle- to- upper-management level, and in some cases reaching down lower in the organization, was one of personal attachment, honor, and obligation not measurable in job values. . . . From a United States point of view, Di Tella did not delegate much authority to these *hombres de confianza*. Instead, he saw them frequently and acquainted them with his views and policies. Inasmuch as they often had to operate in Di Tella's absence they in fact exercised their own authority, but Di Tella was consulted by mail, and important decisions were piled up pending his return.

These *hombres de confianza* he supplemented or balanced with members of his own family, either through descent or through marriage.

With his employees he always dealt person-to-person. He would walk through the factory several times a week, talking with the chiefs and

* The quotations on the following pages are from Thomas C. Cochran and Reuben Reina, *Entrepreneurship in Argentine Culture*, copyright 1962 by the University of Pennsylvania Press. Reprinted by permission.

settling problems on the spot. He listened to the advicve of foreign experts in questions of rationalization and labor-management relations, but he always applied their advice flexibly and opportunistically, adapting it and changing it to suit the preferences and habits of his "S.I.A.M. family." Ten years before the advent of public welfare schemes in Argentina, he had elaborated his own welfare plans

For weddings the company presented one month's salary to those with at least two years of service, up to a maximum of two hundred and fifty pesos. A laborer employed for a year would receive fifty pesos. If both spouses were working for S.I.A.M. at the time of the wedding, they both received the gift. The birth of each child brought a fifty peso gift to laborers of over one year in service. Workers of over twenty-five years' standing were eligible for pensions of sixty pesos a month. A schedule of vacations was established, ranging from ten days for those employed for less than five years up to thirty days for those who had been with S.I.A.M. for more than twenty years.

Where, traditionally, North American industrial discipline has been based on the ultimate sanction of firing, to obtain proper performance by the right man at the right time, in S.I.A.M. firing "was the very last resort, not an expected course of action." Instead, Di Tella used his own person to rally loyalties. This continued after his death. Since his demise the

. . . entire organization was integrated around the symbol of Di Tella in a way that would probably not have been effective in United States culture. The Consejo ruled S.I.A.M. not only through the formal positions of its members but more importantly by virtue of their inheritance of *confianza* from Di Tella. After his death the *patrón* underwent a process analogous to canonization. To preserve the legend of infallibility, his policies were never criticized by the members of the *Consejo*. Wherever the employee went he was confronted with tangible symbols of the man. Pictures of Di Tella hung in every room and a life-sized statue watched over the entrance to Avellaneda. The incoming employee was oriented into the S.I.A.M. tradition by old company men as part of the training process; continuity of the Di Tella symbol was used as a wellspring for company morale.

But such a personalistic mode of business leadership has certain predictable consequences. Let us try to make some of these predictions.

Where the primary purpose of a business organization is to obtain a maximum of profit, executives will strive first to discover what will pay and then mold their actions to that end. But where the recovery of profits is only one end among a number of others, such as the gaining of personal prestige, the search for family security, the building up of ties of kinship and friendship, the enterprise will not function merely to make profits but to underwrite these other ends as well. It will not surprise us, therefore, to find that two American social scientists, William Whyte and Allan Holmberg, say of the Latin American entrepreneur that the "executive first plans what *ought* to be done and then plans as best he can to *make his action pay*."[6]

Second, the *person* of the entrepreneur has primacy over the *operation*. The running of the enterprise is *his* glory and *his* responsibility. From this we can predict he will be unwilling to delegate authority and responsibilities to others. Their mistakes might reflect on his own standing, on his standing in his own eyes and in the eyes of others. From this we can predict several more things. Since other people will not be allowed to participate in the running of the enterprise, except passively, there will be few middle- or lower-level managers who would or could take responsibilities for decisions at those levels. It will not surprise us therefore to hear that in Argentine industry, for example, the top executives supervise many more processes than in North America. According to an Argentine economist, this has further consequences:

to the detriment of the indispensable training and development of lower managerial cadres and of the over-all efficiency of the enterprise, the functional responsibilities of middle and lower management tend to be only vaguely defined. This results in frequent overlapping of duties and responsibilities (which means that more often than not these are not carried out) or in the total neglect of functions which nobody in the organization has been specifically assigned.[7]

Such overcentralization of authority has a second effect. Where primary

6. William Whyte and Allan Holmberg, "Human Problems of U.S. Enterprise in Latin America," in *Human Organization*, Fall 1956, p. 10.
7. Tomás Roberto Fillol, *Social Factors in Economic Development: The Argentine Case*, MIT Press, 1961, p. 61.

loyalty is to the efficient management of the operation, people can discuss their different points of view with regard to the operation. But where the enterprise *is* the person and that person's word must stand, subordinates will not criticize procedures or make suggestions. There will therefore be a high degree of outward conformity. People will agree with the boss, rather than venture suggestions about the operation; they will avoid open disagreement with authority.

But we may note still a third consequence. Where authority is imposed from above, and where people do not participate in decisions, decisions often seem arbitrary and capricious. Authority comes to seem unpredictable; and while workers will accept it, they will also view events with considerable suspicion. People will retreat into the domain where they feel comfortable and safe, the circle of kin and quasi-kin whom one can trust. North American executives who deal with Latin Americans readily assume that Latin American managers and workers alike will respond to them in Anglo-American ways, by "putting all their cards on the table," "giving the other fellow an even break," "being a good sport," "keeping personalities out of this," "refraining from putting things on a personal level," encouraging suggestions and criticisms from subordinates, "sticking to the rules of the game." All of these expectations neglect the central principle of Latin American social relations which grants trust only to those with whom one has close personal relationships and dictates distrust of the outsider.

CITIES

But Latin America is not merely a continent of rural landscapes or industrial locations. Let us remember—from our briefing—that Latin America was conquered and settled by people who came from the European Mediterranean, where living in cities has an ancient past. We have noted how from the outset the colonists "planted" cities, occupying either the capitals of the ancient Indian kingdoms or creating entire new cities to fit their new purposes. As in the Mediterranean, moreover, these cities are not primarily industrial centers, but feed on the countryside that surrounds them. Productive life is carried on in the rural area, but men in the countryside dream of city lights and sounds. "The striking incongruity of the institutional history of Latin America," says the historian Richard M. Morse, is "that the most important job of production has been that of extracting commodities from the soil and subsoil, though the persons who settled the area, as well as the immigrants of

The city dump is close to home for this young girl from a *barrio* in Bogotá, Colombia. (Courtesy *Visión* Magazine)

later centuries, crossed the ocean with the idea of the city in their mind."[8]

Since the days of the conquest, the cities of Latin America have grown apace. In 1900, only four countries in Latin America had more than 10 per cent of their population living in cities larger than 20,000 people. By 1950, however, 25 per cent of the total Latin American population lived in cities of 20,000 people or more, and 17 per cent of their population in cities of 100,000 people and above. This last figure is only 4 per cent lower than Europe, one of the most highly industrialized areas of the world. But Europe also has two-thirds of its labor force in industry, and only one-third in agriculture. Latin America still has two-thirds in agriculture, and only one-third in non-agricultural pursuits. People flock to the cities, but the cities do not have the industrial potential to absorb all this added labor power. How, then, do people from the rural hinterland adapt themselves to living in these burgeoning cities? Listen to Andrew Pearse, a sociologist and scholar of folklore working for the United Nations Educational and Scientific Organization (UNESCO), describing the settlements of the poor in the Brazilian city of Rio de Janeiro.*

General Housing Conditions

One of the characteristic expressions of urbanization in the city of Rio is the growth of *favelas,*[9] in which, according to the most recent survey conducted by the Instituto de Pesquisas e Estudos do Mercado, during 1957, live 650,000 of the city's population of 2 million. In his book, *O Negro no Rio de Janeiro,* L. A. Costa Pinto reports that immediately after Emancipation in 1888 a considerable number of former slaves made

8. R. M. Morse, "Some Characteristics of Latin American Urban History," in *American Historical Review,* Vol. 67, 1962, p. 317.

* From Andrew Pearse, "Some Characteristics of Urbanization in the City of Rio de Janeiro," in Philip Hauser (ed.), *Urbanization in Latin America,* copyright 1961 by UNESCO. Reprinted by permission of UNESCO.

9. The word *favela* in its modern usage was defined by the Instituto Brasileiro de Geografia e Estadística as: (a) a minimum number of fifty buildings grouped together; (b) predominance of huts and barracks of a typical rustic appearance, usually made of planks and galvanized sheets or similar material; (c) unlicensed and uninspected buildings on lands of third parties or unknown owners; (d) not included in the general network of sewerage, running water, lighting and telephones; (e) non-urbanized area, lacking proper division into streets, numbering, feeing, or rating system.

their new homes in the hills which dotted and circumscribed the city. There is further evidence of settlements in Providence Hill at the conclusion of the War of Canudos in the last years of the century, a settlement which also accounts for the origin of the name favela, if we are to accept the investigations of a writer in the excellent weekly journal *Manchete*.[10]

But these two examples must not be thought of as implying that the favela was a characteristic low-class dwelling at so early a period. A more characteristic form of popular housing was the "pig's head" (*cabeca de porco*) and the "bee-hive" (*cortico*), names given to different types of collective dwellings or rooming-houses established usually in what had been large town houses of the rich.

According to the census, in 1890, immediately after Abolition, one-quarter of the population lived in these; i.e. 18,338 families lived in 1449 collective houses, and by 1906 the number had grown to 3041. But from the beginning of the century the movement away from the center of the city had already begun, and in 1904-5 there was a great increase in travel on the suburban railway. Between the 1890 and 1906 censuses, the proportion of suburban dwellers to the total moved from 17.8 per cent to 22.6 per cent while the gross population increased from 522,651 to 811,443. Between 1906 and 1920, the increase in city and suburban population was about equal—approximately 173,000 each—but between 1920 and 1940 the city hardly increased (14,382) while the suburbs went up by 591,886. Thus, throughout most of this period, population increase was taken care of by the existence of available low-rent suburban lands for building, and a fair transport system, though housing standards for the poorer classes were low, and 57,889 houses could be described as "rustic" in the *Estadística Predial* of 1933. One of the important changes which accompanied the growth of the suburbs was the rapid

10. According to this writer, one of the earliest settlements of squatters within the city was made on Providence Hill by veterans from the War of Canudos, described by Euclides da Cunha in *Rebellion in the Backlands*. The hill rises steeply behind Rio's docks, and on the other side overlooks the War Ministry, being chosen on that account by the veterans as a suitable place of sojourn while they daily pressed their claims on the government for compensation and pensions. They gave the hill the name *favela* after the Favela Hill from which the final assault was made on Canudos, so called because of the bitter, stinging *favela* plant which grew upon it in painful profusion. In thus christening their temporary home, presumably they were not only aware of the bitterness of their long wait upon bureaucratic process but also of their anticipated victorious descent on the War Ministry. Later the name *favela* came to be used for similar settlements on the many city hills and even on the flat ground. (See *Manchete*, 1 September 1956, Rio de Janeiro.)

decrease in the number of collective buildings which had been the typical overcrowded dwellings of the poorer classes in the center of the city. It has been suggested that the collective house was a cultural relic of the *senzala* (slave house); at any rate, the changeover from this type of dwelling to the independent, though often improvised and rustic house, marks an important cultural change in one sector of the society.

Perhaps the best accounts of the unstable and marginal life of the suburbs of Rio de Janeiro in the earlier part of the century are to be found in the works of Lima Barreto, the great Negro writer and bohemian, who died in 1922, whose *Clara dos Anjos* is notable in this respect.

As from about 1930, a change in this process took place which led to a very rapid growth of the favelas through a wave of immigration due to both push and pull factors. The year 1930 marked a sudden fall in the world prices for Brazilian agricultural products, and consequently a decline in the low standard of rural livelihood, followed by increased migration from the neighboring states of Minas Gerais, Espirito Santo and Rio de Janeiro to the city. It also marked the beginning of a new political phase in which government efforts were directed to developing industries to supply internal markets, not only to compensate for the unfavorable exchange position which threatened Brazil's power to import, but also as a means of moving towards greater economic independence. The growth of new factories and their demands for a labor force led to dislocation of existing patterns of living, traveling and working. The cost of living rose rapidly along with building costs and real estate values, not only at the center but at the periphery, but the wage rate barely kept up and at times fell behind; thus, while those of the poorer classes already domiciled in the city suffered a worsening of conditions, the new in-migrants found it overwhelmingly difficult to establish themselves in rented houses in the center and suburbs. Furthermore, so great were the suburban increases that the transport system became hopelessly overloaded. When electric trains were introduced in 1937, the immediate result was that during the subsequent six months, the number of passengers immediately increased by 3,948,857. At the present time the appalling *mêlée* at rush hours and the frequent accidents on the suburban lines are enough to discourage the bravest, and result in sporadic outbursts of *quebra-quebra* or wilful destruction of installations by mobs of angry passengers.

The solution to the housing problem which presented itself to the in-migrants was to build their own flimsy improvised houses on the steep hillsides and vacant lands as near as possible to their place of work, and thus participate in the formation and extension of *favelas*.

From 1940 to 1950 conditions worsened steadily, and the gap between wages and cost of living grew while the city population increased by 613,310, largely as a result of migration from the neighboring states. The number of "houses of a rustic type" went up from 66,317 to 89,635 between 1940 and 1949 (counted by the National Yellow Fever Service) i.e. an average increase of 2702 per year as compared with 1060 per year in the seven years preceding 1940.

Making a calculation on the basis of the Yellow Fever Service count the *favela* population reaches approximately 400,000, or about 17 per cent of the population of the city, by 1949. By 1957 it had reached 650,000.

Geographical Determinants of Favela Development

The center of the city of Rio de Janeiro, with its docks and warehouses, administrative, business and shopping center, is an extension of the old city into which were crowded not only the buildings of an old commercial and colonial capital, but also the homes of merchants, servants, lawyers, priests, statesmen and tradesmen. This was modified to become the center of a modern city by cutting through first the Avenida Rio Branco at the beginning of the century, and more recently of the Avenida Getulio Vargas. Today it stands on a "corner" or right angle, with the Atlantic Ocean to the south, and the sheltered Bay of Guanabara to the east. Thus, instead of having a circumference of 360 degrees, as would a city on a river or in the midst of a plain, its hinterland of *terra firma* is confined to 90 degrees. But, to make matters worse, the steep barren-rock mountains of the Serra da Carioca range come down to the coast at this point, leaving for the city area itself a restricted shelf dotted with acute outlyers.

Thus the two directions for the expansion of the city are (a) the southern zone, generally speaking, a thin strip stretching along the southern coast between sea and sheer mountain, obviously an area destined to be an expensive residential quarter or seaside resort; and (b) a segment of hinterland, between the Serra and the Bay of Guanabara, opening out at an angle of no more than 35 or 40 degrees. This is the suburban area above referred to, served by four railway lines. And here, clearly, owing to the acuteness of the angle of the segment, rapid expansion was bound very quickly to proceed to the limits where it could not be served by an adequate transport system. At this point, however, these very geographical peculiarities offered some solution. The mountains and small outlying hills, which had hitherto been regarded as too steep for settlement, and especially for the provision of roads and water, now became optional sites for city workers. In this manner, not only were virtually all the hills built upon, but *favela* settlements spread to cover a number of important level sites, both in the city and in the areas further from the center.

But geographical factors alone do not account for the growth of the *favelas*. A more important cause must be looked for in the socio-economic condition of the nation, especially of the relation between wages and rent in town and country, metropolis and interior.

Some Socio-Economic Conditions of Favela Development

In the year 1948 the average salary in industry was 960 cruzeiros per month and 61 per cent of persons employed in commerce, 76 per cent of manual workers and 50 per cent of persons working in industry, earned under 1000 cruzeiros per month. Of male *favelados*, 52 per cent earned 600 to 1000 cruzeiros, and 26.5 per cent earned between 1000 and 2000 cruzeiros. If a salary of 1000 cruzeiros per month might be considered as allowing the expenditure of 200 cruzeiros per month for rent, what new family houses were still available at this rate were all at a great distance from the center of the city, while the rent of a small apartment nearer in would have cost three-quarters to the whole of the total salary in rent. And so great was the rate of increase of building costs that the Prefecture of the Federal District was forced to revise its original estimate of the cost of a popular house to replace the *favela* dwellings from 10,000 cruzeiros in 1948 to 25,000 cruzeiros in 1949.

In contrast, the declared values of the houses in the *favela* of Esqueleto in 1948 were as shown in Table 6. Thus the average declared value of a house was worth two to three months' salary, and having been built, left its owner without further responsibility for the payment of rent.

The *favela* therefore offered to the in-migrant a means of establishing himself and his family as an unbroken unit in the shortest possible time, and with the least possible outlay, in his own house, in conditions similar and sometimes superior to those of his country home.

Thus in one sense the *favela* performs an inevitable and essential function in the relation between the urban, industrial and rich sector, and the rural, agricultural and poor sector, divided by a quite exceptional socio-economic lacuna. The poverty of the rural areas provides a

TABLE 6

Value of houses in the favela of Esqueleto, 1948

Declared value (in cruzeiros)	Number of houses	Percentage
Up to 1000	194	14.4
1001 to 2000	291	21.5
2001 to 5000	408	30.2
5001 to 9999	131	9.7
Over 10,000	32	2.4
No information	291	21.8

great pool of cheap labor moving steadily to the city, which serves to hold down the level of wages, and the standard of living of the town working class. In these circumstances the progress of industrial organization has reached a point where the pressure of wage-earners obliges the popular leaders of the government to maintain a minimum wage, but not to the point where an organized working-class movement can develop and stand out for a standard of living commensurate with the requirements of city life. The *favela* house is indeed a house of the rustic type, being nothing more nor less than the intrusion into an urban system of life of rural standards of housing, which, according to the 1940 census, made up 65.2 per cent of the homes of Brazilians. What is significant, however, and what is overlooked constantly by the city commentators who weep over the *favelas*, is that though the house-type is "rural," the conditions of life which the *favela* dwellers—by their illegal initiative—have secured for themselves, are rated higher by them in most respects than the conditions prevailing in the rural areas from which the greater number of them have come.

Migration, Social Integration and Cultural Assimilation
In Relation to Family Organization and Structure

The following notes are based on data collected from 279 families covered by a survey done in the *favela* of Esqueleto by the local parish church. It was based on intensive interviews with fathers, mothers and 11-year-old children from 21 families; on general quantitative data assembled from a random sample of the whole *favela* population of the city (taken from publications of the Instituto de Pesquisas e Estudos de Mércado); and on observation.

The Nuclear Family

The nuclear or conjugal family was the usual household unit. That is to say, most households (i.e. 185 out of 279) consisted of father, mother and children of one or both, or adopted children, only. A further 25 families had lost the father (19 were dead and 6 had gone away) but had no other additions. There were a further 23 households in which the nuclear family had lost either father or mother and included other immediate kin, and in almost every case their adhesion to the nuclear family could be explained by the need to substitute for the original father or mother, whose roles as earner or *dona de casa* (head of family), respectively, had been left vacant. Most of these substitutions were effected by married sons or daughters returning to or remaining in their families of origin, with their spouses. Finally there were 17 nuclear families with accretions, most of which could be accounted for by (a) the sheltering of brothers of either spouse who had just migrated from the country and (b) the sheltering of widowed mothers of either spouse. The few remaining households could not be described technically as families.

It must be observed that this pattern corresponded to custom among the rural poor in the areas adjacent to the city from which most of the *favelados* came. The newly married couple is established independently in a roughly built house at marriage. These houses are easily built, and frequently pass from hand to hand. This is also true of the *favela* houses. This pattern is in contrast with that which prevails in the household of the *fazendeiro*, where the nuclear family of the chief frequently lives together with other kin. It is also in contrast with practice observed among the middle class, where joint families and three-generation families were frequent, a situation easily acceptable especially in families of Portuguese and Italian origin, though the younger married women appeared to be discontented with it; the situation was frequently explained in terms of the high level of rents.

The structure of the nuclear family was characterized by four modes of relationship between its members, with each one of which was associated a guiding series of norms. These norms were fully conceptualized and frequently verbalized, departure from them arousing strong moral feelings. The dominant ethic among these families was almost entirely deducible from these norms, or their extrapolation beyond the family.

The *blood relationship* is most important as between mothers and children, committing the mother to unrestrained devotion to and care of the child, and committing the child to affection for the mother and to a willingness to look after her in case of need when he is grown up. In the relations between siblings, and fathers and children, the blood relationship is less compelling, though it contributes to the norms of proper behavior. The situation of the foster child can be used as a test of the relative force of the blood relationship component.

The *relationship of super- and subordination* is based upon the position of authority of the father-of-the-family, in the sense of role rather than biological relationship. According to the norm, the mother must submit fully to this, as well as the children, and a wife may refer approvingly to her husband as "husband and father to me." Authority carries with it an obligation to teach, guide and protect the respective members of the family over whom it is exercised, who in their turn must be obedient. Subject to the father, the mother exercises most of the day-to-day authority with the younger children.

The principle of authority is also supposed to operate amongst the siblings strictly according to age until about eighteen years of age, when the male begins to acquire authority over the female sibling, regardless of age.

Built upon the authority principle, but distinguished from it, there was the *relationship of mutual aid* within the family, based largely on a practical view of the division of labor and the problems of economic subsistence. Each member of the family was expected to contribute to the common good or "family wealth" according to his competence. Father and mother had their respective responsibilities and were not expected to interfere with one another in carrying them out. The principle became more important as the children grew older and the age-attribution of authority weakened. Thus we shall see that this principle was of relatively greater importance in guiding relation within the wider kin group.

Between husband and wife the blood relationship is excluded and its place is taken by the *connubial relationship* in combination with the remaining two. It can be viewed as a continuum between a positive pole of intense mutual affection coupled with exclusively satisfying sexual experience, through varying degrees of affectional fondness, tolerance and indifference to the point where the relationship is broken by separation and one or both the partners seek new mates. It is a critical relationship because of the arbitrary modern manner in which sexual attraction operates to select the marriage partners of the young. This arouses certain expectations which the almost extinct tradition of selection by the parents according to local cultural and socio-economic convenience did not arouse. Moreover, this relationship is critical since a move towards the negative pole is a threat to the total structure of the family. Nevertheless we were frequently reminded that wives were inclined to accept the establishment by their husbands of a new collateral connubial relationship outside the family when their own had become negative, rather than initiate conflict which would end in their husbands leaving the home. In many cases they had come to the city as domestic servants, having been obliged to leave their homes and go to work early. In other cases they had been left on their own by the decease or abandonment of their husbands or fathers, and had come to the city to stay with a relation. In most cases they had only established common-law relations with their present "husbands," who were frequently men who also left their families of origin to find work and a new life in the city. The absence of the family of origin made the contracting of legal marriage unlikely.

The Kin-Group

The nuclear family of the *favelado* is an independent socio-economic unit, but its security is assured and the cultural expectations of its members only fulfilled when the potential network of mutual obligations, freely given services, and affections which link it to kin can be realized in practice. Thus when we speak of kin-group, we do not refer to generalized kin up to a certain degree of removal but to the specific group of kin with which the nuclear family interacts frequently, regularly and intimately. Membership of this kin-group is partly decided by the fact that at marriage the individual moves out of his family of origin but maintains the links with its members in a modified form. But these links are not likely to be strong if his or her marriage partner does not also wish to accept his or her "in-law" family on terms of intimacy or if he or she is unacceptable to them. In the case of all the *favelados* of rural origin which we investigated closely, marriage was preceded by the close and intimate friendship of the two families of the partners, who were thus easily absorbed into the partner's family after the usual periods of *namoro* (early friendship) and *noivado* (engagement). The country families in the smaller sample were all based on legal marriage and had every appearance of stability.

Kin-groups are brought into existence by marriage and relationships within them are celebrated and reinforced by the appointment of their members as godparents as the children arrive. Sometimes non-kin are given virtual status as kin-group members by being made godparents.

Activation of Nuclear Family and Kin-Group in Migration to the City

Of the in-migrant families which were closely observed, there appeared to be two clusters, if considered from the point of view of family forma-tion; (a) those formed before migration, and (b) those in which one and usually both of the partners had already broken away from their family of origin before they migrated and who formed their alliances with persons usually in similar circumstances. The first cluster was characterized by legal marriage, relative stability, planned migration of the family assisted by kin-group in place of origin and already in the city, and continuing close interaction with kin-group. In the other cluster we noted that the wife was not living with her family of origin when she started to live in the city.

Since kin-groups are not independent units but interlocking units, they formed a species of chain, and the majority of in-migrants, whether they came to the city with their families or not, nevertheless came as a link in such a chain, being both preceded and followed by kin in per-sistent movement citywards.

The most important types of assistance given by members of the kin-group to the in-migrant family under the abnormal circumstances of their move to the city were (a) in a few cases, some financial assistance for the move and the initial period of transition; (b) temporary lodging and help in building or acquiring a *favela* house; (c) making the neces-sary contacts to find employment for the main earner of the family.

The Role of the Kin-Group in Favela Life

Most of the rural families studied intensively were able to count on several kin-group families living either within the *favela* or somewhere else in the city. With these families, and these alone, there is constant visiting. It was frequently asserted or implied that the kin-group thus constituted offered the only truly approved area for sociability and the nurturing of close friendship. The men tended to belittle or deny their social activities with their workmates and in the bars, and the women insisted that they avoided intimacies with neighbors, making a point of not going into their houses and forbidding their children to do so.

The exceptions to this rule were in cases of neighbors' sickness, and also the homes of those women who administered remedies of a medical or spiritual nature. A few of the men had had brief experience of the syndicates, but none of them expressed any belief in their usefulness. Anxiety and disapproval were expressed in regard to associating freely with others and to *ajuntamentos* (gatherings), an exception to this attitude being found in the Protestants whose little congregations were free associations whose members entered into a pseudo-kin relationship (brothers-in-Christ, etc.) and who were prepared to take something at least of the responsibility for one another that they would take for genuine kin. But the attitude which prevailed was certainly that of *descompromisso* or the avoidance of extrafamilial obligations and entanglements. One of the corollaries of this pattern of avoidances was the general ineffectiveness of "public opinion" and the relative unimportance of approval and disapproval communicated from outside the kin-group.

A further corollary was the absence of any local neighborhood sentiment, and the only neighborhood joint action observed was the improvement of a road leading to the house of a local "boss," and done under pressure from him, which he was able to exert through certain powers which he had accumulated.

Thus the kin-group emerged as the dominant and almost exclusive sanction group for the behavior of its members. Within it achievements, failures, good and ill fortune were commented according to the common attitudes of the group, subject to individual variations. Advice was given, help proffered and short-term plans made. The new experiences and perceptions of its members, face to face with the ways of the city, were evaluated within it. In addition to these functions it was the first line of defence of the family, and could be relied upon in case of sickness, unemployment, dispossession, accidents, etc.

From Rural Dependence to Urban Independence

The rural families, whether laborers, contract working men or sharecroppers, had all lived in and been accustomed to a situation of dependence on a *patrão* (landowner), whose land they had cultivated and to whom they had looked for a day's work for wages, a house or the right to build a house, land to cultivate on shares or on some other contractual basis, help in cases of sickness or poverty, loans to finance planting—often leading to debt-dependence—protection and political leadership in a non-ideological sense.

It is not suggested that the countryman was servile in behavior or in attitude, but that he was obliged to accept a situation in which he was an inferior partner to a contract, and that all the weight of advantage was on the side of the *patrão*. Should the latter press him too far, then his only recourse was to go elsewhere, but so long as he stayed in rural pursuits, what scanty benefits he might achieve would come to him through one *patrão* or another.

The ideas formed in the country about the nature of social relations and the "inevitability of the boss" persisted in the town, but the modes of dependence are different.

The in-migrant in the town discovered that the government, though not his employer, was his protector, guaranteeing him a minimum wage if he worked, sick benefits, pensions and at least the possibility of hospital beds in the case of sickness, and a variety of legal rights which were his, though they were difficult to understand and secure. He attributed this protective action of the government in favor of the town worker to Getulio Vargas and his collaborators.

As an employee he looks for more than the simple wage nexus, hoping to find a *bom patrão* (good patron) for whom he will work loyally if he can expect what he regards as his right, the occasional loan, help with medicines and intervention on his behalf in his encounters with the bureaucracy, etc.

Accustoming himself to the large enterprise, in which there is no personal boss relationship, he often finds distressing. His wife, if she is a laundress, will also prize highly such a personal relationship with her customers. He realizes that in exceptional circumstances a *patrão* can take on the role of a *pistolão* (protector) who will use his influence to help him in his career, or those of his children, and there are few who believe that ability and industry are more effective than a *pistolão* in getting on in life.

Finally he looks to the saints to protect him and above all to Sao Jorge, especially devoted to the welfare of the poor. Such protection is sought by prayers, the making of *promessas* (vows), and keeping the light burning in front of the saint's image. In special circumstances he will go to the cult-house of the Umbanda or to the Spiritists to enter personally into communication with a strong saint through a medium, hoping that the saint or spirit will be able to manipulate on his behalf the social and natural processes which he can neither understand nor control nor predict.

The cultural assimilation of the country in-migrants can be considered best by recourse to the concept of populism. In its Brazilian setting, populism is a dominant characteristic of contemporary urban culture. Considered from the point of view of the classes with property and influence, it is an attempt to maintain traditional privilege and authority in face of the institutions of constitutional democracy; in face of the breakdown of the system of direct dependency which the archaic rural pattern of socio-economic relations maintained, and its replacement by the powerless independence of the urban worker who is linked to the power-center solely by the cash wage nexus; and in face of the breaking of the social isolation of the rural populace by the rapid development of mass communication and growing literacy.

The ranks of the populist leaders consist largely of new social elements not traditionally associated with large proprietorship, and to a lesser degree of children of family ensconced in the traditional system, but who could not count upon it for a substantial situation. Viewed from this side populism is concerned with political power at the level of the municipality, the state and the Union, which is exercised directly and indirectly through the body of functionaries. It is supported by structures based on clientage in which benefits are handed down in return for votes and personal loyalties in maneuvres. Most of these structures are informal and non-institutionalized and do not coincide with the formal structures of administration.

While the intermediary ranks receive benefits through the allocation of posts in the system of functionaries, jobs, contracts, grants-in-aid of charitable, cultural and sports enterprises, etc., the masses receive them through defensive labor legislation and access to the services of medical assistance posts, sports clubs, religious and cult groups, etc., subsidized through the intervention of populist leaders at various levels, whose names are given due prominence. Populism does not favor the organization of common interest groups or co-operative groups, and power is usually delegated downwards rather than upwards. Representatives are appointed, but they are seldom elected from below. In its appeal to the masses populism uses symbols stressing the protective role of the great charismatic leaders, and the small-scale operators use to the full the confidence in such leaders. While faith in the small-scale operator is frequently lost, that in the great leader is apparently durable.

Coming from a tradition of rural dependence which we referred to above, the city masses still fit easily into this structure. The ordinary propertyless man feels that he is in no position to improve his lot significantly since he does not know either how to obtain his legal rights or how to operate successfully even in the lower ranks of the power and influence structures. He remains powerless without the intervention of a *patrão*, a *pistolão*, the favor of a *pelego* (local boss), or the special action of a saint or manipulator of saints.

Urban mass culture illustrates this situation in an interesting manner. Probably the three most important pastimes of the city populace are: football, *jôgo do bicho* (animal gambling game) and listening to the radio, and nearly all the families bought newspapers from time to time, and most of them regularly. Through these media the in-migrants soon come to share in the urban culture both actively and as observers. The newspapers most commonly read, *O Dia* and *A Luta*, were devoted largely to sport and crime. Each day the reader is likely to see on the front page photographs of the mutilated bodies of suicides and victims of assassinations and accidents. The sensational aspect of the reportage is usually tempered by a note of indignation against the sufferings of the poor, the weak and the innocent, either at the hands of the wicked or through the negligence and heartlessness of the authorities. Leading articles constantly denounce injustices suffered by the poor. The Sunday edition devotes a large section to *macumba*, Umbanda and other forms of Spiritism, and smaller sections to the Protestant and Catholic churches.

It does not take the in-migrant male long to become a *torcedor* (supporter) of one of the great city football teams. He espouses its cause enthusiastically and learns from seeing the matches, listening to radio commentaries and scanning the newspaper, about the great players, their tactics, their strengths and weaknesses. He soon becomes able to take his part in men's group discussions and arguments which center around football. He comes to share the atmosphere of tremendous excitement on Saturday and Sunday afternoons when the football matches and broadcasts are in progress. But it is not only the excitement and the catharsis which follows it that makes football play such an important part in his world. What is characteristic of the football dramas is that the player succeeds on his merits as a footballer only, and neither birth nor influence nor color nor education favor him in any way. Thus the football system of relations is equalitarian, with rewards going according to achievement; it is an alternative and compensatory world in sharpest contrast with the everyday world in which the poor, the black, the illiterate, the man without "connections" is disqualified almost before he starts to play.

Another such equalitarian play world, but one in which even women and children have an equal chance, is that of the universal animal gambling game, the *jôgo do bicho*. It is of minor importance from our point of view that many delinquents are associated with it, that it is a highly lucrative form of exploitation, and that large sums have to be paid out for protection to the representatives of the law charged with the suppression of this illegal but universal game of chance. What is important is that each player knows that all the limiting conditions of his social life have no influence whatsoever upon his chance of winning. Moreover, it is no exaggeration to say that the *bicheiro* (collector of bets) is usually a man who, whatever his moral character, shares the fullest confidence of his unprivileged client in a way that no other role-holder in the society does.

The importance of radio is related to the exceptional predominance of the family and kin-group as the sanction group for the actions and opinions of its members, and therefore as the main arbiter of values, in comparison with other potential arbiters, such as associations, clubs, religious congregations and organizations, class or color conscious group-ings, etc. A radio program is a common experience for some or all members of the family and its contents are therefore immediately subject to the evaluation of the family as a unit. The most widely listened-to pro-grams were (a) popular serials and (b) variety programs with music, singers and humorists. Of the serials by far the most popular depicted a popular Robin Hood of the *sertão* called Jeronimo, himself belonging to a family of landed property, but devoted to the interests of the poor and unprivileged share-cropper, squatter and petty proprietor, who is de-picted as living in the interior at the mercy of the great landlords, be-yond the effective protection of the law, or else subject to the injustices perpetrated by municipal law officers who are depicted as furthering the predatory interests of the harsh proprietor. The oppressed rural peo-ple are shown as quite unable to arrange effective resistance or to take any sort of initiative on their own, but in each episode they are saved by the almost miraculous intervention of the justice-loving Jeronimo.

As regards the other programs which are most popular, they are char-acterized by (a) the use of music of the popular regional traditions, and of the sambas and other types of songs which have been developed by the urban populace, and (b) the devotion to "star" singers, the best known of whom, like the great footballers, have reached fame from humble origins.

Though the cinema is increasingly popular with the town masses in general, the adult in-migrants are not conspicuously interested. Since the great majority of the films are North American, their cultural con-tent is alien and they are difficult to follow because they are spoken in

English with written subtitles in Portuguese flashed briefly on the screen. But the in-migrant children have already learnt the clichés and stereotypes of the North American cinema from the ubiquitous comic books and are nearly all potential cinema fans.

Thus, owing to his background and the socio-economic situation which he confronts in the city, the in-migrant is easily assimilated into those aspects of city culture which partake of what we described as populism. Above all, his pastimes and his religious practices reflect his concern with his powerlessness greatly to improve or even secure his lot by his own and his family's endeavors and his habitual hope for the intervention and protection of a good *patrão*, a political leader or a strong saint. At the same time, though he as yet has not come to see city society as an open one where achievement and talent rather than privilege and position bring advancement, yet he finds great satisfaction in "play-systems" in which the individual's skills and strength bring success and where good luck may fall to any, regardless of his condition.

In his report on the *favelas*, Andrew Pearse has shown us a good bit of the social relations which the migrant develops in adapting to life in the city, and which he adopts to make this adaptation possible. Note that life in the slum is never as disorganized as it seems to the outsider at first glance. People raise families, strive for patrons, attempt to develop meaningful and helpful social ties. Often they rely on traditional cultural patterns to do so. But life in a new urban environment also changes their expectations. This is the aspect that William Mangin emphasizes in a report* on the fate of Quechua-speaking Indians, like those who inhabit Hualcán, who have moved to the coastal city of Lima. Mangin is an American anthropologist who has devoted much time to the understanding of migration in Peru, and has applied this knowledge to active participation in the United States Peace Corps.

Fortunato Quispe, a Quechua-speaking Indian from an hacienda in the mountains of Peru, contracted himself out to a coastal sugar plantation for a year's work in order to earn some cash for a religious festival.

After a year on the coast he took a wife and settled down on the plantation leaving his mountain home for good. He and his wife had seven

* From William Mangin, "Urbanization: Case Study in Peru," in *Architectural Design*, August 1963, pp. 367-70. Reprinted by permission.

children. When their oldest, Blas, was eighteen, he found himself with no job, no possibility of schooling, and under pressure from his father to leave and get a job. The small two-room adobe company house was hardly big enough for the parents and the seven children and the sugar company was mechanizing the plantation even as its resident population expanded rapidly. Blas, who had spoken mainly Quechua as a child, was, at eighteen, fully at home in Spanish. He had visited Lima, the capital city, twice, was an avid radio and movie fan and considered the life of the plantation town dull.

Six months after his eighteenth birthday he and his friend, Antonio, took a truck to the Lima valley and took a bus from the edge of the valley to the city. Having been there before, they knew how to get to the house of an uncle of Antonio's near the wholesale market district. The uncle had heard via the grapevine that they might come. He was renting a three-room house on a crowded alley for his own family of seven, and his maid and her child slept in the small kitchen. He was only able to put them up for one night. They moved into a cheap hotel and pension near the market, and through Antonio's uncle were recruited for a provincial club, Sons of Paucartambo, the native mountain district of Antonio's and Blas' father. Much of their social activity is still with members of the club, and their first orientation to life in Lima was from club members.

Antonio went to work for his uncle, and Blas, who had been robbed of all his clothing from the hotel, took a job as a waiter and clean-up man in a modest boarding house catering to medical and engineering students. He worked six-and-a-half days a week in the pension, taking Thursday nights and Sunday afternoons off. During his first year he saved a little money. He impregnated a maid from a neighboring house, Carmen, and agreed to marry her sometime. Meanwhile, they rented a two-room, one-storey adobe house in a large lot not far from the boarding house. The lot was packed solidly with similar houses and the walks between them were about five feet wide. They had filthy, constantly clogged common baths and water taps for every ten houses and the rent was high. They paid extra for electricity and for practically non-existent city services.

Through a relative of one of the students Blas got a better job as a waiter in a rather expensive restaurant. In spite of the distance and the extra money spent for transportation, it paid to take the job. With the arrival of a second child plus a boost in their rent, they found themselves short of money even though Blas' job was quite a good one for a person of his background.

Carmen, Blas' common law wife, had come to Lima at the age of fourteen from the southern highland province of Ayacucho. She had been sent by her mother and stepfather to work as a servant in the house of a Lima dentist, who was also a land-owner in Ayacucho, and Carmen was to receive no pay. The dentist promised to "educate" her but, in fact, she was not only not allowed to go to school but was rarely allowed outside the house. During her third year with the dentist's family her mother, who had left her stepfather in Ayacucho, rescued her from the dentist's house after a terrible row. Her mother then found a maid's job for Carmen where she was paid. Carmen worked in several private houses in the next few years and loaned a large part of her earnings to her mother. Blas was her first serious suitor. Previously she had had little experience with men and when Blas asked her to come and live with him after she became pregnant, she was surprised and pleased.

In her own crowded house with Blas and their son she was happier than she had been since her early childhood with her grandmother. Although her work was hard, it was nothing like the work she had done in the houses in Lima. They were poor but Blas had steady work and they ate better than she had in any of her previous homes. Her infrequent arguments with Blas were usually over money. He had once hit her when she had loaned some of the rent money to her mother, but, on the whole, she considered herself well-treated and relatively lucky in comparison with many of her neighbors.

She did not have too much to do with her neighbors, mostly longertime residents of Lima than she, and she was afraid of the Negroes in the area, having been frightened as a child in the mountains by stories of Negro monsters who ate children. She found herself being drawn into arguments over petty complaints about children trespassing, dogs barking and messing on the sidewalk, husband's relative success or failure, mountain Indian traits as opposed to coastal Mestizo traits, etc. She was mainly occupied with her son and her new baby daughter, and the constant arguing annoyed Blas more than it did Carmen. Blas had also been disturbed by the crowded conditions. There was no place for the children to play and the petty bickering over jurisdiction of the small sidewalk was a constant irritant. Thievery was rampant and he had even lost some of his clothes since they had to hang the washing outside above the alley. In Lima's damp climate, it often takes several days to dry clothes even partially.

He had been thinking of moving and, although Carmen was settled into a more or less satisfactory routine, she was interested as well. They carried on for another year and another child without taking any action.

When their landlord told them that he was planning to clear the lot and build a cinema within six months, they decided to move. A colleague of Blas' in the restaurant had spoken to him about a group to which he belonged. The members were organizing an invasion of state land to build houses and they wanted fifty families. The group had been meeting irregularly for about a year and when Blas was invited they had forty of the fifty they sought.

The waiter's group came mainly from the same central highlands region and their spokesman and leader was a bank employee who was also a functionary of the bank employees' union. The other major faction was a group of career army enlisted men, including several members of a band that plays at state functions, who were stationed near the proposed invasion site. About half of the group had been recruited as Blas was. Blas himself recruited a neighbor and another family from the Sons of Paucartambo, to which he still belonged.

They met a few times with never more than fifteen men present. They were encouraged by the fact that the government seemed to be tolerating squatter invasions. Several earlier invasion attempts had been blocked by the police and in many *barriadas* [squatter settlements; eds.] people had been beaten, some shot, and a few killed. The recent attitude, in 1954, seemed tolerant, but under a dictatorship, or under any government, the law is apt to be administered whimsically and their planned invasion was illegal. Another factor pointing to haste was the loss of seven of their families who had found housing some other way. Blas was one of those suggesting that they move fast because his eviction date was not far off.

Many barriada invasions had been arranged for the eve of a religious or national holiday. Their invasion site was near the area used once a year, in June, for a grand popular folk-music festival, so they decided to wait until that was over. The next holiday was the Independence Day vacation, July 28th, 29th, 30th; so they picked the night of the 27th. It would give them a holiday to provide a patriotic aura as well as three days off from work to consolidate their position. They thought of naming their settlement after the dictator's popular wife, but, after taking into account the vicissitudes of current politics, they decided to write to her about their pitiful plight, but to name the place after a former general-dictator, long dead, who freed the slaves.

A letter was drawn up for mailing to the dictator's wife and for presentation to the press. The letter stressed equally their respect for the government and their abandonment by the government. They had no hesitation about wringing the most out of the clichés concerning their status as humble, abandoned, lost, helpless and disillusioned but always patriotic servants of the fatherland.

During the last month word was passed from the active meeting-goers, still never more than twenty or twenty-five, to the others and preparations were made. Each family bought its own straw mats and poles for the house, and small groups made arrangements for trucks and taxis. Each household was asked to get a Peruvian flag or make one of paper. No two remember the details of the invasion the same way, but about thirty of the expected forty-five families did invade during the night. A newspaper photographer was notified by the invaders and he arrived about the time the houses were being finished. The members had discussed previously what lots they would take, and how the streets were to be laid out and there was very little squabbling during the first day. By early morning when the police arrived there were at least thirty one-room straw houses flying Peruvian flags and the principal streets were outlined with stones.

The police told them they would have to leave. A picture and story appeared in two papers and by the 30th of July about twenty or thirty more families had come, including some of the old members. A few men, with the help of friends and relatives and, in at least one case, paid workers, had built brick walls around their lots. These families and a few other early arrivals, most of whom are still in the barriada in 1963, proudly refer to themselves as the original invaders and tend to exaggerate the opposition they faced. They were told to leave several times but no-one forced them. A resident, not one of the original invaders, was killed by the police in 1960 during an attempt to build a school on government land. The unfavorable publicity caused the government to desist and the residents cut a lot out of the hillside and built a school.

Blas and Carmen picked a lot about fifteen by thirty meters on the gradual slope of the hill on the principal street. The lot was somewhat larger than most subsequent lots, an advantage of being an original invader.

Blas and some friends quickly expanded the simple invasion one-room house to a three-room straw mat house and they outlined the lot with stones. He worked hard on Sundays and some nights, sometimes alone, sometimes with friends from the barriada or from outside. He soon managed to get a brick wall six-and-a-half feet high around his property.

Many of the residents of barriadas hurry to erect the walls around their lots and then take anywhere from one year to five or ten to finish the house. After about a year of working on the lot and making his "plan," Blas decided to contract a "specialist" to help him put up walls for four rooms. He paid for the materials brought by the "specialist" and helped out on the job. When the walls were done he roofed the rooms with cane, bricked up the windows and put in cement floors. With his first pay check, after finishing paying for the walls, Blas made a down payment on a large, elaborate cedar door costing about $45. With the installation of the door and wooden windows they finally felt like homeowners. They even talked of getting formally married.

About two years later, after a particularly damp winter during which his children were frequently sick, he decided to hire another "specialist" to help him put on a concrete roof. He hired a neighbor who had put on other roofs and he found out that the first "specialist" had sold him faulty cement and had also erected the walls in such a way that it would be difficult to put on a roof. It took considerable money, time and energy to rectify the mistakes and put on the roof, but when it was done, it was a good job and strong enough to support a second floor some day. Meanwhile a straw mat room had been erected on the roof and Blas helps out with the houses of friends and neighbors against the day he will ask them to help with his second floor.

Skilled bricklayers and concreters abound in barriadas and the bulk of the construction in these places is cheaper than on contracted houses. Much of it is done through informal mutual aid arrangements and when contractors are hired they are generally very closely supervised. There is considerable cheating by contractors on materials and many of the specialists hired for roofing and electrical and plumbing installations are not competent. Transport of materials is often expensive but the personal concern of the builder often results in lower prices at purchase. Some barriadas have electricity from the central power plant and public water; the one in this story does not. The front room/shop combination they have in their house is not only fairly common in barriadas but throughout the provincial area of Peru.

Their principal room fronts on the street and doubles as a shop which Carmen and the oldest children tend. Blas is still a waiter and they now have five children. The saving on rent and the income from the shop make them considerably more prosperous than before, but, in spite of their spectacular view of the bright lights of the center of Lima some twenty minutes away, Carmen has never seen the Plaza San Martín and has passed through the central business district on the bus only a few times. She has never been inside the restaurant where

Blas works. She gets along with most of her neighbors and has the company and assistance of a fifteen-year-old half-sister deposited with her by her mother.

Blas and Carmen have a television set which runs on electricity bought from a private motor owner and they are helping to pay for it by charging their neighbors a small amount to watch. It also brings some business to the store.

Carmen and Blas bemoan the lack of sewage disposal, running water and regular electricity in the barriada and they complain about the dust from the unpaved streets.

They are also critical of the ramshackle auxiliary bus which serves them, but, on the whole, they are not dissatisfied with their situation. They own a house which is adequate, Blas has steady work, their oldest children are in school, and Blas has been on the elected committee that runs barriada affairs and feels that he has some say in local government. Since local elections are unknown in Peru the barriadas' unofficial elections are unique. The committee passes judgement on requests from new applicants to settle in the barriada and cut new lots out of the hillside. They also decide on requests to sell or rent. Renting is against the rules of the association. Another important function is presenting petitions and requests to various government ministries for assistance. Until 1960 barriada residents had no legal basis for their ownership of lots. Any recognition by the government in the form of assistance or even taxation was an assuring sign. In 1960 the congress passed a law saying, in effect, that what could not be changed might as well be made legal, and residents of barriadas are to be given their lots. As of 1963 a few land titles had been given out by the government, but the people have been buying and selling for years with home-made titles.

The committees are also concerned with internal order. Barriadas are ordinarily quiet places composed mainly of hard-working family groups, but the public image is one of violence, immorality, sloth, crime and revolutionary left-wing politics. Barriada residents are quite sensitive about this and the committees try to screen out potential trouble makers and control those present. They also try to get as much publicity as possible for the productive work done by barriada people.

The experience of this couple is probably happier than that of the average family but is certainly well within the "typical" range. They feel, in comparison to people like themselves and in terms of their own aspirations, that they have done well. When asked what they would do if they acquired a large sum of money, they both answer in terms of improving their present property and educating their children. There is some resentment of the children, and Blas beats the oldest boy for not doing well in school, and all five children are bedwetters, but they give the impression of a happy family and, although Carmen cried during several interviews, they smile frequently and seem to be getting along. Carmen speaks some Quechua with her neighbors and her half-sister, and has actually improved her Quechua since coming to the barriada. Spanish is the principal language, however, and neither she nor Blas have any strong interest in their children learning Quechua. The children themselves learn some Quechua but they speak Spanish with their peers, and in a group of children it is difficult to distinguish those of recently arrived near-Indian migrants from those of the most *Criollo* Costal families. There is a certain amount of antagonism among the adult barriada dwellers over race, cultural difference, politics, and place of origin. The children, however, are strikingly similar in attitude and have very little of the mountain Indian about them.

The situation of Blas and Carmen is similar to that of many others. They have some friends, some relatives and some income, but they could be ruined by a loss of job or any chronic illness of Blas, and they are aware of it. If there is a potentially disruptive factor in their lives it is that the high aspirations they have for their children are vastly unrealistic. They are sacrificing and plan to sacrifice more for the education of the children, but they overrate the probable results. They say they want the children to be professionals, doctors, teachers, people with comfortable lives, and in this they are similar to most interviewed barriada families. But it is highly unlikely that they will be, unless there are monumental and rapid changes in Peru.

When the children come to this realization they may fulfil the presently paranoid prophecy of many middle and upper class Peruvians who see the barriada population as rebellious and revolutionary.

One thing is notable about both of the reports you have just read. Andrew Pearse showed us how, in an urban environment, people continue to seek patrons, much as they did in the rural area from which they came. But in a large and growing city the chance of finding effective patrons is much reduced. In the rural community your potential patron is a nearby neighbor or a man known to your other neighbors.

But in a city a man can seek for personal contacts and help without finding these. The rich and powerful often live in separate sections of the city, in houses which are walled off from the outside. Life is more impersonal. But at the same time people acquire new expectations. They see new things and they begin to hope that some day they too may own such things or benefit from them. This rising tide of expectations occurs precisely when the traditional social relations and patterns of conduct to which men have been accustomed in the past are slowly dissolving under the strain of city living. This combination of conditions can produce serious social unrest, and sets up pressures toward the creation of a new social order which can guarantee people some measure of participation in the economic and social benefits of modern life.

THE PROBLEM OF ECONOMIC DEVELOPMENT

Much of Latin America still has its face turned to the past. But we have also noted the development of industrial plants, like S.I.A.M., in Argentina; the growth of great urban centers; the rise of professional and bureaucratic middle classes. In Latin America, as elsewhere, men are becoming aware that poverty and misery are not inevitable, and that machines and skills are available to make life more livable, secure, and meaningful. This vision of a fuller life for all has seized the hungry countries of the world like a religion. Where, in fact, does Latin America stand with regard to economic development?

"Development" is a vague term. The newspapers speak of "developed" countries, of "underdevelopment," of countries that are "more developed," while others are politely labeled "less developed." But what is it that is developed or underdeveloped? How can one tell if one country is more or less developed? To render the term more meaningful, we must have a measure of development.

For this purpose economists calculate the total output of goods and services produced by a nation in a given year; this is called the *gross national product*. If you divide this figure by the number of people in a nation, you get the output of goods and services produced in a given year per person. You can compare these figures from year to year, and measure the increase or decrease that takes place each year. That increase is called *growth*, and usually expressed in per cent. If you add up all the figures for the various nations of Latin America, you get the total *gross national product* for the area as a whole, and you can cal-

Women workers, Milluni tin mine, Bolivia. (Courtesy United Nations)

The official caption of this picture reads: "This Indian woman, employed as a laborer at the Oruro mine, Bolivia, keeps her baby with her all day." (Courtesy United Nations)

culate the increases or decreases for each year for the area as a whole. If you do this for Latin America, you see that there was very little growth in the economy during the period from 1900 to 1929; growth could not have been higher than 1.2 per cent. But since the end of World War II, during the period from 1945 to 1960, the gross national product of Latin America increased 5 per cent, while the yearly per capita rate of growth was 2.5 per cent. This is considerably greater than the per capita rate of growth of the United States during the period of its industrial development which was 2 per cent (since 1955 the annual per capita rate of growth of the United States has been only 1 per cent, which has economists worried). The fast rate of growth in Latin America during this "golden period" was achieved because the world at large was willing to pay better prices for Latin America's exports—the ores, oil, and tropical crops of which we have spoken. Since 1958, however, there has again been a downward trend, and the per capita rate of increase has fallen below 1 per cent. Exports have dropped 10 per cent, and prices have decreased. This shows how heavily Latin America is dependent on its foreign trade and economic relations, and how much its development depends on its relations to its chief customers, notably the United States.

But not only has this development slackened off since 1958, even during the "golden period" it was not sufficient to bring Latin America within reach of the industrial nations of the world. The economist Maurice Halperin has calculated that even "if and when Latin America could recover and maintain uninterruptedly its 1945-57 rate of growth, from the moment of recovery it would take it about 55 years to reach the 1957 French or United Kingdom per capital gross national product of 1300 dollars. To attain the 2600 dollars per capita GNP of the United States in 1957, would require close to 85 years." This is also true of the most industrialized countries of Latin America. Brazil, with its 3.5 per cent rate of per capita increase, would pull up to 1957 levels in 45 and 65 years respectively. Argentina would require 90 years to approximate the British and French GNP and 160 to equal that of the United States. "For about half of the republics, with a GNP under 200 dollars and moving at the 2.5 per cent rate, the lapse of time on the average would be 80 and 110 years respectively."[11]

There is, moreover, still another aspect to these figures. One must ask not only *how fast* growth proceeds, but also *what kind* of growth it

11. Maurice Halperin, "Growth and Crisis in the Latin American Economy," in *Science and Society*, Vol. XXV, No. 3, 1961, p. 206.

is. One thing that will immediately strike an economist is that the average increase of agricultural production per person in Latin America during the golden period was only 1.5 per cent. This increase was mostly in export crops, *but not in food crops.* Output of food crops per person has fallen below the levels maintained before World War II. This helps explain the formation of such slums as we have heard about in the accounts of Rio de Janeiro and Lima. Agriculture is not growing fast enough to offer adequate employment in the countryside. At the same time, it does not produce enough food to feed rural people. Hence they come to the city to look for employment.

Economic development would be served if these people could find adequate employment opportunities in industry. But the proportion of the labor force engaged in manufacture and construction has increased only from 17 to 18.5 per cent of the total. This means that industrial development is not proceeding *fast enough* to provide an economic alternative to large numbers of people. It is true that manufacture increased at an annual per person rate of 3.2 per cent. But this was mainly in small shops and enterprises that cannot employ many people; "big" industry represents no more than 15 per cent of Latin America's total industrial plant. This again says something about the position of Latin America relative to the industrialized world. Halperin has pointed out that

For example, in 1955 the United States per capita GNP was eight times greater than that of Latin America, but the per capita consumption of steel in the United States—a basic indicator of the level of economic development—was sixteen times greater. A similar discrepancy is revealed comparing Latin America with other developed countries: the per capita GNP of the United Kingdom was four times higher while per capita consumption of steel was nine times higher. In France the respective amounts were four and seven, and in Austria two and five. Other significant criteria of economic development, such as per capita consumption of energy or copper, more or less coincide with that of steel consumption.[12]

The economic sector in which the greatest amount of growth has taken place in Latin America is in the provision of services. Services includes innumerable different things, ranging from the maintenance

12. *Ibid.,* pp. 207-8.

of police to beauty parlors and nightclubs. In counting the GNP, services are included as well as goods, but there is some question of whether this gives us a realistic picture of development of a non-industrial area. Halperin says about this:

By very definition, such an economy is primarily and basically deficient in production, that is, both in productive capacity and the actual output of industrial and agricultural goods which in the aggregate determine the physical capability of a country to maintain a given standard of living. For an underdeveloped economy, only the production of material goods can have any relevance to growth. Certainly, for a region such as Latin America, an increase in the number of beauty parlors or nightclubs or the size of the police force or other activities that come under the heading of services, whatever their contribution to the joy or sorrow of one or another segment of the population may be, cannot represent economic growth.[13]

Services account for about 40 per cent of the Latin American GNP, and per capita services increased at an average annual rate practically identical with that of the GNP. Consequently it appears that nearly a half of the economic expansion does not really contribute to Latin American growth or to the ability of the region to grow still further. We must not only look at how fast an economy grows, but at the quality of that growth. We have already seen that agricultural employment has not kept pace with the number of people who need jobs. Industrial employment is similarly slow in taking up the employment slack. Where do people find jobs? They enter the service sector, which has showed an increase more than double the rate of manufacturing and construction. "In other words," says Halperin,

the bulk of the labor force released (or in flight) from agriculture swelled the ranks of clerks, bootblacks, newspaper vendors, domestic servants and the like, not to mention the unemployed. This phenomenon at the same time explains the discrepancy between the unprecedented increase of Latin America's urban population and the region's much more modest tempo of industrialization.[14]

13. *Ibid.*, p. 212.
14. *Ibid.*, p. 221.

THE GROWING MIDDLE CLASS

When historians describe the growth of industrialism in Europe, they assign a major role in its development to the "rising middle classes," a third estate with clearly defined interests different from the interests of both aristocracy and clergy on the one hand and peasantry on the other. When observers have attempted to analyze the sources of the wealth and power of the United States, they have often attempted to find it in the strength and solidity of its "middle class," a layer of society made up of people as diverse as independent entrepreneurs, tradesmen, professionals, and government officials, and thought of as being socially "in the middle" between a blue-collared working class and an upper class of industrial tycoons and financial barons.

Many analysts believe that the growth of this middle layer has resulted, in Anglo-America, in a more even distribution of income and political influence, and that therefore Anglo-American society has avoided the polarization between the rich and the poor characteristic of many other societies. This view is held not only by outside observers, but also by many Anglo-Americans themselves who identify themselves as "middle class," and hence possessed also of the virtue of forming the nation's backbone, of fulfilling—in some measure—the promises of the American dream. There can be no doubt that in the Anglo-American experience many individuals did rise from rags to riches, from blue-collar work to white-collar work, and that prodigious amounts of personal energy have gone into the striving to make these transitions possible.

Yet even in Anglo-America some scholars have expressed doubt that upward social mobility, the movement of individuals or groups between positions of lower wealth, power, and prestige to those of higher wealth, power, and prestige has ever been as high as it was claimed to have been in the past; and in the second half of the present century many observers have noted that some segments of the population in Anglo-America do not seem to have experienced much upward social mobility at all. Such questioning poses the rather serious task of collecting reliable numerical information about amounts and rates of social mobility.

Other observers have asked questions about the social causation of the phenomenon. Supposing that it did exist: was it due to a sudden increase of highly motivated individuals in Anglo-America who, in turn, created an upthrust of industry and an expansion of trade; or did

Shoeshine, Bogotá, Colombia. (Bruno Barbey, Magnum)

trade and industry expand for other—economic, social, or political—reasons, and motivated individuals took advantage of opportunities offered them to transcend their previous station in life? Whatever the answers for Anglo-America, these questions imply that societies with a different past and different organization might not present the picture of a "middle class" on the Anglo-American model.

There have certainly been scholars and observers who looked for evidence of an independent and politically cohesive middle class in Latin America. Especially after World War II it became fashionable to point to the beginnings of a Latin American middle class and to predict that, as in Anglo-America, the growth of such a class might produce a widening of democracy, a greater scope of democratic freedom, and greater political stability. These observers hoped implicitly that a Latin American middle class would develop the same virtues and capabilities traditionally associated with the middle class in Europe and Anglo-America. Thus the American sociologist Seymour Lipset in 1960:

The growing middle class in these countries—the countries of Latin America—like its nineteenth-century counterpart, support a democratic society by attempting to reduce the influence of the anticapitalist traditionalists and the arbitrary power of the military.[15]

In a similar vein, the political scientist John Johnson felt that "they possess the equipment for dealing with realities." They "have accumulated in this century . . . valuable lessons in the art of compromise."

The middle sectors have elevated to a new level the art of achieving some equilibrium by balancing a mass of political antagonisms. They have consequently become stabilizers and harmonizers and in the process have learned the dangers of dealing in absolute postulates.[16]

In contrast, the Chilean sociologist Luis Ratinoff has argued that while the middle sectors might well prove progressive during their ascendant phase (when they needed recognition from the established oligarchy),

15. Seymour Lipset, *Political Man: The Social Bases of Politics*, Doubleday & Co., 1960, p. 138.
16. John Johnson, *Political Change in Latin America: The Emergence of the Middle Sectors*, Stanford University Press, 1958, p. 194.

when their claims are met they have more often turned into defenders of the established order against rival claims from below.[17] Thus the Argentine sociologist José Nun even sees in the Latin American middle classes "factors of political instability, whose instrument is the army, and whose detonator is precisely the democratic institutions that those sectors appear to support."[18]

The problem is an old one in the social sciences. By assigning a name to a phenomenon, one hopes to characterize it in some unitary fashion. Thus, categorizing people as "middle class" imputes to them some common characteristics, even perhaps a common will, a common political purpose. Yet, while calling a body of people "middle class" because they stand "in between" those who control the major sources of power and wealth and those who work with their hands may define their social position relative to other bodies and categories of people in a general sense, it says very little about the degree to which the members of such a "class" are similar or dissimilar to each other. Even in Anglo-America the middle class of black Harlem is not like the middle class of the Upper West side of New York; the middle class of a university town like Ann Arbor, Michigan, is unlike the middle class in neighboring mercantile Ypsilanti which services surrounding communities of auto workers and miscellaneous poor; the middle class of an old planters' town like Savannah, Georgia, is unlike the middle class in the thriving industrial town of Atlanta in that same state. In Latin America, with its much greater heterogeneity, its uneven "archipelagic" distribution of centers and zones of enclave, the middle class of an old administrative capital city like Rio de Janeiro is unlike a middle class of an industrial and commercial center like Sao Paulo. Similarly, the middle class of aristocratic and Catholic Popayán in Colombia is unlike the middle class in the thriving coffee-producing town of Antioquía.

Nor does calling a category of people "middle class" do justice to its internal occupational differentiation. Such a category may include members of the so-called "free" professions—soldiers, bureaucrats, shopkeepers, advertising men, controllers of fleets of buses, agricultural extension agents, and liquor distillers—all of whom have very different relations to people above and below them.

17. Luis Ratinoff, "The New Urban Groups: The Middle Classes," in Seymour Lipset and Aldo Solari (eds.), Elites in Latin America, Oxford University Press, 1967, pp. 61-93.
18. José Nun, "A Latin American Phenomenon: The Middle Class Military Coup," in James Petras and Maurice Zeitlin (eds.), Latin American: Reform or Revolution, Fawcett, 1969, p. 147.

Furthermore, calling a body of people middle class tells us little about specific kinds of relationships which link such middle-class people to other groups both above and below them. For instance, in Latin America where restricted resources and deficient organization impede access to resources and power, upper-class families often cannot assign sufficient resources to all their members. Many of the less successful branches of such families are relegated to marginal positions within the economy or polity and fall into positions of personal and social dependence. Younger sons of the wealthy and powerful then often join these declassed relatives in filling the professions; they become doctors, dentists, surgeons, architects, university professors, or military officials. In Anglo-America such people might be classed as "middle class" by an outside observer and indeed so classify themselves; but in Latin America, where family connections underwrite other connections, these people cleave ferociously to their upper-class affiliations, and are often so included by their relatives of superior class position who welcome their services in enlarging the family retinue and influence.

Similarly, Latin America abounds in petty retailers and hungry artisans who play an important part in the distributive services which make up what economists call "the tertiary sector." Economists who think in terms of developed industrial economies often see in the growth of such a "tertiary" sector a healthy sign of a burgeoning economy and believe that such growth guarantees the proliferation of a sturdy middle class. In Anglo-America storekeepers and the owners of craft shops may indeed be categorized as middle class. In Latin America, however, their hand-to-mouth existence, ever on the verge of bankruptcy in the wake of unfavorable shifts of supply, demand, and price, forms the upper fringe of the urban poor rather than anything resembling a sturdy middle class. In addition, other people who think of themselves as middle class do everything in their power to create social and political distance between themselves and this army of unfortunates. Hence, not only are the middle classes more highly differentiated in Latin America but their boundaries also fluctuate in ways which differ from the way boundaries are drawn in industrial North America. This has led to considerable uncertainty and indeterminacy about the size and character of particular Latin American middle classes. Where a Cuban sociologist could argue that, in the years before the advent of Fidel Castro, a majority of Cubans were in fact middle class, an American rural sociologist, Lowry Nelson, who knew Cuba well could write as late as 1950, "This observer is not at all certain that a middle class exists, but there can be no doubt about the upper and lower classes."[19]

Finally, industrialization in the countries of the North Atlantic fringe —Western Europe and North America—produced a large number of independent entrepreneurs and traders, not wealthy and powerful enough to rank with the great captains of industry and commerce, but still independently wealthy and powerful enough to staff a large class of independent "businessmen," with their own economic and political leverage and their own organization. But in Latin America industrial development has always been retarded and sporadic, inhibited by prior industrial development elsewhere. The kind of self-made independent entrepreneur who staffed the middle class in Europe and the United States is largely absent. Where he does occur, he is more often the bearer of European capital or an offspring of the local class of land-owners. Most characteristically, the middle-class person in Latin America works for a large organization created by the state or for a semi-public corporation sponsored by the state.

It is the "dependent" middle class, and not an "independent" middle class, which catches the eye in Latin America. Its members work for the state, and their livelihood thus depends upon the government. They do not make policy; they enact it by processing the claims of the public-at-large. Their capacity to stamp documents and to pass claimants on from one window to the next may give them a sense of social importance, and their ability to favor some claimants over others may yield them a small measure of influence, but all their power is derivative. It comes to them from the top down and depends on policies set in offices to which they have no access. They do not make policy, but they are strongly involved in politics, if by this we mean individual gamesmanship as to who gets what, when, how, and how much.

It is not a politics of independent self-assertion; it is a politics designed to maintain and enhance their liens on existing channels of distribution. They may on occasion favor the claims of another organized group striving for government reform, if it will enhance their security or improve their grip on state resources; most often, they will side with those in power. Hence, as José Nun has noted, they will favor military intervention not because it increases political instability but precisely because it increases political stability for themselves. To the extent that they are employes of an independent state, their security is

19. Nelson Lowry, *Rural Cuba*, University of Minnesota Press, 1950, p. 139.

also enhanced when that state lays claim to a greater share of resources vis-à-vis dominant outside powers. Hence, they are often nationalistic without, however, engaging in a politics of war. Required to underline their separateness from the client population at large, they are forced to exhibit conspicuous leisure and to consume expensive consumer goods as symbols of that leisure—most frequently cars, refrigerators, and radios or television of foreign manufacture or sold by licensed foreign distributors. It is this penchant for commodities produced in North America which renders them vulnerable to exchanging any autonomy they might have for the perquisities of prestige extended to them by others. They trade, as people in middle-class categories in many parts of the globe, independence for reliance on the judgment of other social groups.

To Anglo-Americans their consumption of these "hard" consumer goods may look as if they were purchasing the symbols of independence, but anthropological know-how would immediately tell any observer to beware of situations in which similar symbols are interpreted in the same way. The Latin American middle sectors, utilizing the same symbols of status, may not be traveling in the same direction as the middle class of Muncie, Indiana. They are deeply in debt, and vulnerable to inflation. To the extent that anti-foreign agitation serves as a ritual to attack these evils, it may enlist their emotional support without, however, at the same time, leading to an independent middle-class nationalistic politics.

Their independent political role is further hampered by the fact that they are so frequently involved in individual political strategies of their own. Many of them obtain government jobs through connections with individuals to whom they owe personal political allegiance. A Brazilian sociologist, Helio Jaguaribe, has even said that the state as a whole "consists fundamentally in the exchange of superfluous jobs for votes." It "involves the middle class in an ever-expanding military and civilian bureaucracy by allowing it to nominally render public services but actually providing more or less useless jobs for the political clientele."[20] On the other hand, to get ahead an individual member of the dependent middle class must strive for the approval of those more wealthy and powerful than himself and must act in daily life to win that approval.

20. Hélio Jaguaribe, "Political Strategies of National Development in Brasil," in I. L. Horowitz, et al. (eds.), Latin American Radicalism, Random House, Inc., 1969, p. 395.

In dress, in language, in style of life, in choice of residence, in all the forms of the presentation of self through the observation of forms of etiquette, the aspirant individual seeks approval and certification from above for his aspirations. Educational qualifications become in this game one of the important counters for individual mobility: to get ahead an individual must acquire the kind of education which the upper class values. This has been one of the major factors in favoring retention of a classical and humanist education in Latin America, against the acquisition of technical skills. As of 1958-59 34 per cent of all Western European undergraduates majored in science or engineering, 19 per cent in Africa, 46 per cent in China and the USSR, but only 16 per cent in Latin America. Through proper deportment and behavior the mobile individual seeks patrons or sponsors, and his demeanor is calculated to attract and secure appropriate patrons and sponsors. Advancement goes to those who conform most directly to elite demands. This in turn diffuses both elite standards downward and secures their acceptance by the servants of the elite. Hence, the ritual of demeanor serves both the cause of individual mobility and the cause of maintaining the social system as a whole. Chile, which ranks among the four countries of Latin America where the middle sector is said to be strong, serves as an instructive example in this regard. The Chilean sociologist Claudio Véliz has characterized the relation of the Chilean upper and middle classes as follows:

In fact, in the absence of an alternative set of cultural values and prestige symbols—which the rising middle class proved unable to create —the only possible way of obtaining at least a measure of social prestige is by associating with the traditional aristocracy. This the urban middle classes have done systematically and successfully. . . . The upper classes have not viewed this process with distaste. All they need to do in exchange for impressive financial and political support is to bestow minimal social favors on their eager imitators, and this they have done effortlessly. The two groups have entered into an extraordinarily successful "social contract" which, if Latin America were absolutely rather than relatively static, would most certainly last for a very long time.[21]

21. Claudio Véliz (ed.), *Obstacles to Change in Latin America*, Oxford University Press, 1968, pp. 7-8 (Introduction).

This "social contract" has ever produced a special kind of person, as the American historian Frederick Pike notes wryly:

Chile's urban middle sectors . . . have dedicated themselves to the defense of traditional, upper-class value-judgments. The readily observable traits of the middle class have led to the introduction into the Chilean vocabulary of the word *siútico*. Such a person is a middle-class individual who emulates the aristocracy and its usages and hopes to be taken for one of its members. It is generally agreed that Chile's middle class abounds in siúticos.[22]

While the adherence of the middle-class individual to upper-class values and social connections increases the stability of the system as a whole, it may paradoxically contribute to increased instability within a stable system. When he swears allegiance to a patron-client system, he may—inadvertently—be joining one of a number of political factions operating on the national level. His adherence thus widens the scope of factions and increases the probabilities that they will test each other's mutual strength through opposition and conflict. Certainly none can argue that the rise of the middle class in Latin America has significantly decreased internal conflict. Historians point to 115 successful *coups d'état* in Latin America between the time of the wars of independence and World War I; but between 1931 and 1965 alone there occurred 98 successful challenges to government authority, and innumerable unsuccessful ones. Between 1946 and 1963 there were 3500 insurgencies or insurgency-related events on the continent: and none who counts the numbers of stable and enduring dictatorships in Latin America can be very sanguine about the prognosis for improved democracy.

At the same time, it is the very contradictions to which the middle classes are subject which enhance the contradictions imposed on their individual members. The contradiction between autonomy and dependence, between developing criteria for independent judgment and action on your own, and acceptance, through co-optation or submission of the standards of others, weighs heavily on individual members of the middle class. It is often members of the middle class who, for reasons

22. Frederick Pike, "Aspects of Class Relations in Chile, 1850-1960," in Petras and Zeitlin (eds.), *Latin America: Reform or Revolution*, p. 211.

both individual and general, cannot submit to the role in which they have been cast and become the rebels and revolutionaries pointing the way to alternative choices of action and alternative solutions. A characteristic example in recent memory has been Ernesto Guevara, el *che*, who first merited the title by calling everyone his pal (*che*) in Argentine lingo, and became the symbol of Latin American revolutionaries everywhere as a result of his participation in the Cuban fight for independence from the United States.

PATTERNS OF SOCIAL RELATIONSHIPS

Let us review for a brief moment the recurrent themes in Latin American social relations which we have touched upon again in the course of our discussion of communities, credit arrangements, estates, industrial organizations, and urban slums. These are:

1. the importance of family ties
2. the importance of co-parent relations
3. the importance of patron-client relationships.

Before we turn again to cast another look at the wider problems of Latin America, let us review in more general terms the characteristics of these several ties. They are important because they represent recurring and very stable patterns of organizing people.

Let us remember that in Latin America resources are scarce and unevenly distributed. People have a hard time finding jobs, land, credit, and outlets for marketing their products. Politics has often been unstable and the administration of justice uncertain or arbitrary. To defend themselves against such scarcity and uncertainty, in the wider economic and political field, people therefore rely on the more intimate and more assured ties of kinship, friendship, and personal acquaintance. If we call this set of ties to kin, friends, and personal acquaintances the personal field, then we could say that in Latin America people invest much of their effort in consolidating their personal fields. They increase security in a narrow orbit to counteract insecurity in the wider orbit.

Hence the great stress on family ties. A family will keep in touch with many relatives on the husband's and on the wife's side. The expansion of the network of family ties is greatest among the rich, where people retain contact with some one hundred or two hundred relatives. In this connection, family names are of great importance. In Spanish usage a person carries both his father's name and his mother's name.

Pablo Vásquez Calcerrada is a Vásquez on his father's side, a Calcerrada on his mother's side. In public address he is Señor Vásquez, never Señor Calcerrada; but when he gives his name in a context where family ties are important he will always include both parental names. Similarly, his wife will always retain her own father's name. If Pablo Vásquez marries Soledad Ayala, she will become Soledad Ayala de Vásquez. In Brazil, the mother's paternal name is inserted between the given name and the father's paternal name. Thus if João de Almeida Lara and Maria Lara de Barros have a son Gilberto, his name would be Gilberto de Barros Lara. In both usages, moreover, one can bring in some illustrious ancestor and introduce his name into one's own name, much as people in the south of the United States who are in some way related to the Lees of Virginia will use the name Lee to point up their relation to this important family.

It is among rich and powerful families that the use of family names and of family trees—genealogies—are most important in building a wide network of social ties. The result is that every Latin American country contains a number of wealthy and powerful family blocks whose members aid and abet each other in both business and politics. Moreover, each such great family block is usually surrounded by a fringe of persons who are not kin by blood or marriage but who were servants or retainers for the big families. Many of them were raised in the Big Houses and owe loyalty and support to the family block of which they form a part.

The scope of the kinship network decreases as we move from the rich and powerful to those possessed of lesser wealth and power. Poorer people are able to maintain less contact with kinsmen and have fewer resources to underwrite widespread relations of kin. Their genealogies do not extend as far back as those of the great houses; they have less depth in time as well as less extension in space. Smaller in size and depth than the family blocks of the great families, the network of kin relations remains important nevertheless. Kinship plays a vital part in decisions about who will support whom and whose support will be enlisted on one's behalf.

When we reach the lowest level of society, we shall find the kinship network is still important, but the kinship network frequently shows strains and signs of weakness. This is due to the fact that poor people have the least resources and power of all and are often in direct competition with one another for jobs, land, credit, and protection. It is also due to the fact that in many areas of Latin America marriages among the poor and powerless are frequently unstable. A high percentage of marital unions are common-law unions, entered into by the mutual consent of both partners but not solemnized and supported by a formal marriage. Such unions *can* be just as stable as regular marriages but often are not. In many areas of Latin America inhabited by the poor there is both a considerable turnover of marital partners and a high percentage of households in which the mother raises children without the support of a husband. This is related to the lack of resources. Where neither partner brings significant amounts of wealth or prestige into the family, the union depends for its stability largely on the personal regard of the two partners for each other. If that fails, the desertion of either partner does not materially alter the poverty and social disability of the household. Frequently, therefore, children are raised in broken homes or are legally illegitimate. Thus, often the people who have no wherewithal with which to confront the exigencies of life are also the ones who lack, to the highest degree, the support of kinsmen. In the United States—with its accumulation of great public wealth—we confront this problem through systems of public welfare and social security. In many of the poor societies of Latin America, however, much of the support we mobilize through public organizations is usually left to the private world of kinship; and it is precisely among those most in need that this private world is also weakest.

This is, however, where often the other two patterns of social relation come into play, co-parenthood and patron-client ties. The pattern of co-parenthood makes it possible for a man to extend his network of support to people who are not kin, but to non-relatives who become his quasi-kin as a result of the special ceremonial involved in sponsoring a child at baptism. Co-parents owe each other mutual respect and aid; and a man who has ten children can enlist ten such helpers through baptism of his children alone. This does not mean that the tie of co-parenthood is equally strong everywhere in Latin America. It seems to be relatively weak, for example, in Colombia; but there are also areas where the usual co-parental relation through baptism has been added to through additional types of co-parenthood, extended to other initial events. Thus, in the community of Moche on the coast of Peru the American anthropologist John Gillin noted fourteen types of *compadrazgo*. They included, in addition to baptismal co-parents, co-parental relations involving the midwife who delivered a child, the woman who first cut a child's nails, the person who baptized a child in an emergency, such as a critical illness; the person who first cut a child's hair; co-parents involved in confirmation; the woman who hung the first scapular around a child's neck; engagement co-parents; marriage co-parents; co-parents derived from sponsorship of the ceremony involved in taking down altars or crosses erected by individuals or families on certain religious feasts; housewarming co-parents; co-parents created when a new container of maize beer is ceremonially broached; and co-parents formed during carnival dances.[23] Such a mushrooming of co-parenthood creates many ties. Some are much weaker than others, but all can be mobilized for various social purposes in the course of a person's lifetime. Latin Americans will say, somewhat cynically, that if a man does not have *compadres* he does not get baptized, that is, he lacks help and support. Conversely, to get baptized, he has to have *compadres*. Without them, he is at a social and economic disability.

As we have seen, co-parental ties easily merge into patron-client ties. Often a man will ask his patron to become a *compadre* upon the baptism of one of his children, or he will make an approach to a new potential patron by extending an invitation to sponsor a child at baptism. The tie between a patron and a client is a tie between two persons who are unequal in wealth and power; but the compact between them—which usually remains informal—means that the one of greater wealth and power will help and protect the poorer, and that the poorer in turn will pledge his loyalty and support to the patron in return for favors granted or implied. These ties therefor counteract some of the consequences of social inequality between persons. We can easily see that patron-client ties could not occur between people who are each other's equal; they necessarily imply inequality. They stem from inequality; but they also serve to soften that inequality, building ties of mutual support across the gap created by differences in wealth and power.

It is important to remember that all of these ties are personal ties. They link person to person, in a direct way, without the intervention of complicated organizations. We see, in fact, that the more elaborate economic, political, and social organizations of Latin America rest upon such familial and personal foundations.

This has certain important consequences for the way in which the larger society is built up and out from these personal fields. Where so much of a person's security depends on such personal ties, his loyalties will also be primarily to his kin, friends, and patrons, and only sec-

23. J. Gillin, *Moche: A Peruvian Coastal Community,* Institute of Social Anthropology Publication No. 3, Smithsonian Institution, 1947.

ondarily to larger organizations—government, army, business. He will do business primarily with people who are in his personal field, because he can rely on them and not on others. He will take his concerns to relatives in the government, and they in turn will rely on their personal following to help them keep in office and to enlarge the importance of that office. Where family ties dominate business or service operations politics turns easily into family politics and its corollary, nepotism, the naming of relatives to public office, in order to surround oneself with persons upon whom one can rely. At the same time, where each person plays upon connections of family and friends to gain an advantage, he comes into competition with rival networks of family and friends. Thus, close ties in one direction imply competition, even hostility, in another direction; and the great family blocks, the cliques of co-parents and friends, the leagues of patrons and clients, are frequently hostile to one another and engaged in a social war. On occasion, as we have seen in Saucío and in Tajín, these hostilities may break out in family feuds which are marked by sporadic violence and killing.

This review of the major patterns of social relations makes us realize that the institutions of Latin America rest upon arrangements of people which are ever shifting and hence, in some measure, unpredictable. Each set of kin, friends, patrons and clients tends to maximize its own advantages, always in some measure in opposition to the institutions of the larger society that wish to regulate them, tax them, order them, contain them, and always in some measure also competitive with each other. If we compare the sets of kin, friends, patrons and clients to atoms, and think of the institutions of the larger society as molecules trying to bind these atoms in some stable way, we are led to the conclusion that the stability of these larger molecules is forever challenged by the dance of the component atoms which are continuously trying to change orbits and often escape the cohesive pull of the larger unit altogether. The larger society thus needs unusual power to counteract this centrifugal activity of its parts.

6

Politics

THE *CAUDILLO*

Nowhere has this centrifugal tendency been more evident than in politics. For a century and a half now Latin America has been in continuous political turmoil. When Latin America threw off Spanish colonial rule and asserted its independence in the beginning of the nineteenth century, many Latin Americans hoped for a great birth of freedom and progress. But the glorious dreams of a new future which animated many of the great Latin American patriots quickly turned to ashes. The wars of independence had contradictory results. On the one hand, masses of men rose for liberty and gained arms and military experience in the course of many military engagements. On the other hand, this very movement of liberation gave rise to a type of military leadership which has kept the continent in turmoil for a century or more. Independence produced the *caudillo*, the military chieftain, and much of the history of Latin America to the end of the nineteenth century—and even into the present day—can be read as the history of the rise and fall of *caudillos*, of military strongmen rising to power and falling from it, to be replaced by new seekers after power who rose and fell in turn.

To see what kind of men these were who took the fate of much of Latin America into their hands in the course of the past century, let us examine what is known of the history and personality of one famous caudillo, Juan Facundo Quiroga, who came to be the master of San Juan province under the overlordship of the great Argentinian dictator Juan Manuel de Rosas who controlled Argentina for more than twenty years (1829-52). We are fortunate in having an account of this man from the pen of the famous Argentinian sociologist and statesman, Domingo Faustino Sarmiento. Sarmiento was deeply affected by the con-

The Brazilian northeast has experienced repeated upsurges of banditry—akin to *caudillaje* in organizational terms. The celebrated bandit Lampiaõ and his woman Maria Bonita, killed by the police in 1938. (*Manchete* from Pictorial)

trast he saw between the increasingly prosperous United States of America and Western Europe and the war-ravaged condition of his own Argentina. The United States and Europe seemed to him the embodiment of civilization, his own country the victim of barbarism. At the same time, he had deep sympathies with the barbarians who kept Argentina in permanent political and economic turmoil, the armed cowboys of Argentina, the *gauchos*. Much like writers in Anglo-America who were attracted by the free and disorderly life of the West and Far West of the United States, but understood that cowboys, Indian fighters, and fortyniners would have to yield to a settled agriculture and city life, so Sarmiento both sympathized with the gauchos but longed for a time when the gaucho would have been conquered by civilization. He portrayed Quiroga, the gaucho caudillo, in *Civilización i barbarie. Vida de Juan Facundo Quiroga*, first published in 1845.*

Facundo, as he was long called in the interior, or General Don Facundo Quiroga, as he afterwards became, when society had received him into its bosom and victory had crowned him with laurels, was a stoutly built man of low stature, whose short neck and broad shoulders supported a well-shaped head, covered with a profusion of black and closely curling hair. His somewhat oval face was half buried in this mass of hair and an equally thick black, curly beard, rising to his cheek-bones, which by their prominence evinced a firm and tenacious will. His black and fiery eyes, shadowed by thick eyebrows, occasioned an involuntary sense of terror in those on whom they chanced to fall, for Facundo's glance was never direct, whether from habit or intention. With the design of making himself always formidable, he always kept his head bent down, to look at one from under his eyebrows, like the Ali Pacha of Monovoisin. The image of Quiroga is recalled to me by the Cain represented by the famous Ravel troupe, setting aside the artistic and statuesque attitudes, which do not correspond to his. To conclude, his features were regular, and the pale olive of his complexion harmonized well with the dense shadows which surrounded it.

The formation of his head showed, notwithstanding this shaggy covering, the peculiar organization of a man born to rule. Quiroga possessed those natural qualities which converted the student of Brienne into the genius of France, and the obscure Mameluke who fought with

* The following selection is from Mrs. Horace Mann's translation of *Civilización i barbarie*, in English entitled *Life in the Argentine Republic in the Days of the Tyrants: or Civilization and Barbarism*, New York, 1868.

the French at the Pyramids, into the Viceroy of Egypt. Such natures develop according to the society in which they originate, and are either noble leaders who hold the highest place in history, ever forwarding the progress of civilization, or the cruel and vicious tyrants who become the scourges of their race and time.

Facundo Quiroga was the son of an inhabitant of San Juan, who had settled in the Llanos of La Rioja, and there had acquired a fortune in pastoral pursuits. In 1779, Facundo was sent to his father's native province to receive the limited education, consisting only of the arts of reading and writing, which he could acquire in its schools. After a man has come to employ the hundred trumpets of fame with the noise of his deeds, curiosity or the spirit of investigation is carried to such an extent as to scent out the insignificant history of the child, in order to connect it with the biography of the hero: and it is not seldom that the rudiments of the traits characteristic of the historical personage are met amid fables invented by flattery. The young Alcibiades is said to have lain down at full length upon the pavement of the street where he was playing, in order to insist that the driver of an approaching vehicle should yield the way to avoid running over him. Napoleon is reported to have ruled over his fellow-students, and to have entrenched himself in his study to resist an apprehended insult. Many anecdotes are now in circulation relating to Facundo, many of which reveal his true nature. In the house where he lodged, he could never be induced to take his seat at the family table; in school he was haughty, reserved, and unsocial; he never joined the other boys except to head their rebellious proceedings or to beat them. The master, tired of contending with so untamable a disposition, on one occasion provided himself with a new and still strap, and said to the frightened boys, as he showed it to them, "This is to be made supple upon Facundo." Facundo, then eleven years old, heard this threat, and the next day he tested its value. Without having learned his lesson, he asked the headmaster to hear it himself, because, as he said, the assistant was unfriendly to him. The master complied with the request. Facundo made one mistake, then two, three, and four; upon which the master used his strap upon him. Facundo, who had calculated everything, down to the weakness of the chair in which the master was seated, gave him a buffet, upset him on his back, and, taking to the street in the confusion created by this scene, hid himself among some wild vines where they could not get him out for three days. Was not such a boy the embryo chieftain who would afterwards defy society at large?

In early manhood his character took a more decided cast, constantly becoming more gloomy, imperious, and wild. From the age of fifteen years he was irresistibly controlled by the passion for gambling, as is often the case with such natures, which need strong excitement to awaken their dormant energies. This made him notorious in the city, and intolerable in the house which afforded him its hospitality; and finally under this influence, by a shot fired at one Jorge Peña, he shed the first rill of blood which went to make up the wide torrent that marked his way through life.

On his becoming an adult, the thread of his life disappears in an intricate labyrinth of bouts and broils among the people of the surrounding region. Sometimes lying hid, always pursued, he passed his time in gambling, working as a common laborer, domineering over everybody around him, and distributing his stabs among them. . . .

The most connected account of this obscure and roaming part of his life that I can procure is as follows:

Towards 1806, he went to Chili with a consignment of grain on his parent's account. This he gambled away, as well as the animals, which had brought it, and the family slaves who had accompanied him.

He often took to San Juan and Mendoza droves of the stock on his father's estate, and these always shared the same fate; for with Facundo, gambling was a fierce and burning passion which aroused the deepest instincts of his nature. These successive gains and losses of his must have worn out his father's generosity, for at last he broke off all amicable relations with his family.

When he had become the terror of the Republic, he was once asked by one of his parasites, "What was the largest bet you ever made in your life, General?" "Seventy dollars," replied Quiroga, carelessly, and yet he had just won two hundred dollars at one stake. He afterwards explained that once when a young man, having only seventy dollars, he had lost them all at one throw. But this fact has its characteristic history. Facundo had been at work for a year as a laborer upon the farm of a lady, situated in the Plumerillo, and had made himself conspicuous by his punctuality in going to work, and by the influence and authority which he exercised over the other laborers. When they wanted a holiday to get drunk in, they used to apply to Facundo, who informed the lady, and gave her his word, which he always fulfilled, to have all the men at work the next day. On this account the laborers called him "the father." At the end of a year of steady work, Facundo asked for his wages, which amounted to seventy dollars, and mounted his horse without knowing where he was bound, but seeing a collection of people at a grocery store, he alighted, and reaching over the group around the card-dealer, bet his seventy dollars on one card. He lost them and remounting, went on his way, careless in what direction, until after a little time a justice, Toledo by name, who happened to be passing, stopped him to ask for his passport. Facundo rode up as if about to give it to him, pretended to be feeling for something in his pocket, and stretched the justice on the ground with a stab. Was he taking his revenge upon the judge for his recent loss at play? or was it this purpose to satisfy the irritation against civil authority natural to a gaucho outlaw, and increase, by this new deed, the splendor of his rising fame? Both are true explanations. This mode of revenging himself for misfortunes upon whatever first offered itself, had many examples in his life. When he was addressed as General, and had colonels at his orders, he had two hundred lashes given one of them in his house at San Juan, for having, as he said, cheated at play. He ordered two hundred lashes to be given to a young man for having allowed himself a jest at a time when jests were not to his taste; and two hundred lashes was the penalty inflicted on a woman in Mendoza for having said to him as he passed, "Farewell, General," when he was going off in rage at not having succeeded in intimidating a neighbor of his, who was as peaceable and judicious as Facundo was rash and gaucho-like.

Facundo reappears later in Buenos Aires, where he was enrolled in 1810 as a recruit in the regiment of Arribeños, which was commanded by General Ocampo, a native of his own province, and afterwards president of Charcas. The glorious career of arms opened before him with the first rays of the sun of May; and doubtless, endowed with such capacity as his, and with his destructive and sanguinary instincts, Facundo, could he have been disciplined to submit to civil authority and ennobled in the sublimity of the object of the strife, might some day have returned from Peru, Chili, or Bolivia, as a General of the Argentine Republic, like so many other brave gauchos who began their careers in the humble position of a private soldier. But Quiroga's rebellious spirit could not endure the yoke of discipline, the order of the barrack, or the delay of promotion. He felt his destiny to be to rule, to rise at a single leap, to create for himself, without assistance, and in spite of a hostile and civilized society, a career of his own, combining bravery and crime, government and disorganization. He was subsequently recruited into the army of the Andes, and enrolled in the

Mounted Grenadiers. A lieutenant named García took him for an assistant, and very soon desertion left a vacant place in those glorious files. Quiroga, like Rosas, like all the vipers that have thriven under the shade of their country's laurels, made himself notorious in after-life by his hatred for the soldiers of Independence, among whom both the men above named made horrible slaughter.

Facundo, after deserting from Buenos Aires, set out for the interior with three comrades. A squad of soldiery overtook him; he faced the pursuers and engaged in a real battle with them, which remained undecided for awhile, until, after having killed four or five men, he was at liberty to continue his journey, constantly cutting his way through detachments of troops which here and there opposed his progress, until he arrived at San Luis. He was, at a later day, to traverse the same route with a handful of men to disperse armies instead of detachments, and proceed to the famous citadel of Tucumán to blot out the last remains of Republicanism and civil order.

Facundo now reappears in the Llanos, at his father's house. At this period occurred an event which is well attested. Yet one of the writers whose manuscripts I am using, replies to an inquiry about the matter, "that to the extent of his knowledge Quiroga never attempted forcibly to deprive his parents of money," and I could wish to adopt this statement, irreconcilable as it is with unvarying tradition and general consent. The contrary is shocking to relate. It is said that on his father's refusal to give him a sum of money which he had demanded, he watched for the time when both parents were taking an afternoon nap to fasten the door of the room they occupied, and to set fire to the straw roof, which was the usual covering of the building of the Llanos![1]

But what is certain in the matter is that his father once requested the governor of La Rioja to arrest him in order to check his excesses, and that Facundo, before taking flight from the Llanos, went to the city of La Rioja, where that official was to be found at the time, and coming upon him by surprise, gave him a blow, saying as he did so, "You have sent, sir, to have me arrested. There, have me arrested now!" On which he mounted his horse and set off for the open country at a gallop. At the end of a year he again showed himself at his father's house, threw himself at the feet of the old man whom he had used so

1. The author afterwards learned that Facundo related this story to a company of ladies, and one of his own early acquaintances testified to his having given his father a blow on one occasion.

ill, and succeeded amid the sobs of both, and the son's assurances of his reform in reply to the father's recriminations, in reestablishing peace, although on a very uncertain basis.

But no change occurred in his character and disorderly habits; races, gambling parties, and expeditions into the country were the occasions of new acts of violence, stabbings, and assaults on his part, until he at length made himself intolerable to all, and rendered his own position very unsafe. Then a great thought which he announced without shame got hold of his mind. The deserter from the Arribeños regiment, the mounted grenadier who refused to make himself immortal at Chacabuco or Maipu, determined to join the montonera of Ramirez, the offshoot from that led by Artigas, whose renown for crime and hatred for the cities on which it was making war, had reached the Llanos, and held the provincial government in dread. Facundo set forth to join those buccaneers of the pampa. But perhaps the knowledge of his character, and of the importance of the aid which he would give to the destroyers, alarmed his fellow provincials, for they informed the authorities of San Luis, through which he was to pass, of his infernal design. Dupuis, then (1818) governor, arrested him, and for some time he remained unnoticed among the criminals confined in the prison. This prison of San Luis, however, was to be the first step in his ascent to the elevation which he subsequently attained. San Martin had sent to San Luis a great number of Spanish officers of all ranks from among the prisoners taken in Chili. Irritated by their humiliations and sufferings, or thinking it possible that the Spanish forces might be assembled again this party of prisoners rose one day and opened the doors of the cells of the common criminals, to obtain their aid in a general escape. Facundo was one of these criminals, and as soon as he found himself free from prison, he seized an iron bar of his fetters, split the skull of the very Spaniard who had released him, and passing through the group of insurgents, left a wide path strewn with the dead. Some say that the weapon he employed was a bayonet, and that only three men were killed by it. Quiroga, however, always talked of the iron bar of the fetters, and of fourteen dead men. This may be one of the fictions with which the poetic imagination of the people adorns the types of brute force they so much admire; perhaps the tale of the iron bar is an Argentine version of the jaw-bone of Samson, the Hebrew Hercules. But Facundo looked upon it as a crown of glory, in accordance with his idea of excellence, and whether by bar or bayonet, he succeeded, aided by other soldiers and prisoners whom his example encouraged, in suppressing the insurrection and reconciling society to himself by this act of bravery, and placing himself under his country's protection. Thus his name spread everywhere, ennobled and cleansed, though with blood, from the stains which had tarnished it.

Facundo returned to La Rioja covered with glory, his country's creditor: and with testimonials of his conduct, to show in the Llanos, among gauchos, the new titles which justified the terror his name began to inspire; for there is something imposing, something which subjugates and controls others in the man who is rewarded for the assassination of fourteen men at one time.

Something still remains to be noticed of the previous character and temper of this pillar of the Confederation. An illiterate man, one of Quiroga's companions in childhood and youth, who has supplied me with many of the above facts, sends me the following curious statements in a manuscript describing Quiroga's early years: "His public career was not preceded by the practice of theft; he never committed robbery even in his most pressing necessities. He was not only fond of fighting, but would pay for an opportunity, or for a chance to insult the most renowned champion in any company. He had a great aversion to respectable men. He never drank. He was very reserved from his youth, and desired to inspire others with awe as well as with fear, for which purpose he gave his confidants to understand that he had the gift of prophecy, in short a soothsayer. He treated all connected with him as slaves. He never went to confession, prayed, or heard mass; I saw him once at mass after he became a general. He said of himself that he believed in nothing." The frankness with which these words are written prove their truth.

And here ends the private life of Quiroga, in which I have omitted a long series of deeds which only show his evil nature, his bad education, and his fierce and bloody instincts. The facts stated appear to me to sum up the whole public life of Quiroga. I see in them the great man, the man of genius, in spite of himself and unknown to himself; a Caesar, Tamerlane, or Mohammed. The fault is not his that thus he was born. In order to contend with, rule, and control the power of the city, and the judicial authority, he is willing to descend to anything. If he is offered a place in the army, he disdains it, because his impatience cannot wait for promotion. Such a position demands submission, and places fetters upon individual independence; the soldier's coat oppresses his body, and military tactics control his steps, all of which are insufferable! His equestrian life, a life of danger and of strong excitements, has steeled his spirit and hardened his heart. He feels an unconquerable and instinctive hatred for the laws which have pursued him, for the judges who have condemned him, and for the whole society and organism from which he has felt himself withdrawn from his childhood, and which regards him with suspicion and contempt. With these remarks is connected by imperceptible links the motto of this chapter, "He is the natural man, as yet unused either to repress or disguise his passions; he does not restrain their energy, but gives free rein to their impetuosity. This is the character of the human race." And thus it appears in the rural districts of the Argentine Republic. Facundo is a type of primitive barbarism. He recognized no form of subjection. His rage was that of a wild beast. The locks of his crisp black hair, which fell in meshes over his brow and eyes, resembled the snakes of Medusa's head. Anger made his voice hoarse, and turned his glances into dragons. In a fit of passion he kicked out the brains of a man with whom he had quarreled at play. He tore off both the ears of a woman he had lived with, and had promised to marry, upon her asking for thirty dollars for the celebration of the wedding; and laid open his son Juan's head with an axe, because he could not make him hold his tongue. He violently beat a beautiful young lady at Tucuman, whom he failed either to seduce or to subdue, and exhibited in all his actions a low and brutal yet not a stupid nature, or one wholly without lofty aims. Incapable of commanding noble admiration, he delighted in exciting fear; and this pleasure was exclusive and dominant with him to the arranging all his actions so as to produce terror in those around him, whether it was society in general, the victim on his way to execution, or his own wife and children. Wanting ability to manage the machinery of civil government, he substituted terror for patriotism and self-sacrifice. Destitute of learning, he surrounded himself with mysteries, and pretended to a foreknowledge of events which gave him prestige and reputation among the commonalty, supporting his claims by an air of impenetrability, by natural sagacity, an uncommon power of observation, and the advantage he derived from vulgar credulity.

The repertory of anecdotes relating to Quiroga, and with which the popular memory is replete, is inexhaustible; his sayings, his expedients, bear the stamp of an originality which gives them a certain Eastern aspect, a certain tint of Solomonic wisdom in the conception of the vulgar. Indeed, how does Solomon's advice for discovering the true mother of the disputed child differ from Facundo's method of detecting a thief in the following instances:—

An article had been stolen from a band, and all endeavors to discover the thief had proved fruitless. Quiroga drew up the troop and gave orders for the cutting of as many small wands of equal length as there were soldiers; then, having had these wands distributed one to each man, he said in a confident voice, "The man whose wand will be longer than the others tomorrow morning is the thief." Next day the troop was again paraded, and Quiroga proceeded to inspect the wands. There was one whose want was not longer but shorter than the others. "Wretch!" cried Facundo, in a voice which overpowered the man with dismay, "it is thou!" And so it was; the culprit's confusion was proof of the fact. The expedient was a simple one; the credulous gaucho, fearing that his wand would really grow, had cut off a piece of it. But to avail one's self of such means, a man must be superior in intellect to those about him, and must at least have some knowledge of human nature.

Some portions of a soldier's accoutrements having been stolen and all inquiries having failed to detect the thief, Quiroga had the troops paraded and marched past him as he stood with crossed arms and a fixed, piercing, and terrible gaze. He had previously said, "I know the man," with an air of assurance not to be questioned. The review began, many men had passed, and Quiroga still remained motionless, like the statue of Jupiter Tonans or the God of the Last Judgment. All at once he descended upon one man, and said in a curt and dry voice. "Where is the saddle?" "Yonder, sir," replied the other, pointing to a thicket. "Ho! four fusileers!" cried Quiroga. What revelation was this? that of terror and guilt made to a man of sagacity.

On another occasion, when a gaucho was answering to charges of theft which had been brought against him, Facundo interrupted him with the words, "This rogue has begun to lie. Ho, there! a hundred lashes!" When the criminal had been taken away, Quiroga said to some one present, "Look you, my master, when a gaucho moves his foot while talking, it is a sign he is telling lies." The lashes extorted from the gaucho the confession that he had stolen a yoke of oxen.

At another time he was in need of a man of resolution and boldness to whom he could intrust a dangerous mission. When a man was brought to him for this purpose, Quiroga was writing; he raised his head after the man's presence had been repeatedly announced, looked at him and returned to his writing with the remark, "Pooh! that is a wretched creature. I want a brave man and a venturesome one!" It turned out to be true that the fellow was actually good for nothing.

Hundreds of such stories of Facundo's life, which show the man of superior ability, served effectually to give him a mysterious fame among the vulgar, who even attribute superior powers to him.

BACKGROUND TO CAUDILLO RULE: VENEZUELA

Facundo was a powerful and strong individual personality. But individual personality alone does not explain why so many personalities like Facundo Quiroga should have arisen in Latin America during the nineteenth century. Only a century earlier, under Spanish colonial rule, there had been little opportunity for such men. Under modern conditions, such individuals might seek outlets for their energies in other than political activities. We therefore conclude that there must have been something special about the circumstances that permitted so many men of this type to rise to political power. To gain an understanding of these factors at work, let us look at the circumstances surrounding the rise to power of another great caudillo, this time José Antonio Paéz (1790-1873) of Venezuela. To understand the political system of any society, we must understand first the specific historical processes which have formed the institutions of that society. No real understanding of Venezuelan political life in the period 1830-55 can be gained without some knowledge of its colonial past. For the seeds of anarchy were sown in the colonial period, only to bear fruit when the Spanish administration was swept away by the wars of independence. As we shall see, political anarchy was partially a consequence of the mode of production then prevalent in Venezuela, partly due to the peculiar locus of military power. Both of these features were apparent well before independence was achieved.

Venezuela was a "backwoods" area of the Spanish colonial empire, cursed by a lack of good soil for agriculture, a shortage of cheap Indian labor, and a scarcity of precious metals. That is, it had a short supply of everything which appealed either to the Crown and its bureaucrats or the horde of individual wealth-seekers who forsook the Peninsula for the glitter of the New World. Even most of those who "settled for less" and came to Venezuela to stay must have been bitterly disappointed. One gets the impression that every type of economic activity known to man was tried in the colony, and nearly all of them failed miserably.

When the gold placer mines near Caracas failed to produce a major strike, the would-be-rich turned toward another familiar type of colonial economy. This was commercial plantation agriculture, which attempted to harness to its productive processes what wild Indians could be forced into submission. As elsewhere in the New World where the indigenous peoples lacked a state political organization, the Indians either died fighting or were decimated by disease introduced by Europeans. In desperation, the colonists turned to Negro slavery in the hope of putting together an economy based on growing sugar, tobacco, cacao, and indigo for exportation to Spain.

While this enriched a few individuals, commercial agriculture as a whole proved a resounding failure. Only indigo appears to have been in consistent demand. The magnitude of failure can be gauged from the fact that slaves were constantly freed, until slavery itself was ended shortly after independence. Constant release of slaves in a labor-intensive economy usually indicates that demand is uncertain. As a result, slaves cost their owner more than justified by their productivity.

A second type of land-based economy was cattle raising in the pestilential Orinoco *llanos*. Cattle raising proved the mainstay of Venezuela's economy. The *llanos* region is composed of vast plains (about 600 miles from east to west) lying to the south of the central highlands. This area was (and still is) barely habitable by man. Disease-carrying insects and crocodiles (among other things) await man in the immediate vicinity of the Orinoco. The plains furnish but meager soil for agriculture, and even make poor pastures. Natural barriers were not the only hazard to man in this region; for here a predatory society flourished in which banditry nearly became a social necessity so that some men might survive, albeit at the expense of others.

Llanero society had two basic components. On the one hand, there were those who did the actual herding. This great majority of the *llanero* inhabitants was composed of the flotsam and jetsam of the plantation economy to the north: Indians, Negroes, and the offspring of these with Spaniards who had drifted southward to the cattle lands. Perhaps they were lured by the "free" life of the *llanero* with its attendant possibilities of booty; more likely, because nothing else was available to them in Venezuela.

On the other hand was the small minority of *criollo* cattle owners, who represented the Venezuelan version of the "land-based rich." These wealthy landowners held economic and political power, but can scarcely be said to have reached the opulence achieved in the *criollo* centers of Mexico, Peru, or the Colombian region of New Granada. For if Spain received little from an area she gave less in return. Thus the Venezuelan aristocrats were unable to purchase all the luxuries needed to become as ostentatious and genteel as their counterparts in better endowed regions. Their stock of wealth was reduced still further by the levies of tribute which filled the viceroy's coffers. This constituted yet another economic drain on the region and, quite naturally, produced a great deal of ill will toward Spain on the part of those who had come so far to receive so little.

Since Venezuela could not produce enough to meet its needs, the only hope of the area was trade, an activity largely controlled by Spain. The hub of political and economic life was in the coastal cities of the central highlands, the part of the highland backbone bordering on the Caribbean between Puerto Cabello and Cape Codera. Both the agricultural Valencian area and Caracas are located in this region; and it was from the coastal ports that Venezuelan hides passed on to Spain (and, later, to whoever would have them). Of all the territory of Venezuela, only this small region had both dense urban and rural populations. But, including this "dense" settlement area, only one million people altogether had either chosen or been forced to settle in Venezuela by the year 1800.

Still another factor shaping Venezuelan political life during 1830-55 and after was the nature of Spanish control in the region. Since Venezuela was economically marginal to imperial interests, little effort was spent by Spain in maintaining the area. Although Venezuela acquired the formal status of a captain generalcy, the area was administered by a relatively small number of Spanish bureaucrats.

If Venezuela was shorthanded in secular bureaucracy, the country had even less of the so-called "sacred arm" of the empire operating in her domain. That the church was less interested and less powerful in Venezuela than elsewhere in Latin America should not surprise anyone. For the church depended economically on landed wealth, and Venezuela provided little productive land worth owning. From the beginning of the quest for political independence in 1811 until 1836, Venezuela lacked an archbishop, a dignitary to whom it was theoretically entitled. When an archbishop finally arrived in the country in 1836, General Paéz was able to throw him out with impunity for refusing to participate in the swearing in of the national constitution.

It appears that Spanish control over Venezuela depended heavily on the presence of regular army troops which could put down any uprising. But even in this crucial aspect of colonial policy, Spain apparently cut corners. At the turn of the nineteenth century, when Spanish authority in the region had already been challenged by the conspiracy of 1796 there were but 8000 regular troops in the area. While it might be argued the 8000 well-organized troops could keep a poorly organized population in subjection indefinitely, the behavior of these troops, commanded by the captain-general, suggests that Spanish control over the region was shaky. Their operations resembled those of active terrorists rather than those of obedient force backing up a well-established authority. Striking exhibitions of naked royal power were apparently needed to demonstrate to the population of Venezuela that Spanish authority should be recognized. Thus we read that the anti-royalist conspirator, José Maria España, met the following fate in 1799:

Nine days later he was hanged in the *plaza* of Caracas: it was ordered that his head, placed in an iron cage, be sent to La Guaira, and that mangled pieces of his body be placed in baskets and distributed in various towns throughout the country.[2]

Terrifying as this may sound, Spanish terrorism was largely directed against lesser *criollo* wealthy. That the more powerful *criollos* had to be treated with greater care is suggested by the fact that no powerful *criollos* were treated in the above fashion until 1808.

Considering the weakness of the Spaniards in Venezuela, it is not surprising that Venezuela was one of the hearths of anti-Spanish rebellion. Venezuela was in fact the first South American country to proclaim its independence (1811). It was here that Bolívar was born (Caracas); here that Francisco Miranda, the "Morning Star of the Spanish American Revolution" (and son of a prosperous Caracas merchant), spawned intrigues carried out on three continents; and it was here that the English first tried to establish a commercial beachhead on the continent of Latin America.

As an area vital to rebel strategy, bloodshed was intense during the War of Independence. Not only did the Royalists attempt to wipe out centers of separatist sentiment, but a bloody civil war exploded between the *llaneros* and the *criollos*. As a result of this civil war alone, which reached its peak intensity in 1814, the *criollo* class was nearly exterminated. Due to the combined actions of the *llaneros* and the

2. Casto Fulgencio López, *Juan Bautista Picornell y la Conspiración de Gaul y España,* Ediciones Nueva Cádiz, Madrid, 1955, pp. 282-83.

royalist forces, Venezuela was completely ruined by the War of Independence.

One of the most interesting questions relating to the achievement of independence is why Latin America broke up into so many small and weak countries instead of forming a few large (and stronger) states. It seems strange that Venezuela, so backward in the colonial period, and in such ruin after the War of Independence, should attempt to go her own way apart from Colombia. The first explanation is historical. As noted earlier, the wealthy class of Venezuela had to pay tribute to the viceroy of New Granada. When Venezuela became independent, the wealthy landowners interpreted Bolívar's Gran Colombia Scheme as a perpetuation of the colonial system. As we shall see, these men did not want to contribute to the maintenance of any government, least of all to one governed from Colombia.

Secondly, when Bolívar considered forceful annexation of Venezuela, Venezuela had a military advantage over Colombian troops. Venezuelan military force did not consist of a regular army but of *llanero* cavalry. This highly mobile cavalry had the advantage of fighting in the *llanos*, an environment which of itself would have claimed as many lives as the cavalry. For men unaccustomed to the rigors of the *llanos* died like flies from its pestilence. Perhaps this military ascendance in Venezuelan territory was itself sufficient to ensure the country's independence.

Once independent and thrown back on its own resources, Venezuela faced grave problems. Above all, it had to adapt itself to producing for the world market after three hundred years of producing for a controlled colonial economy. As Bolívar pointed out, Venezuela had no money to buy anything and little to sell. A strong government was needed, first to obtain necessary foreign loans, and second to ensure that export quotas could be maintained.

While the first task of government proved to be fairly easy, the second did not. For any government in Venezuela was faced with a lack of resources, non-support by key segments of the population, lack of an organized means of force to implement its will, and absence of authority. Given these conditions, it is not surprising that fifty armed revolts took place between 1830 and 1900, many of which were successful in overturning the government.

One of the great paradoxes of Venezuelan political life under Paéz was that although government was conceived of as a device to aid the wealthy, the wealthy did not or were not able to support a strong government. Why this should be the case cannot be answered simply: we can, however, offer some suggestions.

First, government tends to become a thing in and of itself once it is firmly established. If it is endowed with resources (e.g. in the form of taxes), it can become a power in its own right. This power was dreaded by the wealthy landowners of the country who feared that the growth of a strong central power would curtail their authority in their own domains. Not only did they refuse to pay taxes, thus causing the government to go ever deeper into debt via foreign loans, but some of them attempted periodically to take over the government outright. While it has been often pointed out that this allowed the successful conqueror to enrich himself from the resources, it also kept the government weak.

Secondly, the wealthy landowners feared one another, thus precluding any kind of class unity which would have led them to support a government devoted to their common interests. Each man had a domain independent of any other man's. At the same time, there was considerable economic pressure to increase herd size, in order to have more hides to sell into the markets of the world. The time-honored response to this was cattle-rustling, accomplished simply by turning one's *llaneros* loose on a neighbor's herds. A good part of the banditry which was rife, at least during the early years, consisted of this type of activity. Fear of encroachment by neighbors was also a powerful political tool to array against power seekers like Paéz. He constantly had to defend himself against such charges, which were contrived to bring about his fall.

Thirdly, Venezuela's wealthy did not constitute one homogeneous social class, enjoying a similar degree of control over similar resources. Here we must take issue with the traditional view of Latin American society, which states that there are but two social classes, "the rich" and "the poor." In Venezuela (and elsewhere) there were two types of "wealthy": those whose wealth was based upon land (owners of cattle estates and owners of commercial agricultural plantations) and those whose wealth depended upon cash transactions of one type or another.

L. Vallenilla Lanz, a noted Venezuelan historian, has pointed out that a serious conflict developed between these two classes during the colonial period, which intensified during Paéz' regime.[3] As in other Latin American countries, this class opposition led to two "schools" of

3. L. Valenilla Lanz, *Cesarismo Democrático*, Tipografía Universal, Caracas, 1929, p. 106.

political thought. In Venezuela, these were called *godos* (Goths) and *liberales*. The *liberales* were in the main composed of land-based wealthy who moved to the cities to carry on business, while the *godos* were those whose wealth depended on money transactions.

However, no one has attempted to explain why these two classes should be antagonistic. Let us suggest a possible answer. Since the cattle estates held the key to Venezuela's economy, and each estate was a separate domain, the estate owners had no need to cooperate with the money-based rich. If demand for hides went slack, the estate owners could fall back on their domains. But if demand went slack and currency inflation began, the money-based rich were bound to suffer. Here, in a nutshell, is the basis of the conflict between wealth based on money and wealth based on land.

While the political ideologies of the wealthy in Latin America have long been held up to ridicule, we note that in Venezuela the basic ideological differences between the two groups seem to appear perfectly rational. The *godos* wanted a strong central government which would be able to regulate production for export and thus ensure that no debasement of the currency would occur. On the other hand, the *liberales* wanted to secure their local autonomy and naturally demanded a weak government.

Conflicts among the wealthy by themselves do not explain why no stable government emerged in Venezuela. Venezuelan political life was characterized by still another great paradox. Although land-based and money-based wealth may have dominated the economic life of the country, they did not control the means of force required to implement stability.

As mentioned earlier, military power in Venezuela was held during this period by the *llaneros* rather than a regular army. For those who held wealth in the form of land, however, this proved to be a problem, since the experience of 1814 had demonstrated that the *llaneros* were not content to follow their dictates blindly. Much has been made of the *llanero* turnabout in the War of Independence, but too much emphasis has been placed on the political significance of this "change of allegiance." Whether or not the *llaneros* perceived any great political differences between royalists and patriots is open to question. These rude men were certainly lacking in political sophistication. It appears, rather, that they did not favor either side but followed whatever leader could offer them the most booty.

Given the questionable loyalty of the *llaneros* and their military ascendancy, we might ask how anybody managed to hold them down at all, let alone mobilize them into a coherent force. It may be suggested that only certain types of men were capable of doing this. Certainly one attribute which a *llanero* leader had to have was outstanding courage. In addition to unquestioned bravery, it has been suggested that the leader needed to be skilled in warfare (tactics) and have sound knowledge of the geographical territory he moved in. Finally, it may be suggested that a leader had to be able to consistently distribute some sort of booty to his followers.

If these are the qualifications for the leader of the *llaneros,* it is not surprising that General Paéz was leader of Venezuela for so long. For he was the embodiment of these qualities. No one was able to rally the *llaneros* behind him as well as Paéz, and do it as consistently. The other facet of his success was that he was able to serve as a mediator between the *llaneros* and the land-based wealthy. His great forte is summed up in historian Richard Morse's apt phrase—he was able to "derange the predictable interplay of hierarchical class interests."

In spite of the fact that Paéz was able to balance class interests by virtue of the fact that he was a *llanero* leader, all governments in Venezuela were destined to be weak, including his own. For in balancing class interests, Paéz had to keep his source of force, the *llaneros,* from applying their force against his other pillar of support, the land-based wealthy. And without applying some sort of leverage against the land-based wealthy, he could not gain sufficient revenue to create an independent economic fund of power. Hence it may be said that Paéz' rule was "weak-man" rather than "strong-man" rule. This pattern of "weak-man" rule continued until the discovery of oil and the attendant growth of a new money-based capitalist group began to alter class relations in the twentieth century.

THE PARADOX OF CAUDILLO POWER

From this account we can see some of the factors involved in caudillo rule:

1. Competition among the wealthy and their unwillingness to finance a strong central political machine.

2. The fact that military power was not concentrated in a national army or police, but that many men—in all walks of life—could acquire arms, carry arms, and use them to further their own interests. There were always available groups of armed men looking for a leader who

could promise booty and leaders looking for armed groups of retainers to seize booty.

3. That in an important sense caudillo rule was not strong-man rule, but weak-man rule. Pillage had its limits, and if one man did not deliver booty, another could rise up to challenge his right to leadership. Therefore there existed a continuous danger that one political leader whose power was on the wane could be overturned by another whose star was rising.

4. That the caudillo had to make up for his deficit in resources by projecting his personal image. His personality was vital in holding together his band of followers and cowing the potential opposition. We have seen to what extent Facundo possessed the ability to make men yield to him and fear him, to what extent he possessed the faculties of independence, courage, and cruelty. The caudillo had to be bold and able to dominate other men by force of his personality. He must be, as Latin Americans say, *macho*—male or masculine. Men must be dominant over women—this is one aspect of being a *macho*. But equally important is the ability to show dominance over other men. Look back to our discussion of the role of men and women in the family, and remember that the home is the domain of the woman, but that it is her husband who represents the family in public, in trade or work or politics, in relation to other heads of households. In the public sphere, where men deal with men, rewards go to the man able to subdue and dominate other men. In this he must be willing to play the game to the limit, to be ready to use violence, even to kill. There is no "splitting of the difference." The successful caudillo must be ready to *imponerse*, impose himself on others, or be conquered by others in turn.

Yet a caudillo must also be shrewd, "savvy" in relations with other men. He must dominate men and manipulate them. But ultimately his power is dependent on whether or not he is capable of delivering the "payoff." As long as he is able to gather wealth through violence, manipulation, extortion, he has largesse to distribute, and largesse buys loyalty. As long as the men who flock to his banner gain by their association with him, they will be loyal to him. Hence the staying power of a caudillo depends not merely on his capacity to dominate others by physical force or to manipulate others, but also on his capacity to search out new sources of wealth to distribute to his followers. This capacity is the equivalent of Anglo-American "business acumen." All too often, caudillo ventures are one-shot treasury-raids; the caudillo seizes the government and distributes the contents of the treasury. When the supply of wealth dries up and no other sources of wealth are forthcoming, the armed followers of the caudillo begin to desert him and to look for alternative leadership. The more limited the supply of wealth in a country, therefore, the more rapid the turnover of caudillos. Thus Bolivia, one of the most impoverished countries of Latin America, at one time averaged one violent change of government per year. In contrast, a man like Paéz held power for thirty-three years in Venezuela (1830-63), because he controlled enormous cattle estates in a country where beef was the economic staple. This wealth on the hoof ensured the loyalty of his fierce cowpunchers. Yet even he was ultimately defeated by rival contenders, as was Manuel Rosas, the great caudillo of Argentina to whom Facundo Quiroga owed his ultimate loyalty.

This shows us some of the weakness of this weak form of strong-man rule. As long as one man is able to dominate others, manipulate them, and buy their loyalty, he will be able to hold the reins of power. But there are always potential rivals who may grow dissatisfied and willing to undermine his position. If they can counter his stratagems and begin to uncover alternate sources of wealth on their own, they will attract others and the original band of retainers will begin to dissolve.

VIOLENCE IN POLITICS

The classic moment for the abandonment of a leader comes at a moment of public violence, when potential rivals meet head-on. We do not think of violence as a means of settling disputes, but in the many occasions of political violence which occur in Latin America there is implicit a kind of vote. On the occasion of an uprising or a seizure of government, men must take sides—*declararse*, in Spanish—declare themselves for either one man or another. This mode of arriving at political decisions is not merely a form of random violence, but has an orderliness and predictability of its own. In the following selection William S. Stokes, a political scientist, analyzes the types of violence which are employed in the Latin America political process.*

Introduction

Violence seems to be institutionalized in the organization, maintenance, and changing of governments in Latin America. The methodology of

* Excerpted from William S. Stokes, "Violence as a Power Factor in Latin American Politics," in *Western Political Quarterly*, Vol. V, No. 3, September 1952, pp. 445-68. Reprinted by permission of the University of Utah, copyright holder.

force is found in advanced and in backward countries, in Indian, *mestizo,* and white republics, in the large states and in the small ones, in urban and in rural areas, in agricultural and in industrial organization, in the beginning of the twentieth century, in the present period, and in the early, middle, and late nineteenth century—in a word, wherever and whenever Hispanic culture is to be found in the Western Hemisphere.

Force is a unifying factor in Latin-American political culture, yet the fact of geographical and ethnic differences and of varying rates of social and economic development leads to the logical inference that the mobilization of violence for political purposes is not likely to revolve around one simple formula. This is, however, exactly what is done when the general term "revolution" is employed to describe all use of force in Latin-American politics. Violence is, instead, a highly developed technique for obtaining power. Direct action procedures include *machetismo, cuartelazo, golpe de estado,* and revolution. The monopolization of the power factors of the state by a single political leader, a group, or a class sometimes renders unnecessary the direct employment of violence, and in such cases the methods of *imposición, candidato único, continuismo* and election (in the Anglo-American sense) may be selected. These are, of course, outwardly peaceful methods of obtaining and maintaining power, but they rest upon a foundation of force.

At the very least the research scholar and the practitioner in international relations alike should attempt to reconcile the fact of force with such idealized interpretations of Latin-American politics. The primary objective of this paper is to describe the anatomy of violence in Latin-American politics. In addition, the implications of such violence in international relations must be subjected to some examination.

"Machetismo"

Machetismo is a crude, primitive method of mobilizing violence primarily in local, rural politics but occasionally in national, urban areas as well. The term emanates from the word "machete," the general utility knife employed widely throughout Latin-America. In an extractive, agricultural economy guaranteeing little more than subsistence to the majority of the people, poverty is seldom or ever so great as to deny the rural resident his machete. It is a major implement in the construction of habitation, the production of foodstuffs, and in the establishment of political power. To survive, the rural inhabitant must develop proficiency in its use, and the process of becoming expert begins as a child. Whoever can command the authority represented by the machete in rural areas possesses political power of an important nature and automatically constitutes a factor to be reckoned with in the affairs of government.

If it could be demonstrated that no political leader has exercised sufficient discipline over the rural masses to employ their collective strength in direct action, then it might be possible to argue that *machetismo* no longer characterizes Latin-American rural politics. However, leadership of a highly personal nature can readily be observed in Latin America. The matters that vitally concern the rural resident include distribution of government patronage, rights to water holes and grazing areas, military service to the central government, road building in lieu of payment of taxes, and adjudication of social disputes. In many instances, the leader who exercises authority and issues judgments on such issues is the *alcalde, jefe de operaciones militares, comandante de armas,* or official in the church hierarchy. But on the other hand the political leader might very well possess no official position at all. That his power exists there is no denying; his authority is so well known that almost anyone in the area of his jurisdiction can identify him as *el que manda* (the one who commands). This kind of absolutist personal leadership is local, rural *caudillismo.*

Many writers, Latin-Americans included, have associated *caudillismo* with the violent struggle for leadership among the generals in the early independence period, and hence terms such as the "Age of the Caudillos" and "Men on Horseback" are common in historical literature. It is correct to define *caudillismo* as a principle of personal leadership in politics, but it cannot be restricted to any one age or period in Latin American history. Indeed, its origins are to be traced in part at least to the feudal institutions of Spain and Portugal and to the nature of government in the colonial period. *Caudillismo* as personal authority, as a substitute for direction and control by institutional means, such as law, is to be found in all periods of Latin American development, including the present. Nor is it accurate to think of the *caudillo* solely as a man on horseback, for he may be a civilian, such as Carlos Antonio López of Paraguay, García Moreno of Ecuador, Estrada Cabrera of Guatemala, and Fulgencio Batista of Cuba (who although a sergeant in the army did not even learn to ride a horse until after he had first achieved power!).

The determinants of leadership in Latin American politics have never been investigated with sufficient objectivity and scholarship to permit definitive generalizations. How are personal qualities, education and professional training, religious and other social beliefs, location in a rural or urban area, and affiliation with organizations and institutions related to the development of leadership? We do not know. In my own field experience I have known *caudillos* who fitted various physical and psychological patterns. The *caudillo* exists, however, and exercises an almost omnipotent personal authority in his designated area, an authority his people will respect without question to the point of enforcement on the field of battle. He is in his own person law, constitution, party, flag, and political principle.

Although Latin American rural communities are frequently isolated by poor communication facilities, the local *caudillos* are thrown into contact from time to time (to divide the spoils of government, for example), and occasionally, in activities such as drinking, card playing, carousing, and brawling a man so stands out that the others automatically accept his authority and extend to him their loyalty. When this occurs for an area as large as a province or a department, institutional means for resolving major issues of public controversy have been created which frequently may be entirely disassociated from the formal structure of government. The sectional *caudillos* are usually the group from which "available" presidential candidates are to be found. When a sectional leader commands the loyalty of all other major *caudillos* in the country, then a *jefe máximo* (or *caudillo supremo*) is recognized, and if he wants the presidency he will have it; he assuredly will determine who *will* have it. This procedure for the establishment of executive power is one that is essentially based upon violence, because any leader at any time may challenge the hierarchy of power, with immediate local, sectional, or national conflict resulting. Indeed, case studies of *machetismo* can be discovered somewhere in Latin America at all times, although most frequently in the local areas.

Widespread evidence of *machetismo* at the national level can still be observed among backward and advanced countries alike from time to time. Thus, for about half of the year 1947 Paraguay was in what news dispatches termed "civil war," and ever since April, 1948, Colombia has been in a state of violence that includes geographically almost the entire country. When no one *caudillo* can peacefully subjugate existing opposition, when one or more challenges claim to "supreme power," *machetismo* becomes a costly and time-consuming methodology for establishing authority. Among seventy nation-wide examples of *machetismo* in Colombia in the nineteenth century, one conflict alone took approximately 80,000 lives, and the struggle which covered the years 1899 to 1903 took about 100,000 lives.

The *caudillo supremo* produced by *machetismo* may govern by means of harsh measures including *estado de sitio* (state of siege), but on the other hand, his stature may be such that no challenges of importance may be directed against him, and he might well become *un presidente simpático*. In any event, it is doubtful that a *caudillo* can long maintain himself in power, no matter how mechanized and up-to-date his military and police systems, unless he has a large body of popular support (*tiene gente*). Detailed analysis of the politics of the republic of Honduras convinced me that the major reason the Liberals of that country were not a force in government in the period 1933-49 was that they lacked the kind of leadership required to capture support. They simply did not have a national *caudillo*. The defection of the Liberal party in Colombia in recent years with such tragic consequences lies primarily in divided leadership, with no one man sufficiently strong to command. For the *caudillo* is, above all else, a man who can command (he is *muy hombre*, or *un presidente macho*, literally, a stallion president). In his Labor Day speech of May 1, 1944, General Perón declared: "I believe that programs, as revolutions, should not be announced, but simply carried out." What a magnificent exemplification of authoritarianism! The *caudillo* thinks the acts in terms of absolutes, and in active politics "for" or "against" are sole choices. In the language of speeches, and in day-to-day communication words like "inflexibly," "inexorably," "unchangeable," or "instantly" appear frequently. The president refers to his "'supreme power"; he is not merely president but *el Presidente Constitucional*; all the symbols of power and status he puts forth openly; if he has a Ph.D. degree he is "doctor"; and if he is a general as well, he will be *El Presidente Constitucional de la República de . . . el doctor y general. . . .* The *caudillo* meets situations with lordly equanimity; he can't be an ordinary president; he heads a "Restoration Movement" (for example, General Odría of Peru, 1950); he is a regenerator, *benemérito*, restorer, defender of the constitution, pacificator. Government by *caudillo* tends to be authoritarian, intolerant (law of *desacato* of Argentina), personal ("my government," "my administration," "my people," nepotism, graft), antiscientific, and violent. But it should also be pointed out that in most instances it probably tends also to be representative of majority opinion.

"Cuartelazo"

Cuartelazo (sometimes called sargentada or golpe de cuartel), a more highly developed, complex method of organizing and changing governments than machetismo, has its focus in the barracks (cuartel). Its classic pattern is the treason of a single barracks, the pronunciamiento, manifiesto or grito, the march on centers of communication, sites of military supplies, the exchequer, government headquarters, and ultimately the capital itself, the announcement to the populace that the government has changed hands, and finally the appointment of a patriotic junta to guide the country in the interim period. Even the most cursory examination of illustrative cuartelazos reveals that it is a mistake to think of the technique as involving massive, overpowering military force repressing the legitimate desires of the people. To be successful the cuartelazo requires consummate skill in the selection of leadership, the drafting of a program, the equating of the power factors, the technical problems of logistics, and the drafting of at least a temporary series of policies to meet the most pressing problems of government when power is obtained. He who would play barracks politics must know his fellow officers and men well indeed to suggest that they follow his leadership in a calculated plan of treason. Betrayal by a single officer or soldier means at least ignominious failure in the venture and possibly death by firing squad.

The cuartelazo's success depends upon capturing the support of other centers of military power as well as that of public opinion. This is a problem which effectively deters all but the most well-prepared politician. Many Latin-American armies, particularly those in the South American area, have been trained by German technicians, whereas the navies have been trained or inspired by the British. In the century of air power, the plane must be considered, and as a competing unit with the older vested interests in the area of defense, it can constitute a delicate source to be placated. Even assuming that a barracks has been captured and that it is able to obtain sufficient support from other segments of the armed forces to justify some optimism for success, what about the civilian caudillos in both the rural and urban areas? As has already been demonstrated, they also command power in politics, including from time to time the authority to plunge an entire country into civil war. Thus, it usually develops that the successful cuartelazo involves substantial support from the sectional leaders, the leading university and professional men, and the leaders of several of the principal political parties in the country.

When the politics of the *cuartelazo* have been organized with skill, the change in governments is likely to occur with a minimum loss of life or property. Excellent illustrations of well-planned and maturely executed *cuartelazos* include those of Argentina in 1930 and 1943. General José F. Uriburú combined a section of the army with strong civilian groups and announced to the acting president on the morning of September 6, 1930 that he was marching on the capital. When he reached the *Casa Rosada* that evening about six o'clock, the acting president resigned and fled. Then General Uriburú demanded the allegiance of the military commanders who had not participated in the *cuartelazo* (which he promptly received), issued a manifesto detailing his general policies, dissolved the legislature, and issued a decree making himself provisional president. The major details of the *cuartelazo* of June 4, 1943, are known, but this classic should be studied in complete detail. General Pedro P. Ramírez, war minister in the government of President Ramón S. Castillo, hoped to advance to the presidency through party nomination and election. This aspiration was put in jeopardy by the open hostility of the president, and Ramírez then conspired with his friends in the important *Campo de Mayo cuartel* about twenty miles outside Buenos Aires for organization of a *cuartelazo*. President Castillo learned of the conspiracy, called a cabinet meeting at about 2:00 a.m., and ordered the arrest of Ramírez. This was the signal for General Ramírez to call for the march, and General Rawson began leading about 8000 troops from *Campo de Mayo* to the *Casa Rosada*. Although the *cuartelazo* was superbly executed, it appears that the head of the Navy's Mechanical Training School either was not advised of the plan or refused to affiliate himself with it, for he offered a defense, and in the resulting military action forty lives were lost. The first troops from the *Campo de Mayo* arrived in the capital about 7:00 a.m. and surrounded the *Casa Rosada;* by noon they had occupied the central police barracks, the *Banco de la Nación,* and other government offices. By three o'clock in the afternoon the troops controlled the radio stations, and in the evening of June 4, General Rawson announced to the crowds that he was president. Communiques indicated that Colonel Juan D. Perón (the leader of the "colonels" group in the *cuartelazo*) was made chief of staff of the army. By eight o'clock in the evening, the excitement was over, the streets were cleared, and it was evident that the *cuartelazo* was successful. Former President Castillo and his cabinet had taken refuge on a mine sweeper.

Cuartelazos may thus involve a single *cuartel,* as in Argentina in 1943, or a series, as in Venezuela in 1948. They also gravitate naturally to the capitals where military, political, and economic power are usually concentrated. On the other hand, *cuartelazos* have been consummated successfully which bypassed the capital in the initial stages of the violence. General Manuel Odría of Peru, for example, by his "Proclamation of October 27" (1948) began the "revolution of Restoration" from Arequipa, about 470 miles southeast of Lima, the capital. General Odría's three-day almost bloodless march persuaded President José Luis Bustamante to flee first to Argentina and later to New York.

"Golpe de Estado"

The *golpe de estado,* frequently called the coup d'état, and sometimes referred to as *golpe militar,* with the noun *derrocamiento* being occasionally employed along with the descriptive phrase *desplazar del poder,* is the fastest, the most difficult to plan and implement successfully (short of genuine revolution), and potentially the most dangerous of the forceful methods of establishing and changing governments in Latin America. The *golpe* is a direct assault on power—almost always personal in Latin American countries—which means the immobilization of the president either through assassination or detention. The possibilities of success are obviously enhanced if the president's cabinet, high-ranking members of the armed forces, and the head of the police system can be seized when the assault on the president is consummated. The *golpe de estado* is distinguished from the *cuartelazo* by the fact that professional military experience is less needed, and by the procedure of attack which bypasses the *cuartel* entirely. Whereas considerable military skill is required to capture the loyalty of troops and lead them successfully against a major *cuartel,* even a civilian with literary, professional, or scholarly training can, assuming ingress to the casa *presidencial,* blow out the president's brains and proclaim a change in governments. The *golpe,* then, is a forceful method of organizing and changing governments which definitely permits, even encourages, civilian participation.

Inherent in the technique is ecstatic excitement for leaders and masses alike, for the *golpe* guarantees that a "bad" *caudillo* can be replaced by a "good" one, that "justice" can be substituted for "injustice," *immediately,* without the time-consuming and demoralizing limitation of such institutional restraints as law or constitutions. To the predilection toward extremism in politics in Latin America is added the factor of extreme speed and flexibility. The leader can ascertain easily and quickly the extent to which public opinion has been conditioned to the

Political rally in favor of General René Barrientos, Cliza, Bolivia, 1965. The slogan adorning the photograph of the general, reads: "Service to my people is my profession." (Cornell Capa, Magnum)

kind of change in administrations he is attempting. Politically, his status might well be nothing one moment, everything the next; his *golpe* might be rejected upon its announcement and he, himself, put to flight or captured and subject to penalties that might include death.

Yet the *golpe* is not spontaneous combustion in the field of organizing and changing governments. As with the *cuartelazo,* mastery of the element of politics within the environmental framework of each Latin American country is required by the successful politician (some of whom have participated in many *golpes* during a lifetime). The first step in the process is almost invariably the organization of the cadre of leaders and subleaders. To cement loyalty and guarantee incentive, the *jefe supremo* of the proposed *golpe* is likely to appoint his key personnel in advance. Sometimes there is no need to carry on any propaganda whatever prior to the assault; public opinion might be favorably disposed toward a change by the ineptitude of the incumbent. If this is not the case, however, then media of communication are required to attack the government, more frequently than not (unfortunately for the research scholar who faces the task of separating objective evidence from falsification), through lies, slander, and license. As insurance against failure, the *caudillo* should have an airplane, an automobile, or other means of locomotion ready for immediate departure. Recognition by the United States and other major powers is no longer a primary determinant, if it ever was, for the existence of a government, yet it is undeniably true that immediate recognition of a new regime might have a positive effect on public opinion in the Latin American country concerned. The leaders, therefore, endeavor to plant competent diplomats in the several capitals to negotiate speedy recognition. Timing is of the utmost importance, and although circumstances vary from country to country, Sundays and holidays, when the official offices are closed and the president probably is separated from his major supporters, are to be preferred.

The recent political history of Bolivia provides excellent case studies of the *golpe de estado.* Eight different men occupied the presidency from 1930 to 1943. One resigned under pressure, one committed suicide or was murdered, two transmitted power peacefully, and the others were forcibly ejected. The most dramatic and the most completely analyzed *golpe* in recent years took place on July 21, 1946, in connection with the government of President Gualberto Villarroel who obtained power by *cuartelazo* on December 20, 1943, possibly with official aid from the Argentine government. It was so well planned and executed that when the junta's assassins cornered President Villarroel in his own offices and shot him, then threw him, still alive, from the second-story window where a mob seized the body and hanged it from a lamp post, the belief was common in the United States, despite very convincing evidence to the contrary, that this was a popular movement.

Revolution

The history of Latin America from independence to the present time is a history of violent struggles of "ins" versus "outs," but it is not a history of revolutionary movements designed to remold the institutional bases of Latin-American life. By "revolution" I mean "fundamental change in the nature of the state, the functions of government, the principles of economic production and distribution, the relationship of the social classes, particularly as regards the control of government—in a word, a significant breaking with the past." Revolution so defined is rare in Latin America, and even mass participation in violence is only occasionally found. It is an obvious and inescapable fact that revolution is too big and too difficult a power mechanism to employ in Latin America with any frequency. Problems of leadership, ideology, policy, planning, logistics, and timing are all maximized in genuine revolution.

Profound institutional transformations have taken place in Uruguay since the first decade of the twentieth century, but such changes have not occurred in an atmosphere of revolution, despite the ferocious violence of the nineteenth century. The Liberal revolution in Central America which began in the 1870's dramatically established in theory the doctrines of the liberal-democratic state and attempted some institutional changes, such as relations between Church and State. But the revolution lacked sustained vitality and continuity, and its effect was shadow rather than substance. Systematic research might well reveal that revolutions have been under way in various Latin American countries in recent times, such as in Brazil from 1930 to 1945, in Argentina since 1943, and in the Dominican Republic from the 1930's to the present. The Cuban revolution assuredly deserves study. But I would also argue that the only clear-cut illustration of revolution in Latin America since independence is the Mexican revolution, which began in 1910-11 and which continues to exist as the dominant characteristic of Mexican economic, political ,and social life today. Despite the difficulties of mobilizing violence in revolution, of all the forceful methods of organizing power in Latin America, it is probably the most democratic. Revolution is the only method which invites mass participation and renders imperative the formation of decisions on basic issues of public policy by virtually all members of the state.

"Imposición"

Imposición is a nominally peaceful method of organizing power in which the dominant political element in the state hand-picks a candidate and then rigs the election to guarantee victory. Its major principle is the presupposition of success for the privileged candidate. That being the case, the opposition must never become convinced that an *imposición* is operating because then there logically is no further premium in maintaining peace and force is likely to result. The conditions under which *imposición* enjoys maximum possibilities for development include: (1) the existence of a *caudillo* of such stature, power, and personal popularity that no opposition dares stand against him; (2) a government firmly in power; (3) the principal parties or major elements of political strength in the country in agreement on the same candidate for supreme power. Even under the most favorable conditions, however, *imposición* is exceedingly difficult to exploit, and only the most mature, prepared, and experienced individuals or groups have been able to utilize it successfully.

A firmly established, confident government can, of course, openly announce support for a particular candidate and successfully carry through a campaign. On the other hand, such a course invites the opposition to unite and opens the way to charges of official unfairness which might result in undesirable violence. The typical *imposición* usually begins, therefore, with an official announcement from the highest sources in the state that the government is neutral and will guarantee free, fair elections. These protestations of impartiality and fairness are repeated continually throughout the campaign through all the media of communication. The president frequently will issue an impressive order to all government personnel calling attention to the principles of representative democracy and outlining specifically the provisions of the electoral law relating to proper conduct by government employees.

The government is likely to encourage a large number of candidates to offer their names in the election. The politically ambitious *caudillo* can reason thus: if the election is really fair, perhaps the vagaries of public opinion will favor his candidacy; if an *imposición* is under way, perhaps he is the chosen candidate of those who are manipulating power. All during the campaign the perpetrators of the *imposición* carefully select and sharpen for effective use the methods required to insure success, whether they be control over the nominating machinery, registration fraud, appointment of key personnel at the polls, intervention in the *escrutinio* (official check of balloting), or cruder techniques involving purchase of votes or employment of violence through party workers, the police, or the armed forces.

If the election in an *imposición* is adroitly rigged, power will be maintained or changed peacefully, and the press and even scholars will hail the experience as a final demonstration of the democratic aspirations of the country. On the other hand, long experience has made most Latin American politicians and the politically conscious citizenry exceptionally sensitive to fraud, and an *imposición* has to be very ably executed to forestall violence. In Mexico, for example, every change in power from the fall of Díaz to the *imposición* of General Manuel Ávila Camacho in 1940 was followed by armed revolt. Another good illustration of improper handling of *imposición* is President Carlos Arroyo del Río's attempt in 1944 to transfer the presidency of Ecuador to Miguel Angel Albornoz. His ineptitude permitted the opposition to execute a successful *cuartelazo* and install José Maria Velasco Ibarra in power. Velasco Ibarra attempted the *imposición* of Mariano Suárez Veintimilla in 1947 and failed.

"Candidato Unico"

Candidato único, or an election in which there is but one candidate running, occurs occasionally when a *caudillo* develops who is so overwhelming in stature that no other political figure dares oppose him. An excellent illustration is General Manuel Odría of Peru who obtained power by *cuartelazo* in October, 1948, then developed his position so strongly that he was able to run for the presidency on July 2, 1950, without opposition. When so employed, however, it becomes an open, blunt repudiation of representative democracy and opens the administration to attack at home and abroad. More frequently the astute *jefe supremo* of the country will select *imposición* as a more subtle, mature method of realizing his objectives. For an outstanding *caudillo* it is a relatively simple matter to persuade a respectable, distinguished man to run against him, with the understanding that the dummy candidate will receive enough votes to make the campaign appear authentic and to maintain his honor.

"Continuismo"

Continuismo is a peaceful, constitutional methodology for maintaining a chief executive in power beyond the legal term of his office. From time to time a *caudillo* will discover at the termination of his tenure that no one wishes to challenge him. He might even be approached by representatives of major power groupings in the country with the appeal that he continue in office. If the constitution prohibits re-election, then *continuismo* must be embraced. This usually involves amending the constitution, drafting a new document (in which the major change will be a section providing for temporary abrogation of the no re-election article), enactment of legislative statute, plebescite, or judicial interpretation. Russell H. Fitzgibbon's important study of *continuismo* in Central America and the Caribbean presents in detail some of these techniques.[4] But *continuismo*, like the other forceful and peaceful techniques for organizing political power, was in use before the period covered by the Fitzgibbon study, and it applies not only to the small countries in the Caribbean and Middle American area but to the larger countries of south America as well. The new Argentine constitution of 1949, for example, eliminated the no-re-election clause of the document of 1853 in order to permit General Juan Domingo Perón a second term of office.

Elections

Finally, the electoral method of organizing power has been employed at least once in all of the Latin American countries. It is my hypothesis, however, that elections in the Anglo-American sense for the determination of executive leadership are resorted to mainly in Latin America when more satisfactory methods have for one reason or another proved inadequate. Election under such circumstances is not likely to produce a strong, popular leader, but the technique may provide time for reassembling and again bringing into play the more fundamental bases for determining political power.

If the assumption of force in Latin American politics possesses validity, the question quite fairly can be raised: Why have elections at all? The reasons include the following: (1) The need for the friendship and financial assistance of the United States dictates at least superficial

4. R. H. Fitzgibbon, "Continuismo in Central America and the Caribbean," in *Latin American Quarterly*, Vol. II, No. 3, 1940, pp. 55-74.

respect for the idiosyncrasies of that country in the field of organizing and changing governments. (2) Elections have a public-opinion role to perform for the government. Through the media of communication the government can help to strengthen the conviction that it has chosen the right candidate. (3) Elections are also useful to the opposition which can employ the campaigns to build up moral justification for revolt. (4) There is the belief that the electoral technique of the liberal-democratic state should be developed as the most satisfactory procedure for organizing and changing governments.

Concluding Implications

The thesis of violence in the organization, maintenance, and changing of governments in Latin America is susceptible of considerable demonstration through ample objective evidence. As democracy is assumed to be imperative to American foreign policy in the Western Hemisphere, and as it is evident that violence tends to characterize politics in the Latin American countries, it is only logical that a strong effort should be made by the Department of State of the United States to eliminate violence. Two main approaches stand out for consideration. One is associated with the name of the late Lawrence Duggan, who argued that we could never further the development of democracy in Latin America by supporting the landed oligarchs or the reactionary army and church groups. Instead, he insisted, we should extend our aid and assistance to the labor unions, which, if they achieved a position of power in Latin American politics, would strive for democracy. What Mr. Duggan did not make clear was that the major unions, during the time he was advocating his policy, were dominated by militant communists. If they were to achieve power it seems reasonably clear that they would offer modest support indeed for such principles of the liberal-democratic state as individualism, the basic freedoms, and parliamentary organization. It is fair, however, to agree with Duggan that failure to support the labor unions in all probability would mean retention in some countries and development in others of clerico-military authoritarianism, almost as much opposed to democracy as is communism.

The other approach, one that seems to be widely accepted, is that political instability in Latin America finds its origins in economic distress among the masses. The concomitant argument is that if the Latin American countries are assisted in raising their living standards, democratic procedures will in some way result. The fact that violence has a long history even in the most advanced Latin American countries, such

Sacred and secular protectors of the miners of Oruro, Bolivia. The man in the foreground, wearing the traditional Oruro Devil's mask, is president of the Oruro Devil Fraternity, organized in honor of the Virgin of Socaván, the protectress of the miners. The miners' monument in the background, sculpted in the best tradition of proletarian art, reflects the left-wing party and union affiliation of the miners. (Courtesy United Nations)

as Argentina, negates for me so simple an explanation. Furthermore, it is instructive for us to observe that right-wing authoritarianism as exemplified by Perón's *justicialismo*, and left-wing authoritarianism, as exemplified by the Mexican Revolution or *Aprismo*, also call for higher material standards of living for the masses.

My own research has led me to the conviction that the problem of violence is much more basic and a good deal more complicated than either of these approaches would suggest. There is much evidence which leads one to believe that there is no one simple cause for violence, which, if removed or corrected, would produce stable, democratic politics in the Anglo-American conception. It seems more defensible to me to argue, first, that Hispanic culture tends everywhere in Latin America to dominate in the power sense; second, that the institutions of Hispanic culture such as the family, church, army, educational institutions, and economic systems, are essentially authoritarian in nature, hence, conditioning the individual to more frequent acceptance of processes of dictatorship, including violence, than processes of political democracy.

The Hispanic family, characterized by stratified inequality of rights, duties, and responsibilities based upon differentiations of age, sex, and other factors; the church, hierarchical, authoritarian, and absolutist in both organization and dogma; the educational system, with its theories of exclusion which reduce the extent of educational services to a few, its segregation of the sexes, particularly in the primary and secondary fields, its discouragement of women in higher education, and its widespread retention of scholasticism in method; the exaggerated importance and influence of the army in social and political life; and an economic organization which discourages individual initiative, imagination, and enterprise, and which seeks solutions through collectivism—all these are data in support of the generalization that the individual is constantly conditioned to authoritarianism. If the hypothesis here presented is valid, then it is possible to say that Point Four and the program of the United Nations in respect to Latin America, both of which assume that modification of one aspect of Latin American culture—the economic—will produce attitudes conducive to the development of democracy, are doomed to confusion and disillusionment.

Indeed, the eradication of force and violence takes on monumental proportions, for it implies fundamental re-organization of large parts of an entire way of life. Effective exploitation of those few aspects of Hispanic culture which tend toward the development of political democracy, and modification or elimination of the many that do not, presuppose almost unlimited time, power, and material resources, which are denied to any one state, such as the United States, or collection of states, such as the United Nations or the organization of American States.

In this connection the question might well be raised as to whether the employment of violence in organizing political power in Latin America necessarily negates the principles of representative democracy. Or, to put the issue in another way, to what extent have governments established by force lacked majority support? Is it possible that Latin American political culture has developed procedures for measuring and representing opinion different from but as valid as the techniques of election, initiative, referendum, and plebiscite of the Anglo-American and Western European states? This is a subject on which firm judgments already exist, but I submit that it is an area of research which might profit through comprehensive elaboration. Systematic analysis of the pathology of violence in Latin American countries is a necessary introduction to mature and meaningful speculation on the meaning of the phenomenon in terms of both comparative government and international relations. The definition of terms and the survey of selected case studies found in this paper point to the obvious conclusion that other facets of the broad, fundamental problem of the nature of power in Latin American politics require research. The most important of such areas include: (1) the development of techniques for determining accurately where power is to be found in such areas as the appointment of personnel, the formulation of policy, the administration of the functions of the state, and the adjudication of competing interests; (2) an analysis of the nature of power and its classification and application to given circumstances, including the extent to which it is personal; the extent to which it is institutional, associated with the family, church, army, or economic organization; and the extent to which it is structural and found in federal, unitary, executive, legislative, or judicial forms; and (3) an evaluation of the pattern of power from the standpoint of its relationship to forms and philosophies of government.

THE ROLE OF THE MILITARY IN
MODERN LATIN AMERICAN POLITICS

The following selection by Ronald Schneider, a professor of Political Science at Queens College, deals with military influence on the civilian government of Brazil.* The explicit and overt importance of the Armed Forces in the government of Brazil has increased, because with the growth of the state mechanism and the decline of consensus among the holders of institutional political power, it has become the only agent independently strong enough to implement decisions. It is not wise, however, to consider the Armed Forces only as an institution, growing relatively stronger in its interaction with other institutions. Another student of the Brazilian military, Alfred Steppan,[5] also a political scientist, has argued that the military should often be considered a dependent rather than an independent variable. That is, the military commanders cannot take controversial positions without running the risk of splitting the Armed Forces into opposite camps. That the Brazilian Armed Forces are not a single homogeneous political actor is abundantly clear from the Schneider selection, especially in those sections dealing with the events of 1950-55. Thus, before the military will act it must have external, non-military support. It has been argued by José Nún that the source of this external support is in the growing middle class, which provides the Armed Forces with its officers.[6] With Steppan we would argue that the middle class is too vast and heterogeneous a category to provide a single stimulus. In addition, Steppan argues that social origins do not provide a basis for decision making but that present conditions and opportunities do.[7] His research suggests that the military officers have a great deal of contact, not with a massive, heterogeneous middle class but with local political, industrial, and technical notables, who themselves may affect different sections of middle-class opinion through control of mass media communications. A later selection, by Locker and Goff, describes some of the forms these connections may take.

Since the establishment of the Republic, there have been very few periods in Brazilian history that have not been marked either by military revolts or by heavy Armed Forces tutelage of the government. In

* Excerpted from Ronald Schneider, *The Political System of Brazil*, Columbia University Press, 1971, pp. 37-69. Reprinted by permission.
5. Alfred Steppan, *The Military in Politics: Changing Patterns in Brasil*, Princeton University Press, 1971, pp. 56, 65.
6. José Nún, "A Latin American Phenomenon: The Middle Class Military Coup," in James Petras and Maurice Zeitlin (eds.), *Latin America: Reform or Revolution*, Fawcett, 1969.
7. Steppan, *The Military in Politics*, pp. 54, 94.

the recurrent struggle between legalism and political activism within the Brazilian military, the latter had long been substantially stronger than depicted by most historians and many contemporary observers. Neglect of this fundamental fact, and the corresponding over-emphasis of the role of civilian politicians and political movements, has distorted interpretations of Brazilian political development. . . .

1889-1930

Although not apparent to the casual observer, whose attention was generally drawn to the political debates of the Congress and the articulate expression views by representatives of civilian interest groups as carried in the generally free, if conservatively oriented press, the Armed Forces exerted important influence on national political life throughout the period of the Old Republic. . . . Their favorable image—that they were largely above politics, or were at least disinterested watchdogs of the national welfare—was in part a historical carry-over from the past. It was also, in part at least, a result of the fact that no competition between national parties existed in Brazil. Indeed, there was no real electoral competition for power and office at the national level. Once the system shook down around the turn of the century in the so-called politics of the governors, the dominant coalition of forces headed by São Paulo and Minas Gerais, with Rio Grande do Sul, Rio de Janeiro, and Bahia playing secondary roles, selected the next president. With the powerful state machines falling into line behind a choice influenced heavily by the incumbent president and important financial interests, the lesser states were left with little choice but to adhere. On those few occasions when a real contest seemed possible, the military took an active part in the campaign.

Throughout this period, military figures were actively involved in the political life of the states, albeit more often behind the scenes than in the spotlight. . . . With the beginning of the political decay and institutional deterioration of the Old Republic at the end of World War I, the military was at the center of every crisis. . . . By 1928, the republican regime in its nearly four decades of existence had reached the same point of deterioration, and the oligarchic system a parallel degree of political decay, as had been the case with the Empire in the mid-1880's. . . . The electoral process was highly fraudulent, national parties were nonexistent, and protests against the inequities of the established order were increasingly met with repression rather than compromise and evolutionary reform. The federal executive, while frequently arbitrary, often lacked the compensatory merit of strength and effectiveness. The political representatives of the patriarchal and "oligarchic" regime could not point with pride to outstanding accomplishments to justify their continued stewardship of the nation. Or rather, when they sought to do so, they were convincing only to themselves, while appearing hypocritical and self-seeking to an increasing proportion of the politically conscious public.

As long as elections might lead to change, there was no strong popular base for revolution. But the people were aware that never in the history of the Republic had the government's candidate lost. Moreover, only on two widely separated occasions had the electorate been given even the shadow of a real choice rather than just an opportunity to ratify the decision of the powerful state machines. . . . In this context the presidential succession of 1930 turned out to be the last chance for the old republican system to demonstrate significant flexibility or adaptability. But the course of events from late 1928 on demonstrated that Brazil's political crisis was one both of men and institutions.

The core of the revolutionary movement that eventually triumphed in October, 1930, was composed of the *tenentes*, who had gained conspiratorial experience as well as a degree of popular renown during the four years of their armed struggle against the government of Arthur Bernardes (1922-1926). During 1928-1929, they were able to win additional adherents to their cause within the officer corps, exploiting their growing dissatisfaction with the regime's policies.

The successful revolutionary movement of 1930 was a heterogeneous amalgam of groups desiring sweeping political changes if not a new social order with elements, which although violently opposed to the incumbent administration and the president's hand-picked successor, were devoid of any wish for more than modest political and administrative reforms. In both its civilian and military components—each crucial to its success—the revolutionary coalition was essentially, indeed almost exclusively, bourgeois in nature. . . .

Presidential succession was the issue that coalesced the fragmented opposition forces into a single movement cohesive insofar as its immediate objective—attainment of power—was concerned. In 1929, the world market crisis combined with a record coffee harvest to thwart government price-support policies and trigger an economic recession. Elements linked to industry, finance, commerce, and services began to react strongly against economic policies favoring export-oriented agricultural producers. Against this background, an unusually strong opposition coalition was forged to contest the 1930 presidential election. When outgoing President Washington Luis of São Paulo broke with tradition and sought to impose another *Paulista* as the official candidate, Minas Gerais' political leaders threw their support to the "Liberal Alliance" slate headed by Getulio Vargas, the Governor of Rio Grande do Sul. Julio Prestes was announced the winner, but the Liberal Alliance refused to accept the allegedly fraudulent results and launched a revolt in October, 1930. Alarmed at the prospect of civil war and impressed with the visible decay of the old regime in face of this challenge, the high command of the Armed Forces, after a good deal of maneuvering by generals with key commands, stepped in and forced the president to resign in favor of a *junta*, which it was hoped by some participants might prove a viable alternative to the revolutionary forces.

1930-1946

Vargas became provisional chief executive at the head of a very heterogenous movement. Although the *tenentes* and some "young Turk" politicians desired a real social revolution, they lacked any coherent plan; other groups wished only to correct the evident deficiencies of the old political system. They agreed only upon a new electoral code incorporating the secret ballot, proportional representation, a system of electoral courts, and extension of the franchise to include women. Following an unsuccessful "Constitutionalist" revolt centered in São Paulo in July, 1932, a Constituent Assembly was elected, and in 1934 conferred a four-year presidential term upon Vargas. During this time both the communists and the local fascists (known as Integralists), thriving in a situation where less ideological parties failed to take root, sought Vargas' overthrow by violent means. In November, 1937, Vargas staged a coup with the acquiescence of the Armed Forces' leaders, assuming dictatorial powers and decreeing a semi-corporative "New State." By absorbing into his regime important elements of the dominant state machines, he was able to bend the existing political system to his wishes and adapt it to his needs. Thus he was able to govern without a formal party structure while maneuvering to neutralize critical military elements.

Vargas' fifteen-year stay in power, although interrupting Brazil's tradition of constitutional government, helped to break the hold of the traditional elite groups and brought new elements into the political arena. Moreover, Vargas gave impetus to social and economic developments that subsequently tended to give a broader base to Brazilian experiments with representative regimes in the 1946-1964 period. Yet more than anything else the Estado Novo reinforced authoritarian tendencies and corporatist structures which proved barriers to the development of a pluralist system.

. . . In an environment of sustained industrialization and urbanization, the civilian elite groups expanded significantly through the addition of industrial, commercial, and professional elements. The bureaucracy grew substantially in numbers in the wake of broadened governmental activities and came to play an important role in the formulation and execution of national policies. Assumption by the federal government of responsibility for the welfare of urban labor gave the group a new interest in politics and established the image of Vargas as the "Father of the Poor."

With the triumph of Allied arms in World War II, pressure grew in Brazil for a return to representative Government. Vargas reluctantly called general elections for late 1945 and political parties were allowed to organize. Important political and military groups—including not only the traditional opposition, but many of the Army leaders long associated with the dictator—doubting the sincerity of Vargas' new found democratic inclinations, brought about his involuntary but peaceful departure from office in October. (The return of the Brazilian Expeditionary Force from the Italian campaign, where it had fought to defend and extend democracy, was a major factor in Vargas' fall.)

The Dutra Regime

The candidate Vargas eventually endorsed, General Eurico Gaspar Dutra, his long-time War Minister, was elected in December, 1945, and gave Brazil five years of orderly if uninspired government. The Constitution of 1946, which remained in effect until 1967, re-created a federal system, with a presidential executive and a bicameral national legislature. It included numerous social welfare provisions and institutional restraints on arbitrary exercise of power—the former in response to the Vargas experience and the latter in reaction against it. Although Dutra was a career Army officer, it can be said with substantial justice that he strove conscientiously to act as a democratic President, albeit with a strong leaning toward conservative positions.

Thus Brazil's return to constitutionalism began as had the Republic itself and the post-1930 experiments, with the civilian political groups indebted to the military for having ousted the "decadent" regime. Indeed the striking fact about Brazil in the immediate postwar period is not the Armed Forces' assumption of responsibility for intervening in politics on behalf of the civilian democratic elements, but the latter's acceptance of this as a proper and legitimate function of the military as a national institution—a tendency which was manifested again in less unqualified terms in 1954 and 1964. The selection of military candidates for the presidential succession of 1945 involved questions of political tactics, if not strategy, as well as recognition that the "re-establishment of democracy" required the sponsorship of the Armed Forces. . . .

The nature of the political party system that emerged in 1945 set significant limits on what could be attempted, much less accomplished during Dutra's administration. At the same time, Vargas' continuance as the potentially dominant figure in two of the three major parties largely inhibited their development along modern programmatic lines or into the institutionalized vehicles for political modernization. Anti-Vargism was the unifying factor and guiding principle of the National Democratic Union (UDN), while the power-oriented Social Democratic Party (PSD) subordinated to emotional issues of Varguismo, while personal and regional differences stemming from the Estado Novo epoch would generally override the class and interest similarities between the UDN and PSD and keep the latter in increasingly uneasy alliance with the Brazilian Labor Party (PTB). Only in the wake of the 1964 revolution—a decade after Vargas' death—would a permanent realignment be imposed upon the parties by the military to supplant an alignment along the cleavages of 1945.

The PSD, pre-eminently the party of the *situacionistas,* or political "in" groups, supplied the majority in the 1946-1950 Congress, occupied the largest share of executive positions in Dutra's cabinet, and controlled the greatest number of state administrations. Essentially non-ideological in its orientation, the PSD combined the dominant state machines of the post-1930 period, chiefly rural based, with the businessmen and industrialists who had benefited under the authoritarian interlude from Vargas' increasing orientation toward economic development. A high proportion of the new bureaucratic elite, whose ranks had multiplied through the steady expansion of government activities during the Vargas era, also leaned toward the PSD, whose ranks were further swelled by those who sought advantage from associating themselves with the administration party in Brazil's patronage-oriented "cartorial state." Essentially, these groups wanted more of what they had been receiving from the Estado Novo and pressed Dutra for special favors as well as increased support for programs beneficial to their diverse interests. Indeed, the PSD was more a loose confederation of regional parties than a unified and coherent national organization. In 1946, it bore a striking resemblance to the state-based republican parties of the pre-1930 regime, in spite of the fundamental changes that had taken place in Brazilian society since that time.

In its early years, the UDN was as much an alliance of political "outs" as the PSD was a coalition of the holders of power. With bifactionalism the predominant pattern on the local level in rural areas, the UDN label was often adopted by the political chief or clan that was not linked to the state interventor's power structure. Thus, in much of the country the UDN was not distinctively different in its social base or policy objectives from the PSD. Similarly, in the cities, the UDN was heavily supported by commercial-industrial interests, many of whose members opted for the PSD. While the pro-Vargas center-conservative PSD attracted many middle-class voters linked to the expanding government bureaucracy, the UDN recruited heavily from among professional men and white-collar employees of the private sector. It was also strong among intellectuals and students, who at that time were intensely anti-Vargas on juridical and libertarian grounds; in the cities, the UDN was a liberal party in the classic sense. As a minority party, it became accustomed to the role of public critic, although various of its component interests negotiated with the government for what patronage and favors they could extract.

The PTB, at the beginning of Dutra's presidential period, was more significant for its potential than for its existing strength. It suffered from organizational deficiencies and was an effective electoral force only in the major industrial centers. Yet few politicians could be blind to the fact that with the continued mobilization of urban groups and development of the working class it would almost surely continue to grow. With Vargas at its head, the PTB would be a formidable power contender and hence merited respect beyond its 1945 electoral performance.

The re-establishment of a representative legislative organ and the emergence of political parties would in any case have seriously affected the operations of the policy-making mechanism and administrative machinery. But the undermining of executive authority was accentuated in the 1946-1950 period by the fragmented and factionalized nature of the parties, constitutional provisions and structural modifications designed to decentralize power, and the political style of the new

President. Dutra was a military man of previously authoritarian leanings who was so determined to govern entirely within the limits of the recently reinstituted formal democracy that he failed to take a strong role in resolving the difficult adjustments necessary if the representative system of the renewed Republic was to demonstrate the effectiveness required for long-run viability.

Thus, Brazil failed to receive strong and imaginative presidential leadership in the period of transition from a relatively closed discretionary regime toward an open, competitive, and representative system. While characterized by great freedom and exceptional stability, the Dutra years were hence also a period of lost opportunities. Although many of the vices of the Estado Novo were eliminated, its major virtues were also lost, and a number of the less desirable features of the pre-Vargas system re-emerged. Instead of liberal democracy being "legitimized" by its achievements in the aftermath of authoritarianism, its shortcomings were too often underscored by a policy of drift and accommodation with retrograde forces. The conservative Republic became a breeding ground for a new brand of populism that would alter the nature of political life and quality of participation without effecting a new synthesis between the forces of tradition and modernization.

This peculiarly Brazilian form of populism, combining features of urban machine politics with personalism and emotional appeals with effective performance in the realm of patronage, assumed several distinct forms in the decade after 1948. . . . The several strains of populism shared in common an appeal to the poorly assimilated mass urban population fed by heavy migration from the countryside, plagued with the insecurities of city life, and dissatisfied with its level of living. The restless but largely non-radical middle sectors also gave substantial support to populist politicians. Although this tendency was still not evident during the Dutra years, it grew in importance through the crisis of the 1950's and was crucial to the "Janio phenomenon." Left betrayed and disoriented by Quadros' resignation in August, 1961, the middle sectors would be important to Goulart's early successes before giving support to the movement which overthrew him.

The Vargas Regime: Prologue to 1964

The rise of populism was matched during the 1950's by a reaction within the military, which also helped contribute to the political confrontation that brought about a fundamental system change in the mid-1960's. Thus, these interrelated developments are crucial to an understanding of the collapse of the representative regime.

Indeed, to a very considerable degree, the 1964 coup was a reflection, if not direct continuation, of the political crisis and military interventions of 1954-1955, which saw the final elimination of Vargas and a struggle over whether the victors of the 1955 elections should be allowed to take office. What the Armed Forces did and refrained from doing in 1954-1955 had a profound impact upon their actions in 1961 and 1964, and the roles of the main actors in the 1964 crisis are intelligible only against the background of the positions they assumed a decade earlier. For the leaders of the 1964 coup and Goulart's military supporters had not only held key command positions in 1961, but had been junior generals or senior colonels during the 1954-1955 crisis. In fact, many had played consequential roles in the 1945 deposition of Vargas, and their memories of the 1937 coup, the 1930 Revolution, and even the *tenente* revolts of the 1920's were those of participants as well as observers.

This continuity of leadership, which necessitates a close examination of the 1950's for an adequate understanding of the 1960's was nearly as pronounced on the civilian side, with the physical absence of Vargas after 1954 more than offset by the pervasive influence of his political legacy and the prominent role of his political heirs, particularly Goulart. Among the civilian leadership of the post-1964 governments, Pedro Aleixo, Vice President under Costa e Silva (1967-1969), had been speaker of the Chamber of Deputies during the mid-1930's, government leader under Quadros, opposition leader through the Goulart regime, and majority leader under Castelo Branco. His predecessor as Vice President, José Maria Alkmim, had also been active in national politics for over three decades, as had many congressional leaders and holders of ministerial posts in the military-headed administrations. Thus, to the degree that the 1963-1964 crisis was a replay of the 1953-1954 polarization and military intervention, analysis of the demise of the Vargas government is crucial to comprehension of the breakdown of the system itself a decade later.

Vargas' inability to cope with changing conditions, which led to the chain of deepening crises, can be understood only in terms of the situation in which he came to power and particularly the divisions within the Army that developed in the early 1950's. Elections within the influential Military Club had long been one of Brazil's most significant political barometers. The victor in 1948 was the highly professional Salvador Cesar Obino, with General Leitão de Carvalho, one of the most intransigent legalists, as his vice presidential running mate. The salient issue about which military politics had come to revolve in the early postwar years was that of petroleum policy. While the Dutra administration was relatively favorable to the idea of United States participation in the exploration and development of Brazil's inadequate petroleum reserves, an increasingly vocal nationalist current in the Armed Forces opposed foreign investment in and control over such a strategic resource. In large part, the alignment of this question arrayed the pro-United States politicians of the Italian campaign against leftist and pro-Vargas elements. Leitão de Carvalho joined a number of other retired generals in founding the Center for the Defense of Petroleum and the National Economy (CEDPEN), and Obino, who was far from an unconditional admirer of the Dutra government, permitted debate of this question within the Military Club (to which all Army officers belonged). General Julio Caetano Horta Barbosa and ex-*tenente* leader Juarez Tavora were the major antagonists in this dispute, dating back to the time when the former had served as head of the National Petroleum Council under Vargas and adopted a policy contrary to that followed by the latter when he had been Minister of Agriculture. Since basic legislation in this field was under active consideration in Congress during the 1948-1950 period, the matter remained at the forefront of military concern. The 1950 Military Club elections thus centered on the question that was also one of the major issues in the concurrent presidential campaign, that of economic nationalism. Vargas had placed increasing emphasis upon this theme in his effort to gain broad popular support for a bid to return to power as constitutional president. At least equally important to the ex-dictator as the response of the electorate was the attitude of the Armed Forces, who, as they had been able to oust him from office in 1945, could still effectively veto his candidacy. In this context the victory of a "nationalist" slate, in the Military Club balloting in May removed the major threat to Vargas' political comeback. Elements hesitant to commit themselves to a candidacy which might be aborted by the Armed Forces now foresaw sufficient military support for the ex-president.

. . . Where the Dutra administration had tended to open the petroleum field to foreign investment, at the end of 1951 Vargas submitted a bill calling for the creation of a mixed (government and domestic private capital) corporation to explore and exploit Brazil's petroleum reserves. Thus, the military's running debate on the oil question came to center around the administration's proposal, making the Vargas policy an issue within the Armed Forces. Vargas may well have thought in terms of the 1950 Military Club election and his War Minister's attitude that a nationalistic petroleum policy would win him increased Army as well as civilian political support. In fact, it was to have the opposite effect: a victory within the arena of military politics for the opponents of radical nationalism, whose anti-Communist sentiments were aroused by the leading role assumed by the Communist Party in the "Oil Is Ours" campaign for "national economic emancipation." As would prove the case for Goulart in 1964, Vargas confused a temporary swing in military opinion with the beginning of a basic, long-term shift in orientation. Even during this period of quite moderate and democratic behavior by Vargas, important military leaders outside the regime's power scheme (with the officers of the World War II Expeditionary Force as the movement's backbone) launched a strong campaign against its pillars, particularly War Minister Estillac Leal. The victory of the nationalist slate within the Army's "class" organization in 1950 had resulted not only from the popularity of their political views, but perhaps even more from their championing of a new promotions law and pay bill. Thus, that election was not necessarily the mandate for radical political positions that the relatively small group of ideological leftists saw in it. The May, 1950, balloting had taken place before the outbreak of the Korean War, an event that rallied the veterans of the Brazilian Expeditionary Force (FEB) to the side of the United States and gave a powerful impulse to anti-Communism among the officer corps as armed conflict in Asia dramatically reinforced "cold war" thinking insofar as an important sector of the Armed Forces was concerned.

In 1951, then, the alignment within the military, which had been relatively favorable to Vargas when petroleum policy was the line of division, shifted markedly over the question of Brazil's attitude toward the Korean conflict. This impingement of international considerations led very directly to a serious deterioration of Vargas' organized military support or "dispositivo," which was built upon the leftist nationalist current within the Army.

As a result of the pressures from the sectarian leftist minority in the Military Club, War Minister and Club President Estillac Leal had found himself pushed toward radical positions, which cost him support from the less exalted nationalist elements. By the end of 1951, the anti-

Estillac forces had organized to contest the upcoming elections. Among the founders of the "Democratic Crusade" (Cruzada Democrática), as the movement called itself, were such major figures of the 1964 coup and Costa e Silva regime as Lieutenant Colonel Sozeno Sarmento, Captain Mario David Andreaz, Major Edson Figueiredo, and Lieutenant Colonel Joao Bina Machado.

In March, 1952, Vargas, under heavy pressure from the center and right, dismissed Estillac and signed a military agreement with the United States that had been fiercely opposed by the left-nationalist faction. In this changed environment the Military Club elections of May, 1952, saw Estillac Leal soundly defeated by the strongly anti-Communist Crusade ticket headed by General Alcides Etchegoyen and Nelson de Melo. (Both were ex-chiefs of police of the Federal District; the latter was also a hero of the Italian campaign.) In the aftermath of this blow to the left, a series of Military-Police Inquiries (IPM's, a Brazilian form of quasi-judicial proceedings conducted by the military services) dealt severely with leftist and ultra-nationalist officers. The increasingly dominant faction within the military advocated cooperation with the United States and was highly sensitive to the freedom of action which the Communists seemed to be enjoying under Vargas.

. . . Vargas' cultivation of labor and appeals to nationalism in the latter half of 1953, like the "independent foreign policy" of Janio Quadros in 1961, can best be understood as an attempt to offset the unfavorable impact on the working class of a deflationary program of economic stabilization. At the same time, as part of his policy of balancing moves welcome to the right with measures popular among the left, Vargas increasingly voiced anti-imperialist sentiments and advocated statist solutions to problems of economic development.

As would be the case in the early 1960's, inflation served as the catalyst of social tensions and raised the dilemmas of financial policy which the administration had sought to avoid, making it necessary to disappoint the groups it was most seeking to court. Wage restraints and credit restrictions, essential as they might be for economic reasons, seriously undercut Vargas' efforts to build up political support among labor and the new industrialists. The cost of living in 1952 had risen 21 per cent, compared to 11 per cent for each of the preceding two years: in 1953 it threatened to go even higher. The middle class was badly squeezed by the rise in prices, while labor was demanding substantial wage increases rather than kind words and gestures. Thus, wage policy was to prove a critical factor in the collapse of Vargas' conciliatory strategy and the politics of confrontation which replaced compromise in 1954.

Vargas' problems were accentuated by the inauguration of the Eisenhower administration in the United States. Under the influence of Treasury Secretary George Humphrey and Secretary of State John Foster Dulles, willingness to use public funds to aid Brazil's development programs was replaced by a policy of insisting that United States private investment would do the job if the Brazilian government would create a sufficiently attractive climate. The Joint United States-Brazilian Economic Development Commission, which had made a notable contribution since it began to function in mid-1951, was to be phased out of existence, with no commitment to finance the projects it had agreed were essential to Brazil's development. The new United States government did not conceal its opposition to the Petrobras law, which established a state monopoly over petroleum exploration and exploitation, while United States private interests were vocal in condemning it as Communist inspired. Vargas' foes were not loath to exploit this new difficulty. The President reacted by increasing the nationalist tenor of his public pronouncements. Vargas had already extended his economic nationalism into the field of profit remittances during 1951 and 1952, when the overvaluation of the cruzeiro led foreign firms to send their profits home instead of reinvesting them in Brazil. In December, 1953, he struck back at United States investors' attacks upon the Petrobras law by denouncing the "sabotage" of Brazil's developmental efforts by private enterprises with international affiliations. This tactic of attributing Brazil's economic troubles to external factors had substantial success in diverting resentment stemming from the economic austerity away from the Vargas administration.

This stress on nationalism, which struck a responsive chord not only among the urban working class but also with a very large proportion of the middle sectors, did not prove at the time to be the unifying force its intellectual advocates expected it to be. The identification of nationalism with basic societal as well as economic changes, caused by the very vocal role of the radical nationalists in championing the causes Vargas espoused for populist rather than revolutionary reasons, led to apprehension among many middle-sector elements.

By the end of 1953, in fact, as would be the case ten years later, there was a propaganda war going on between the rightist opponents of the Government and those who hoped to turn anti-foreign capital sentiment against the domestic free-enterprise system. Polemics largely replaced dialogue as radicalizers of both extremes played upon class interests and the tensions and insecurity produced by the processes of modernization. In particular, the conservative propagandists strove to drive a wedge between the urban middle sectors and the working class by depicting the political rise of the latter as a threat to the former and grossly exaggerating the extent of the "Communist threat."

More sharply than in 1945 and very much as would be the case in 1964, the backbone of the anti-Vargas movement was an alliance of the UDN with the strongly anti-Communist wing of the Armed Forces. Lacerda had proposed, as he would again in 1955 and as would finally be done in 1964, Armed Forces' establishment of a "state of exception" in which corrupt and subversive elements would be purged from the body politic and political institutions overhauled to prevent the resurgence of another "Vargas-type" regime. While relatively few important figures within the UDN or the military were ready for such a drastic interruption of the democratic process they had restored in 1945, the seeds for a new intervention had been sown.

The victory of the Democratic Crusade in May, 1952, had been in large part a function of many of middle-of-the-road officers reacting against the leftward swing of the Club, which they saw as introducing dangerous divisions into the officer corps . . . [But] once having performed their surgical intervention, the vast bulk of the officer corps would favor leaving these matters to the interim regime headed by the Vice President.

Since most officers turned against Vargas only after the military had been drawn into the crisis by an incident in which one of their colleagues was killed, they were not highly concerned with the outcome of the elections. But the politicized minority, particularly those who had attended the National War College (Escola Superior de Guerra, ESG) was very much involved in the question of presidential succession. The founder of the ESG, General Cordeiro de Farias, harbored political ambitions, as did his successor as commandant, Juarez Távora. The War College brought together many civilian politicians, journalists, and businessmen with officers of all three services above the rank of colonel. It was the arena for the development of a doctrine of national security that saw Brazil's future as firmly allied with the western Christian world in its confrontation with the Communist bloc. This doctrine held that the rapid emergence of a strong Brazil would best result from cooperation with foreign initiative, technology, and capital.

The military movement that was to result in Vargas' ouster and death made its first overt move in February, 1954, with the issuance of the so-called Colonels' Manifesto. In this rather curious document—which, although bordering on an ultimatum, reflected certain legalist scruples —a group of eighty-two colonels and lieutenant colonels expressed their strong dissatisfaction with the neglect of the Armed Forces' needs for modernization of equipment, their concern over labor agitation, and their disapproval of corruption in the nation's political life. (Among the signatories were officers who) were active in future military crises and remained influential after 1964. . . .)

Vargas' nearly immediate removal of Goulart as Minister of Labor, rather than satisfying his critics, was taken as a sign of weakness calling for escalation of the offensive. Vargas responded by turning up the volume of his nationalist pronouncements, introducing a bill to create a government power complex (Electrobras), and, on May Day, proclaiming a doubling of the minimum wage scale. This move, so similar to Goulart's decision to pull out the stops on "basic reforms" in March, 1964, was taken against the advice of Vargas' economic experts and represented a willingness to alienate important groups in order to solidify his leadership of the workers.

The Military Club elections of May, 1954, confirmed the strength of essentially anti-Vargas forces within the Army. The victors were Canrobert da Costa (War Minister under Dutra) and Juarez Távora. . . . Many centrist officers had moved over to support the anti-Communists in the wake of the pro-UDN press's campaign against Vargas' alleged plots for a coup to continue in office beyond 1955. At the same time, the propaganda campaign against the Vargas regime was stepped up by the UDN. The diabolically effective "crusader" Carlos Lacerda led the attack through the pages of his daily *Tribuna da Imprensa,* as well as speaking with devastating impact from every available platform. Returning to his apartment in Copacabana from one of these sessions shortly before 1:00 a.m. on August 5, the founder of the militantly anti-Vargas "Popular Alliance against Theft and a Coup" was the object of an assassination attempt—the bungling of which by Vargas retainers would instead cost the President his life. For while Lacerda was merely wounded in the foot, his companion, Air Force Major Rubens Florentino Vaz, was killed.

Colonel Joao Adil de Oliveira's vigorous investigation undertaken on Air Force initiative . . . soon had the culprits in hand. But since they were linked to Vargas' chief bodyguard, damage done to the President's position was irreparable. Vagas strove to ride out the storm, but his efforts to arouse popular support fell flat, as daily revelations about the "sea of mud" surrounding the presidency alienated public opinion. War Minister Zenobio da Costa held the Army in line, although with increasing difficulty, but the Air and Navy Ministers lost control of the situation. All attempts to find a "constitutional" road out of the crisis ran up against Vargas' unwillingness to be disgraced (and later possibly punished) and the opposition's solidifying view that any solution short of his departure from the presidency would be a temporary palliative at best. Air Force brigadiers subscribed to a statement demanding the President's resignation, and opinion in the Naval and Military Clubs moved quickly in the same direction.

Vargas avoided the humiliation of a second deposition by committing suicide on August 24. He left behind a shrewdly designed political testament that immediately transformed him from tragic failure into martyr. Instead of mass demonstrations against his regime, the country was swept by a series of attacks on Vargas' enemies and against such symbols of United States imperialism as the American consulates in several cities.

Although Vargas was dead and most of his close associates pushed out of the center of the political arena, the tension between pro-Vargas and anti-Vargas forces continued to dominate the political scene. The Café Filho administration, composed of a mixture of nearly all the non-Vargas forces, including the Dutra wing of the PSD, assumed a caretaker role in keeping with the fact that the country was already in the advanced stages of campaigning for the October, 1954, legislative and gubernatorial elections, with the presidential balloting little more than a year away. The outcome of the elections of October 3, 1954, held only 40 days after Vargas' death and, as Café proudly stressed, without a state of siege having been imposed in the interim, was a relative stand-off between the heirs and the foes of Vargas. The presidential elections a year later gave a slight plurality to Kubitschek and Goulart running on a PSD-PTB coalition ticket, with the former receiving nearly 470,000 votes more than the UDN's Juarez Távora, and Labor Party national chairman Goulart edging Milton Campos for the vice presidency by less than half that margin. On November 8, the military ministers were informed of Café Filho's proposal (allegedly made on his doctor's advice) to turn the presidential office over temporarily to Carlos da Coimbra Luz, who as presiding officer of the Chamber of Deputies was first in the constitutional line of succession. The ties of the new Acting President to the coup-minded officers and their UDN allies were widely believed to be quite close if not truly intimate. Whatever mistrust the supporters of the victorious candidates harbored with regard to the intentions of Café Filho—who consistently guaranteed that they would be inaugurated if confirmed by the electoral courts—their suspicions of the new Acting President were far greater. Many doubted that Café was really ill and saw his hospitalization as a move to clear the decks for those articulating a coup. While War Minister Henrique Teixeira Lott debated with himself whether or not to turn over the War Ministry to the individual chosen by Luz to replace him, General Odylio Denys, Commander of the Eastern Military Zone (the present-day First Army), organized a powerful military scheme to thwart the Acting President. Only in the pre-dawn hours of November 11 was Lott informed of their plans and invited to join as the movement's titular leader. With his acceptance, the troop movements began, and by morning the capital was securely in their hands. The PSD presiding officer of the Senate was sworn in over UDN protests as the new chief executive, with Café Filho barred by force from reassuming the presidency.

Since no documentary proof was ever presented of plans to mount a coup to keep Kubitschek and Goulart from office—as distinct from a strong desire to do so on the part of Lacerda and some junior officers—the "preventive coup" was to persist as a bone of contention within the military as well as in the broader political arena. Lott and his associates, who considered themselves to have acted to preserve legality, were denounced as having engineered an unjustified coup. In the 1960 presidential campaign, for example, Lott's sponsorship of the "movement to a return to existing constitutional means" was criticized as a cover for a naked power grab. The question of "legality" in this episode was never to be clear, but rather to remain highly ambiguous in succeeding crises as assertion continued to take the place of demonstration. While the "August 24" and "November 11" groups in the military (named after the dates of Vargas' ouster and Lott's coup) would be numerically far inferior to the centrist majority, in periods of political polarization the latter would tend to do nothing, leaving the initiative to the more militant minorities.

In this instance those who won the battle and even the campaign eventually lost the war, for the defeated "anti-Communists" would constitute the backbone of the 1964 movement which overthrew Goulart and took power themselves. Having ousted Vargas in 1945 only to see him elected President in 1950, subsequently driving him to suicide in 1954 only to have his political heirs triumph in the 1955 elections, and finally witnessing the defeat of the Vargista forces at the polls in 1960 only to watch them come back to power the next year, the Armed Forces would act decisively to end this Vargas succession in 1964, destroying in the process Brazil's experiment with a competitive democratic regime and open political system.

In Schneider's account of the intimate relationship between the Brazilian military and civilian power-holders, he emphasizes the institutional relationships of government and military in terms of the power available to each. However, a discussion of institutional relations alone frequently obscures the actual behavior which gives shape to these institutional arrangements. In Latin America, the *golpe*, for example, is a common enough occurrence to have developed its own form of etiquette, or rules of comportment. Some insights into this etiquette is provided by Colonel E. P. Gonzalo Briceño Zevallos, Secretary of the Peruvian *junta* responsible for the *golpe* of 1962.*

July 12, 1962
Director of La Prensa
Lima, Peru

Dear Sir:

I address this note to you on behalf of the Government Junta, with reference to the article entitled "How the Palace Was Captured and Doctor Prado Overthrown," which is published on page four of today's edition.

It is the opinion of the government, undoubtedly shared by the directors of *La Prensa*, that though the press has many clear rights it also has the duty to tell the truth in an objective fashion and without distortion. The government further believes that your own and other publications have strict ethical principles that serve as the only censorship acceptable to newspapermen.

The exact version of the events as recounted by Colonel Gonzalo

* From Colonel E. P. Gonzalo Briceño Zevallos, "A Description of the Seizure of Power in 1962," in Paul Sigmund (ed.), *Models of Political Change in Latin America*, copyright 1970 by Praeger Publishers, Inc. Reprinted by permission.

Briceño Zevallos, Chief of the Army Commandos, will demonstrate to you the inaccuracy of the article in *La Prensa*.

The government does not wish to limit in any way the freedom of the press, which permits differences of opinion, but it zealusly defends objectivity in the service of the high principles of true journalism.

I would be very grateful, sir, if you would publish this note and the enclosed article.

> *Sincerely,*
> *Julio Vargas Prada*
> *Secretary of the Governing Junta*

The Facts

1. Colonel (Briceño) and his officers stand in front of the tanks facing the government palace.

2. The ultimatum is read twice, with a time limit of two minutes after the last reading.

3. Commander Lombardi, presidential aide, indicates that the President will receive the Colonel but that the palace troops will not open the front or side doors.

4. The Colonel orders a tank to open one of the front gates of the palace.

5. General Ciriani, Chief of the (presidential) Military Household, without his aides, stands in the center of the ceremonial patio of the palace.

6. The Colonel enters, followed by eight officers in a double column.

7. The Colonel salutes the General, as do his officers, and identifies himself as Chief of the Army Commandos and Representative of the Joint Command of the Armed Forces, wishing to speak to the President of the Republic.

8. The General and the Colonel, followed by their officers, enter the palace, led by the Chief of the Military Household, using the street door. Thereafter, they enter the presidential office.

9. The President is standing behind his desk, surrounded by ministers, relatives, friends, and other people, among whom is Sr. Pedro Beltrán.

10. The Colonel salutes the President, identifies himself, and says: "I am ordered by the Joint Command of the Armed Forces to invite you to please accompany me."

11. The President addresses the Colonel, his officers, and the public,

nervously at first, but always correctly and with decorum in his actions and words.

12. Cheers are heard, some get angry, others shout, and the national anthem is sung; but there are no acts or gestures that are not in keeping with the momentous occasion.

13. After the President has put on his overcoat and scarf, the Colonel sends for his baggage. The Colonel assures those present that the President will receive courteous treatment, in keeping with his high office, and that he guarantees his life. These words are pronounced calmly and firmly in the midst of absolute silence.

14. The Colonel then speaks to the President and says: "Mr. President, please accompany me," and the President answers, "I am ready, Colonel," and walks toward the palace guard.

15. Those who wish to accompany the President are told that they may do so up to the ceremonial patio of the palace.

16. When the group arrives at the place where the station wagon is parked, the Colonel addresses the President and invites him to sit where he pleases. The President chooses the center seat and lends a helping hand to the Chief of the Military Household. At that moment, the officers are ten steps away from the President and the gentlemen who accompany him. The Colonel is beside one of the doors and a captain is behind the steering wheel. At no time have enlisted men intervened, since they had not yet entered the palace.

17. Many people, among them ministers, aides, and relatives, wish to enter the vehicle but are stopped by the Chief of the Military Household, who is authorized by the Colonel to enter the car and, together with Commander Rivero Winder and the Minister of Aeronautics, to be transported to its destination.

18. In the struggle to enter the vehicle the Colonel is pushed, and as a result is forced to raise his voice in order to be heard; he warns of the imminent danger to the life of the President and others present should one of the ten security latches on the eight hand grenades and two charges of TNT that he carries be accidentally loosened. Commander Mezett is one of those closest to the Colonel, who keeps pushing him; despite his technical knowledge, (Mezett) is obviously unaware of the grave danger to those present.

19. It is common among commando teams to carry grenades and TNT on the belt in this fashion, with very sensitive security latches in position.

20. The Colonel permits the relatives of the President to follow in their own cars, which they do in the company of his aides and In-

terior Minister Elías Aparicio, who was permitted to follow in spite of the ordering of his arrest.

21. In the station wagon, the seating order is as follows: in the front seat, the Captain driving, and General Ciriani and Colonel Briceño; in the center seat, the President and the Aeronautics Minister; in the back seat, the aide with two commando officers; standing on the right running board, a captain of the commandos.

22. The station wagon is escorted by two armored vehicles, one in front and one behind, followed by two cars.

Conclusions

The correct attitude and behavior on both sides was remarkable. In accordance with their education and dignity, neither the President, the Colonel, nor the others present acted in a discourteous or insulting fashion.

Any other account of the events, especially if told by a witness, is an evil and ill-intentioned act and an attack on the prestige of the armed forces.

The events that took place did not ruffle the calm of the commandos, since such situations are routine in the light of their training, as is proved by the weapons they each carried, in spite of which no one was harmed. This is proof of the self-control, confidence, and responsibility with which the army commandos acted.

Any serious discussion of power arrangements in Latin America must include an account of the forms in which power is organized by the overseas metropolis. The penetration of metropolitan political power has greatly increased in the twentieth century and particularly since the Second World War, diminishing the political autonomy of the Latin American elite in all its component forms. While the organization of power may have a distinctive Latin American style, exemplified by Colonel Vargas Prada's note to *La Prensa*, the source of such power has progressively been drawn from the United States government.

THE POLITICS OF INTERVENTIONISM:
THE U.S. IN THE DOMINICAN REPUBLIC

In the following selection, Fred Goff and Michael Locker, editors of the North American Congress of Latin America Report, examine the proliferation of political techniques that the metropolis has employed in the Dominican Republic in recent years. Their analysis, entitled "The Violence of Domination: U.S. Power and the Dominican Republic,"* traces the growth of United States dominance in the political organization of the Dominican Republic.

The massive U.S. military intervention in the Dominican Republic during 1965 greatly clarified the political situation throughout Latin America. Just as Viet Nam focused U.S. interests in Asia, so the Dominican intervention objectified North American intentions throughout the hemisphere. In both places Washington made it painfully clear how far it is willing to go to maintain control over the Third World. The more subtle guises by which the U.S. tried to manipulate events since the days of gunboat diplomacy were stripped away when 20,000 soldiers stormed ashore to crush a nationalist rebellion in Santo Domingo. For most Latin Americans the official reasons offered to justify this action were patently false. To all but most North Americans it was obvious the Dominicans had their independence stolen in order to benefit U.S. economic, political, and military interests. The violence that flared to the surface in this confrontation is buried inside every other covert and overt mechanism the United States utilizes to control the Third World. Domination breeds violence and the potential for organized revolution.

In many respects the Dominican Republic is a small carbon copy of Cuba. An island republic close to our shores, it lives on a sugar-export economy, has a large Negro and Spanish population, and suffers from a history marked by violent, cruel dictatorship and U.S. intervention. American efforts to dominate the country stretch back to the early 1800's, culminating in the Spanish-American War and the gunboat diplomacy days of Theodore Roosevelt, Taft, and Wilson.

Plagued by long-term economic stagnation, extensive debts to European bankers, and by political chaos, the country was invaded in 1898 by a U.S.-supported secret military expedition led by a wealthy exiled Dominican merchant. The venture failed, but in 1903 and again in 1904 revolts broke out and political leaders, vying for control, sought U.S. protectorate status. Troops landed temporarily to "protect" a sugar estate and lend support to a pro-United States faction; Kuhn, Loeb

* From Irving Louis Horowitz, et al. (eds.), Latin American Radicalism, copyright © 1969 by Random House, Inc., pp. 249-91. Reprinted by permission of Random House, Inc.

and Co., a large New York banking house, took over the foreign debts and floated a $20 million bond issue.

In a dozen years from 1904 to 1916, the United States moved from the Roosevelt Corollary to full-scale Marine occupation of the Dominican Republic. First we collected customs, then we forbade insurrection in order to maintain stability, then we held elections with warships in the harbor and sailors or Marines at the polls, then we demanded full control over internal revenues and expenditures as well as over customs, then we demanded the disbanding of the Army and establishment of a Guardia Nacional (Constabulary); then we sent the Marines.[8]

Domination Through Occupation: 1916-1930

U.S. military occupation forces literally ran the country for eight years, ignoring even the fiction of a "Dominican government." In strikingly contemporary language the commanding U.S. admiral announced the occupation:

. . . for the purpose of supporting the constituted authorities and to put a stop to revolutions and consequential disorders. . . . It is not the intention of the United States Government to acquire by conquest any territory in the Dominican Republic nor to attack its sovereignty, but our troops will remain until all revolutionary movements have been stamped out and until such reforms as are deemed necessary to insure the future welfare of the country have been initiated and are in effective operation.[9]

In order to stabilize the financial situation, the military government repressed nationalist forces through a program of "disarmament and pacification." In two eastern provinces, Seibo and San Pedro de Macoris, where large American sugar estates were established, Dominicans took to the hills, harassed the plantations, and conducted guerrilla warfare. The Marines, terming them bandits, hunted the insurgents down mercilessly, terrorizing the local population and committing atrocities. By 1920 the repression, combined with the award of disputed land to United States and Dominican latifundistas, raised nationalistic passions almost to the point of full-scale rebellion. Alarmed, the plantation operators banded together under the leadership of an American, Edwin Kilbourne, to pacify the area. With a new Marine Commander they organized local squads of native Dominicans familiar with the terrain. A program of peaceful inducements was initiated

8. John Bartlow Martin, *Overtaken by Events: The Dominican Crisis from the Fall of Trujillo to the Civil War*, 1966, p. 28.
New York, 1928, Vol. 2, p. 777.
9. Sumner Welles, *Naboth's Vineyard: The Dominican Republic, 1844-1924*, 2 vols.,

after limiting the guerrilla forays and the more important leaders were persuaded to surrender. "The Marines unquestionably sowed the seed of anti-Americanism throughout the Republic," especially in the eastern provinces. To this day "in some towns the anniversary of their departure is celebrated as a holiday."[10]

Most of the social and economic programs established during the occupation collapsed when the troops formally withdrew in 1924. But even before withdrawing, the United States insisted on maintaining control over customs until all foreign debts were paid, forced the adoption of a U.S.-drafted electoral code, and further strengthened the National Police as a substitute for the old politicized army. Trained and officered by American Marines, the police quickly became the most organized and powerful force throughout the island. It was through this structure that Rafael Leonidas Trujillo made his way, assiduously cultivating friendships with the American officers, conspicuously demonstrating cooperation and cordiality. As he climbed the promotional ladder, with the aid of favorable American recommendations, he mastered the one essential rule for gaining and sustaining political power in the Republic, an understanding that the base of domestic power is rooted primarily in the United States.

Domination Through Dictatorship: The Era of Trujillo

When the National Police was transformed back into the army in 1928, Trujillo assumed the role of chief. Maneuvering carefully behind the scenes he engineered a fake uprising followed by the seizure of cities and the confiscation of weapons on the pretext of preserving order and preventing bloodshed. "One of Trujillo's greatest concerns in this plot was to insure that the government he established would be recognized by the United States."[11] Close contact with the American legation and his influential old Marine Commander, Colonel Cutts, guaranteed Trujillo U.S. support and ultimate success.

Once in power Trujillo proceeded to erect a pervasive and repressive totalitarian regime. The army was his private instrument of coercion and terror; the oversize officer corps benefited materially and enjoyed privileged status. At home and abroad he developed a huge espionage apparatus providing the kind of intelligence needed to predict events

10. Martin, *Overtaken by Events*, p. 29.
11. R. D. Crossweller, *Trujillo: The Life and Times of a Caribbean Dictator*, New York, 1966, p. 62.

and manipulate people. By recruiting their sons Trujillo cleverly forced most of the oligarchy into collaboration; blackmail, threats, and economic pressure compelled virtually every man of ability to serve him. Torture and assassination awaited those who resisted. Political opposition was erased or manipulated by co-option, imprisonment, exile, or murder. The Generalissimo personally selected all the national and local appointments, and his own party, manned by an endless string of relatives and cronies, administered a sizable social-welfare program. Every official, high or low, was subjected to constant rotation, public humiliation, or sudden elevation on short notice by orders from "El Jefe."

Beyond this traditional caudillo system, Trujillo constructed a fantastic personal economic empire. "At the most, . . . other [caudillos] had wanted money for its own sake, or for luxury, display, bribery, or a political purpose. Trujillo, far more than any of them, saw in the entire economic process a source of dominion as potent as the army, as strong as the most rigid political structure."[12] Funds collected from the public and from illicit operations were invested in every conceivable agricultural and industrial enterprise; monopolies usually followed. Import-export taxes and license fees facilitated the harassment and eventual takeover of corporations dealing in foreign trade, the lifeblood of the economy. Moreover, U.S. commodity shortages at the end of World War II raised prices on agricultural exports and propelled the island's elite into relative prosperity. After centralizing banking operations, Trujillo could sell any of his unprofitable businesses to the state for a large profit and make timely reacquisitions. It has been estimated that between 65 and 85 percent of the entire economy eventually ended up in his hands. The monetary fortune accumulated from this empire was not trivial, and the variety of devices it afforded for exercising power was crucial to maintaining the regime.

In the late forties and during the fifties, Trujillo made his move for the most coveted prize in the Dominican economy—the cane sugar industry. A sharp rise in postwar sugar prices attracted Trujillo's attention, but with the exception of relatively small properties held by the Vicini family the entire industry was owned by foreign capital—mainly United States. Fully aware of the financial and political complications involved in entering this economic sector, he proceeded cautiously. After acquiring a small independent mill in 1948, he pushed forward

12. *Ibid.*, p. 123.

with the construction of an enormous milling installation, Río Haina, that was put into production in 1953. In order to supply enough cane, he acquired large tracts of land from Dominicans, Canadians, Puerto Ricans, and finally Americans with small holdings. The largest single sugar complex on the island, La Romana, subsidiary of the American-owned South Puerto Rico Sugar Co., was then handed the technical task of building a railroad for the efficient transportation of cane and managing the entire operation on a profit-sharing basis.

These accomplishments pushed Trujillo into the largest economic deal of his reign—acquisition of the prized U.S. West Indies Sugar Company. A product of the Marine occupation and the efforts of anti-guerrilla expert Edwin Kilbourne (president and director of the company), West Indies was the largest geographically dispersed sugar complex on the island: four high-volume mills, along with 30,000 head of cattle, considerable pasture land, coconut plantations on Samana Bay, some coffee fincas, and a great deal of underdeveloped land. Unlike La Romana with its powerful South Puerto Rico Corp. connections to Kuhn, Loeb and Co. and Rockefeller interests, West Indies could not elicit enough political influence to bring about U.S. intervention. After some pressure was applied and the word of Trujillo's desire to buy got out, the stockholders negotiated a favorable figure ($35,830,-000) in three cash installments. As for South Puerto Rico, Trujillo realized its technical skills were not replaceable and its powerful connections could be mutually advantageous in raising the island's U.S. sugar quota.

The sugar acquisitions demonstrated that Trujillo still retained his keen understanding of power relationships within the United States as well as the limitations they imposed on his actions. Geographic proximity and the economic strength of the United States forced any Dominican government to depend on close and cordial relations with powerful U.S. citizens. To this end, Trujillo devoted boundless energy and resources in the form of business deals, sex, flattery, campaign contributions, bribes, blackmail, even murder. Joseph E. Davies, the archetype of Trujillo's influential American, was a multmillionaire corporate lawyer (with a major interest in General Foods) turned New Deal diplomat. In 1931, Davies visited the Republic for President Roosevelt and brought back a highly favorable assessment of the new regime, which led, in turn, to a lifesaving moratorium on debt payments and opened up new lines of credit. A long friendship ensued; Davies visited often to serve as financial counsel on business ventures and fiscal policy.

Along with Davies, industrialist Herbert May, construction tycoon Felix Benítez Rexach, diplomat-businessman William Pawley, and the molasses dealers A. I. and J. M. Kaplan served as Trujillo's economic liaison with the U.S. financial and business community.

Trujillo never found an equivalent to Davies in the political sphere of the U.S. Establishment, though he managed to significantly influence governmental decisions and public opinion through a chain of well-paid politicians, lawyers, journalists, and lobbyists. Nobody knows how many millions of dollars were passed directly or indirectly to Senators, Representatives, Executive Department employees and other powerful Americans in public life who might protect and promote Trujillo. Such dignitaries, critics as well as supporters, were often invited to his private fiefdom, wined and dined, provided with women and then secretly photographed. The "blackmail photographic library was extensive."

In conjunction with these unsavory tactics, Trujillo produced a continual barrage of propaganda geared to project a favorable image of the Dominican Republic and its benevolent leader. Elections were staged, figureheads occupied the president's office, the capital was "beautified" and anti-Communism took on the trappings of a holy crusade. In order to inflate the country's importance, extravagant foreign embassies were maintained, glamorous trips undertaken, and a world's fair hosted in the capital. In a most clever move to obtain the influential good will of American and European Jewish leaders, an offer was made in 1940 to admit 100,000 Jewish refugees on very liberal terms. Most of these programs and many others were of course meaningless, but in public relations terms they would have to be judged a success. A countless number of public officials and newsmen praised the nation's "progress built on stability" and cooperated with its operations out of innocence, stupidity, or greed.

After 1955, Trujillo built a Congressional power base in the United States centered around his periodic attempts to enlarge the island's share of the extremely lucrative U.S. sugar quota. Since 1934, the United States Government has subsidized the price of raw sugar to regulate supply and stabilize prices for domestic refiners and industrial consumers. A tonnage quota is assigned by Congress (primarily the House Agriculture Committee) to exporting nations and domestic growers guaranteeing the producer a high price and thus assuring delivery. Cuba had always been a preferred nation in the system, receiving the largest quota (providing approximately one-third of all sugar consumed in the United States) by reason of its position as the world's greatest producer. Since the dollar stakes were high and most of the Cuban ventures constituted very substantial American investments, the Cuban lobby exercised considerably more leverage than Trujillo and South Puerto Rico Sugar.

Thus, it was not until the Cuban Revolution fundamentally altered power relations inside the United States that the Dominican Republic had a chance to sell its greatly expanded sugar exports at preferential quota prices. As United States-Cuban relations deteriorated and Castro cut back sugar production during 1959-60, Trujillo's lobbying in Congress began to bear fruit. By July 1960, the Cuban quota was cancelled and the Dominican Republic received the largest portion of its subsequent redistribution. Cane production soared and the value of sugar exports doubled.

Yet Castro's revolution was obviously a mixed blessing. On June 14, 1959, Dominican exiles launched an invasion from Cuba which, though unsuccessful, shook Trujillo's regime to its roots. Torture, arrests, and assassinations of prominent Dominicans followed, and for the first time in thirty years, opposition on a large scale developed. By January, 1960, in an unprecedented event, the Roman Catholic Church finally denounced the Trujillo regime. During this same period huge arms expenditures began to sap the economy's strength. In a fit of desperation, Trujillo lashed out in an assassination attempt on an archenemy, Venezuela's social democratic President Romulo Betancourt. The Organization of American States (OAS) was called into session, Trujillo was denounced, and economic sanctions were imposed.

U.S. support for OAS condemnation and sanctions demonstrated how far Trujillo's U.S. power base had diminished. U.S. investments failed to increase after the early fifties because of the dictator's drive for total monopoly over the economy and massive corruption. Washington's preoccupation with revolutionary Cuba provided the impetus for a change in policy; in order to alter the traditional nonintervention policy of the OAS and legitimize the destruction of Castro's "dictatorship," a precedent for hemispheric intervention would first be established vis-à-vis Trujillo's regime. Soon after Castro's rise to power, Trujillo and his advisers recognized this dilemma. Survival was possible only by eliminating Castro (to restore the status quo in the Caribbean and U.S. support through "nonintervention") or, barring this, creating a completely new power base resting on an alliance with Cuba and the Eastern bloc. Obviously the latter course placed Trujillo's interests above those of the United States and was therefore fraught with danger. But after thirty years of unscrupulous rule the Generalissimo was hardly prepared to step down without a struggle.

A plot to overthrow Castro in August, 1959, financed by Trujillo, attempted to foster an internal uprising backed by a foreign invasion (from Florida and the Dominican Republic). But the Eisenhower Administration was not yet prepared to back such drastic moves and the CIA hampered the invasion operations. When the Cuban-based conspirators double-crossed Trujillo's agents the plot failed miserably. Without Castro's removal relations continued to deteriorate: "The Department of State increasingly viewed the Dominican tyrant as an embarrassment, an awkward inheritance from an earlier time, now lingering too long imperiling the future and unwittingly preparing the way for Castroism."[13] Increased U.S. reliance on Dominican sugar imports strengthened the push to stabilize the situation by removing Trujillo. Diplomat-businessman William Pawley, along with his close friend Senator George Smathers (D.-Fla.), visited El Jefe to plead for his abdication in order to facilitate a smooth transition toward democracy. Trujillo refused to comply, military assistance and arm shipments were terminated, and Ambassador Joseph S. Farland contacted the growing internal underground before the United States vacated his diplomatic post in May, 1960.

By this time Trujillo had already moved to offset his increasing isolation through an informal alliance with Cuba and the Eastern bloc. "The two Caribbean outcasts agreed to stop fighting each other and to concentrate on their other problems."[14]

The Communist Party was legalized and only Russian disinterest prevented the establishment of close political relations with the socialist countries. The disestablishment of the Catholic Church and the expropriation of all U.S.-owned property were urged in public. But in contrast to these anti-U.S. moves, Trujillo desperately tried to protect the country's much-valued sugar quota from OAS-inspired sanctions. His lobbyists and diplomatic representatives went to work in and outside the government on the close-knit sugar community. Lawrence Myers, head of the Agriculture Department's sugar office, Thomas Murphy, deputy to Myers, and William Case, an official in the sugar office, were secretly contacted. The lobbyists convinced Representative Harold Cooley (D.-N.C.), powerful Chairman of the House Agriculture Committee, to block legislative moves by the Eisenhower Administration to suspend the quota. When Congress adjourned without final action, executive power prevailed through an order imposing a special

13. *Ibid.*, p. 421.
14. *Ibid.*, p. 424.

tax on Dominican sugar, thereby abolishing windfall quota profits. Kennedy's rise to power gave Trujillo's lobbyists a new chance to alter U.S. policy. State Department consultant and sugar company executive Adolf A. Berle, Jr., and Under Secretary of State Chester Bowles were reached in an effort to have the special sugar tax lifted. Moreover, a special lobbyist (Igor Cassini) convinced Joseph Kennedy that a revolutionary situation was developing and that it would be helpful to send a special envoy to Ciudad Trujillo to assess matters. The State Department's top troubleshooter, Robert Murphy, paid an informal visit and again sought a liberalization of the regime. It was clear to the Kennedy Administration that support among the Latin Americans for anti-Castro activities (including the Bay of Pigs) rested in part on anti-Trujillo moves. Without a power base in the executive branch of the United States Government the Dominican dictator was helpless to determine his own fate.

The failure of the Murphy mission set in motion the final stages of a CIA-supported plot to assassinate Trujillo. Chiefly organized by some of his own military officers, the assassination was successfully carried out on May 31, 1961. As an obstacle to, rather than an instrument for, domination, the Great Benefactor had to be removed.

Domination Through Stabilization: 1961-1963

With Trujillo's disposal the Kennedy Administration had to choose between maintaining order through support for the remaining repressive apparatus and hated Trujillo cronies or gambling on democracy and social change by favoring the anti-Trujillo forces. U.S. priorities were clearly spelled out by the President in a Cabinet session soon after Trujillo's death.

> There are three possibilities in descending order of preference: decent democratic order, a continuation of the Trujillo regime or a Castro regime. We ought to aim for the first, but we really can't renounce the second until we are sure that one can avoid the third.[15]

In effect, Washington simultaneously attempted to maintain stability and order while encouraging democratization and minor social change. In classical fashion the New Frontiersmen submerged Dominican interests under North American needs. For six months the United States hesitated to dismantle the old structures now administered by Tru-

15. Arthur M. Schlesinger, Jr., *A Thousand Days: John Kennedy in the White House,* Boston, 1965, p. 769.

jillo's last figurehead president, Joaquin Balaguer, but really in the hands of Trujillo's remaining relatives, military officers, business associates, and gangsters. The island was wracked by bloody repressions and severe unemployment, while the United States encouraged Balaguer to "liberalize" and "democratize" his regime. Conservative and left opposition against Trujilloism without Trujillo sought continued suspension of the U.S. sugar quota to restrain the regime's excesses. Kennedy, realizing this was his most powerful weapon, had to postpone moving against the Trujillistas until the U.S. military, the CIA and its cooperating organizations could penetrate the country's shattered infrastructure, create a conservative alternative regime, and thereby control events. By the end of 1961 a conspiracy of Dominican generals was combined with a show of U.S. naval power offshore near Santo Domingo to force the last of the Trujillo family to leave the island.

The first real political organization after Trujillo's assassination sprang up within the oligarchy, petty bourgeois and professional classes who formed an anti-Trujillo civic-minded association which later became the Unión Cívica Nacional (UCN) political party. In order to gain a base among the youth and intellectuals, the UCN entered into an unholy alliance with the strongly nationalist 14th of June Movement (IJ4). This alliance, however, was quickly sacrificed in January, 1962, for control of the U.S.-backed interim Consejo de Estado (Council of State) government which was charged with maintaining stability and holding elections the following December. The United States demonstrated its strong backing of the council by lifting economic sanctions, restoring military assistance, extending $25 million in emergency credit, and authorizing the purchase of additional sugar under the premium quota price.

The ending of sanctions and the reestablishment of a Dominican sugar quota was undoubtedly crucial. The cane sugar industry is the largest industrial operation on the island and the leading contributor to the government income in the form of taxes, foreign exchange, and employment. Privately South Puerto Rico Sugar's La Romana produces one-third of the cane output, while the former Trujillo holdings, taken over by the Consejo, produce a little less than the remaining two-thirds. In 1962 over 90 percent of Dominican cane went to American ports, and under a newly enacted sugar quota act, both South Puerto Rico Sugar and the interim government retained influential lobbyists to jack up quotas even further.

A fundamental question confronting the Consejo and subsequent governments revolved around the fate of the confiscated Trujillo properties. These represented approximately 65 percent of Dominican industry in fifty-seven different product sectors, 35 percent of the arable land, and 30 percent of the animal husbandry. It was an open secret that the UCN hoped to distribute the holdings to favored private interests if they won the upcoming elections.

During the 1962 electoral campaign the Partido Revolucionario Dominicano (PRD), headed by twenty-five-year exile Juan Bosch, presented a platform advocating distribution of Trujillo land to landless campesinos, formation of cooperatives, an increase in agricultural wages, construction of small town communal eating halls, public works, and development of new industry around untapped mineral resources to reduce unemployment. The general object was to diversify agriculture and to create a consumer economy.

Despite repeated setbacks and unforeseen complications the holding of elections was guaranteed by the frantic but thorough manipulations of U.S. ambassador John Martin, a man with strong ties to the ADA (Americans for Democratic Action) liberals in the United States. For example, at one crucial juncture, Martin wrote:

> Then I called the senior Embassy staff and Williams together, told them what I was doing and told them we must slow down the Dominican reaction before it got completely out of control. We must immediately talk to all important Dominicans—explain the situation, urge everyone to await developments, and reaffirm our determination not to abandon the Republic. We divided up the people we could see—Consejeros, political party leaders, government, sugar men.[16]

Domination Through Infiltration: The Bosch Government

The defeat at the hands of Bosch's social democratic PRD, which received 60 percent of the December, 1962, vote, caught the UCN and its conservative backers by surprise. But Bosch, a self-educated intellectual from humble origins, knew his government would not last long; thirty hours before the polls opened he told a television audience:

> I do not wish to be a candidate because I know the PRD will win the elections and if it does, the government . . . will be overthrown in a short time on the pretext that it is Communist.[17]

As a skeptical business community looked on, Bosch negotiated a

16. Martin, *Overtaken by Events,* p. 164.
17. Juan Bosch, *The Unfinished Experiment: Democracy in the Dominican Republic,* New York, 1965, p. 123.

$150 million line of credit with a Zurich-based consortium to finance his larger development projects, a departure from the usual U.S. sources. Next he cancelled an oil refinery contract, which Esso, Texaco, and Shell had negotiated with Trujillo and the Consejo, because of the large profits which would leave the country.

Despite these initiatives toward financial independence, Bosch found it necessary to seek United States aid. The Kennedy Administration hoped to make the Dominican Republic a "showcase of democracy" as a counterweight to Cuba. Nevertheless, Bosch found U.S. financial backing hard to obtain. Former businessman Newell Williams, AID director for the Republic, commented: "Ever since Bosch has been in, we've been turned down." Later, toward the end of Bosch's first one hundred days in office, Ambassador Martin noted, "We had committed something over $50 million to last year's Consejo but not a cent for Bosch."

Several aspects of his administration alarmed native and United States investors. An effort was made to rescind several sugar contracts negotiated by the Consejo. While advantageous for U.S. sugar purchasers, these contracts meant a loss of several million dollars in foreign exchange for the Dominican Republic. Former Ambassador Martin wrote:

> The Department [State Department] instructed me to inform the Dominican Government that its failure to honor legitimate contracts with U.S. sugar firms would certainly have most serious repercussions for the Bosch government and might even lead to an invocation of the Hickenlooper amendment which would end AID to the Republic.[18]

Within a week of Bosch's inauguration, *Business Week* attacked him for proposing a "revolutionary constitution" and land reform "which would prohibit operations of U.S.-owned sugar companies. An official of La Romana expressed the fear that Bosch's government might make the Puerto Rican "mistake" of subdividing the cane lands. "To break up the Company's lands would wreck Romana." Concern over constitutional provisions about business operations was a constant theme in discussions between U.S. representatives and all Dominican governments. Much later during the U.S. invasion and occupation of the Republic in 1965, U.S. negotiators demanded that the "rebels," who were fighting for a reinstatement of the 1963 Constitution, modify several of its articles. They were especially troubled by Article 19, giving workers

18. Martin, *Overtaken by Events*, p. 355.

the right to profit sharing in both agricultural and industrial enterprises; Article 23, prohibiting large landholdings; Article 25, restricting the right of foreigners to acquire Dominican land; Article 28, requiring landholders to sell that portion of their lands above a maximum fixed by law, excess holdings to be distributed to the landless peasantry; and Article 66, prohibiting expulsion of Dominicans from their own country. American negotiators in 1965 proposed an amendment to exempt owners of sugar plantations and cattle ranches, the largest of these being South Puerto Rico Sugar's La Romana.

The Constitution also upset the Roman Catholic Church, especially for its articles legitimizing divorce, secularizing education, declaring juridical equality of legitimate and natural-born citizens, and for failing to mention the 1954 Concordat with the Vatican. Papal Nuncio Emanuele Clarizio and Msgr. Thomas Reilly (a U.S. citizen working in the country under the authority of the Vatican) both visited Bosch, seeking constitutional changes. When the Constitution was promulgated without changes, the Church declined to send a representative to the official ceremony.

In short time, inflated anti-Communism flourished and began to undermine Bosch's legitimacy. Even civil-libertarian Ambassador Martin kept constant pressure on Bosch with advice like the following:

> I recommended Bosch couple any changes with other measures—repeal of the old de-Trujilloization law and enactment of a law providing for the trial of military personnel by military tribunals. . . . I recommended that Congress adopt a resolution declaring it the sense of the Congress that communism was incompatible with the Inter-American system . . . and that it enact a Dominican version of the Smith act. . . . I recommended he hold back on agrarian reform if it entailed confiscation laws.[19]

In practical terms, Martin's anti-Communism reinforced the irrational charges of Dominican rightists which further undermined Bosch's government. A favorite target of right-wing generals was the Inter-American Center for Social Studies (CIDES). Run by a Rumanian-born naturalized American, Sacha Volman, CIDES received its funds and direction from the American-based Institute of International Labor Research (IILR). The IILR in turn was headed by U.S. social democratic leader Norman Thomas and its secretary-treasurer was Volman. All but a fraction of IILR's budget came from the J. M. Kaplan Fund, which was exposed in 1964 by Congressman Wright Patman as a con-

19. *Ibid.*, p. 487.

duit for Central Intelligence Agency funds. Immediately after the armed forces overthrew Bosch, CIDES was sacked and closed while Volman fled the country. Ironically, the military was, in effect, charging a CIA operation was riddled with Communists and Communist sympathizers, though it is now clear CIDES' covert purpose was to assure strong U.S. influence in the PRD and Bosch's government.

Earlier this same Institute of International Labor Research played a crucial role in Dominican politics. At the time of Trujillo's assassination (May, 1961), Juan Bosch was teaching at the Costa Rican Institute of Political Education which Sacha Volman set up in 1959 with CIA funds channeled through the J. M. Kaplan Fund and the IILR. Immediately after Trujillo's assassination Volman was the first man Bosch sent to the Republic to survey the political situation and recommend strategy for the PRD. During 1962 he proceeded to organize a 300,000-member peasant league (FENHERCA), which played a key role in providing Bosch's PRD with the critical countryside vote in the election (approximately 70 percent of the Dominicans live in rural areas). But once the votes were in Volman abandoned FENHERCA and one of the PRD's strongest bases of organized support deteriorated.

With Bosch in office, Volman reoriented his energies and resources into organizing CIDES, a planning-research center for the government and a training institute of young political organizers and administrators. CIDES was to provide most of the state planning as well as the crucial technical and professional talent for running the government and the infrastructure of the PRD. The Kaplan Fund contributed $35,-000 which was supplemented by grants from several other U.S. foundations and government agencies. A $250,000 grant from the Ford Foundation (administered by Brandeis University and ADA leader John P. Roche) paralleled CIDES' work within the government civil service administration. Along with other similar programs, the U.S. Government was thus able to penetrate and manipulate the social democrats (PRD) in the Dominican Republic as well as the government they formed.

As it turned out, the involvement of J. M. Kaplan in the IILR and its Dominican offshoots (FENHERCA and CIDES) was not a fortuitous occurrence. This Caribbean sugar and molasses speculator had arranged a monopoly of Dominican molasses sales during the latter years of the Trujillo era. Introduced to Bosch by Norman Thomas, Kaplan became the Dominican president's personal emissary to business and political circles in New York and Washington. In reality, Kaplan's interest in Bosch's government, both in terms of channeling CIA funds to Volman's operations and maintaining a favorable image for Bosch among his powerful U.S. friends, was directly related to his sugar and molasses operations and associations. One month before Bosch was overthrown Kaplan suddenly decided that his administration was infiltrated with Communists and he withdrew his influential support. This vital break signaled the collapse of Bosch's power base in the United States.

But the Kennedy Administration never placed all its bets on infiltrating and controlling the social democratic PRD in order to guarantee U.S. domination. In what amounted to a schizophrenic policy, the Kennedy Administration, while supporting Bosch, simultaneously trained and equipped the antireformist forces that eventually brought down his regime—the armed forces and the police.

> . . . the United States-trained police joined the Army in ousting President Bosch, following which both the police and the antiguerrilla units, trained during 1963 by a forty-four-man United States Army Mission, were used to hunt down Bosch's non-Communist partisans in the name of anti-Communism.[20]

Bosch never directly confronted the graft-ridden and top-heavy military with its large officer corps and oversize portion of the national budget: "Had I ever made even a single change in the military command, my government would have lasted only weeks, perhaps only days." Nevertheless, the military chafed under several aspects of his administration, especially the abrogation of a special military privilege —the right of trial solely by military tribunals. And, in his last days in office, Bosch fought the purchase of six British warplanes which included a 20 percent kickback for top air force officers.

Although Bosch did curtail military graft, the primary reason the armed forces turned against him was more complex, and behind it lies the specter of Cuba. Batista and his officers' first stop after fleeing Castro's revolutionary militia was San Isidro Air Force base on the outskirts of Ciudad Trujillo.

> The issue that united all those military officers who opposed Bosch for various reasons was the alleged growing Communist influences in his government. For the officers, Communism was neither an ideological, economic, or imperialistic system but only meant as they recalled the case of

20. Edwin Lieuwen, *Generals vs. Presidents: Neomilitarism in Latin America*, New York, 1964, p. 127.

the Cuban revolution, destruction of the armed forces and death to the officers; and rumors that Bosch's Party was arming a militia seemed to give credence to their fears.[21]

The Dominican officers were not used to acting alone, however. Judging from accounts like the following, they were given the go-ahead to overthrow Bosch by their U.S. advisers:

Cass [Bevan Cass] was having problems of conscience about Bosch. As our naval attaché, he was obliged to urge Dominican officers to support Bosch, but he himself had misgivings about Bosch's attitude toward the Castro Communists . . . and didn't know "how much longer I can go on supporting him like this" . . . he was probably our most influential attaché.[22]

Led by the air force tank commander, Elías Wessin y Wessin, and Trujillo assassin Antonio Imbert Barrera, the armed forces deposed Bosch on September 25, 1963.

The cross-purpose policy of backing both the right and left went even deeper. The AFL-CIO Latin American trade union federation, ORIT, split the PRD-oriented labor movement with the formation of CONATRAL, a pro-U.S., parallel confederation of Dominican unions organized along the anti-political Sam Gompers line. Aiding in the training of anti-Bosch unionists was the American Institute for Free Labor Development (AIFLD), a bizarre hybrid of AFL-CIO, big business, and U.S. Government interests. Not surprisingly, CONATRAL exhorted the Dominicans one week before the coup, through a one-page newspaper advertisement, to put their faith in the armed forces to defend them against Communism. Shortly after the coup most other labor leaders were in jail, hiding or had sought asylum.

Ambassador Martin, never overwhelmingly enthusiastic about Bosch, nevertheless sought the State Department's view on the utilization of American warships for reinstating Bosch. The Department refused to intervene unless a "Communist take-over" was imminent. Bosch's downfall was the final blow to the Kennedy hope for peaceful social reform in Latin America. The extremely weak power base in the United States advocating such a program—certain intellectuals, social democrats, some of Kennedy's advisers and a section of the CIA—was no match for threatened business interests, generals, and liberals who put anti-

21. H. J. Wiarda, "The Politics of Civil Military Relations in the Dominican Republic," in *Journal of Inter-American Studies,* Vol. II, No. 4, 1965, pp. 465-84.
22. Martin, *Overtaken by Events,* pp. 504-5.

Communism ahead of social change. It should be remembered that Caribbean policy in the early sixties was dominated by a preoccupation with Cuba and the incipient spread of Fidel Castro's revolution. For businessmen, journalists, and State Department officials, the legitimacy of Bosch's administration rested on its ability to contain, through whatever means necessary, the small Castroite left (primarily the nationalistic 14th of June Movement). As mentioned above, Martin went so far as to strongly recommend the enactment of a Dominican Smith Act. Bosch refused. And for the influential power base in the United States concerned with Cuba, this ruled out large-scale support, and therefore survival.

La Romana, already in economic difficulty, was worried about extended strikes, land confiscation, and the disappearance of their cheap labor supply. Exporters, shipping lines, and dock workers feared a loss of business. East Coast sugar refiners and their industrial customers realized an occlusion of their precious commodity from the one large remaining Carribbean source would trigger wild gyrations in sensitive sugar prices. For an industry still shaky from an earlier Caribbean storm, the mere prospect of "another Cuba"—with the attendant loss of an ample supply of cane at stable prices—was too much to bear. Moreover, a crucial development within the sugar industry strengthened the hand of anti-Bosch *golpista* forces. A shortage created by Cuban developments temporarily drove the price of world sugar far above the subsidized U.S. quota rate. This guaranteed the Dominican sugar interests a profitable outlet for their commodity in the event of reprisals by the Kennedy Administration. In effect, the Dominican right was gambling on the traditional U.S. willingness to recognize any reactionary government after a decent period of mourning for a departed constitutional order. Bosch was never prepared to deal effectively with a right-wing coup. The early deterioration of Bosch's peasant support organized by CIA-backed Sacha Volman through FEN HERCA cut him off from the countryside. Mishandling of his labor support, combined with splitting of the labor confederations by U.S.-trained organizers, deprived Bosch of his most effective weapon against a right-wing coup—a mass-based movement which at any time could be armed to counteract the military. With the cooperation of some reform-minded disgruntled young officers this might have been possible, but Bosch refused to condone the use of violence. What could have been his strongest base of support, an organized labor and peasantry, had been infiltrated and manipulated by the United States.

Domination Through Manipulation: The Triumvirate

Kennedy, seeing the golpe as a heavy blow to the Alianza, refused to recognize the new regime and suspended aid; but Kennedy was assassinated. In an effort to gain U.S. diplomatic recognition and economic aid a new government, the so-called Triumvirate, dramatically announced it was threatened by an incipient guerrilla movement aided by Fidel Castro. Actually, some June 14th Movement leaders took to the hills shortly after Bosch's downfall, but the arms they acquired were apparently obtained through a CIA agent (Camilo Todemann) and proved useless. When the guerrillas surrendered, they were mercilessly tortured and executed. The plot produced the desired effect, for one of President Johnson's first foreign policy shifts was to recognize the regimes in the Dominican Republic and Honduras. On the same day (December 14, 1963), Thomas Mann was appointed Assistant Secretary of State for Inter-American Affairs. The subsequent Dominican government was headed by Donald Reid Cabral, former auto dealer, close friend of U.S. business and member of the oligarchy. Realizing his power rested with the military, Reid turned his back on the officers' contraband and smuggling operations, thereby winning their tacit support.

The Reid government put an end to economic and social development. With the shelving of the 1963 Constitution, the Bosch reform legislation, and the Zurich consortium credit, large numbers of United States businessmen turned again to the Dominican Republic. George Walker (of the Mellons' Koppers Company), a close Reid friend, had made a visit to the Dominican Republic during the Consejo period (Reid was one of the seven Consejo members) on behalf of the Businessmen's Council on International Understanding. Walker "had brought in high-level U.S. industrialists to study the former Trujillo properties and advise the Consejo what to do with them." It was from these operations that Bosch had hoped to partially finance his social reforms. But Walker recommended gradually selling or leasing the properties to private investors.

The Midland Cooperatives of Minneapolis, Minnesota, landed an oil refinery contract. Falconbridge Nickel Mines, a Canadian-American concern, announced plans to build a $78-million refinery. The Inter-American Development Bank and the AFL-CIO launched a joint housing project. The World Bank gave $1.7 million for a hydroelectric study, replacing the one Bosch intended to finance with European capital.

And there was more. At the same time, plagued by plunging world sugar prices, Reid continued Bosch's austerity program and received International Monetary Fund (IMF) and AID credit and loans as well as a $30-million loan from six U.S. commercial banks.

During the Bosch regime the 18,000 workers at South Puerto Rico's La Romana had won a 30 percent increase in their meager wages. Under Reid, that contract was broken and in February, 1965, one much more favorable to the company was negotiated with a parallel or "ghost" union set up by La Romana. Since low wages are crucial for profits in this marginal industry requiring surplus labor, the company greatly benefited from Reid's antilabor policy. Reid had previously declared a state of siege in Santo Domingo to offset a general strike called by the Sindicato Independiente de Choferes. By spring of 1965 the country was $200 million in debt; there were rumors of a Reid campaign to sell the former Trujillo properties, now in the hands of the state, to private investors; the armed forces were carrying on increasingly flagrant and publicly known contraband operations; and Santo Domingo itself was facing a serious water shortage—Reid had discontinued the renovation and expansion of the city's water system initiated by Bosch. One other persistent rumor was that Reid was planning to rig the promised elections to insure his victory. More than one commentator was led to observe that only U.S. support kept Reid in power.

Meanwhile, in exile, Bosch and leaders of the Revolutionary Social Christian Party (PRSC) agreed on the Pact of Río Piedras, a plan to cooperate in overthrowing Reid and restoring the 1963 Constitution. In a more secret move, Bosch also reached a similar but more tenuous agreement with the ex-Trujillo servant and conservative, Joaquín Balaguer. Both agreements involved utilization of disparate military factions in the projected overthrow of Reid Cabral. Many of the conservative senior officers were riding high on corruption involving import rackets. The younger and lower-echelon officers were easily approachable by the various anti-Reid factions who also feared cancellation or manipulation of the promised elections. These clandestine accords, combined with deteriorating economic and social conditions in the country, especially in Santo Domingo (unemployment was as high as 40 percent), precipitated the coup in April, 1965. It is quite possible that in the early hours of the uprising as many as three or more separate military factions were vying for power: one faction supporting Bosch, another Balaguer, and one right-wing faction supporting Wessin y Wessin. And it was at this point, when the military split and broke into internecine combat, that the Dominican crisis made international headlines.

Domination Through Intervention and Occupation

Within three days the constitutionalist forces routed Wessin y Wessin's troops while the other military faction wavered. Obviously the crucial question was whom the United States would back. There is no doubt that the PRD leadership was counting on rather automatic U.S. support for the return of the legally elected Bosch government. It seems they were convinced of U.S. democratic intentions. At the point when the constitutionalists were in control of Santo Domingo—April 27—the United States could have prevented bloodshed and chaos, furthered the development of social reform and destroyed the anti-reformist military forces by supporting exiled Juan Bosch. It was simply a matter of permitting Bosch to reenter the country to take command of the constitutionalist forces. On several occasions Johnson confidant Abe Fortas and ex-Ambassador Martin visited Bosch in San Juan, Puerto Rico, making it clear that Washington would not support his return to Santo Domingo. The FBI and CIA kept him under constant surveillance and thwarted his various overt and covert attempts to return.

Public statements not withstanding, the Johnson Administration decided on April 24 that it would send in the Marines if the rebels gained the upper hand. A massive buildup of troops and equipment was set in motion. When the United States made it apparent, through Ambassador William Tapley Bennett, Jr., that it was going to back the Wessin forces and that the rebels would have to fight or surrender, the PRD civilian leadership passed to the rebel military commanders, who by this time had armed and organized a sizable proportion of the civilian population within Santo Domingo.

On April 28, when it became clear that Wessin's forces had been routed, the Marines landed, ostensibly to evacuate Americans, but in reality to bolster the military and lay the groundwork for U.S. occupation. This whole process was portrayed as a response to a rump military junta set up by U.S. military attachés and led by Wessin's ally Colonel Bartolomé Benoit. The Marines quickly solidified the fractionalized military forces; wavering elements realized the rebels were doomed in the face of U.S. firepower. The so-called "neutral" landing force quickly equipped the junta units with badly needed radios, food, weapons, medical supplies, and logistic support. Surrounding Santo

U.S. Marines interrogating a Dominican citizen, summer 1965. (Charles Harbutt, Magnum)

Domingo, they succeeded in containing and eventually splitting the rebel forces.

In effect, the rebel movement's power base passed from the political leadership to the barrel of a gun. For the first time in recent Dominican history Santo Domingo was in control of Dominicans completely independent of the United States. Without PRD leadership, with its links to the United States, particularly to the social democratic liberal community, violence and destruction on a massive scale were inevitable. The rebels' independence became most apparent to the American embassy staff when the constitutionalist forces twice approached the Georgia plantation Ambassador William Tapley Bennett, Jr., for the negotiation of a cease-fire. Bennett agreed to talk only if the rebels gave up their arms (i.e. surrendered). And after they refused, his response was obvious scorn and the threat of annihilation. When confronted with an independent political force the United States' response was military violence.

The effects of the rebels' independence and consequent power were tellingly demonstrated when the United States threatened to destroy the constitutionalists by a full-scale attack, including bombing, on the rebel-held sector of downtown Santo Domingo. This attack was deterred, partly because the rebels threatened to set off explosives in the banks (including Chase Manhattan and First National City), the headquarters and offices of many U.S. businesses operating in the Republic, the electric plant and the telecommunications center, all of which were within the rebel-held sector. The United States backed off and thereby demonstrated some of its true interests.

The stated reasons for American military intervention are still veiled in confusion, primarily because many of the official documents have never been made public and the political figures who formulated and executed the policy are still in power. In President Johnson's first public statement on April 28, 1965, the United States intervened to "give protection to hundreds of Americans who [were] still in the Dominican Republic and to escort them safely back to this country." The President's statement was based on embassy and press cables which exaggerated the constitutionalist threat to American lives. Dispatches described firing squads holding terrorized American tourists at gunpoint in the Embajador Hotel. Moreover, the heads of assassinated victims were supposedly paraded through the streets of downtown Santo Domingo. In reality, from the outbreak of the rebellion not one American civilian was killed by accident or on purpose by constitutionalists.

By April 30, President Johnson, after reiterating the purported threat to American lives, hinted at another justification for intervention:

> . . . there are signs that people trained outside the Dominican Republic are seeking to gain control. Thus the legitimate aspirations of the Dominican people and most of their leaders for progress, democracy, and social justice are threatened and so are the principles of the inter-American system.[23]

By May 2, however, President Johnson clarified the above:

> The evidence that we have on the revolutionary movement indicates that it took a very tragic turn. Many of them trained in Cuba, seeing a chance to increase disorder and to gain a foothold, joined the revolution. They took increasing control. What began as a popular democratic revolution that was committed to democracy and social justice moved into the hands of a band of Communist conspirators. . . . Our goal, in keeping with the great principles of the inter-American system, is to help prevent another Communist state in the hemisphere.[24]

The charges of Communist infiltration and control have been refuted by liberal journalists who were on the scene, liberal Senators such as J. William Fulbright, noted resident researcher at Stanford University's Hoover Institute, Theodore Draper, and Juan Bosch himself. While agreeing that Communist conspiracies are a real danger to democratic revolutions, they proceed to question the strategic influence of the small and fractionalized Dominican Communist parties. Given such criteria one could delegitimize any revolution threatening U.S. interests by uncovering a handful of Communists. Undoubtedly Communists are present in every Third World conflict today; but, from a radical perspective, there is no reason to assume Communists cannot also be bona fide nationalists. The supposition that a Communist Party member will place the interests of an international Communist conspiracy above those of a nationalist revolution cannot be substantiated from a historical or practical point of view. It should be noted that the international Communist conspiracy within the rebel movement never appealed for Cuban, Soviet, Chinese, or any other Communist aid, even while under severe duress.

What, then, were the real motives and circumstances of the U.S. intervention? American liberals and social democratics, including Tad

23. "Statement by President Johnson, April 30, 1965," Committee on Foreign Relations, p. 54.
24. "Statement by President Johnson, May 2, 1965," Committee on Foreign Relations, pp. 56-57.

Szulc, Dan Kurzman, J. William Fulbright, and Theodore Draper all agree that the troops intervened to bolster the flagging junta forces. But they fail to offer any comprehensive explanation of why the United States opposed a return to a democratic order under the constitutionalists. In their opinion, faulty information about the rebel forces was supplied and evaluated by competent policy makers who were overly preoccupied with Cuba and anti-Communism. After meticulously refuting the Administration's "cover stories" Draper awkwardly concludes: "We .still do not know what was behind the anti-Bosch campaign." The key to this perplexing question lies in an analysis of why the United States supported the right-wing junta forces. Johnson and his advisers knew from past experience they could control the military and thus guarantee U.S. domination; however, the constitutionalists, with their independent, armed civilian cadres, presented a more formidable obstacle to manipulation.

The liberals offered no comprehensive explanation for U.S. intervention because they were hopelessly confused about the priorities and objectives of U.S. policy. They assumed the primary goal was to promote democracy and social welfare, and the intervention, with its support of the right-wing military, became a paradox. But if one assumes the most important U.S. foreign policy objective is maintaining control and domination over Dominican development, the intervention and occupation becomes quite logical. Johnson and his advisers knew from past experience they could penetrate, manipulate, and control the military, thus guaranteeing U.S. domination and its consequent benefits; the constitutionalists, however, lacked a formal structure to penetrate and were willing to employ illegal and violent means which frustrate manipulation. Given the objective of domination, President Johnson had little choice about which side to support.

The forces determining U.S. priorities and objectives in the Dominican Republic were rooted in powerful American economic interests and domestic political considerations. The U.S. corporations with a direct and indirect stake in the outcome of Dominican events had ready access to U.S. Administration officials, and when the April, 1965, rebellion broke out they most likely expressed their deep concern. A considerable number of individuals with financial, legal and social connections to the East Coast sugar complex were well stationed throughout the upper echelons of the U.S. Government. For example, prominent New Dealer and Johnson confidant Abe Fortas was a twenty-year director of the Sucrest Corporation, the third largest East

Coast cane refiner. State Department expert and adviser to several presidents on Latin America (including Kennedy and Johnson) Adolf A. Berle, Jr., was postwar Board Chairman of Sucrest as well as a large stockholder. OAS Ambassador and special envoy to the Dominican Republic Ellsworth Bunker was past Chairman, President, and thirty-eight-year director of the second largest East Coast cane refiner, the National Sugar Refining Co.; roving Ambassador W. Averell Harriman (sent to Latin America by Johnson to explain the Dominican intervention) is a limited partner in the New York banking house of Brown Brothers, Harriman, which owns approximately 5 percent of National Sugar's stock. Molasses magnate J. M. Kaplan is a heavy contributor and influential adviser to many Democratic Party candidates and the ADA. State Department consultant and ex-U.S. Ambassador to the Dominican Republic (1957-1960) and Panama (1960-63) Joseph S. Farland has been a director of South Puerto Rico Sugar Co. since 1964. Former Deputy Secretary of Defense Roswell Gilpatric is the managing executive partner of Cravath, Swaine and Moore, the Wall Street legal counsel for National Sugar. Wall Street lawyer Max Rabb, in the firm of Stroock, Stroock and Lavan (legal counsel for Sucrest), was a member of the National Committee for Johnson and Humphrey.

The whole East Coast sugar industry, which is dominated by National Sugar, Sucrest, and the largest U.S. refiner, American Sugar Co., is directly dependent on sizable Dominican sugar and molasses imports. Any disruption in supply, as happened after the Cuban Revolution, would threaten price stability and earnings in this narrow margin of profit industry. The ability of these as well as many other corporations to either place people directly in the government or have access to important government officials was and is a major factor shaping the priorities and objectives of American foreign policy vis-à-vis the Dominican Republic. Even without direct economic interests it would be difficult, if not impossible, for these gentlemen to resist or escape the assumptions and inclinations inculcated by their economic and social milieu.

The domestic political considerations operating in favor of intervention were even more subtle than the economic forces at work. Any foreign country (especially in the Third World) which attempts to become truly independent by freeing itself of American economic, military, and political manipulation and control is easily branded in the U.S. public media as Communist. The financial and military interests affected by such a move have direct access to the mass media and other organizations shaping public opinion. This could be used as leverage against those political officials responsible for protecting their interests. No domestic political figure can afford to risk the charge of being soft on "communism" which, for all practical purposes, means losing control over actual or potential (1) investments and trade opportunities returning high profits, (2) markets for goods and services, (3) sources of cheap labor, (4) sources of cheap or strategic raw materials, (5) military strategic bases, and (6) influence and votes in international regional organizations. Particularly after the Cuban Revolution any U.S. President would be vulnerable, and therefore sensitive to, a situation like that confronting President Johnson in April, 1965. The decision which had to be made was painfully clear. Rather than risk failure by backing a nationalist government promoting democracy and social reform, Johnson intervened militarily to insure U.S. control and head off any domestic political threat from U.S. financial and military interests. In short, domestic political interest again took priority over Dominican democracy and independence.

With the U.S. occupation, domination and control in the Dominican Republic became, for all practical purposes, absolute. Military operations involving over 30,000 U.S. troops were coordinated out of the office of General Bruce Palmer and not by the Brazilian Inter-American Peace Force Commander-in-Chief. The Assistant Secretary of State for Economic Affairs, Anthony M. Solomon, went to the Republic to coordinate the work of more than sixty U.S. officials "acting for all practical purposes as the civilian government in the Dominican Republic." The U.S. Special Forces' "Operation Green Chopper" flew units throughout the country to inquire about the political views of the citizens at large, to distribute food, and to promise public works.

Once Santo Domingo was militarily secure, the Johnson Administration moved to reestablish control through economic, political, and social manipulation. Rejecting an original plan of establishing a provisional government with the former Bosch minister of agriculture, Silvestre Antonio Guzmán, as head (the "Bundy formula"), the Johnson Administration finally settled on a plan similar to one described by Tad Szulc of the New York Times:

> In Washington highly authoritative officials told me that the Administration favored a plan for Dominican elections within six to nine months. The authorship of this idea was ascribed to Assistant Secretary [of State for Inter-American Affairs, Jack Hood] Vaughn, with the explanation that

the State Department was hoping for a victory at the polls by Joaquín Balaguer. . . .[25]

The State Department had been in touch with Balaguer, in exile in New York, through Washington lobbyist I. Irving Davidson. Davidson represented at one time or another Ecuadorean sugar interests, Israel military interests, the Somoza and Duvalier dictatorships, and served as intermediary for Texas oil magnate Clint Murchison in an illegal Haitian meat packing deal involving Bobby Baker.

To further extend its political control, the United States forced out the military junta headed by Imbert, cutting off U.S. funds which were supplying the government payroll. By September, 1965, U.S. negotiators were able to put together a provisional government headed by Hector García Godoy, formerly Bosch's foreign minister and subsequently vice-president of Balaguer's Partido Reformista. The U.S. objective for this administration was to maintain stability and hold elections which would further legitimate a U.S.-backed government. In effect, Washington was creating a pro-U.S. political atmosphere and party within the country. Aiding mightily in this task was an OAS mission headed by Ellsworth Bunker, and U.S. gifts and low-interest loans amounting to over $100 million.

Bosch returned from exile in September, 1965, and under strong domestic and foreign pressure, agreed to run in the upcoming elections. Well-known social democratic and liberal Bosch sympathizers Norman Thomas and Victor Reuther argued that only through elections and the subsequent establishment of stable democratic government would the occupation troops leave the island. Obviously, no meaningful election could be held without the participation of the PRD and their candidate Juan Bosch. Thomas, Reuther, civil rights leader Bayard Rustin, lawyer and New York Reform Democrat Allard Lowenstein, Sacha Volman, and others organized the Committee on Free Elections in the Dominican Republic. They told Bosch they would send a team of "independent unofficial observers" (eventually seventy) to oversee the elections, and through their presence, help moderate possible fraud and coercion. Unbeknownst to Bosch and all but one or two of the committee observers, Allard Lowenstein held several private talks with U.S. officials in Santo Domingo and on the eve of the elections made a secret agreement with Ambassador Ellsworth Bunker. If Bosch won, Bunker would publicly state U.S. support for his election. And if Balaguer was the victor, Lowenstein promised to use his considerable influence to encourage a public statement of support.

25. Tad Szulc, *Dominican Diary*, New York, 1965, p. 313.

Though nearly blind and over eighty years old, Thomas made a three-day visit to the Republic at election time to lend his prestige as head of the committee. Upon his return to New York immediately after the election, Thomas, accompanied by Lowenstein, made a press statement that was interpreted as a personal endorsement of the election's freedom and fairness. In the eyes of many liberals who had opposed Johnson's intervention policy, the committee's presence and Thomas' statement legitimized the elections. However, the Dominicans who cooperated with the committee (most of whom were Bosch sympathizers) felt betrayed by the premature statement. The committee and most Americans avoided the key question: How can you hold a free election in a country occupied by foreign troops who invaded to prevent one of the two main candidates from assuming the presidency? Even more convinced than in 1962 that he would be overthrown if elected, Bosch first refused to run. After being persuaded otherwise, however, he conducted a campaign aimed at educating the electorate about problems facing any Dominican government. An atmosphere of fear pervaded the country and he never left his heavily guarded Santo Domingo residence to campaign among the peasantry and pro-urban strongholds.

The candidate favored by the United States, the oligarchy, most of the armed forces, the Church and the U.S.-backed Dominican Labor Confederation, CONATRAL, was Joaquín Balaguer. The ex-Trujillo servant won handily amidst charges of fraud, coercion, and political pressure tactics. The much needed peasant backing organized in 1962 for the PRD by CIA-financed Sacha Volman was missing. Apparently, Volman had agreed, in accordance with U.S. State Department wishes, to remain outside the country during the campaign. It was obvious to most Dominicans that the United States was backing Balaguer and that a Bosch victory was unacceptable. Never close to U.S. social democrats and ADA liberals—the Kennedy operatives for controlling the PRD—Johnson literally constructed a new pro-American power base (Balaguer's party and government) that was largely dependent on, and subservient to, United States interests.

Domination Through Stabilization And Infiltration: Balaguer's First Year

Balaguer's election victory in June, 1966, vindicated U.S. intervention and occupation in the eyes of the Johnson Administration and its supporters. A new Constitution was drawn up and most of the U.S. objections to the 1963 document were excluded. Financial and technical resources were quickly brought to the assistance of the new regime. Supplementing generous loans and grants were nearly five hundred Americans serving in official capacities, creating a virtual parallel government. An outfit known as the International Development Foundation, financed and staffed by the Central Intelligence Agency, replaced Volman's operations in the training of anti-Communist peasant leaders. The U.S. sugar quota was substantially raised to bolster revenues. On top of $3 million in military assistance, the Pentagon sent sixty bilingual advisers to train a 3400-man "elite" army brigade in riot control and counter-insurgency. In addition, AID was spending $800,000 on "public safety" (police training). The military received upward of 40 percent of the national budget; approximately 40 percent of the labor force was unemployed.

Satisfied that the situation had been stabilized, United States business flocked to the Republic to make new investments in housing construction, land and tourist development, and agri-business. Strikes were virtually outlawed for one year, the government austerity program (geared to alleviating the foreign debt) frozen, and in some cases it forced reduction of wages. And a program for selling the state-owned properties was instituted. Meanwhile, left political parties were thoroughly infiltrated while the return of many feared ex-Trujillistas into positions of authority brought about a rise in political assassinations and terrorism. Periodically the Dominican press carried reports of sporadic guerrilla warfare in the countryside.

Conclusion

The U.S. intervention and occupation had several far-reaching consequences. Large segments of Dominican society, especially the urban youth, were further alienated from the traditional political leadership with its links to the United States. Anti-Americanism became even more deep seated. As one Dominican author observed, the intervention "fully revealed those who were culpable for our underdevelopment." As a result of the struggle, during the late spring and summer of 1965 a whole new power base was created and two opposing camps were strengthened, reinforced, and polarized to the extent that few observers feel there will be a peaceful reconciliation. The people were armed with as many as 20,000 firearms which they still possess; they saw how their commando units could hold off and even defeat the regular army; the right-wing military elements acquired new equipment and supplies while solidifying their ties to the U.S. Armed Forces.

The more international effects of the intervention were a further weakening of the Organization of American States and the United Nations. Professor W. Friedman of the Columbia University Law School described how the United States did not even pretend to be guided by international law: "It [U.S. intervention] departs from the principle that international law does not permit interference on the ground of an objectionable political ideology." The "joint" military action in the Dominican Republic was the first such "cooperative" venture in the history of the hemisphere and set the precedent for the creation of a permanent Inter-American Peace Force.

In the United States the intervention led more liberals to conclude that Vietnam was not simply a mistake, but rather part of a new approach to foreign relations. The official policy of nonintervention in the internal affairs of Latin American nations which had been proclaimed with varying degrees of credibility since December, 1933, was officially reversed. A less noted though significant effect was the weakening of the Peace Corps' political independence. Frank Mankiewicz, then director of the Corps' Latin American operation (and later Senator Robert Kennedy's press secretary) made a special trip to Santo Domingo to oppose the threatened en masse resignation of a sizable number of volunteers as a protest against U.S. policy.

Juan Bosch once again left the Dominican Republic after the 1966 election, declaring that "there is no democratic exit from the present situation." It became clear that the constant priority of United States foreign policy was the maintenance of control and domination for the unequal benefit of U.S. interests. The mechanisms for achieving this objective varied from brutal suppression to subtle manipulation, with a conscious preference for the latter. Military occupation gives way to U.S.-trained and -financed "national" organizations whose dependency is invisible only to North Americans. Democracy, social progress, and independence are subservient to the primary objective and readily disposable if they jeopardize U.S. authority. What is conspicuously absent from most left-liberal and social democratic interpretations is an analysis of political and economic forces within American society. Interests, associations, and structures, rather than intentions and rhetoric, largely determine the motivational forces that shape foreign policy. While the Kennedy and Johnson administrations employed different mechanisms of domination—political vs. military—their objectives remained the same. Kennedy had strong enough links to the PRD through ADA liberals and social democrats to take a chance with democracy and muted nationalism; he hedged his bets by stepping up military assistance. But Johnson lacked Kennedy's connections and when revolutionary nationalist forces took up arms the ability of the United States to maintain effective control, short of occupation, was undermined.

The fate of peaceful democratic modernization in Peru, Brazil, Ecuador, or the Dominican Republic, pivots on the political, corporate, and military structures of American society. This is what the Cuban revolutionaries profoundly understood and the American people, including liberals from the Church, university, and the professions, have never confronted. Those who define Latin American problems primarily in terms of conditions external to the United States and offer assistance based on this assumption will only perpetuate U.S. domination. Without fundamental change in American society, violent confrontation is inevitable.

ASPECTS OF POPULAR REVOLUTION: MEXICO AND CUBA

While the preceding selections demonstrate that there is no dearth of violence in Latin American political life, most of the violence is committed in the process of maintaining the political order rather than transforming it. Revolutions which transform the political power bases and reorient the productive priorities of nations have been relatively rare in Latin America, particularly when compared to the incidence of *golpes*. Yet the possibility of revolution is ever present, and on occasion this possibility has reached fruition. We now turn to examine two of the revolutions which have occurred in the twentieth century—that of Mexico and that of Cuba.

These two revolutions provide a study in contrast. As the late Frank Tannenbaum, a pioneer in the study of revolution has pointed out, there were enormous differences in the pre-revolutionary societies of these two countries, as well as sharp contrasts in the revolutionary process itself.[26] Here we are interested in one of the sharpest contrasts between the two revolutions: that of the relationship of the revolutionary leadership to the agrarian masses. In each case, the agrarian masses made the revolution possible. In both cases the revolution was made partly in the name of the agrarian masses. Yet the relationship between the agrarian masses in Mexico and the state is much different

26. Frank Tannenbaum, *Ten Keys to Latin America*, Random House, Inc., 1960, pp. 218-27.

The Mexican Revolution produced many inspiring popular leaders, such as Pancho Villa—the "Centaur of the North." Here shown in 1916, Villa had deep roots in the northern countryside, especially in Chihuahua. (Culver Pictures)

than the same relationship in contemporary Cuba. In the former, the Mexican peasantry appears to be alienated from the state, and still fighting some of the same battles as in 1910. In Cuba, the rural proletariat and peasantry seem to have an active stake in the revolutionary government.

For much of the Mexican peasantry, the revolution has been singularly unrewarding, and in that sense, a tragedy. Carlos Fuentes, an eminent Mexican novelist, makes this point in his review of John Womack, Jr.'s excellent book, *Zapata and the Mexican Revolution.** For many, the names of Zapata and Pancho Villa are synonymous with the revolution. Fuentes' account is concerned with the present fortunes of the Morelos peasantry, and with their role in the revolutionary process.

During the summer of 1962 I visited the villages and rice fields in the State of Morelos. We were a small group of Mexican writers and our purpose was to investigate and denounce the murder of Ruben Jaramillo by the state troops. Jaramillo had been the agrarian leader of Tlaquiltenango. During his lifetime, he had defended the integrity of the *ejido* or communal lands, against the voracious encroachments of real-estate dealers who wanted to create a suburban tourist haven for nearby Cuernavaca. The metropolitan investors insisted that the region would profit from the influx of affluent vacationers and that Jaramillo was standing in the way of progress. The *agrarista* chief held his ground; let the capitalists have the beautiful but barren lands to the west of Tlaquiltenango; the communal lands were the livelihood of his people and his people were not about to relinquish their rights and their roots in order to become waiters, gardeners, or soda-pop vendors.

But the investors had gone too far: plans had been drawn, officials had been bribed, urbanization works already had been started. So one morning the intransigent Jaramillo, along with his pregnant wife and three stepsons, was hauled from his home by the state troops, mounted on an army truck, and taken to the lonely plateau where the ancient pyramid of Xochicalco stands. There, facing the misty blue hills and the deep grey gorges of the Sierra Madre, Jaramillo and his family were shot to death. Their blood stained, once again, the carved frieze of the

* From *The New York Review of Books,* March 13, 1969, pp. 5-11. Copyright © 1969 by NYREV, Inc. Reprinted by permission.

plumed serpent that devours its own tail around the base of the Toltec temple.

Jaramillo's secretary received us in a simple brick hut. He was a bald middle-aged man with a big curly moustache and the face and hands of a smooth brown Buddha. He was indistinguishable from the *campesinos* around him, except for two details that marked him as a literate man: he wore, in the hot, vibrant night, a black waistcoat, and a gold-plated ballpoint pen conspicuously stuck out of his shirt pocket. He was gentle and proud, sad and firm in his speech and manner. Yes, he had been warned by the state officials to lay off. He knew who was responsible: a well-known and virtually untouchable Mexico City financier, in collusion with the Governor of Morelos, who, by the way, had been involved in the killing of Emiliano Zapata forty-three years before. We all knew that the only man finally responsible for the actions of the Mexican army was the President of the Republic. Yes, he would probably have to flee and go into hiding. The real-estate people would probably win this time.

We did not try to hide our outrage; he remained serene. He looked at us, at our city clothes, at our dove-blue Renault parked near the tropical veranda full of hammocks and flower pots. "No coman ansias," he murmured with wry sympathy, "Don't feed on anguish." He stood up and went into the hut. A few minutes later, he came out carrying a black, battered old dispatch box, placed it before us, and opened it. With great care he unfolded the almost golden sheets of paper. "These are our titles to the common lands of Tlaquiltenango. The land was ours in Indian times. The King of Spain recognized it as ours; we lost it to the planters and then Zapata fought and got it back. Here is Emiliano's own signature. They don't have these papers. We do. They prove our right to exist. And I will never lose them, even if it costs me my life."

He put the papers back in the box and hurried into the hut. The next day, when we came back, he was gone. Where? *Quien sabe!* Nobody knew. The last of the *Zapatistas* had taken off with his sacred writ; it was almost as if the enemies of *agrarismo,* by murdering Jaramillo, had achieved nothing: they had not been able to destroy the papers, the one concrete piece of evidence of the reality of the communal existence, work, memory and hope. Stronger than murder, the titles to the land were even stronger than justice, since justice itself could be founded only upon that holy bit of parchment signed by an ancient father, the King, and by a sacrificed brother, Zapata. I imagined the little secretary as a wandering guardian of the seals, humble and obscure, but sure of his true power and eventual triumph because he held in his hands the final proof of legitimacy: the written word.

"In early 1914," writes John Womack, Jr. in his exemplary history of the *Zapatista* revolution, some emissaries from a Mochiacan rebel came to [Zapata's] camp at Pozo Colorado, to see whether he was sincere. What was he really fighting for? How could he prove it? (Zapata) showed (the Anenecuilco documents) to his visitors. 'Por esto peleo,' he said. 'This—not these titles, but this record of constancy and uprightness—I am fighting for.' "[27]

It would be tempting to interpret Mexican history as a battle between sacred texts and profane reality. The eyewitness chronicles of the Conquest written by Hernan Cortés and Bernal Díaz del Castillo are great Renaissance epics: they signify the arrival, in the New World, of a new world, that of sixteenth-century Europe with its growing confidence in individual enterprise, its sense of moral risk, its assault on hierarchy. The reality of the Spanish Counter-Reformation soon put an end to that: the Old World transferred the rotting structures of feudal absolutism (for such was the Spanish paradox) to Mexico. The enlightened, paternalistic Law of the Indies passed by the Crown under pressure from benevolent missionaries were in harsh contradiction to the actual working conditions in the mines, forests, and *encomiendas* of the colony. Moreover, our founding fathers (mostly landed members of the creole elite) bequeathed us, along with independence, the liberal Constitution of 1821, inspired by the American and French revolutions. But the masks of Jefferson and Montesquieu hardly fitted the children of an ascendant, but defeated Indian theocracy and of a conquering, but already decadent European autocracy.

With the blessings of formal democracy, the oppression of the *campesino* communities continued without hindrance; the native Mexican landholder now invoked, not the rights both divine and *de facto* of the conqueror, but the free play of economic forces. When the Reform Laws of Benito Juárez broke the dead hand of the Church holdings, the liberated lands were sold on the open market. It was not the *campesinos* who could buy them back, but the new class of proprietors, who became the backbone of the thirty-year Porfirio Díaz dictatorship.

What does this proliferation of legal texts actually cloak? Perhaps a grave problem of identity and its attendant question: from what does

27. John Womack, Jr., *Zapata and the Mexican Revolution*, Alfred A. Knopf, 1969, pp. 371-72.

legitimacy spring in a country that denies its rapist Spanish father and condemns its treacherous Indian mother? The feeling of being orphaned has been sublimated by attributing paternity to the objective, aseptic legal text, much as if it were the incarnation of an undefiled act of genesis. He who possesses the text also exercises the *patria potestas*. And since the text delivers us from the degraded condition of bastards (similarly, the image of the dark-skinned virgin, Guadalupe, saves us from the fear of being sons-of-a-whore: we now see our Mother pure and enshrined) we should willingly renounce our unprotected freedom as children of the left hand for the privileged, if submissive, status of subjects of the right.

The legitimation of the bastard, the identification of the orphan, is achieved through the authority of the text and thus becomes the basic moral condition of a society ruled from the top, sustained and suffered from the bottom. To renounce a name and a place, however lowly, in the rigid pyramid, means losing one's self, again, in the deserts of populist illegitimacy. Whether it be the civil register, a membership card of the Party of Revolutionary Institutions or the Federal Constitution: Mexicans need a solid text that gives them an identity by referring them to a paternalistic authority.

From this rationalization springs the unbroken line of succession of power in Mexico: Aztec Emperor-Spanish Viceroy-Republican Señor Presidente. "Mexicans are incapable of governing themselves democratically; they need a benevolent, guiding father who flexibly implements the broader meanings of the law": this conclusion, openly voiced by the *científico* bureaucracy of the Díaz regime (who used to read Spencer and Comte), is now urbanely muttered, along with the appropriate reflections on the nature of *realpolitik*, by their modern-day heirs, the ruling managers of the P.R.I., the Banker's Association, and the Chambers of Commerce (who read Burnham and Rostow).

The marvel of Zapata and his movement was that in this maze of conflicting texts and realities the *campesino* communities of Morelos should have maintained, through the centuries, a continuing sense of their identity and the legitimacy of their social, cultural, and economic claims to the land. "Like a wound, the country's history opens at Anenecuilco." This quote from the Mexican historian García Cantú aptly heads Womack's study. Indeed, not the least of Zapata's achievements was that his movement not only destroyed the objective structure of feudal land tenure, but also wounded the subjective justifications of the almost metaphysical Mexican status quo. For only in appearance were Zapata's claims to rights based on the legal texts of Anenecuilco another extension of the rightist scriptural theory.

This theory contains an implicit acceptance of the necessary *écart* between text and reality, between juridical promise and administrative implementation. It contains, furthermore, a no less implicit approval of the fatal compromise, between the purity of the ideal text and its outright violation in practise. Madero defied Díaz's legitimacy as the heir to the 1857 Juarista Constitution because he felt that the old dictator had not achieved that compromise; violations were too flagrant. On reaching the Presidency, Madero himself believed that to strike the right note of equilibrium was quite sufficient. Madero was not a revolutionary: he was an apostle of textual legitimacy. Zapata was a revolutionary: and his scandalous belief was that men should fight, starve, strike back, suffer sickness, burn, hide in the mountains, and never relax until finally the text and the reality should be one and the same.

Madero was eventually unwilling to be anything more than an honest broker for the Establishment, which Don Porfirio ran with a heavy hand (his blood-chilling motto was, "Kill them while they're hot"). Zapata's break with Madero over his lack of a decisive agrarian policy is particularly well dealt with [by Womack], although one would desire fuller treatment of the causes of Madero's downfall at the hands of the very forces he had naïvely left intact: the traditional army, big landholders, and foreign interests. Indeed, the sacrifice of Madero is a case history of *don'ts* for revolutionary Latin America: his immense democratic good will, his respect for the free speech, parliamentary debate, freedom of the press, and electoral rights were nothing but frothy dreams so long as the basic, anachronistic structures remained intact. This is the lesson which Castro learned in Cuba, which, in the Dominican Republic, Bosch did not, and which Frondizi, in Argentina, or Belaúnde in Peru, could not.

In 1915, after the triumph of the national uprising against Huerta, three significant forces comprised the revolutionary spectrum: first, Pancho Villa's confused, violent army of uprooted peasants, local bandits, ambitious politicos, adventurous intellectuals, and St. Cyrien military strategists; secondly, the wide front of the rising national bourgeoisie under the Constitutionalist banner of Carranza; and finally, the campesinos of the Zapatista movement, deeply rooted in the South. From today's perspective, it would be facile to claim that any of the three factions was exclusively representative of the revolutionary spirit. The Mexican Revolution was too much a spontaneous, undoctrinaire movement. It was an act of national self-recognition. Villa's cavalcades up and down the national territory showed the strong intuitive need to break away from the closed compartments of Mexican life, to contaminate Mexico with its own songs, colors, slang, passions. The Constitutionalists, who finally conquered and remained in power, represented the broader, more abstract and rational purposes of the national design. But in choosing to study the locally limited movement of Zapata, Womack has pinpointed precisely what the Revolution was about at its profoundest level. "The people want their rights respected. They want to be paid attention to and listened to." These are Zapata's words and the fact that they were pronounced by a Mexican *guerrillero* at the beginning of the century makes them no less contemporary, both for Mexico and for most of the rest of the world.

Only this profoundly civilized self-awareness can explain, first, the apparently natural talents of the Zapatistas. Applied to guerrilla warfare in their campaign against General Juvencio Robles and Huerta's Federal Army, Zapata, the so-called "Attila of the South," was the first of the line of strategists—Castro and Guevara, the NLF fighters in Algeria, Giap in Vietnam—that have made the guerrilla the natural defensive arm of a locally based culture. The Zapatistas thought of themselves as people who knew how to live together in one place with a sense of the tension between the values of tradition and the limited possibilities of happiness through progress. Guerrilla warfare was the intuitive extension of that awareness; it was the defense of a freely accepted tension against a brutal, inflexible tension imposed from outside.

The story of Zapata's "little war" reads like contemporary headlines. A powerful and remote authority declares martial law in Morelos, and, incapable of distinguishing among the cultural components of the rebellion, also fails to distinguish rebels from villagers; in attacking the latter, it swells the rebel ranks. Villagers and rebels, in the process, discover that they *are* indistinguishable from each other; the rebel's uniform is the *campesinos'* work clothes. Since military forces thus defeats political purpose, social terrorism supplants them both. A drastic program of pacification through resettlement is pushed through; General Robles, it seems, has already thought of strategic hamlets in 1914. The wealthy planters lobby furiously in Mexico City for more and more troops, bigger campaigns, harsher methods. But escalation only binds the villagers and *guerrilla* bands closer together and finally brings them under the unified command of Zapata.

The "reconcentration" of villagers fails because as soon as the local population sees a Federal Army column approaching, they flee to the hills. The column fruitlessly sacks the abandoned village and goes away. The inhabitants filter back, now convinced *Zapatistas,* Zapata is free to make the Revolution on the march; his officers are ordered to lend their "moral and material support" to villages presenting titles and filing reclamations for the land. The military victories of the Federal Army become more and more Pyrrhic. The rebel guerrillas cannot be concentrated in one place for formal battle, where they can be fixed and annihilated; they attack swiftly, then disperse and establish new, invisible headquarters. The camouflage of the *guerrillero* is a cultural fact; he knows the land because he *is* the land, humanly re-created and situated. Robles is soon reduced to defending urban enclaves; the countryside belongs to the guerrillas. And the rebel chieftains learn to synchronize their attacks, so that in a single day the Federal Commanders will have to expect half a dozen raids without knowing whether they are major attacks or simply divertive ones. Demoralization from within, menaced by the northern legions of Villa and Obregón, the old elitist army that Madero had not dared to touch finally caves in.

The people of Morelos had rewon their land. After the eighteen months of the guerrilla came the year of freedom. . . . Indeed, Zapata's agrarian movement was a tiger lurking in the Morelos ranges and forests. In retrospect, one can now see it wrapped in the shadows of history, nurturing the promises of a local culture, knowing that its time (I employ the crucial distinction made by Octavio Paz) was not the linear, positivistic measure of the West, but rather the circular, cosmogonic revolution understood by the aboriginal mind. A time symbolized by the self-devouring deity that witnessed the murder of Jaramillo. The people of Morelos had waited for their time to come with the patience of inevitability. Then the spark of revolution flashed and caught fire for an incredible year, from the summer of 1914 to the summer of 1915: the long, lonely, unforgettable year of an impossible Arcadia. The price, the strength, and the weakness of this revolution was its isolation. It was a radical revolution, as profound and limited as its roots. . . .

Zapata and his chiefs, of course, were themselves villagers, field hands and sharecroppers; their authority sprang from local councils and rested on fidelity to the texts they were about to make forcefully real. On this basis, a politics of confidence arose. "Significantly, Zapata never organized a state police; law enforcement, such as it was, remained the province of village councils." Zapata's personal aura never degenerated into authoritarianism or pride; as Womack points out, the man never went too far from "the guts and flies and manure and mud of local life." Military chiefs were forbidden to interfere in village affairs, and when Zapata himself had to arbitrate local troubles, he always limited his action to enforcing decisions that the villagers had already reached on their own.

For the first time in Mexico, it was not a remote bureaucracy, not an all-too-present military authority that made decisions in the name of the people. The people themselves, through the cooperation of village leaders, fashioned the new levers of power and the new means of livelihood from the bottom up, unhindered by rigid programs, fusing the traditional agencies of local society and the momentum of the Revolution. The *Zapatista* chiefs proclaimed that the partition of lands would be carried out according to the customs of each pueblo. If a pueblo wanted the communal system, it would have it; but if it chose to divide the land in order to admit small individual property, so it would be.

Word was sent to the villagers: reclaim your lands. Technically this problem was solved by appointing agrarian commissions "charged with the survey and division of lands." The situation recalls the demands of those European university students who are demanding the right to collaborate professionally with the working classes rather than with private enterprise. In Mexico, scores of graduates from the National School of Agriculture went to work in the field with the agrarian commissions set up to legalize claims, survey the land, and determine boundary lines. In six months, the *"ingenieritos"* from the city won the respect of the local villagers; together, they assured the renaissance of the hundred odd pueblos of Morelos, which finally came into possession of their local farm land, the stands of timber, and the irrigation facilities.

Legally, the revolution was made. Practically, it was necessary that a state razed by civil war be restored. Rather than take on the more complex responsibilities of the old haciendas the free campesinos of Morelos stuck to the staple products of the pueblos; in one summer they restocked Morelos with beans, corn, chile peppers, tomatoes, chickpeas, chickens and onions. As local production rose, so did local consumption. Prices were kept low and inflation was avoided.

In such clear relief the character of revolutionary Morelos emerged: in the very crops people liked to grow, they revealed the kind of community they liked to dwell in. They had no taste for the style of individuals on the make, the life of perpetual achievement and acquisition, of chance and change and moving on. Rather they wanted a life they could control, a modest familial property in the company of other modestly prosperous families whom they knew, and all in one place. (Womack, p. 241.)

The text and reality had become one. The campesinos of Morelos had achieved the modest, profound dream for which they had fought so hard. Far from being hopelessly anchored in resignation, they had shown that a campesino culture could escape its presumed fate and achieve a humane and functional civil and economic organization on a local basis. They had shown that Mexicans *could* rule themselves democratically. But the very values of the system proved to be its undoing; the Morelos Arcadia cut against the grain of the national design. In effect, the vision of the National Mexican State presupposed a withering away of provincial peculiarities in favor of a much wider enterprise; little Morelos had to be sacrificed to greater Mexico, the dynamic, responsible, unscrupulous, centralized force that was taking shape around Carranza and his ambitious chieftains, Obregón and González.

It would be unfair to say that, once the remnants of the Díaz regime had been shattered and *Carrancismo* was in power, the popular democracy of Morelos was threatened by a new form of reaction. Rather a national revolution faced a local revolution. The latter was based on accepted common traditions; the former had to elaborate and impose a national plan for progress. In Morelos, the people's intimate knowledge of one another favored direct democracy; the nation as a whole was unknown to itself. Where did the common bond lie between Sonora cattle ranchers and Yucatán plantation workers, between Mexico City intellectuals and several million isolated Indians?

Zapatismo could not solve problems as they came; local ethics were clear, concise, and irrevocable, local culture was homogeneous. The national revolution, however, felt it had to centralize energies in order to transform a heterogeneous society and create a modern infrastructure in a country lacking in communications, electric power, and administrative coordination. The Morelos revolution could be internationally irresponsible; the national revolution had to stand the constant pressure of North American power and the explicit menace of foreign intervention. Zapatismo knew it could rely on the common sense of a democratic people who knew and respected both one another and a locally approved law. On the other hand, the national revolution could impose its abstract laws only by falling back on consecration of the authoritarian father figure and the sacred text that assured his legitimacy. That the Political Constitution of 1917, which embodied the basic agrarian demands of the Zapatista movement, was written into this text was, perhaps, the only possible measure of its local success.

When, in the winter of 1915, the government forces of General Pablo González swooped down from Mexico City into Morelos, the dream was over. González was as brutal as the Huertista General Robles had been. But where the Zapatistas could fight victoriously against the henchmen of the old regime, they faltered, however courageously, in their struggle against the new national forces. With González, it was not the old planters who came back. It was the new merchants, the ambitious little lawyers, the promoters, who arrived. They had been waiting in the wings for the opportunity to establish the rights of a national bourgeoisie cloaked in the mantle of modernity and progress.

Zapata fought on grimly, firm in his loyalty to a revolution "rooted in local pride and grief." But now he fought in order not to die, a hunted fugitive, helpless against the rising national bourgeois tide. When he was murdered by Carranza in 1919, the heirs of Constitucionalismo were about to accept Zapatismo as the local wing of the national revolutionary movement, as an eccentric experience that offered limited solutions. This is how Zapatismo has come down to us: shadowy, profoundly rooted, sometimes corrupted by the powerful forces imposed on the country by capitalist development (Zapata's own son, Nicolás, became a wealthy, cynical and oppressive oligarch), sometimes winning small battles, seduced by stability and a thin prosperity; sometimes brutally suppressed as in the case of Jaramillo, its primitive cohesion shaken by the mobility and porousness of the new Mexican middle class; and sometimes seemingly lost forever in its own brooding nostalgia for Arcadia and its grief over the sacrifice of the legendary leader. At times almost an irrelevant anachronism. . . .

But Zapatismo, as the profound aspiration of people capable of participating in the decisions that affect them, as a rebellion against the fate of subservience, Zapatismo has not spoken its last word. For the Revolution has not had the last word in Mexico. The urgent, dynamic bourgeoisie that came to power with Obregón in 1920 has now become a calcified political class. It created the conditions for Mexico's considerable economic progress in the past fifty years; it created these conditions by realizing that its existence as a class depended on revolutionary measures. Agrarian reform meant better methods, higher production, fewer hands in the fields and more hands in the factories; nationalization of natural resources meant cheap fuel for industrialization, better social conditions, rational conservation and long-range planning. Till the end of the Cárdenas presidency in 1940, economic development was accompanied by a sense of social duty; only thus, thought Cárdenas, would the inevitable inequities of capitalism be corrected and its programs made coherent. Without social justice, the national market would never reach that 50 percent of the population that still was and is, rural.

Unhappily, the spirit of Cardenismo (historically coincidental with Roosevelt's New Deal) was quickly abandoned once its revolutionary methods had assured the New Class of sufficient power, wealth, and stability. Centralized politics became a screen for quick, profitable, socially irrelevant investments. "The Revolution" became an empty slogan piously invoked by bankers, corrupt union leaders, and official speech makers. More and more, Mexico's economy became a model of uneven distribution (4 percent of the population receives 50 percent of the national income) and myopic credit structures. Small loans are given only for short terms and high interest, and thus restricted to highly remunerative and/or speculative mercantile operations; large credits are absorbed by national and foreign monopolies. The mask of this *nouveau-riche* boom is there for any tourist to see, in shops, hotels, residential districts, and luxury spas. But sixty years after Emiliano Zapata rose up in arms, almost half the population of Mexico is still illiterate, a third never eats bread, a fourth consumes neither meat, milk, nor fish, and 12 million people still walk on their bare feet, in a country where shoe manufacturers, for lack of a local market, have to export part of their product. The metropolitan markets are saturated, while the 25 million people who live in the countryside languish. Yet it is thanks to their sacrifices that Mexico has become a partly industrialized nation.

A few years ago, I accompanied ex-president Cárdenas on a tour of rural districts in the states of Michoacán and Jalisco. Everywhere we went—the dusty hamlets near Guadalajara, the lush Urupan valleys, the baked lands around Jiquilpan—where agrarian reform had been honestly administered, where the campesinos had been able to count on technical assistance, modern machinery, seed and fertilizers, price stability and protection from middlemen, the *ejido* or collective farm had been a success. The *campesinos* had again shown that, if dealt with fairly, they could rule themselves. The reverse side of the story was dramatically brought home to us by a white-thatched, nut-faced old *campesino* in Jalisco. I remember his words vividly: "When Cárdenas gave us the land, we became free for the first time. For generations, we had been like slaves to the big *hacendado*, we had been chained to the *hacienda* through debts that passed from fathers to sons. Then we were free, the debts were cancelled, and we became masters of our corn-growing *ejido*. Many left, it is true; they went to Guadalajara, even to Mexico City, and began to work in the factories. They were paid better.

"We stayed at the *ejido* and tried to prove we could make it. At first we were protected, the agrarian officials lived with us and knew us. But later things changed. People we didn't know were named as officials. Rich people began buying the farm land, small plots, one after the other, until all together they formed new *haciendas*. It was useless to protest. These people were old government functionaries, and they had named the new agrarian officials. Our demands ceased to be listened to. The bigger farms got the machinery and soon we were forced to go back to work for them, or to the cities and the factories, or up to the United States as *braceros*. Also, there was no protection against the mill owners. We know what our harvest is really worth; the mill owners will only take it at half the price. Many children are born here; it is becoming difficult to feed them. We feel we are not moving. Who will listen to us?"

While the Mexican revolution appears to have failed Zapata's heirs in the state of Morelos, the Cuban revolution has involved a different orientation toward its rural masses. Although the Cuban rural proletariat and peasantry were never committed to the actual fighting of the revolution (Fidel Castro's rebel army never numbered more than 2000 men) in the way that the Mexican peasants were, they have been the primary beneficiaries of the revolution.

Robin Blackburn, one of the editors of the *New Left Review*, traces the course of the revolution from its historical bases in the following selection.* His work provides a description of power alignments in pre-revolutionary Cuba, as well as the manner and composition of the revolutionary coalition that overthrew the Batista dictatorship. Black-

* From "Prologue to the Cuban Revolution," in *New Left Review*, Vol. 21, No. 4, 1963, pp. 52-91. Reprinted by permission of the editors of *New Left Review*. Mr. Blackburn will soon publish a much expanded version of the essay as part of a study of the Cuban Revolution.

burn makes it very clear that the Cuban revolution was not the work of any single social grouping or class, but the result of the coalescence of numerous popular forces against imperialist domination of a plantation society.

The Debility of the Bourgeoisie

Havana's extensive and resplendent suburb of Marianao offers a vivid image of the Cuban bourgeoisie in the days of its prosperity. Its posthumous presence is eloquent: in the cemetery itself the marble vaults of the rich are fitted with internal lifts, air-conditioning and telephones. . . .

The nascent bourgeoisie of the first decades of independence had, along with all other sections of the Cuban population, suffered catastrophically from the collapse of the 20's. In the space of one year the national income of Cuba was cut by 63 per cent; 20 Cuban banks with 334 branches and deposits of 130 million dollars were forced to close, and by 1939 foreign banks held 83 per cent of all Cuban deposits. The recovery and rise of the class began with the Second World War. High sugar prices refloated the whole economy; profits once again rapidly accrued to Cuban capitalists. The value of the sugar crop rose from 110 million dollars in 1940 to 256 million in 1942, and to 677 million in 1947. Bank deposits rose from 138.9 million dollars to 727.3 million dollars in 1951, while the proportion of them held by Cuban banks climbed from 16.8 per cent in 1939 to 60.2 per cent in 1955.

However, the absolute (and ostentatious) monetary wealth of this class concealed its relative economic weakness. The invasion of U.S. capital which ended the traditional aristocracy in the countryside, shackled and stunted the bourgeoisie which succeeded it. Simple percentage figures reveal the extent of U.S. control over the Cuban economy: 40 per cent of raw sugar production was U.S. owned, 23 per cent of non-sugar industry, 90 per cent of telephone and electrical services, 50 per cent of public service railways. Moreover, these figures show only the scale of U.S. investment. The mode of investment was at least equally important, for it typically took the form of the establishment of subsidiaries by U.S. companies with participation by local Cuban capital or, alternately, participation by U.S. capital in already established Cuban concerns. These industries were dependent on the U.S. parent company for essential supplies, and it was often on the sales between the two that real profits were made. Lone Star Cement, U.S. Rubber,

American Agricultural Chemicals, Firestone, Procter and Gamble, and others profited by arrangements of this kind. Cuban capital was thus invested not in competition but in collaboration with U.S. capital. The result was the structural integration of the Cuban bourgeoisie within the economy of an alien capitalism. For as the French economist François Perroux remarks: "When a large firm sets up a concern in a small country, the concern is doubtless situated in the so-called 'national' territory of the smaller country. In reality, however, it belongs to the firm's own area."[27] The de facto situation was clinched juridically. A reciprocal trade treaty in 1934 guaranteed Cuban sugar a preferential U.S. market and in return secured U.S. manufacturers a privileged entry into the Cuban market. Hence forward it was usually worthwhile for a Cuban industrialist to set up a plant in Cuba only if he could do so under some arrangement with the large U.S. corporations.

The most decisive and glaring result of this integration was that Cuban capitalists had to limit their field of operations to the boundaries set for them by North American neo-colonialism. Only sectors of the Cuban economy complementary to most of the United States could be developed. This confiscation of its economy condemned Cuba to extreme underutilization of its resources, and blocked any real economic growth. The sugar sector represented 80 per cent of exports in the 50's and provided 25 per cent of the national income. Yet sugar production was 500,000 tons lower in 1956 than it had been in 1925. In 1956 the sugar companies owned or controlled 188,000 caballerías of land; yet only 74,000 caballerías of cane were cut. These vast uncultivated estates made a mockery of Cuba's heavy food imports—in 1958, 80 million dollars worth, or 25 per cent of Cuba's food consumption, was bought abroad. The island's other greatest natural resource suffered even worse neglect: Cuba possesses the world's largest known deposits of nickel, but they were almost entirely unexploited. The United States Government owned the deposits and kept them simply as reserves. Inevitably, the Cuban economy failed to gain any real productive impetus. The repatriated capital siphoned off to the U.S.A. amounted to 369.1 million dollars net disinvestment between 1952 and 1958. GNP rose by a derisory 1.4 per cent per annum between 1951 and 1958, or at a slower rate than the population. In a work-force of 2,700,-000, unemployment ran at 700,000 men for the greater part of the year.

It is clear then that the Cuban capitalist class could not properly be

27. François Perroux, "Large Firm-Small Nation," in *Presence Africaine*, No. 38, p. 43. Cf. also F. Perroux, *Coexistence Pacifique*, Paris, 1961.

described as a "national" bourgeoisie. All major sections of Cuban capital were compromised in the exploitation of Cuba by U.S. capital and collaborated as subordinates in prolonging the retardation and stagnation of the economy. The term "national" bourgeoisie is made still more inappropriate by the strikingly deracinate and expatriate composition of the Cuban capitalist class. The island's largest "Cuban-owned" sugar enterprise was the property of Julio Lobo, a naturalized Cuban of German origin (original name Wulf), who owned sugar plantations throughout the Caribbean and a flourishing brokerage business in New York. Cuba's largest native industrialist was Burke Hedges of "Textilera Ariguanabo," a naturalized Cuban of U.S. origin. The largest rum-producing company, Bacardi, was owned by two families, the Espins of French origin, and the Boschs of German origin. The largest Cuban-owned bank, "El Trust Company of Cuba," was owned by the Falla family of Spanish origin. Spanish citizens, moreover, accounted in 1943 for a full 16 per cent of all the "merchants and businessmen" in the census. The Cuban bourgeoisie, in fact, lacked almost any homogeneity or "history."

A final consideration is important. One sector, and one sector alone, of the Cuban economy showed autonomous dynamism under the neo-colonial regime: speculative construction. De luxe apartment blocks, gleaming hotels, colossal casinos shot up in Havana, which witnessed 80 per cent of all construction in Cuba in 1957. Immense windfall profits were made in the property market; and a substantial rentier stratum was created. Personal incomes from urban rents ran at 99 million dollars in 1956, and at a further 74 million dollars from rural rents. A significant proportion of this boom was provided by tourism. But it was a distinctive kind of tourism, drawn predominantly neither by cultural, not even particularly by climatic attractions, but by commercialized vice—prostitution and gambling. The call-houses and casinos of Havana were an international version of the classic "safety-valves" of bourgeois society. The fundamental image of it in the United States was of an exotic but adjacent red-light district. This aspect of Cuban society was not merely of picturesque significance; it was of some psychological importance for the character of the Cuban bourgeoisie. The contrast has often been made, most eloquently and originally, by Frantz Fanon, between the dynamic entrepreneurial bourgeoisie of nineteenth-century Europe and the corrupt and enfeebled administrative bourgeoisie of the Third World today. Fanon's description is now classic: "It is only psychologically that it [the bourgeoisie of the Third World] identifies with the Western bourgeoisie from which it has learnt all its lessons. It imitates the Western bourgeoisie in its negative and decadent period without having made the initial efforts of exploration and invention which themselves created this Western bourgeoisie. At birth the national bourgeoisie of the colonial countries identifies with the final stage of the Western bourgeoisie. . . . It is already senile without ever having known the impatience, the fearlessness and the voluntarism of youth and adolescence. . . . This bourgeoisie, mediocre in its efforts, in its achievements, in its thought, attempts to mask this mediocrity by prestige achievements at the individual level, by the chrome of American cars, by Riviera holidays, by week-ends in neon-lit night-clubs."[28]

In an article which notably enriches the sociology of this class in the Third World, Claudio Véliz describes the specifically Latin American variant of it: "Finally, the outbreak of the Second World War created a new situation which opened unprecedented opportunities for rapid industrial growth. European and U.S. exports ceased to need Latin American markets and, in the vacuum thus created, a fantastic mushrooming of industry took place. The consequences of this were obvious. In less than a decade, the leadership of the urban middle sectors became extremely wealthy. Using their access to the sources of power and their influence with the bureaucracy, they allocated tenders, granted licences, exercised the traditional rights of patronage, and, even without outright corruption, accumulated considerable fortunes. . . . Thus in a relatively brief period of time, the violently outspoken reformist leaders of 1938 became the sedate, technically minded, and moderate statesmen of the 1950's. Once their foot was in the door, there was no more talk of demolition: now the problem was how to get inside the mansion of privilege. . . . Now, throughout the continent, the middle sectors are willing and ready to outdo the conservatives in their devotion to established institutions. . . . Social-climbing has thus become a political institution. It is perfectly true that this is a well-known aspect of all social change. Europe has even produced a complete gallery of caricatures and stereotypes around the ridiculous figure of the nouveau riche. But Latin America has improved on the old style by making this a mass phenomenon."[29] It was thus of some significance that the Cuban bourgeoisie could not successfully "borrow" identity

28. Franz Fanon, Les Damnés de la Terre, Maspero, Paris, 1961, pp. 113-51.
29. Claudio Véliz, "Obstacles to Reform in Latin America," in The World Today, January 1963, pp. 18-30.

from an established oligarchy. Social snobbery, however, ran rife in Havana. Spanish titles were eagerly bought and gossip columns running to several pages, with payment for insertion, helped to subsidize the newspapers and magazines. Thus while Cuba's wealthy classes were unable to prevent the upstart "Sergeant" Batista from running the country, they consoled themselves—until 1952 at any rate—with barring him from the Havana Yacht Club because of his Afro-Chinese ancestry.

More important, however, was the distinctive cast of the Cuban bourgeoisie itself. If the "administrative" bourgeoisie of the Third World which Fanon and Dumont denounce represents an immense decline from the classic "entrepreneurial" bourgeoisie of the West, the Cuban bourgeoisie in many ways represented a debasement of even this type. The markedly parasitic character of this class in Cuba could not but have a significant effect on its cohesion and consciousness. Its ignoble role and image within the U.S. economic and socio-affective system made it almost impossible for it to have a morale of the kind which is vital to a class's political and social efficacy. A dominant social class must believe in its own necessity. The Cuban bourgeoisie was too compromised: it was never able to achieve real confidence and combativity. . . .

The Fiasco of the Institutional Order

The classic Latin American power structure, from Independence to this day, may be summarily described. Wealth lies in the hands of an oligarchy of landowners and businessmen, more or less aristocratic or arriviste according to the country. The property regime remains untouched, no matter what the formal political system. Surface turmoil—electoral campaigns, cabinet intrigues, armed uprisings, military putsches—is directly proportionate to structure stability. The ruling class preserves the status quo indifferently through anarchy, autocracy or "democracy." But its various institutional instruments, the classic trio, have undoubtedly been: the Church, the Army, Political Parties. The character of each of these in Cuba is worth some examination.

Church

The Catholic Church has been a major institutional buttress of the social order everywhere in Latin America. Its economic, political and ideological power was so great in the nineteenth century that in most countries it posed the only issue which seriously disturbed the unity of the oligarchy. In the twentieth century aristocratic anti-clericalism has become an anachronism, and in nearly all Latin American countries the Church has assumed a simple, general role of social and political reaction (Colombia is perhaps the only country where lay Catholicism achieved such a pitch of fanaticism in the post-war period that oligarchic anti-clericalism was preserved). For this purpose, an extensive ecclesiastical apparatus is necessary, comprising an economic base (Church lands, Vatican subventions, contributions of the faithful, etc.), local training institutions (seminaries, colleges), a numerous personnel (flourishing priesthood), a publicity network (press, radio), and a pervasive lay presence (voluntary organizations). In most Latin American countries these conditions are amply met.

Cuba, however, was an exception. Churches existed only in the rich suburbs and old city centers. The priesthood was woefully inadequate to its ostensible flock: there were only 725 priests in the whole island, 1 to every 7850 parishioners (the comparable ratio for Chile is 1 for 2750, for Venezuela 1 for 4350, for Colombia 1 for 3650). Furthermore, the overwhelming majority—75 per cent—of these priests were not Cubans at all. They were Spaniards dispatched from Spain to maintain the Cuban Church. The hierarchy itself was Hispanized: the Archbishop of Santiago, Enrique Pérez Serantes, who intervened on Fidel Castro's behalf after the Moncada attack in 1953, for example, was a Spaniard. This phenomenon was a product of the Independence Wars, when the Church had identified itself so completely with Spanish cause that it gravely weakened its local strength in Cuba. After Independence, Catholicism in Cuba became much more a diffused cultural presence, providing an (often adulterated) popular imagery and mythology, rather than a powerful and oppressive social institution. The findings of a Catholic Action Survey, based on 4000 interviews, showed that: "One of every three adult Catholics never made his first communion, and only one in four fulfilled the Easter precept. Very many marriages lacked canonical validity, and considerably more than half of all Cuban Catholics approved of divorce. Religious ignorance was appalling. . . . Superstitions were revealed to be flourishing. . . . The Bayamo district, for example had two priests and ten spirit-worship centers (i.e. for the Afro-Cuban cults. R.B.). Here one inhabitant in nine gave spirit worship as his sole religion. Vast numbers of others mixed . . . primitive jungle rites with the Christianity they professed to the point that one Cuban in four admitted having gone at some time to placate the spirits or get their advice."[30]

30. B. Macoin, *Latin America: The Eleventh Hour,* New York, 1962, pp. 108-9.

Thus, when the Revolution came, the Church was unable to put up any serious resistance. The comparison with, say Argentina, is instructive. The social program of Perón was infinitely less radical than that of the Cuban Revolution, yet when the Church joined the opposition a successful uprising was almost immediately precipitated. Faced with a far greater challenge in Cuba, it was helpless. The Church was politically a broken reed in Cuba.

Political Parties

. . . The typical political formations of nineteenth- and early twentieth-century Latin America made up an almost indistinguishable dyad, the Liberal and Conservative Parties. This couplet was found throughout the continent: in Mexico, in Venezuela, in Colombia, in Ecuador, in Chile. Almost everywhere, the sole substantial difference between these alternate factions of the oligarchy was their attitude to the Church. The Liberals were anti-clerical, the Conservatives ultra-montane. The economic regiments of each were virtually identical. Political rule by one or the other was indifferently civilian or military: there were as many Liberal Dictators (e.g. Guzmán Blanco in Venezuela) as Conservative Presidents (e.g. Montt in Chile). Together they formed what might be called the Twin-Party System. Despite their sociological and political identity, however, the two parties became established institutions with, in many countries, a significant degree of continuity and tradition. In some countries they have survived down to the present. In the most Catholicized country in Latin America, Colombia, the Liberal-Conservative opposition dominates formal political life to this day.

It is against this background that the political parties of independent Cuba should be seen. There, as elsewhere, a Liberal and a Conservative Party were formed, and the two parties furnished the Presidents of the initial decades of the Republic: Estrada Palma, Gómez, Menocal, Zayas. This was also the period of repeated and regular U.S. intervention: 1906-1909, 1912, 1915, 1917, 1920. The creaking and corrupt parliamentary façade of the Cuban Republic was successfully sustained by U.S. military presence. This phase came to an end with the ascension to power of the Liberal Gerardo Machado in 1925, and the onset of the world depression. The economic and social effects of the sugar slump has already been noted. Machado installed a sanguinary personal dictatorship which lasted until 1933, when a wave of student *attentats,* followed by a general strike, forced him into exile.

In this revolutionary situation, senior officers of the Cuban Army in collusion with the U.S. Special Representative in the island, Sumner Welles, established a conventional conservative government. Symbolically, the President in this last flickering hour of the traditional regime in Cuba, was the aristocrat Carlos Manuel de Céspedes, grandson of the latifundist author of the Declaration of Yara. Three weeks later he was overthrown, and his class effectively disappeared from Cuban history.

The Revolution of 1933 was the achievement of a coalition of university students and army sergeants, which seized power on September 5. Ramon Grau San Martin, leader of the Student Directorate, became President and Fulgencio Batista, the stenographer-sergeant leader of the insurgent non-commissioned officers, became Chief of Staff. The revolutionary government nationalized the island's U.S.-owned electrical company and promised to distribute land to the peasants. Four months later Batista, urged on by Sumner Welles, who regarded the revolution as "ultra-radical" and "'frankly communistic," suppressed his student allies, murdered their left-wing leader Antonio Gutiérrez and abandoned their program of reform and anti-imperialism. A socialist jacquerie that had broken out in the countryside was brutally quelled. The United States immediately recognized the new regime.

Batista rules as de facto dictator for six years, from 1934 to 1940. In 1940 he was elected President against Grau in a relatively open plebiscitary election. But effective parliamentary law was suspended for a decade; it was only really resumed again as the Second World War drew to a close. Batista himself inaugurated Cuba's second—and last—parliamentary period. Convinced that he could win an open election, he allowed one. His candidate, Carlos Saladrigas, lost, although only by a narrow margin. To general surprise, he accepted defeat and retired to Miami with the spoils of office.

The interlude was to be brief. The second parliamentary period failed even more wretchedly than the first in establishing stable and meaningful political parties, let alone a working parliamentary system as such. The Cuban political scene was an inextricable confusion of volatile and venal factions, devoid of any program or ideology, competing avidly for office and wealth. A North American political scientist has described the nineteenth Assembly: "More or less nebulous majority and minority blocks took form with *líderes* or leaders nominally in charge of each."[31] The old Conservative and Liberal Parties had shown

31. William S. Stokes, *Latin American Politics*, New York, 1959, p. 444.

no staying power: after the 1933 Revolution they were shadows of their former selves. The victor of the 1944 election was Grau San Martin. Grau was head of the Auténtico Party (Partido Revolucionario Cubano), theoretically left-wing and faithful to the ideal of the 1933 Revolution. Yet the Autentico Party won both the 1944 and 1948 elections (when Carlos Prío Socorrás became President) in coalition with the ultra-right Republican Party. The Autentico government was in alliance with the Communist Party from 1945 to 1947; in 1947 it turned on the party and purged the trade-unions of Communists; but the major Auténtico trade unionist, Eusebio Mujal, who became secretary-general of the Cuban Confederation of Labour (C.T.C.) under Prío, himself later defected to Batista—supposedly the sworn enemy of the Auténticos. The opposition showed little more coherence. The successful coalition in the 1940 election which supported Batista included the National Party, the Democratic Party, the National-Democratic Party, the Communist Party, the Conservative Party and the Liberal Party. Under the Auténtico regimes of the early post-war years, the major opposition party was the newly formed (1947) Ortodoxo Party. This had no independent political or socio-logical content; it was founded by the Auténtico Senator Eddy Chibás in protest against Auténtico corruption, and its only platform was the "broom." Anarchic violence and terrorism were endemic. Despite the return to parliamentarism, the politics of *pistolerismo* were still rife. The U.S. scholar William Stokes remarks: "Important terrorist cells, clubs and movements continued to exist . . . the 1948 election was marked by the exploding of bombs in ministeries, the machine gunning of prominent figures, including officers of the student body of the University, the discovery of a cache of arms on the University Campus."[32] In the seven years of Auténtico government, no serious social legislation of any kind was passed. An attemped purge of the army failed to remove important Batistianos. The single public political issue was corruption. And it is certain that if the 1952 election had been held, the candidate of the Ortodoxo Party would have won campaigning solely on the issue of Auténtico venality. Grau was reliably believed to have stolen the ceremonial emerald embedded in the Chamber of the Cuban Senate. Prío surpassed his predecessor; the end of his administration saw a frenzied, wholesale plunder of public funds. A *Time* magazine report captures the flavor of the Cuban Parliamentarism of the period, and of the tone of comment on it in the United States. Reminiscing about those "seven years of riot-

32. *Ibid.*, p. 383.

ously rotten government," it recalled the final exit of José Alemán, Minister of Education in the Grau government, from Cuban political life: "On the afternoon of October 10, 1948, he [Alemán] and some henchman drove four Ministry of Education trucks into the Treasury building. All climbed out carrying suitcases. 'What are you going to do, rob the Treasury?' joshed a guard. 'Quien sabe?' replied baby-faced José Alemán. Forthwith his men scooped pesos, francs, escudos, lire, rubles, pounds sterling and about 19 million dollars in U. S. currency into the suitcases. The trucks made straight for the airfield, where a chartered DC-3 stood waiting."[33]

The true character of the parliamentary regime was conclusively revealed by the manner of its termination. Just as the interlude had begun at Batista's fiat, so Batista ended it, when he wished and how he wished, without bloodshed. On the night of March 10, 1952, he effortlessly and almost single-handedly reassumed control. There was no resistance, scarcely even token opposition, from the Government Party, the legislature, the executive, the press or the judiciary. No government was ever more supine; no coup smoother.

A final foot-note completes this miserable record. It is striking that even today, in the most extreme adversity and under intense U.S. pressure, the exiled Cuban bourgeoisie has failed to produce a single large, stable, counter-revolutionary party. The Auténtico and Ortodoxo parties have disappeared along with their predecessors. In Miami a myriad of minuscule and fratricidal cliques dispute their abysmal heritage.

Army

The Army has, of course, historically been the prime instrument of oligarchic domination in Latin America. Its officer corps has been overwhelmingly recruited from aristocratic and merchant families. In the twentieth century it has provided a certain limited escalator for sons of professional families and white-collar groups. But the attraction of right-militarist ideologies has nearly always neutralized the class origin of these new entrants, and absorbed them into a reactionary and repressive elite. The innumerable coups and counter-coups which mark the Latin American scene have normally been essentially sub-political products of inter-service or inter-officer rivalry. The oligarchic character and role of the armed forces has remained unaltered.

The Cuban Army of the first decades of the Republic is unmistakably of this kind: it was a small, U.S.-created force designed by West

33. *Time* Magazine, April 21, 1952.

Point officers to replace the revolutionary army of the War of Independence which the U.S. expeditionary corp had deliberately disbanded a decade before. Its early history was uneventful. However, with the accession of Machado (himself a General) to power in 1925, the Army became directly compromised with the prevailing dictatorship. Then, when Machado was overthrown in 1933 and Céspedes installed as the New President something unique in Latin American history happened. In alliance with revolutionary student groups, the sergeants of the Cuban Army led the enlisted men in a revolt against their officers. The four-hundred strong officer corps barricaded themselves in Havana's Hotel Nacional, which had just been proclaimed by Sumner Welles a place of refuge for all U.S. citizens in the fighting. . . . Welles and his assistant, Adolph Berle, interposed themselves between the officers and the insurgents in the lounge of the hotel. Negotiations finally secured the withdrawal of all United States citizens from the building. The sergeants' and student forces stormed the hotel, and half the officer corps lost their lives in the fighting, and in their subsequent imprisonment. The remaining lost their positions. The traditional military elite was annihilated overnight. Nothing like this had ever happened in Latin America. There had been "colonels'" and even "lieutenants'" revolts before when junior officers, influenced by nationalism or an inchoate reformism, had risen against senior officers of an older generation (the Brazilian *tenente* revolts of the 20's were of this kind, and Peronism in its initial phase had much of this character). But there had never been an assault on the whole officer class from the ranks below it. As Edwin Lieuwen writes: "The Cuban revolution that brought Fulgencio Batista to power in 1933 was unique in being a mutiny of the rank and file, which toppled the old officer corps along with the government."[34]

The Sergeants' Revolt destroyed the Army as an instrument of traditional oligarchic rule. It did not replace it with a stable institution of middle-class character. Here, as elsewhere, the Cuban bourgeoisie failed to create its own institutions. Batista, a man of Afro-Chinese descent and peasant origin, converted the Cuban Army into a personal machine. His friends and fellow-sergeants monopolized the command structure of the armed services. Batista increased the size of the army from 12,000 to 16,000 men, raised the pay of officers and men, and allocated 22 per cent of the budget to military expenditure. However,

---

34. Edwin Lieuwen, *Arms and Politics in Latin America*, New York, 1961, p. 61.

despite this fortification, the Batista machine was politically isolated, since it possessed no real roots in local class formations. It was thus forced to make such internal alliances as it could, within the limits set by the U.S. international and economic policy of the period. The dictatorship remained, of course, the guarantor of the capitalist order in Cuba, but this was because of the context external to it, not because of its class content or ideological orientation. Within the limits of this context, its policy was purely opportunist.

Thus, the distinctive feature of the first Batista dictatorship was its "social" policy. A period of intense labor unrest, rural uprisings and brutal repression, culminating in an unsuccessful general strike in 1935, followed by the installation of the dictatorship. In 1937, however, Batista changed his tactics. Fearing the growing isolation of his regime, he began to make overtures to the trade-union movement. In 1939 he allowed the formation of the Cuban Confederation of Labour, of which a Communist (Lazaro Peña) became Secretary-General. Thenceforward, the Cuban working-class won a number of important concessions. Minimum wage-levels, an eight-hour day, a month's paid annual holiday and guarantees against dismissal were secured. Many of these provisions were even, at Communist insistence, written into the new Constitution proclaimed in 1940. The "Report on Cuba" of the I.B.R.D. (International Bank for Reconstruction and Development) was later to comment: "The political strength of organized labor . . . has become very great since the political and social revolution of 1933. . . . Before the 1933 Revolution the Government was usually on the side of employers in disputes with the workers. Since, the pendulum has swung so far to the other extreme that it is now employers and investors who complain that every issue seems to be settled against them." By the end of the first Batista dictatorship, Cuban labor legislation was among the most advanced in Latin America. It was against this background that Batista was able to win a genuine victory in the elections of July, 1940.

When Batista seized power again in 1952, he immediately attempted to re-create the entente which had won him popular support before. Eusebio Mujal, the Auténtico Secretary-General of the C.T.C., was summoned to the Presidential Palace and a working agreement was arrived at. However, this alliance at the summit failed to "take" at the base of the union movement. The Communist Party, which had supported the Batista regime in the 40's, was now cool. The rank-and-file of the unions were almost as mistrustful of Mujal as the I.C.F.T.U.

was enthusiastic. In 1955, for instance, the sugar workers staged a successful national strike in defiance of Mujal's instructions.

From 1957 onwards, as the Revolutionary forces consolidated their position in the Sierra Maestra, while the urban resistance of the 26th of July Movement increased its activity in the towns, the dictatorship became more and more isolated. An assassination attempt against Batista, an unsuccessful general strike and an abortive naval revolt followed in quick succession. As student workers and even naval officers went over to the opposition, the regime struck out blindly in retaliation. The more isolated it became, the more it relied on terror to survive, and the more it increased its isolation. By 1958, it no longer had any support outside itself: it was a pure apparatus of terror and extortion. In the second period, the Batista regime was personified in the international gangsters and adventurers who bedecked it at all echelons. Rolando Masferrer (El Tigre), a Spanish renegade from the Republican Army in the Civil War, ruled Oriente Province with a private army of 2000 para-military terrorists whose characteristic insignia were the baseball-cap and the mobile short-wave radio patrol car (*micro-onda*). Meyer Lansky, a Russian-born and U.S. naturalized gangster identified by the Kefauver Committee as one of the six most powerful racketeers in the United States, controlled Havana's vast gambling concerns and built the last and most lavish of Cuba's luxury hotels, the Riviera. Amadeo Barletta, an Italian who had been a member of Mussolini's General Court, monopolized Cuba's lucrative Cadillac concession and was the island's largest newspaper owner. In men like these, the carnal character of Cuban capital found its last and purest expression. Their predominance marked the impending collapse of the regime. The end came suddenly: within four weeks of Guevara's march on Santa Clara, although his armies were still in the field, Batista fled by air with retainers and treasury to Ciudad Trujillo in the Dominican Republic. Alone, Masferrer's army in Oriente fought on into January.

The Batista dictatorships were the most distinctive and durable institutional product of pre-revolutionary Cuban society. It has been seen how Batista's power was originally founded on the destruction of the old officer class in the army. After a period of wholesale repression, the regime attempted to acquire a popular base by means of a tactical alliance with the trade-union and political organizations of the working class—a rapprochement facilitated by the Second World War. It was at no point, however, a populist phenomenon of the recognizable Latin American kind; it had more affinity with those demagogically "social" dictatorships which mimic the programs of populism without its character as a movement. These *dirigiste* simulacra of populism have been almost as common as populism itself in Latin America: Odría in Peru, Ibáñez in Chile, Rojas Pinilla in Colombia have provided notable examples. When Batista reassumed power in 1952, he tried to repeat this formula, but with decreasing success. The dictatorship, which came to be infiltrated with expatriates, swiftly became hated by all sections of the population. By the end, its armed apparatus stood alone. It had always been an arbitrary and contingent structure. It became a senseless and untenable one. Although the military strength of the regime was still ostensibly great, the evacuation of December 1958 was inevitable.

Aspects of the Revolution

. . . What social forces overthrew Batista? This crucial question can only be answered by some attempt at a precise assessment of the scale and structure of the revolutionary movement in Cuba.

It is, in the first place, clear that in both military and political terms the decisive revolutionary organization was the guerrilla army of the Sierra Maestra. The urban resistance of the 26th July Movement, although of considerable psychological importance, was politically and strategically a secondary phenomenon. What was the real character, then, of the Rebel Army?

A current North American version of this force is that it consisted of a peasant rank-and-file, "officered" by young "middle-class" revolutionaries. As all armies have a plebeian rank-and-file, the argument goes, the social character of an army is uniquely determined by its officer corps: the Rebel Army had "middle-class" officers, therefore it was a middle-class army. For it was the "desertion of the middle-class—on which Batista's power was based—that caused his regime to disintegrate from within and his army to evaporate." Thus the Cuban Revolution itself "was essentially a middle-class revolution that has been used to destroy the middle-class."[35]

It is true, of course, that Batista objectively preserved the capitalist order in Cuba. But it is quite inadmissible to pass from this to the conclusion that Batista's power rested on the middle class. A passing acquaintance with Cuban history should be enough to avoid this error: Batista's power rested on the army and on support from the United States. Because the vast mass of the middle class was the passive spec-

35. Theodore Draper, *Castro's Revolution*, New York, Praeger, 1962, pp. 23, 10.

tator of Batista's coup, the thesis asserts that his power was based on it. Similarly, despite the evident fact that the vast mass of the middle class was the passive spectator of the revolution against Batista, his downfall can be attributed to it. The young revolutionaries of the Sierra Maestra were often of middle-class origin, but it is absurd to conclude from this that the middle class in any way acted as a class through them. The truth is that the middle class as a class took almost no action either to support or to overthrow Batista. Its nature and history had not equipped it to play any such role.

So much for the middle-class character of the Rebel Army. The complementary argument, that the social origin of the guerrilla rank-and-file should be discounted, since all rank-and-file soldiers are peasant or working class, is equally aberrant. The "rank-and-file" of the Rebel Army were, of course, volunteers, and as such qualitatively distinct from conscripted or professional soldiers. The conundrum that the "Cuban Revolution was essentially a middle-class revolution that has been used to destroy the middle-class" is quite empty: it is based on no more than some elementary category confusions.

Returning to the real questions posed by the Rebel Army, the first and simple fact to register is the tiny size of the force operating in the Sierra Maestra. Probably at no point throughout the war did the entire Rebel Army number more than 1500-2000 men in arms.

Having said this, however, some—cautious—characterizing remarks are obviously possible. The social origins of the rebel leaders were mixed. Many came from middle-class backgrounds—but did not have middle-class occupations—they were too young. These comprised the important student element in the Revolution (Raúl Castro, Faure Chaumon). Some had professional qualifications: lawyers (Fidel Castro, Osvaldo Dorticós), doctors (Faustino Pérez, René Vallejo), teachers (Francisco País). Some were white-collar workers (Abel Santamaría, Jesús Montané of the Moncada attack). Others were drawn from the urban unemployed (Camilo Cienfuegos, Ephigenio Almeijiras) and the peasantry (Ciro Redondo, Guillermo García). It has been seen how meaningless it is to call this heterogeneous group a "middle-class force." If any single term is applicable, the majority of them might be described as revolutionary intellectuals in the sense in which the Declaration of Havana speaks of a revolutionary intelligentsia. In the plundered and subordinated Latin American societies of today, the formation of a dissident intelligentsia in revolt against the social order as a whole (and often its own inherited social milieu) is a widely attested phenomenon. . . .

Turning to the base of the Rebel Army, a number of considerations are important. In the first place, there is no doubt that the great majority of the guerrilla fighters in the Sierra Maestra were peasants—probably about 75 per cent. A private may not define the character of a professional army; a volunteer unquestionably defines the character of a guerrilla army. In this sense, the Rebel Army was certainly a peasant force. Furthermore, a successful guerrilla force cannot be considered in abstraction from the social field in which it operates. The two form a socio-ecological whole. In Mao's famous image, if the guerrilla fighters are fish, the rural population which hides them and sustains them is the water in which the fish swim and without which they cannot live. In Cuba, this indispensable medium was the destitute peasantry—the poorest in the island—of the Sierra Maestra. The character of the Rebel Army was thus doubly peasant: it was peasant both in its men and in its maintaining milieu.

However, to say this is not to say that it "represented the Cuban peasantry." The sheer size of the army precluded this in any literal sense. There were perhaps 1200 peasants in all in the Rebel Army; the rural population of Cuba is 3,000,000. Moreover, the geographical area of the rebellion was a very specific one: the backward mountainous region of Oriente Province. The peasantry of this zone—numbering some 40,000 families—was not typical of Cuba as a whole: it was a small subsistence peasantry, growing beans and malanga on rented plots, and —in the north—coffee as a cash-crop. This mountain peasantry was economically and culturally distinct from the rural proletariat of the sugar-plantations of the Cuban plains. Che has said: "we ought to mention, out of respect for the truth, that the first territory occupied by the Rebel Army, made up of survivors of the defeated column that had arrived aboard the Granma, was inhabited by a class of peasants different in its cultural and social roots from those that dwell in the regions of extensive, semi-mechanized Cuban agriculture. In fact, the Sierra Maestra, locale of the first revolutionary base, is a section that serves as a refuge to all those country workers who struggle daily against the landlords. They go there as squatters belonging to the state or some rapacious landowner, searching for a piece of land that will bring them some wealth. They must fight continuously against the exactions of the soldiers, always allied with the land-owning power; their horizon does not go beyond a document to the title of their land. The soldiers that made up our first guerrilla army of country people came from the part of this social class which shows its love for the possession of land most aggressively, what expresses most perfectly the spirit catalogued as petty bourgeoisie; the campesino fights because he wants land for himself and for his children; he wants to be able to manage it, sell it and make himself rich through his work."[36]

Thus, apart from the numerical limitations of the Rebel Army its geographical composition was not representative of the Cuban rural world as a whole. It was never simply "the Cuban peasantry in arms." It was, rather, an authentic expression of the dramatic encounter between a dedicated revolutionary leadership and the mountain peasantry of the Sierra Maestra. The survivors of the Granma were able to strike root in the mountains solely because they demonstrated their program in action. Guevara has described how the tiny guerrilla band passed from being "merely tolerated" by the peasants to being concretely helped, supplied with food, information, and, most important of all, recruits: "This was not due to any miracle but only to our program of action in the question of agriculture and schooling." By the summer of 1958 the Rebel Army administered an area of 5000 square miles; it had carried out an agrarian reform which included the distribution of 6000 head of cattle, and had established 25 schools. By the end of the war, significant sections of the Sierra Maestra peasantry had been radically politicized. The impact of this experience on the revolutionary leadership was equally profound. Again, Guevara writes: "The men who arrive in Havana after two years of arduous struggle in the mountains and plains of Oriente, in the plains of Camaguey, in the mountains, plains and cities of Las Villas, are not the same men ideologically, that landed on the beaches of Los Colorados, or who took part in the first phase of the struggle. Their distrust of the campesino has been converted into admiration and respect for his virtues: their total ignorance of life in the country has been converted into a knowledge of the needs of our guajiros; their flirtations with statistics and with theory have been fixed by the cement that is practice."[37] The juncture between the revolutionary leadership and the mountain peasantry was to have immense importance for the future of the revolution.

It remains to make some brief comment on the character and extent of the urban resistance of the 26th July Movement. The strength of this resistance varied regionally. It was most active in Eastern Cuba, particularly in Santiago, where País had great popularity. There was

36. Che Guevara, "Cuba: Exceptional Case or Vanguard in the Struggle Against Colonialism," in *Verde Olivo*, April 9, 1961. English translation, *Monthly Review*, July-August 1961, p. 59.
37. *Ibid.*, p. 69.

also an effective group in Cienfuegos. The Havana resistance, despite the presence of revolutionary student groups like the Directorio Revolucionario, was relatively weak. The average numerical strength of these groups is suggested by Robert Taber's revealing account of the abortive general strike of April 9, 1958. Taber, who was in Cuba with the resistance, relates how the Havana 26th July Movement claimed it would produce two thousand "front-line fighters" for the expected clashes during the strike. The strike was a failure over most of the island, including Havana. Taber comments: "The two thousand adequate armed and trained 'front-line fighters' did not exist. It is doubtful that there were two hundred."[38] Thus at no time did the resistance in Cuban cities compare as a force with, say, the F.L.N. in Algiers. The composition of the groups in the towns was varied. According to a former member of the Havana 26th July Movement, Javier Pazos, "of the militants in the action groups, some were students, others were workers who were either unemployed or sick of a corrupt trade union in league with Batista."[39] At the same time, the political and social composition of the leadership of the urban resistance does not seem to have been markedly different from that of the Rebel Army—there is no real basis for opposing one to the other, as has sometimes been done. Armand Hart and Faustino Pérez, head of the Havana section, Osvaldo Dorticós and Emilio Aragonés, chiefs of the Cienfuegos group, Faure Chaumon and Louis Wanguemert, leaders of the Revolutionary Directorate, are all prominent members of the revolutionary regime today.

These, then, were the effective historical forces which overthrew Batista: a handful of revolutionaries leading minuscule units recruited from the mountain peasantry of Oriente Province supported by even smaller, sporadic resistance groups in some of Cuba's towns. By the end of the war, Batista still had 30,000 men in the field, equipped with tanks, artillery, helicopters, jet-fighter bombers. How was the apparently miraculous rebel victory possible?

The real history of the war against Batista was the way in which a small group of revolutionaries was able to awaken political consciousness against the regime in almost every section of Cuban society. From the beginning, the guerrillas depended for their existence on the goodwill of the mountain peasantry. If the guerrillas were to do more than simply exist in the mountains, they had to enlist the active help and support of the peasantry. Once they were established in the Sierra

38. Robert Taber, *M-26: Biography of a Revolution*, New York, 1961, p. 19.
39. Javier Pazos, "The Revolution," in *Cambridge Opinion*, Vol. 32, p. 21.

Maestra, their task was to transform in the island as a whole resigned acceptance of the regime into positive hostility. They succeeded in this, and it was enough to destroy Batista. The real role of the Rebel Army, then, was not just military. As soon as the existence of the guerrillas in the Sierra was made known to the population as a whole [by Herbert Matthews' reportage of February 1957], the entire character of the opposition to Batista changed. Prior to the rebel invasion, the opposition to the regime had been so inadequate that in 1955 Batista had virtually staged a mock coup against himself in order to smoke out those he distrusted. From February 1957 onwards, the resistance to Batista acquired a permanent focus in the Sierra Maestra, which assisted—and united—even opposition groups at that time extremely antipathetic to the 26th July Movement and to each other, from Prío's Organización Auténtica to the Communist Party. From March 1958 onwards, the rebels in the Sierra were able to reach the civilian population of Cuba directly through the Radio Rebelde, which became an extremely important political weapon. Thus, although the almost universal hostility that had been aroused throughout the island was translated into action only by the minuscule but suicidally brave Rebel Army and urban resistance, this was quite enough to complete the demoralization of the army and persuade its leaders that further fighting was useless. By the end, Batista's regime was hated everywhere in Cuba, and its own paid personnel were deserting it. The military and political credit for its defeat was unchallengeably that of the Rebel Army. Proof of this was provided by the tumultuous welcome which met Fidel's triumphal progress along the whole length of the island from Santiago to Havana.

At the same time, the astonishing history of Batista's overthrow was only possible because of the particular historical nature of Cuban society. Compared with all other revolutionary wars of the last decades, Cuba's was short: almost exactly two years. Compared with all revolutionary armies, Cuba's was tiny. The speed of its victory was possible because the enemy it fought was fundamentally so weak. No coherent ruling-class had ever established stable domination of the Cuban Republic. There were no powerful institutions or ideology to oppose: only the isolated and opportunist Batista machine. In this light, the otherwise magical victory of the insurrection becomes rational. More, the very character of the revolutionary regime which succeeded it—which so much puzzled the world in the following years—becomes explicable. The unprecedented hallmarks of the revolution—in lack of party or an ideology—were the logical product of a pre-revolutionary society which

The revolution triumphs in Havana, January 1, 1959. (Burt Glinn, Magnum)

itself lacked any decisive institutional or ideological structures. There were no institutions in Cuba of a kind to force the revolution, over decades of testing struggle, to create iron counter-institutions of its own, as happened in Russia and China. There was no enveloping, pervasive reactionary ideology to combat either. The enemy was a starkly corrupt and asocial machine. Its character determined the condition of its overthrow. . . .

The triumphal entry of the Rebel Army into Havana captured the imagination of the world. The events which followed it came as a thunderbolt to foreign observers. Their tempo and scale was utterly unforeseen outside Cuba. The cataract speed of the social and political revolution in Cuba was far faster than that of the comparable progress in Russia and China after the conquest of power. Within six months of the entry into Havana, a radical Agrarian Reform was realized. Within twenty months nearly all U.S. property in Cuba was expropriated. Within twenty-two months the vast majority of Cuban firms were expropriated. Within thirty months a U.S.-backed counter-revolutionary invasion had been fought and defeated. Within thirty-six months Fidel Castro announced that he was a Marxist-Leninist and that the Revolution was a Marxist-Leninist Revolution. Within forty months he had publicly denounced the de-facto Secretary-General of the new Cuban Revolutionary Party for, in effect, Stalinism. Within forty-two months Cuba was officially recognized by Russia and China as an integral part of the Communist world. Within forty-six months it was the scene of the first international nuclear crisis.

What caused this evolution? How was it possible? The war against Batista was fought, as we have seen, with the almost universal support of the Cuban population but with the active participation of only minuscule groups. The next question to ask is what kind of social panorama did the Rebel Army debouch onto, when it came down from the mountains and into power? So far in this study, deliberately only the top layer of Cuban society has been examined. It is now necessary to consider its "Lower Depths." The following major exploited groups can be distinguished:

1. Urban Proletariat. 400,000. The working class was highly organized in (often very corrupt) unions. It was divided by a wide fan of wage-differentials, running from a typical textile worker's wage of 40 dollars a month to an electrical worker's 500 dollars. It had a considerable political tradition, although of a markedly economist kind.

2. "Petit Bourgeoisie." Perhaps 250,000. The term can only be used in

a very analogical sense. It covers essentially an army of petty traders, domestic servants, waiters, entertainers, and procurers. This proliferating, parasitic mass was created by the combination of unemployment with the luxury life styles of the local rich and the tourists. The exact size of this group is difficult to estimate. Many of them were seasonally employed, and so might be included in the next category.

3. Unemployed. 700,000. The number of those unemployed for the greater part of the year was almost double that of the working-class itself. The unemployed were mainly encamped in the shanty towns which surround Havana and other urban centers. About half of them found jobs in the countryside during the sugar harvest as cane-cutters. The rest, if they were lucky, might find a few months work each year in construction, or might temporarily join the previous or subsequent groups.

4. Rural Workers. 570,000. Like the urban working-class, this group was divided into different sections. The major differentiation was between mobile laborers and those workers permanently employed in the sugar-mills, on cattle ranches or on tobacco *vegas* [plots; eds.]. The 50,000 mill-workers were an economically privileged elite in the countryside: they received a total annual income equal to the total payment of over 500,000 cane-cutters.

5. Minifundist Peasantry. Perhaps 250,000. There were about 135,000 minifundia (farms under 50 hectares and averaging 15 hectares) in Cuba. According to the 1946 census, 35 per cent of these peasants were small tenant farmers, 25 per cent were small-holders, 25 per cent were share-croppers (*partidarios*). Ten per cent were squatters (*precaristas*) and 5 per cent were sub-tenant farmers. However the census certainly under-estimated the number of share-croppers and squatters. Many of the eloquently-named precaristas seasonally moved into the category of cane-cutters.

These five categories comprised the main exploited classes and excluded groups of Cuba. Together, they numbered something over 2,-000,000 out of an employable work-force of 2,500,000-2,750,000.

This tabulation must be set against some general comments on the oppressed classes of Latin American societies, however brief and inadequate. The central, determining fact of Latin American history has been the failure of the bourgeoisie to complete its task of transforming the economy. The incomplete development of this century has produced probably the most profoundly fragmented and disintegrated societies in the world. The economic failure of the bourgeoisie allows the most advanced modes of production to co-exist with the most primitive. The exploited classes, who together constitute the vast majority of the population, are segregated into divided minorities. A serf-life peasantry is imprisoned within feudal relationships. Semi-employed agricultural workers are exploited by a plantation economy. An urban proletariat works modern capitalist industry. A white-collar force precariously depends on a corrupt and over-staffed State apparatus. A mass of unemployed, sub-proletarians, petty parasites and Lazzaroni stagnate in swarming bidonvilles. Ethnic differences—Pre-Columbian American, European, African, Asian—add vertical divisions. This complex fragmentation is undoubtedly the greatest single barrier to revolution in Latin America today.

However, as against this, the ramshackle social order undermined both town and country. The ubiquitous influence of foreign capital creates an important proletariat without producing an enlarged countervailing bourgeoisie—and the growth of industrial employment and urbanization in turn leads to the creation of large numbers of unemployed on the edge of the towns. At the same time the rural areas, despite the backwardness and oppression which reign in them, are also strikingly vulnerable. Both Spanish and Portuguese colonial empires were more successful at establishing towns and cities than at effectively colonizing the rural interiors. The imposed feudalism of Latin America always remained to some extent inorganic, bureaucratic and city-based. The intimate bond between feudal lord and serf was never effectively re-created in the New World. The land-owner, even when he lived on his land, never wholly acquired feudal authority over the serf population of Indians and escaped or freed slaves. Only in those countries where the population is almost wholly European (e.g. Argentina and Uruguay) has a stable rural order been established. Elsewhere the "backlands," "interior," and "Sierra" have been a constant source of revolts; even Guajiros of Spanish origin become "Indian."

In Cuba, these epicenters in the social order were present in an extreme form. The weakness of Cuban rural society was particularly acute. Lowry Nelson noted a striking absence of social institutions (schools, churches, etc.), a high rate of geographical mobility among all groups, and a lack of "name-consciousness"—even large villages often possessed no name. Officially rural illiteracy was 40 per cent, but it was in fact much higher. According to the 1943 census over half of the permanently co-habiting couples in rural Oriente Province were unmarried. Nelson's questionnaires reveal that the rural population felt itself to be an alien territory: the first demand was for improved communications; the second for educational facilities. An outbreak of socialist jacqueries in the countryside in August-September, 1933, revealed the potentially elemental forces which could be unleashed in the Cuban countryside. Sugar workers took over thirty-three mills establishing what they called soviets. The army immediately attempted to suppress these rural soviets, but many fought on bitterly for months.

At the same time the existence of 700,000 permanently unemployed or under-employed in both town and countryside constituted an immense breach in the whole society. This mass was not even exploited in the relationships of production: it was simply excluded from them altogether. It had no stake or foothold in the social order at all. No more radical destitution and expulsion can be imagined. In the case of both the rural work-force and this vast interzonal flotsam, one crucial fact is clear; there was an almost complete lack of any social or ideological integration of these groups into the normative structure of society. No such thing as an "inclusive" or "parent" society existed.

In the towns, the Cuban working-class had a history which was significant in a quite different way. The countryside, the semi-employed and the unemployed existed outside any regulating ideological or political universe at all. The urban working-class, on the contrary, was for most of its history integrated into the most highly structured ideological organization in Cuba—the Communist Party. Two facts are enough to show how important the historical role Communist Party was in Cuban society. The Cuban C.P. was in relative terms the most successful Communist Party in Latin America. In Cuba it was the only durable political party produced by the pre-revolutionary Republic. It was a serious social and political force uninterruptedly from its foundation in 1925 to the fall of Batista in 1959. No other Cuban political party could match this record.

The Cuban Communist Party, then called the Partido Communista de Cuba, had for its first general secretary the student leader, Julio Mella, later murdered in Mexico by Machado agents. During the 1933 revolution the party carried out an abrupt right-left zig zag in its political line; at one point it attempted to push through a deal with Machado, giving him support in return for government recognition of the Trade Unions, then, after Machado's overthrow, it opposed the Grau regime from an ultra-left position. These maneuvers certainly inhibited the influence of the party in the revolutionary process and disoriented its militants, setting a precedent for both opportunist and sectarian policies. However, the party emerged organizationally strengthened from the vents of 1933-34, especially in the trade union field.

Trade unions had existed in Cuba since the late nineteenth century; their leadership at first tended to be anarcho-syndicalist though by the early 1930's the Communist Party dominated the most impoartant national trade union federation. But at this time the unions were still comparatively weak. Thus the party had a certain influence among the sugar workers but it was unable to co-ordinate the seizure of mills and the formation of rural soviets in 1933. As the Sugar Workers Union Conference later commented: "Organization in general trailed behind the evolution of the struggle as it developed from day to day—the seizure of the sugar mills, the attempted creation of soviets, the arming of the proletariat." In 1935, at the forum plenum of the Central Committee of the P.C.C., the policy of the Popular Front was adopted, in line with the general change of policy within the Communist movement after the seventh congress of the Third International. Henceforth the party devoted all of its energies to union organization. The new general secretary who succeeded Villena after his death in 1934 was Blas Roca (Francisco Calderio), a militant of the shoe-makers' union. The I.B.R.D. Report on Cuba later commented: "From 1933 to 1947 the Communists by superior industriousness, devotion, training and tactical skill—all of which qualities their bitterest critics emphasize—succeeded in attaining practically complete control of the Cuban labor movement." After 1937 the unions as has been seen, were able under Batista to win important gains for the working-class. This naturally attracted support for the party. In 1939 it was legalized under the name Unión Revolucionaria Communista and 80,000 people attended a celebration meeting in Havana. In 1942 a coalition with Batista was marked by the presence of two Communists in his cabinet (Cuba had declared war on Germany, though she was not involved in the fighting). In the elections of 1944 the party backed Batista's candidate under its new name, Partido Socialista Popular (P.S.P.). Its membership, registered with the Electoral Tribunal, was 122,000, of whom about 15,000 were cadres. The party had become the only mass party of the Cuban working class. After 1947 its strength declined as the Auténtico Government systematically purged the unions and persecuted the party; prominent Communist unionists, like Jesús Menéndez (secretary-general of the sugar workers' union) were shot to death by Auténtico gangsters. However it was too strongly rooted in working-class traditions to be eliminated. The 1950 elections revealed continuing support for the P.S.P. as it received in Havana only 10,000 votes less than the Government coalition.

However, the stamina and success of the party was bought at a price. The P.S.P. identified itself with only the economist aims of the working-class. This incapacitated it for revolutionary leadership. It was unable either to build the necessary alliance of revolutionary forces or to formulate the requisite revolutionary strategy. Batista's coup of 1952 was greeted with a call for honest elections and this policy was maintained until the summer of 1958 when the party rallied to the rebels. The opportunism of the party's politics, especially its quite uncritical support for Batista from the late thirties to 1944, was accompanied by a fervent adherence to Stalinism in all matters of an ideological nature. The party's membership and influence was certainly on the wane by the fifties with the emergence of a genuine and uncompromised revolutionary leadership.

Nevertheless, it must be emphasized that the Communist Party in January, 1959, represented a major and lasting force in Cuban society, which no revolutionary regime could ignore or easily displace. The I.B.R.D. report paid it its truest tribute: "It must be remembered that nearly all the popular education of working people on how an economic system worked and what might be done to improve it came first from the anarcho-syndicalists, and most recently—and most effectively—from the Communists.

These then were the major forces of the poor and exploited in Cuba: an abandoned rural population, a destitute mass of unemployed, and a relatively compact and disciplined urban proletariat. The revolutionary potential of each was incapsulated in diametrically opposite forms: non-integration into any ideological or organizational structure, integration into an extremely militant and articulated structure.

Finally, some comment is also needed on the inarticulate and inchoate forms of consciousness which were to be found among the Cuban poor. In the first place, what may be called the African tradition is extremely important. Very little can be understood about Cuba until it is realized how ethnically African a country it is. Some 25 per cent of the population is of more or less pure African descent and the number of mulattos is very considerable: census figures are not an accurate guide to how many. The overwhelming majority of Afro-Cubans have been in manual occupations, particularly in the rural labor force. These descendants of the Cuban slave population have retained strong elements of an African identity. Caribbean and Brazilian (in contrast to North American) slaves went mainly to large plantations; despite the unbelievably cruel conditions on these plantations the slaves were able to preserve a certain collective consciousness and continuity of identity. Thus African religious ideas are clearly dominant in the Haitian Voodoo and the Cuban *ñañigo* cults, whereas black religious movements in the United States have until recently been almost purely Christian; Afro-Cuban music and dance forms are much closer to African originals than are North American variants.

The political expression of this African identity was a tradition of continuous insurrection and rebellion which lasted to the early decades of the century. The first slave revolts in the continent occurred in Cuba in 1525, only thirteen years after the resistance of the Indian leader Hatuey had been crushed. In the nineteenth century there were many revolts and conspiracies usually involving several thousand slaves and originating in Oriente—notably in 1812, 1827, 1843 and 1879. Afro-Cubans played an important part in the Independence wars—the very name given the Independence fighters, *mambises*, was of African origin. The last Afro-Cuban uprising in 1912, led by Evaristo Estenoz, was only suppressed after U.S. marines had intervened and 3000 Afro-Cubans lost their lives. After 1912, the African political tradition merged into the general currents of Cuban radicalism. In particular, the Communist Party was always distinguished by its large number of Afro-Cuban leaders. The famous Realengo 18 Rural Soviet, which held out against Batista's armies right into the early months of 1934, was led by an Afro-Cuban Communist, León Álvarez, Jesús Menéndez, whose murder was one of the most notorious episodes in the Grau Government, was an Afro-Cuban. Today such prominent members of the former P.S.P. as Blas Roca (editor of Hoy), Lázaro Peña (Secretary-General of the C.T.C.), Severo Aguirre (I.N.R.A.), and Carlos Olivares (Ambassador to Moscow) are all of partly African origin. At the same time, the associations and traditions of the Africans in Cuba have been present in the Fidelista Revolution almost from the start. Raúl's column in the Sierra Maestra was affectionately known as the "Mau-Mau." A typical post-revolutionary illustration of the tradition is provided by a recent speech of Fidel's at a meeting in Oriente, ethnically the most African of Cuba's provinces: "In the past when voices were raised in favor of liberation for the slaves, the bourgeoisie would say 'impossible, it will ruin the country'; and to instill fear they spoke of the 'black terror.' Today they speak of the 'red terror.' In other words; in their fight against liberty they spread fear of the black; today they are spreading fear of socialism and communism."[40]

A second current of radical consciousness among the Cuban poor was provided by popular Christianity. It has already been explained how the

40. Fidel Castro, *Speech*, July 26, 1962.

Church was unable to play its normal reactionary institutional role in Cuba. In this vacuum, there became prevalent what Gerald Brennan has called the "heresy" that consists in "taking very literally the very frequent allusions in the Scriptures to the wickedness and consequent damnation of the rich and the blessedness of the poor." Perhaps the Cuban worker or peasant read the words of the Virgin Mary with the same reaction as the Spanish worker: "In her great song of triumph, charged with an un-mistakeable prophetic meaning, she had rejoiced that the mighty had been put down from their seats, and the poor exalted, that the hungry had been filled with good things whilst the rich had been sent empty away. He [the worker] might be forgiven for seeing in such words an expression of class feeling!"[41] In this form Christianity provided a moral critique of the venality and oppression of pre-revolutionary Cuba. Today a revolutionary slogan reads "He who is against the poor is against Christ." The three bearded wise men in the small wayside Christmas crib sometimes look uncannily like Karl Marx and Fidel Castro. Pictures of Christ and Fidel side by side in a Cuban home are very common. Spanish priests have been expelled and "heresy" reigns undisputed. It is noteworthy that today relations between the Holy See and the Revolutionary Government of Cuba are cordial.

A final pervasive form of consciousness in Cuba was, of course, nationalism. Because Cuba's independence was late and incomplete, it was an "advanced" nationalism from the beginning. The hero of the Second Independence War, José Martí, was able in the perspective of the 1890's to be the most radical of all the great Latin American liberators. He saw with anguish that Cuban independence, which was costing Cubans such immense losses in the war against Spain, might be confiscated from them by the nascent imperialism of the United States. The social content of Martí's anti-imperialism appeared at first to be classically petit-bourgeois. But as a leader of the Cuban liberation movement he discovered that in the Cuban conditions of his time: "The people—the oppressed masses— are the real leaders of revolutions." He saw his task as "uniting all the real forces of labor against those who strangle freedom with their corruption, their plunder, and their luxury." His last words called on Cubans to "halt the spread of the United States over the West Indies, after which it will with added force descend on our lands of America" and urged them to prevent "the opening in Cuba, though its annexation by the imperialists, of the road that must be barred, and which we are barring

41. Gerald Brennan, *The Spanish Labyrinth*, Cambridge University Press, Cambridge, Mass., 1962, p. 80.

with our blood, of the annexation of all the nations of our America by the violent and brutal North that despises us." When the Republic was finally established, it became clear that Cuba which had perhaps fought hardest against Spain, had acquired the least independence. Systematic subjection—economic, political, cultural—to the United States ensured that Cuban nationalism retained and developed the radical character that Martí gave to it. Because the Cuban bourgeoisie was structurally integrated into the neo-colonial economic regime, nationalism became a force directed against the whole social order, not merely the imperialism power. The continuity of Cuban nationalism receives material expression in the Second Declaration of Havana which opened seventy years afterwards, with Martí's dying words.

These, then were the mass forces and the collective consciousness which awaited the arrival of the Rebel Army in Havana. It was their immense driving-power which turned the insurrection of a tiny minority into a tumultuous total revolution. How were their energies released? How did the rebel leadership succeed in mobilizing the exploited classes of Cuba?

Three decisive factors may briefly explain how the revolutionary elite of 1956-58 became the mass revolutionary force of 1959-63. The first two reveal the extreme importance of the relatively developed character of the Cuban economy as compared with that of Russia in 1917 or China in 1949. First and most obviously the communications network in Cuba—transport, tele-communications, and newsprint—was very highly developed; in some sectors it had effectively reached saturation point. This sophisticated system of communication provided the indispensable technically perfect conditions for the astonishing mobilization of 1959-60. The absence of a political party was compensated by a television radio and transport system which allowed immediate, electronic contact between the revolutionary leadership and the working people of Cuba. In the critical early days of the rebel regime the importance of this physical substitute for a political organization can scarcely be overestimated.

Secondly, the crucial economic conditions of mobilization were provided by the sheer, maldistributed wealth of the Cuban economy. A radical Agrarian Reform, a 50 per cent reduction in urban rents, a massive housing and schools construction program. A wave of 25 per cent-30 per cent wage-increases—these measures brought almost unbelievably rapid and visible benefits to Cuba's disinherited classes. Agricultural production rose considerably. There was a great increase in the output of cheap textiles, clothes, shoes, cigarettes and beer, and a corresponding decline in luxury consumption. Altogether the sum effect of these measures was to transfer 15 per cent of the National Income from property-owners to wage-workers within the space of about a year. A redistribution of this kind is historically unprecedented. No revolution before has ever been made in a country rich enough to permit such a transfer. The demonstration effect of it must have been overwhelming.

Thirdly, the political condition of the united élan of 1959-60 was the quality of the revolution's leadership. The tactical skill, dramatic flair and political vision of Fidel, Raúl and Che was of the highest order. The Revolution was unchallengeably consolidated in its first two years, before serious economic difficulties and political threats materialized. From 1961 onwards, North American fury had been aroused by the expropriations of the previous summer, and the blockade, flight of technicians and drop in investment had produced the first food shortages. But by the time the Cuban bourgeoisie began its exodus to Florida and the United States government decided to destroy the Revolution, it was too late. The Revolution rested unshakeably on the enthusiastic, armed participation of the majority of the Cuban people.

A final remark should be made. The fusion of the rebel leadership and the broadest mass forces in Cuba sealed the revolution. The problem of revolutionary institutions, however, remained. An unavoidable concomitant of the revolution's special history has been that, in the absence of equivalents to the soviets of 1917, institutions of socialist democracy have had to be "handed down" from the leadership. This accounts for a number of false starts. For example, Che commented on one experiment: "The main defect of the *Consejos de Técnica Asesor* [set up to ensure the participation of elected workers' representatives in the organisation of the factory] is that they were not created under pressure from the masses. They are a bureaucratic creation, introduced from above in order to give the masses an organ they had not demanded." [*Obra Revolucionaria*, May, 1961]. As had been seen, the special nature of pre-revolutionary Cuban society made the overthrow of Batista possible without a real political organization or ideology. In a different way, the special nature of Cuban society allowed the creation and consolidation of a mass Revolution in an unprecedentedly short period of time, still without a political organization or ideology. But thereafter, in the long-term task of socialist accumulation, and the mortal struggle with the United States, both were inevitably needed. The Cuban road to Communism was open. Today, when Cuba has crossed the threshold into a plural Communist world, the tension between the distinctive values of the "uninstitutionalized" character of its Revolution, and the imperative needs of its new economy and society, continues.

One of the many problems facing the revolutionary Cuban government is that of liquidating the profound heritage of imperialism on the island. A prominent example of this heritage is the penchant for North American consumer goods that many Cubans developed during the era of North American hegemony over the island. The possession and acquisition of these goods, although not possible for the majority of poor people in Cuba, became a way in which individuals determined their status vis-à-vis other individuals. José Yglesias, a North American novelist of Cuban descent, describes how some Cubans are desperately keening for these goods and services which are now scarce or absent in revolutionary Cuba:*

One of the times that Jorge, the young man who needed a pair of pants to ask for his girl's hand, came out of the windups he practiced in front of my room, his eyes fell on my feet, and he stepped back with surprise and admiration. I had put on leather thong sandals bought in Greenwich Village that I wore only around the Bitirí, and he had failed to notice them earlier because it was nighttime when he arrived with his friends. "My God, look at those sandals!" he said to them. "José has La Enfermedad!" And we all laughed because *La Enfermedad*—The Sickness—is an illness that attacks only young males.

The most common symptom of La Enfermedad is a penchant for tight pants; any of the clothes young men wear in Europe and the States, in fact, would qualify as *tremenda enfermedad*. "If you dress well—that is enough," I was informed by a fifteen-year-old who was in the first stage of the illness. "They suspect you and DOP (Orden Pública) will pick you up. You look close, though, and you will see that they wear their uniforms real tight. But do not say it and do not say La Enfermedad in front of them—it is like criticizing them, you know what I mean. All the young people feel like me, José, they hate the UMAP. They want to dress well. Do you want to sell your sunglasses?"

The first stage of the illness is nonpolitical: the young man is mainly seized with longing for stylish things, most of which are unobtainable,

* From José Yglesias, *The Fist of the Revolution*, copyright © 1968 by José Yglesias. Reprinted by permission of Pantheon Books, a division of Random House, Inc.

and he spends much of his time trying to get them or talking about them. (The vision is somewhat behind the times; the ideal style is the Italian designers' of four years ago or early Pierre Cardin: they do not know Mod and it might shock them.) They are restless and unhappy that they cannot get such clothes and angry about the revolutionaries who frown on them. In the last stage of the illness, they are counter-revolutionaries; they despise everything about the Revolution and are only waiting to reach that magical age of twenty-seven, when they can apply to leave the country.

Girls cannot catch La Enfermedad. Whatever a girl does to make herself noticeable and attractive is cause for approbation, sometimes expressed aloud as a "piropo"—"Take me home with you, my dear!"—or silently with a complete parabola of the men's swivel eyes. I liked to think that I could spot a Party member in a group of men: he was the one whose eyes braked in mid-course when a pair of flowering thighs went by. A young, handsome Party member of the Committees for the Defense of the Revolution was explaining the mentality of La Enfermedad—"Men with such values can be enticed into counter-revolutionary activity. . . ."—when a good-looking blonde went by, and someone with us exclaimed, "Look at that! Couldn't that entice you?" The Party member took a quick look, laughed, and said, "I have been cured of that!" But obviously he approved of all the aids—the hair dye, the cinch-waist belt, the aggressive brassiere, the tight skirt—that tempted him to look. "Aha, he is lighting a cigarette," the other said. "It makes him nervous!"

The fifteen-year-old with La Enfermedad wasn't recognizably hooked —he wore baggy pants, a nondescript shirt, ordinary shoes—and I met him at an unlikely place for someone with his interests. Perhaps not for he had a consuming hunger for girls, and the occasion was the graduation of 250 girls at Los Pinares as "lot leaders." They had spent three months there learning tractor driving and practical techniques in horticulture in order to become foremen of the twelve thousand women already signed up to work in the mesa. Since it was also International Women's Day, a program was planned, and I caught a ride up to Los Pinares, a half-hour uphill drive from Mayarí, with some women of the Federation of Cuban Women. Toward the end of the program it began to rain and we got back in the jeep for cover; two boys got in back with me and one of them turned out—in time—to have La Enfermedad.

The boys horsed around, and I spent most of the time talking to the driver of the jeep and two of the women who sat in front. But before the boys left, I asked the one if he was attending the horticultural technology school at Los Pinares. The jeep driver turned around and with a sarcastic smile said, "Not him, he is one of the frogs of the town." It was a perfect name for him: he showed up everywhere during the six weeks left to me in Mayarí, and I got to calling him El Sapito, the little frog.

He was a familiar young man; he got on a first-name basis with you—without permission and no matter what your age—after one encounter, and was apt to stop you on Leyte Vidal with much fanfare to ask you to change a ten. It was obvious he did not need to change the ten; he just felt it was a debonair thing to do. He got to dropping by the Bitirí, whether he had seen me on the street or at El Parque, because it gave him status; he liked draping himself over a chair, one leg swinging from an arm of it, and asking for a cigarette, which he smoked with many gestures and then flicked away into the bushes with great élan.

But the first time I saw him after the ceremonies at Los Pinares, he told me quite soberly that he was leaving the next day for the Soils and Fertilizers School in the Sierra Maestra; he was taking a bus to Bayamó and from there walking or hitching his way up the mountains. Until a few days earlier he had been working as an apprentice at a garage near the Palace of Justice, but he had decided that being a mechanic did not appeal to him; he went to the Party and told them he wanted to go away to study. "I do not know much about soils and fertilizers, but I can keep studying and working at it and then studying some more and get somewhere. Right?" At the moment he had just returned from Party headquarters, where he had shown them his sixth-grade diploma and a letter from his block's Committee for the Defense of the Revolution attesting to his good character. He shook hands when he went away, and I said to myself that no one could call him a frog of the town now; he was set and on his way.

Three days later he was back. The class he was to have joined had already left, as had many throughout the country, to work in the countryside for forty-five days. El Sapito was told to return on May 1, and he had a six weeks' vacation, he said, before he got down to work. I asked him if he were going to cut cane around Mayarí or get involved in some other voluntary work. "I might do that," he said, but I could see it had never occurred to him. It was a Friday night and he had come to see the weekend show at the Bitirí. The chairs in front of my room were a good place to watch for friends arriving that he could join.

"José, are you sure you are an American?" he said. "The first time I saw you I thought you were from one of the ships. I like to meet the sailors from the ships. Zing, as soon as I hear there is a ship at Guatemala or Nicaro I get on the bus and go there. A Greek once sold me a pair of sunglasses for fifteen dollars and I sold them for thirty! Pretty good, eh?" I nodded.

"How do you say, Give me a cigarette? How do you say socks? and condoms, how do you say condoms?" He practiced each a couple of times. "You do not have to teach me how to say Chiclets. Or Chesterfields or Lucky Strikes or Camels. But I like Chesters the best. I have to get some Chiclets and Chesters. I am invited to a wedding and I want to have some to impress the girls. I want to walk in chewing a Chiclet— oh man! I hear there is going to be a ship at Guatemala soon."

He sat up in the chair in order to reach into one pocket. He looked around and showed me a pack of condoms. "They are Chinese. See the butterfly on the cover? We call them Butterflies. Not because of the picture, oh no. It is because they have a short life. If you have not done it for a couple of days, you can shoot right through them!"

You didn't have to answer El Sapito. He kept right on talking, assured you were interested.

"The Greeks have the most to sell," El Sapito continued. "They always want to get laid. They say, Fuck-fuck signorina. I take them to a couple of loose ones in Mayarí who do it for five dollars. They just do it on the side, you know. There are no more women of *la vida* and you do not want to do it with them. You get syphilis and your hair falls out and your teeth go bad. I go to a woman in Cueto. She gives it to me any time I want.

This woman was a servant at a house on our block. I put in some time with her—you know, talking and convincing her I was all right. I knew she would do it because she was past her time—thirty years or more so she would not marry—and why should she not get what is coming to her? I told her I loved her and she let me. Now I go to Cueto every time I want it. Only it is not so convenient. I need to catch a girl right here. Right? Is it true that in the United States all the girls do it? Oh man, how I would like that! I would wear myself out.

I had a girl lived right next door. She still does, but it is all over. Not because of me—I still want to. It was last year. I was fourteen and she was eighteen, so one day when there was no one in our houses—I had been watching for the chance—I asked her over. I have something to tell you, I said. I was shaking I was so nervous. I told her, Oh I want you to know that although I am only fourteen I have been watching you and I love you so much I do not know what to do. I was looking down when I said this. Seeing I love you so maybe we can make love? And she said,

Look, if you do not tell anyone then maybe we can do it. But she would not do it then because it was too dangerous.

So one night we met at the Secundaria Básica, the new school across the field from the Reforma Urbana. It is dark there at night like the mouth of a wolf. No one comes by. Why would they? She did it for the first time. I told her, Get on four points. I saw that position on one of the postcards I have. A good thing I remembered, because she said, How are we going to do it? She did not want to lie down and get dirty. I said, From behind, get on four points. So she got on four points and I lifted her dress. There was such a spout of blood I thought she had been injured. I got scared I would be jailed or something. Then I remembered that she was eighteen and I was fourteen, so they could not do anything to me. What a relief!

That was the only time I did it with her. I do not know why but she got angry with me. She started saying *usted* to me. As if I was some stranger she did not know well. Then she stopped talking to me altogether. She had become engaged to a fellow in Guaro. You know, I do not think the poor fellow is passing it to her yet. He is going to have to marry her to get what I got. But you know how women are. I worked a couple of weeks for the cigarette distributorship and she wanted to get Aromas, the mild cigarette. So she spoke to my sister for me to get her some. But not to me. I got them for her.

I do not have a girl now, except that woman in Cueto. There is no time. But maybe up in the Sierra I will get a girl. Not maybe, sure. You pick one out and work on it and you got her. I also want to get a pair of sunglasses and a pair of sandals. You cannot get them just like that. You have to get a prescription. Oh man, sunglasses! That is something with el feeling—sunglasses! That is an American word, feeling, right, José? I would like to have one of those Italian suits. Real tight, oh what a feeling! But I could not wear it, of course. In Havana maybe. But here in Mayarí the DOP picks you up right away. Sunglasses and sandals okay, but no tight clothes. Not me.

You know, José, I once got picked up by the DOP. Not once, twice. They keep an eye on you when they see you with a foreign sailor. They saw me. I bought some Chiclets and Chesters, for the next day I was going to an engagement party. I went to the party and I passed out some Chiclets. The girls got the feeling and then I thought I would pass out a couple of Chesters. I reach in my pocket and all I have is Aromas. That is not too bad but I want to make a big impression. I went home to get the Chesters, but I did not get there because the DOP picked me up and searched me. All they found was the Aromas. What luck!

The next time I brought it on myself. But I did it for the feeling. I bought a pack from a sailor and at the cafeteria I took one and leaned against the wall like this and I smoked the Chester like this, letting the smoke right out. You can smell those American cigarettes in a room full of people smoking. They are very special, they have feeling. So they took me to DOP headquarters and they made me take off all my clothes. But all, and they asked me where I got the Chesters and I told them I bought them. They looked at me and said, Do you have more? I said no. Okay, they said, you can go home. They kept the Chesters. That is all they did."

"How much did you pay for those shoes?" El Sapito asked.

They were Hush Puppies. "Twelve dollars," I said.

"You can sell them for a hundred," he assured me. "You should sell the sunglasses. You can get thirty like I did."

I saw him on Leyte Vidal two days later. He had borrowed a bicycle and was riding around on it looking as if he had the feeling. He called me over and took a piece of paper from his pocket. It was a prescription for sunglasses. "I had to lie a little," he said. "I said I drove a motorbike for the Army. Now I have to go to Holguín to buy them. They do not have the kind I want here."

"I guess Cubans like sunglasses so much," I said, "because the sun is so bright here."

"Oh no, it is for the feeling," he said. "Say, José, did I tell you I danced with one of those girls that night at the Bitirí? There was a bunch having a party for one getting married, remember? They were most of them *gusanas* from Holguín and one went out on the dance floor with me. I got up real close. I hold my left hand in hers this way, I pull it all the way back and she has to get close to me. I put a real shine on it and she acted as if she did not notice it. Then she said I should visit her in Holguín. Her father would be glad to receive me since I am a nice boy. Wait until I get the sunglasses and then show up at her house. She is going to notice it then!"

Chepi, the maintenance man, came out of the pizzeria to talk to me, and he simply stared at El Sapito as if saying, I know kids' stories are mostly lies, and El Sapito found a reason to leave. On Sunday, Chepi said, the pizzeria would open, a reminder that we had a date to eat there on the inauguration. "There is not much else they can fuck up," he said; the opening had been long delayed. "But they may find something."

Rosebushes and shrubbery had been planted a week ago in the beds along the sidewalk, and round metal tables set into the terrazzo floor of the open dining room. Over each table brilliantly colored umbrellas—

yellow, blue, green—blossomed; they were in the shape of inverted tulips, and yielded slightly, femininely, to the breeze: a modern setting from which to look, with one's back to Leyte Vidal, at my favorite view from Mayarí, the valley with the winding river and the horses and cattle grazing. On Sunday, the waitresses wore wine-colored uniforms with white cuffs and collars, and they moved among the tables, as the moment drew near, as if enchanted, readjusting the black wire chairs and the settings to their sense of perfection. On the other side of the ropes stretched at waist height along the sidewalk, the crowd watched and talked.

The sun waned, the mountains in the distance turned blue and purple, then black; and the crowd in the street grew. After the first hour, I signaled to Granda who was watching the girls get the dining room ready, and told him when he approached that I hoped he would have a table for me and my friends. Granda told me not to worry, they would have a table for me. I was glad he didn't ask me how many we were, for I didn't know. Chepi knew everybody and a whole new crowd I had not met came over to talk while we were outside the ropes. The waiting made Chepi impatient: it was one of those inefficiencies he could not bear.

He became ironic, then sarcastic. He laughed at himself for having given up being an independent mechanic, hiring himself out for a job at a time, and having taken a regular job with a pizzeria. "Working for INIT is a *jamón*—a ham—an easy job," he said with disgust. "I think I am going to marry in another month. She is a girl of poor family but a good girl. That is a problem now, too, getting married. I like to dominate my wife and that is not so easy any more. Nothing is so easy any more. You see, they will not get one fucking pizza served tonight."

He was one of three sons of a Spaniard—Chepi did not know what part of Spain his old man had come from—who had worked hard and established two stores in Mayarí. His brothers all went to school and did well. "But I was dumb, I still am dumb," he said. "God, I am so dumb." He left school, worked around the courthouse for awhile, then left for Nicaro and did "brute's work" clearing out swampy areas; but by 1957 he had done several different types of work around the plant, been a *garrotero* lending money out at high interest, owned his own car, and saved ten thousand dollars. "Then I got a fistula on my backside and I went to Havana to get it cured. There was no hospital here then."

He got the fistula cured, but he did not come back to Mayarí because he had been a little too active in the Movement and his mother told him it was dangerous to come back. "Do not think I was a bit revolutionary like everyone tells you now that he was," Chepi said. "One reason I did not leave Havana was that I was leading la dulce vida. I had found a house full of little girls. They ran around in little panties, for they were smooth above, nothing to show there. The first time I went I had not had a woman for five months because of the fistula and I was surprised to be given a little girl. I thought I would never stop fucking. I went back every day."

But Chepi did not have La Enfermedad. He had not bought a new pair of pants in a couple of years, but he did not care. He told it to you —as he avowed that no one could beat the United States in a war—because these were facts and he had respect for facts. "And what government of Cuba has done as much for the country as the present one? None. The public works! The planting and the modernization! And they are honest—not one takes a penny for himself!" It was while he was saying this that he and I both noticed that Victor Bermúdez, the head of DOP, was staring at our table, trying to get my attention; Chepi blushed and then waved at Bermúdez. Bermúdez only nodded at him but beckoned to me. He wanted me only. As I went toward him, I knew—for I had seen Bermúdez earlier, before he caught my eye, gazing at the others at my table with a serious, appraising look—that he was not happy about the company I was in.

But Bermúdez seemed only to want to show me the inside of the kitchen. He took me around proudly with Granda and the regional head of INIT. There were walk-in refrigerators, many work surfaces, built-in ovens, two stoves: they were not making the mistake of the Bitirí, with its tiny kitchen and cramped space. We drank a glass of Spanish sherry in the kitchen and wished the pizzeria success. Yet when I went back, I looked at the collection of young men at my table and wondered why Bermúdez had been disappointed with the company I kept on so gala a night for the Revolution in Mayarí. There were Jorge, and Eider Cesar, the sports teacher, and El Chino, the electrician, and Hugo Ramírez, the young barber, all with varying degrees of devotion to the Revolution but none a counter-revolutionary.

There was one I didn't know and hadn't seen around Leyte Vidal till that night. The others didn't seem to know him well, but he introduced himself and said I was to call him El Rubio. When we broke up around midnight, he said he lived in the Reforma Urbana and would walk my way. The narrow sidewalk along Maceo made it necessary to walk close and then I could smell his cologne. I had not seen him in Mayarí because until two or three days ago he had been in Havana, where he had had a temporary job as a male nurse in a hospital. "But I could not keep the job," he said. I volunteered that I knew the government was now filling jobs that were not physically demanding only with women. He nodded reluctantly. "I have a month of doing nothing before I go to my next job, which is in agricultural production in Las Villas. A hard job."

When we got to the Bitirí, I realized that he had walked past the block where he should have turned off. He had been telling me, at my request, how they got water up to the third floor of the Reforma Urbana—a tedious process with a pail on a rope—and he was too polite, I thought, to tell me I was taking him past his home. But his face lit up as the orchestra in the dining room began playing for the last show of the evening and he said, "If you are not going to retire, I should be pleased to keep you company." I said I was only going to sit in front of my room and smoke a cigarette. He took that as an invitation and joined me. I was to smoke several more cigarettes before he finally left.

"Aaah, listen to that music," he said. "I have spent the last three days in my room, not going out, just listening to my radio. I have a radio but I would like to have a transistor. I like to lie in bed and put on the dim light in my room and listen to music. What else is there to do? I used to have a lot more things in my room. I had red damask curtains and I hung them over the wall behind the bed, but one has to sell those things to get other things. Or I spend the day desiccating insects, I like to do that too. I do them for the schools here, for their science classes. I inject them with formaldehyde and they are desiccated in a day or two. One day this week that is all I did.

I have a lock on my room, I like privacy. I live with my mother and my sister and my niece and they do not come into my room. I have had a lot of adventures but now I can spend hours in my room just listening to the radio. I am trying to take myself in hand. I have a fiancée in Havana and I have a lot of things to think about. I went out tonight because it is Sunday, and I am glad I did because I met you. It is interesting to meet people from other countries. You used to meet them in Havana. How I would like to travel! That is what I think I would like to do now—get a job on a merchant ship and travel. I think I would like to go to the United States. Not to stay there but to go on to places in Europe I have heard about. Like Greece.

One of my sisters lives in your country. She went there right after the Revolution to join my father. He has been there a long time. They live in Brooklyn, New Jersey. Do you know that place? I have asked them to send me a phonograph. I have records of feeling music but I cannot play them. And rock-and-roll. The Beatles. Do you know them? They are very hard to get here. Like everything. I am going to spend two years at *cara al campo*—face to the country, that is what they call work in agricultural production. I do not like it but I have to do it.

I can do anything. I was fourteen when I first went to Havana alone. Now I am twenty-two. That was not the first time. I went the first time with my mother and my sister because my sister had to go to a hospital there. I was twelve but I got to like Havana, and when we came back and I had a quarrel with my family, I took off for Havana alone. I already had friends there. I got a job in the mornings, another in the afternoons and evenings. And one on Saturdays. And I went to parties. Do you like parties? I like to do everything because I do not like to have people tell me stories—I like to be the one to tell the stories. Oh, I had a very good time in Havana.

I like adventures. That is why I want to get a job on a ship that will take me to the places I want to see. In 1958 when the Rebels were winning more and more I started back to Mayarí, but at Camagüey they were not letting buses go on to Oriente. I got stuck there for a whole month. I slept in the bus station the first night. And when I ran out of money, people gave me things to eat. Some nights I would sleep in someone's home or in a hotel or on a bench. I got to know many people in Camaguey and I had many adventures. I was never so happy in my life, it was so free and easy and friendly. You have to be careful about friends, though. That is one good piece of advice my mother gave me."

"Is he a friend of yours?" El Rubio said in a low voice, and looked toward the dining room. El Sapito was skipping across the lawn toward us. El Rubio frowned.

"Oh José, I got a prescription for sandals!" El Sapito said. Then recognized El Rubio: "José is a friend of mine. I did not know you knew him."

El Rubio smiled tolerantly.

"Where did you get your sandals?" El Sapito asked him.

"From a Greek for five dollars." Then he turned to me: I got them so cheap from him because he was drunk, or they would have cost more."

"I am going to get mine in Holguín," El Sapito said and took out his two prescriptions. "When I get my sunglasses. Have you got a cigarette on you?"

El Sapito sat on the arm of the other's chair, not noticing El Rubio's chagrin. "I been dancing again. Close up. This one fitted right in." He got up and began to move around to the hot music from the dining room. "I have to learn more steps."

El Rubio got up. "I can only dance well on the loose. When I am up against the girl only one thing responds. The other day I was with one who was too short and it pressed into her belly. So when they played a bolero I had the excuse to bend my knees and crouch and get it in the right place!"

El Sapito grabbed himself. "I have to go right back. It will end soon and I have to get her out on the floor one more time." He started off and then turned around. "I see you later, José. El Rubio is a good friend of mine."

"He is just a neighbor," El Rubio said. "I do not tell him much. He talks too much. Not like the friends I had in Havana when I was his age. We did what we wanted and our mothers did not find out. He is the way I was before I ran away to Havana, trying to get girls and going to the country for animals when you could not get a girl. I used to take a rope with me and go for a walk in the country. I kept the rope inside my shirt so no one would guess. I tied the rope around their necks —goats or calves—and pulled them down. Their heads bent down toward their bellies from my pulling and they spread their back legs and I would mount them! Oh, the things I did as a boy!

It is not so good, don't you agree, that there are no more women of *la vida*. Now men have to masturbate and that is weakening. You have to make such a mental effort. And then we do not get the proper food to be able to respond. Of course, not when you are young like my neighbor there. But he does not know what he is missing with this Revolution.

In Havana I used to go to the *fiestas de percheros*—the clothes-hanger parties—when I was younger than he. A friend took me. He had been to them before and he invited me. No, you did not pay any money. It was a party at someone's house and you just got together for fun. We went in and everyone got introduced to each other if they did not know each other from before. Then you had a drink and there was a little talk and joking. Then you got given a clothes hanger. Everyone got one—it was to hang your clothes on. I whispered to my friend to tell me what to do and he said, Take your clothes off and hang them up.

But the lights were all on and I said I would keep my shorts on. My friend said, Do not be a fool, take them all off. I did, but I was greatly embarrassed and my insect would not stand up. I kept my hands in front of me and sat in a chair apart. Then a girl came over laughing and took my hands away and touched it with her hands. She leaned over a little and put one of her breasts in my mouth. I liked that I must admit.

While I was doing it, a fag came over and kneeled on the floor and sucked me. I kept my mouth on that breast and my hand on her other one. I got so drunk that night I had to chew a lot of Chiclets so that my mother would not suspect when I got home. But I had to get up from bed to throw up and my mother half suspected it was not just indigestion.

I went to a lot of clothes-hanger parties after that. Sometimes two perverted women would lie on a mattress while the rest of us watched them. Then someone would turn off all the lights and we would each grab a girl and have a wonderful time all night. If we were broke, we went to the Parque Central or the Prado and walked until some homosexual talked to us. They would pay me five or ten dollars to play with me and nothing said later. I do not like those fags who act like girls in the street and talk to you like you are their fiancé. There was an old American with a young wife, he used to ask me to their room to watch me lie with his wife while he masturbated. Then we went out together and everything was perfectly normal. I respected him a lot.

None of that is possible any more, because the UMAP took all those people if they had not already left. Anyway, I am taking myself in hand. I have a fiancée and her parents approve of me. Now all I would like to do is travel, for I did everything there was to do in Havana in those days. Except for one thing. I did not get to go to that theater in old Havana with the shows and movies."

7

Concluding Remarks

If we compare the immediate present with the age of the *caudillos,* we can observe important features of continuity and change in the organization of power in Latin American societies. Numerous writers have stressed themes of continuity in Latin American political life; some of these themes are: political personalism (an eschewal of responsible, institutional political structures in favor of politics centered in labyrinthine interpersonal networks); lack of recognizable political ideologies (at least in European terms); structural authoritarianism (of which persistent military intervention is only one example); and continued bondage to overseas metropolises.

To stress continuity alone would obscure some fundamental changes in the political order, particularly those changes that have occurred between elites and masses (themselves quite changed) since the age of the caudillos. No longer is it possible for *hacendados* with a group of *peon* retainers to dominate the political structures of countries, as in the heyday of the caudillo order. The whole social order which spawned these types has been superseded by more advanced systems of productivity, even in the highland areas of Peru, Mexico, and Bolivia where they were once pre-eminent. In a word, many different kinds of what the anthropologist Richard N. Adams refers to as "power domains" are now present in Latin America.[1] Part of our discussion, then, has to center on the proliferation of ways of organizing power that have evolved in this century.

In addition to outlining some of the major changes in Latin American political life, it is useful to note that even those continuous features of

1. R. N. Adams, *The Second Sowing,* Chandler, San Francisco, 1967, p. 39.

politics have been subject to substantial modification. When trying to analyze a particular trait in a particular culture, it is imperative to look at the *context* in which the trait occurs. It is very possible that a trait may appear to be continuous, in structural terms, but the context in which it occurs has changed radically, altering the function of the trait itself. Thus, for example, we can note from the Schneider article that much of high-level policy in Brazil involves personalist cliques within the army; hence we could point to the continuity of political personalism within that country. But, as the anthropologist Anthony Leeds points out, the masses are now severed from the political process, whereas once they too were to be found in one sort or another of personalist power domain.[2] We cannot let the continuity of personalism in the system obscure the fact that it has come to be the province of the "classes" at the exclusion of the "masses," when once it involved both.

Perhaps the clearest way to deal with the issues of continuity and change in Latin American political structures is to focus on the structural aspects of present power relationships and see how they compare with past alignments. As a starting point we can consider two traditional sources of elite power—metropolitan and Latin American—and try to outline some of the major changes since the caudillo period. Then we can consider the changes between the Latin American elites and masses for the same time span. To us, the major changes in these relationships seem to be the following:

1. Metropolitan intervention in the political organization of Latin America has vastly increased in scope and complexity. This intervention has progressively entailed a diminution of the power wielded by the Latin American elites in their own domains, compared to the power wielded by the metropolitan elites. It has correspondingly involved increased dependence on the metropolis on the part of the elites, coupled with progressive circumscription of their autonomy and initiative within their own countries.

The increasing interlocking between metropolitan and Latin American elites has involved an effort to rationalize production, in the capitalist sense of the word (cut costs, enhance profits); as this process has been carried out, it has involved a divorce between the masses and the elites in every respect. The masses are either committed to forms of obsolete production in the countryside, which are more untenable every year, or

2. A. Leeds, "Brazilian Careers and Social Structure: A Case History and a Model," in D. Heath and R. Adams (eds.), *Contemporary Cultures and Societies of Latin America*, Random House, Inc., 1965, p. 384.

living as pariahs in the over-burdened cities, where many cannot find licit means of livelihood. There is no simple way for either of the elites to incorporate the masses into an organic relationship based on long-range national development.

3. The masses have the alternative of organizing or being organized into one form of socialist revolution, if only to ensure their physical survival, or simply being defined out of existence. Whereas once the masses were diverse (peon, Indian, open peasant, shacktown dweller), the differences between them have now become minuscule; they are the outsiders, the economically irrelevant. Let us consider each point in turn.

First, metropolitan power has progressively increased at the expense of both the Latin American elite and the masses. Paradoxically, this tendency has increased since the wars of independence. Comparing our account of Venezuelan *caudillaje* with Locker and Goff's description of the Trujillo regime in the Dominican Republic, one can note that the methods and power of the U.S. State Department are infinitely more diversified and efficacious than those of the supposedly all-encompassing Spanish colonial bureaucracy. From Goff and Locker we can observe some of the myriad ways in which the new imperial order both creates new power domains while penetrating many old ones as well. In the case of the Dominican Republic, new ways of dealing with the masses were spawned within governmental agencies of the metropolis itself. Thus trades-union activities relating simultaneously to governmental welfare policies and national electoral politics were created by a complex partnership between the C.I.A., American labor unions, and a philanthropic foundation.

It is not only that the metropolis generates new forms of organization in Latin America, it also has different target populations to control in different ways than did the traditional elites. Perhaps the growing penetration of the organs of the state into the countryside provides the most spectacular example of this point. Traditionally the countryside has been more or less detached from a direct incorporation into national political life and subject to a series of more or less personalistic power domains which composed whole social systems in and of themselves. The relationship between hacendado and peón is not a simple matter of social control of one class by another, although this relationship is not understandable without this aspect; it also involves a series of mutual obligations, prestige and deference behavior, and cultural idiom to make the roles comprehensible to their players. All of these things considered together made it possible for both to be mobilized together (not opposed to each other) in caudillo bands or even in the Brazilian pattern of *coronelismo*.

But the population of the countryside has since come to enjoy a diminished economic status from the period of *haciendas* or even vigorous peasantries. The course of the twentieth century, particularly since the Second World War, has led to a mass exodus from the countryside into the *callampas* and *favelas* of the cities. The remaining peasant or rural worker is increasingly an economic marginal man, and in that status has rapidly come to be a political liability for the modernizing elites. At this juncture, the complicated social relations of another century are transformed into the unitary problem of how to control the marginal man of the countryside. Into this breach have plunged national armies in search of guerrillas in Cuba, the Dominican Republic, Columbia, Bolivia, and Guatemala, to name a few examples. But the army is not as it was in the past; it now has available the advice and counsel of the metropolitan armed forces and intelligence services, and a fair amount of its hardware as well. It knows and studies the manuals on counterinsurgency, distilled from another war half way around the world.

It is not the countryside alone that gives rise to concern on the parts of both the Latin American elites and their metropolitan counterparts; both the urban masses and even the middle classes are looked upon as potential troublemakers. Nothing looks stable and progressive in this sphere of society, and it is best handled by a mixture of outright repression, populist manipulation, and a smattering of welfare programs to muffle the grumbling from below. In this milieu, it is perhaps the trait of populism which deserves most attention. From Pearse's study of the Rio de Janeiro favelas we can note that the essence of populism appears to be that the poor and others with no direct access to power still count on receiving aid of a welfaristic nature from those in power. The response of the Latin American elites has been to ideologically cater to these desires and demands, as well as to develop some of the bureaucratic structures necessary to implement a fraction of them.

On the face of it, the new populism appears to be a continuation of the old personalism, which is now coated with an institutional rather than an interpersonal cast. Where once a caudillo dealt directly with his henchmen, populist leaders reach urban masses with personal appeals via modern means of communication, often with great emotional impact. Yet populism is not the old personalism, no matter what the reaction of the lower classes may be to it. In the first place, this form of populism involves no sharing of power whatsoever, and even less room for maneuver by the underdog than *caudillaje*. Second, the lower classes are seldom mobilized for anything other than electoral politics. That is to say, their actual participation in politics is less than it was in the past century. They vote and go home; they are not being welded into a permanently mobilized group of activists, on behalf of democracy or anything else.

This is not to say that the old personalism has disappeared; rather that its social context has been reduced. The anthropologist Anthony Leeds, among others, has noted recently that there is a nearly impermeable boundary between what he calls the "classes" and the "masses," which roughly correspond to our "elite" and "masses." In his study on Brazilian careers and social structure, Leeds notes that only the "classes" (found in the upper sectors of urban areas) are tied together, actually and potentially, by sets of interpersonal relationships of the traditional style; the masses are excluded. We could note similar occurrences of exclusion throughout Latin America, and offer a partial explanation: as the masses have become increasingly irrelevant to the means of production, and as power has become increasingly centralized, the need for considering the masses as an important political entity has decreased. Correspondingly, the need for the classes to associate in any way with the masses has reached the zero point, except for the function of control. The masses do not even have the kind of leverage that the rubber tappers in the Amazon had against the store owners in Itá (threat of vanishing and defaulting on credit), which led to a proliferation of the godparent (*compadresco*) tie. Power, once more up for grabs and diffused throughout society, has been increasingly the province of the metropolis and the Latin American elite.

But even the elite itself has not been free from the strictures of the metropolis. Both Blackburn for Cuba, and Locker and Goff for the Dominican Republic point out the increasing dependency of the Latin American elite, politically and economically, on the Colossus of the North. While the elite now has more tools of power at its disposal (more modern armies, advisory agencies, foreign credits, etc.), all these tools are increasingly mortgaged to the United States. This growing dependence, in its extreme form, has even led the elites to become a minor parody of their North American counterparts in a social sense, marked by elaborate consumption of luxury items manufactured in the United States. Far from being a model of some traditional aristocracy, much less a national bourgeoisie, the Latin American elite are a dependent class of power brokers between American imperialism on the one hand and the

Latin American masses on the other. The metropolis, for its part, does not even seem to trust the initiative and autonomy of the Latin American elite very far, and seems to assume more and more of the functions of government at the elite's expense.

Our second major focus on change in Latin American political organization concerns the increasingly tight connection between the metropolitan and Latin American elites in economic terms. In our briefing on Latin America, it was noted that Latin America is hardly devoid of modern industry and commerce. One can find immensely costly and sophisticated industries (oil in Venezuela, steel in Brazil), some proliferation of consumer goods, particularly in cities, and complex banking and credit institutions in any Latin American country. Since World War II there has been a noted increase in all these areas throughout the continent.

Yet as we also pointed out earlier, this development is by no means uniform; if anything, the new businesses have tended to be centered in a few places, and many displace far more people from older forms of economy than they can provide for. As Halpern indicates, the spread of new forms of commerce and industry may actually sharpen, rather than eliminate, the already sharp contrast between hinterland and metropolis, between city and countryside. It may also serve to bring the problems of a dying countryside into the cities in the forms of burgeoning shantytowns bursting with people who can find no gainful employment within the confines of the new economies.

Not everyone is losing his means of livelihood in Latin America, however; the elite seems to be much more prosperous than ever before, and elements of the middle sectors in the cities have made some salary gains and achieved the ability to consume. What is the shape of this prosperity, and what are its terms and conditions? For the elite prosperity seems to be based on their partnership with the metropolis in the financial, rather than the productive, aspects of this development. The scope of the new economy, in both technological and financial terms, has long ago outstripped the capacity of the Latin American elite to implement it on its own, even if it had the political autonomy to do so (or even the inclination). Even in the agrarian sector, much less costly than the industrial, we can note from Blackburn and Goff and Locker the technical and financial complexities involved in running plantations on small Caribbean island societies.

That the Latin American elite holds property titles to quite diverse enterprises should not obscure the fact that credit manipulation and control is essential for this diversity and also as a weapon to use against non-conforming elements of any would-be national bourgeoisie. The anthropologist François Bourricaud, writing of the Peruvian elite, states:

The oligarch's first aim is the control of a sector of which he can be the master, the *patrón*. From this strategic position, which is a necessary course (distribution of credit, or more generally of favors and privileges of all kinds), he lies in ambush to draw his tribute. His whole art consists in making himself unavoidable.[3]

Such a statement has wide application generally in Latin America as well.

The elite, then, is by no means traditional, but fully incorporated into the mainstream of international capitalism on the level of high finance, albeit as a junior partner to its counterparts in the more developed countries. The anti-traditionalism of the elite extends to everything but some elements of life style; it is sharply focused, popular opinion to the contrary, on a rationalization of the economic and social order on the terms of the two elites—the metropolitan and the Latin American. To implement rationalization, cost accounting in productivity is a large factor, and wages and personnel must be kept at a minimum to maximize profit. That means that there simply is not enough room for all of the job seekers to find full-time employment, because there is not enough of a new economy to provide the jobs. Nor can there be any guarantee that the economy will develop with national interests like full employment as a goal, because the economy is geared to metropolitan demands and sanctions. Herein lies the dilemma of the Latin American elite: as economic development of a *restrictive* nature increases, the divorce between elites and masses becomes more absolute.

Finally, we must look at changes which are occurring in the masses themselves, as their conditions of life are undergoing the greatest transformation of all. Having been progressively left in the lurch by changes which they did not initiate, increasingly defined outside of the existing structure of opportunity, and progressively stripped of upper-class patronage, they appear to be developing their own methods of dealing with crisis. The Cuban and, to a lesser extent, the Mexican revolutions have demonstrated that popular revolution is not impossible in Latin America.

3. François Bourricaud, *Structure and Function of the Peruvian Oligarchy*, Comparative Studies in International Development No. 2, Washington University, St. Louis, 1966, pp. 23-24.

Identification of Che Guevara as a member of a guerrilla band operating in Bolivia. Guevara was killed and his band dispersed in 1967 by Bolivian rangers operating with advice and training by United States agencies. (Wide World Photos)

Indeed, the possibility for them seems to grow in direct proportion with the inability of the elites to find a place for the masses in the institutional matrix of the new society. The Cuban experience shows that the masses may come to view the elites in much the same way, although excluded from a different matrix.

But the road to revolution is not a simple linear path, nor is it inevitable that popular forces will everywhere win the day and usher in the new society. Latin America is also a continent of failed revolutions, of revolutions betrayed or aborted. Fuentes' analysis of the Mexican revolution provides one example of this failure: less spectacular failures have occurred in Guatemala in 1954 and in Bolivia, where a revolutionary government of fourteen years was overthrown by a military *golpe*. Recently in Peru and Brazil peasant leagues gained momentum early, then ebbed and waned as the repression intensified. From 1948 onward peasant violence in Colombia has cost a quarter of a million deaths by conservative estimate, yet the oligarchy has not tumbled from power. Nor has the peasantry of that country been molded into a genuinely revolutionary force. Even the guerrilla war of the out-country is no surefire route to success; witness the demise of Che Guevara, in the jungles of Bolivia, killed, with a handful of companions for lack of peasant support, by the army.

Yet the key to the issue of revolution versus elimination must be provided by the masses themselves, and with those alienated sections of the urban middle classes which produce Castros and Guevaras as well as status-seeking consumers. It is precisely this combination that made Cuba possible, and provided an alternative image of what the human condition in Latin America could be like tomorrow.

Bibliographical Notes

For readers who either wish to pursue given topics further or to consult the original sources cited in our work, we have compiled a short annotated bibliography for each section. Selections appearing in the text are marked with an asterisk.

1. BRIEFING ON LATIN AMERICA. For those unfamiliar with the over-all economic and political geography of Latin America, we recommend R. Kingsbury and R. Schneider, *An Atlas of Latin American Affairs,* Praeger, N.Y., 1965. The historical dimensions underlying the economic and political geography of the continent are highlighted in S. and B. Stein's excellent short book *The Colonial Heritage of Latin America,* Oxford University Press, N.Y., 1970.

In order to understand the economic structure of Latin America, it is necessary to understand the relationship of Latin American economies to those of overseas metropolises. Particularly helpful in this respect are: R. N. Adams' *The Second Sowing,* Chandler, San Francisco, 1967; A. Gunder Frank, *Capitalism and Underdevelopment in Latin America,* Monthly Review Press, N.Y., 1967; D. Chalmers, "Developing on the Periphery: External Factors in Latin American Politics," in J. N. Rosenau (ed.), *Linkage Politics,* Macmillan, N.Y., 1969; M. Halperin, "Latin America in Transition," in *Science and Society,* Vol. XX, No. 4, 1956 pp. 290-319, and M. Halperin, "Growth and Crisis in the Latin American Economy," in *Science and Society,* Vol. XXV, No. 3, 1961, pp. 195-228.

2. INDIANS AND EUROPEANS. The nature of early contacts between colonizers and Indians was shaped to a considerable degree by the varied nature of the Indian populations themselves. The developmental levels of Indian cultures at the time of colonization ranged from simple hunting and fishing cultures in Patagonia to the densely populated states of the Inca and Aztec. A straightforward summary of the results of these contacts is provided by E. R. Service, "Indian-European Relations in Colonial Latin America" in *American Anthropologist,* Vol. 57, No. 3, American Anthropological Association, Menasha,

Wisc., 1955, pp. 411-25. An account of the intricate history of these relationships from colonial times to the present for Mexico and Guatemala is E. R. Wolf, *Sons of the Shaking Earth*, University of Chicago Press, 1959.

In our presentation we have relied on the accounts of actual participants in these early contacts, drawing from the following sources: H. Staden, *The True Story of His Captivity,* translated and edited by Malcolm Letts, George Routledge and Sons, London, 1928; P. de Cieza de León, "The Travels of Pedro de Cieza de León A.D. 1532-50," contained in the second part of his *Chronicle of Peru,* translated and edited with notes and an introduction by Clements R. Markham, Hakluyt Society, Second Series, No. 68, London, 1864; A. de Zorita, *Life and Labor in Ancient Mexico: The Brief and Summary Relation of the Lords of New Spain,* translated and with an introduction by Benjamin Keen, Rutgers University Press, New Brunswick, N.J., 1963.

Ethnographic descriptions of present-day Latin American Indian cultures can be found in J. H. Steward (ed.), *Handbook of South American Indians*, Bureau of American Ethnology Bulletin 143, Washington, D.C., 7 vols., 1946-59; and R. Wauchope, ed., *Handbook of Middle American Indians*, vols. 6-8, University of Texas Press, Austin, 1967-69.

3. COMMUNITIES. Here we are concerned with the varied forms of rural communities in Latin America, with particular emphasis on the networks of social relationships that exist within communities, and also those relationships that link communities with larger socio-political entities. Among the general works that provide a synthesis of these relationships are: E. R. Wolf, *Peasants*, Prentice Hall, Englewood Cliffs, N.J. 1966; E. R. Wolf, "Types of Latin American Peasantries: A Preliminary Discussion," in *American Anthropologist*, Vol. 57, No. 3, 1955, pp. 452-71; R. Stavenhagen, "Classes, Colonialism, and Acculturation," in I. L. Horowitz (ed.), *Masses in Latin America*, Oxford University Press, N.Y., 1970, pp. 235-88.

The emphasis on this section lies on materials drawn from ethnographic accounts of communities and relationships. While there are many good descriptive acounts of rural communities in Latin America, we found the following particularly useful in our preparation: G. and A. Reichel-Dolmatoff, *The People of Aritama*, University of Chicago Press, 1961; M. Harris, *Town and Country in Rural Brazil*, Columbia University Press, N.Y., 1956; R. N. Adams, *A Community in the Andes*, University of Washington Press, Seattle, 1959; G. Foster, *Tzintzuntzan*, Little Brown, Boston, 1967; N. Whitten, *Class, Kinship and Power in an Ecuadorian Town*, Stanford University Press, 1965; W. Stein, *Hualcan* * Cornell University Press, 1961; C. Wagley, *Amazon Town,* Macmillan, N.Y., 1953; R. Murphy, "Credit Versus Cash: A Case Study,"* in *Human Organization*, Vol. 14, No. 3, Fall 1955, Society for Applied Anthropology, Washington, D.C., pp. 26-28; O. Fals Borda, *Peasant Society in the Columbian Andes: A Sociological Study of Saucío,* University of Florida Press, 1955.

Culture and personality aspects of these relationships are examined in G. Freyre, *The Masters and the Slaves,* A. A. Knopf, N.Y., 1946; and O. Paz, *The Labyrinth of Solitude*, Grove Press, N.Y., 1963.

4. THE ROLE OF RELIGION. Much of the literature on religion in Latin America is concerned with popular aspects of Catholicism rather than the formal organization of the Church itself. The literature on religious practices of poor peoples is emphasized at the expense of information on the religious practices of elite groups. This bias has carried over into our own work. Apart from citations from Wagley, Stein, and Paz, all *op. cit.*, the following works examine facets of popular Catholicism: E. da Cunha, *Rebellion in the Backlands*, translated by S. Putnam, University of Chicago Press, 1944; R. della Cava, *Miracle at Joaseiro*, Columbia University Press, N.Y., 1970," D. Gross, "Ritual and Conformity: A Religious Pilgrimage to Northeast Brazil," in *Ethnology*, Vol. X, No. 2, 1971, pp. 129-48; T. de Azevedo, "Popular Catholicism in Brazil: Typology and Functions," in R. S. Sayers (ed.), *Portugal and Brazil in Transition*, University of Minnesota Press, 1968, pp. 175-81.

Popular Catholicism is not the only form of religious expression in Latin America; there are many other forms of folk religion, and recently parts of Brazil have seen an upsurge of Protestant Pentecostalism. This latter phenomenon has been studied by Emilo Willems in *Followers of the New Faith*, Vanderbilt University Press, 1967.

The relationship of the Catholic Church to social change in Latin America has recently been dealt with by E. de Kadt in *Catholic Radicals in Brazil*, *R.I.I.A.*, Oxford University Press, London, 1970, and also in his article "Religion, the Church and Social Change in Brazil," in C. Veliz (ed.), *The Politics of Conformity in Latin America*, Oxford University Press, N.Y. 1967.

5. THE HUMAN SIDE OF THE ENCLAVE ECONOMY. Just as the sort of economies found in Latin America vary widely, so do the webs of social relationships which articulate these economies. Our selections have attempted to locate the human component in these economic systems; additional works suggested below were picked by using the same criterion.

Materials which exemplify the penetration of ancillary variants of modern capitalism can be found in many of the works already cited in Section III. Particularly relevant are Wagley (store keeping in the Amazon), Foster (debtors and creditors in a Mexican village), and Murphy (rubber tappers and traders in the Amazon). For a good discussion of the arrival of modern commerce in traditional Indian areas, see R. Waterbury, "Urbanization and a Traditional Market System," in W. Goldschmidt and H. Hoijer (eds.), *The Social Anthropology of Latin America*, Latin America Center, UCLA, 1970, pp. 126-53; and M. Nash, *Machine Age Maya*, American Anthropological Association Memoir 87, Menasha, Wisconsin, 1958.

Latin America has seen many forms of large estates throughout its history, ranging from the slave plantations of colonial Brazil and the Caribbean to the cattle ranches of Southern Brazil to the highly mechanized sugar plantations of Cuba and the Dominican Republic. Particularly useful for our discussions of these estates have been J. A. B. Beaumont, *Travels in Buenos Ayres and The Adjacent Provinces of The Rio de la Plata*,* James Ridgway, London, 1882; G. Freyre,* *op. cit.*; C. Jayawardena, *Conflict and Solidarity on a Guianese Plantation*, Athlone, London, 1963; S. Stein, *Vassouras*, Harvard Uni-

362   BIBLIOGRAPHICAL NOTES

versity Press, Cambridge, 1957; E. R. Wolf, op. cit., 1959; F. Ortiz, Cuban Counterpoint: Tobacco and Sugar, Random House, N.Y., 1970; E. Williams, Capitalism and Slavery, Capricorn, N.Y., 1966; J. Steward, et al., The Peoples of Puerto Rico, University of Illinois Press, 1956.

In addition to these monographic accounts, many novels portray life on large estates, two of which are: J. Guimarães Rosa, The Devil To Pay in the Backlands, A. A. Knopf, N.Y., 1963; and J. Amado, The Violent Land, translated by S. Putnam, A. A. Knopf, 1965.

Dimensions of the industrial growth of Latin America are provided by T. Cochran and R. Reina, Entrepreneurship in Argentine Culture, University of Pennsylvania Press, 1962; W. Dean, The Industrialization of São Paulo, 1881-1946, University of Texas Press, 1970.

In the past decade there has been an enormous growth of literature on facets of city life in Latin America. While much of the literature has concentrated on the spectacular growth of shantytowns in major Latin American cities, there are some general works about the evolution of urban life. These works are reviewed in some detail by R. M. Morse in his "Recent Research in Latin American Urbanization: A Selective Survey with Commentary," in Latin American Research Review Vol. I, 1965, pp. 35-74.

Among the many recent works on the shantytowns are: W. Mangin, "Latin American Squatter Settlements: A Problem and a Solution" in Latin American Research Review, Vol. II, No. 3, pp. 65- ; Andrew Pearse, "Some Characteristics of the Urbanization of Rio de Janeiro,"* in P. Hauser (ed.), Urbanization in Latin America, UNESCO, N.Y., 1959, pp. 141-205; T. Ray, Politics of the Barrios of Venezuela, University of California Press, 1969; W. Mangin, "Urbanization: A Case History in Peru,"* in Architectural Design, Aug. 1963; L. Peattie, The View from the Barrio, University of Michigan Press, 1968.

Diverse aspects of urban social relationships are discussed in A. Leeds, "Brazilian Careers and Social Structure," in American Anthropologist, Vol. LXVI, 1964, pp. 1321-47; A. Strickon, "Class and Kinship in Argentina," Ethnology, Vol. I, pp. 500-515; F. Pike, "Aspects of Class Relations in Chile, 1880-1960," in J. Petras and M. Zeitlin (eds.), Latin America: Reform or Revolution, Fawcett, N.Y., 1968, pp. 202-19; E. R. Wolf, "Aspects of Group Relations in a Complex Society," in American Anthropologist, Vol. LVIII, 1956, pp. 1065-78; S. W. Mintz and E. R. Wolf, "An Analysis of Ritual Coparenthood (Compadrazgo)," in Southwestern Journal of Anthropology, Vol. VI, 1950, pp. 341-68.

The present state of the literature on the rise of the middle classes can be characterized as more polemical than substantive; there are many thoretical perspectives, but little systematic relationship between theory and empirical data. Some of the range of opinion can be sampled by consulting the following works: J. Nun, "A Latin American Phenomenon; The Middle Class Military Coup" in Petras and Zeitlin, op. cit., pp. 145-85; R. N. Adams, "Political Power and Social Structure," in C. Véliz (ed.), The Politics of Conformity in Latin America, Oxford University Press, N.Y., 1970, pp. 15-42; S. M. Lipset, "Values, Education and Entrepreneurship," in S. M. Lipset and A. Solari (eds.), Elites in Latin America, Oxford University Press, N.Y., 1968, pp. 3-60;

J. Johnson, *Political Change in Latin America—The Emergence of the Middle Sectors,* Stanford University Press, 1958; L. Ratinoff, "The New Urban Groups: The Middle Classes," in Lipset and Solari, *op. cit.,* pp. 61-93.

6. POLITICS. During the past decade or so there has been a great florescence of the study of politics in contemporary Latin America. In the past few years many articles have been reissued in paperback editions in anthology form. In our view, the following compilations are very useful for understanding the human side of politics in Latin America. Petras and Zeitlin, *op. cit.,* C. Véliz, *op. cit.,* C. Véliz, *Obstacles to Change in Latin America,* Oxford University Press, N.Y., 1968; R. Stavenhagen, *Agrarian Problems and Peasant Movements in Latin America,* Doubleday, Garden City, N.Y., 1970; I. L. Horowitz, J. de Castro, and J. Gerassi, *Latin American Radicalism: A Documentary Report on Left and Nationalist Movements,* Random House, N.Y., 1969; I. L. Horowitz (ed.), *Masses in Latin America,* Oxford University Press, N.Y., 1970.

For our discussion of the *caudillo* period we have used D. F. Sarmiento, *Life in the Argentine Republic in the Days of Tyrants: Or Civilization and Barbarism,** translated by Mrs. Horace Mann, New York, 1968; and E. R. Wolf and E. C. Hansen, "*Caudillo* Politics: A Structural Analysis," in *Comparative Studies in Society and History,* Vol. IX, 1967, pp. 168-79.

Violence and militarism are dealt with in W. Stokes, "Violence as a Power Factor in Latin American Politics,"* in *Western Political Quarterly,* Vol. 3, 1952, pp. 445-68; R. Schneider, *The Political System of Brazil,** Columbia University Press, 1971; A. Steppan, *The Military in Politics: Changing Patterns in Brazil,* Princeton University Press, 1971; and E. P. Gonzalo Briceño Zevallos, "A Description of the Seizure of Power in 1962," in P. Sigmund (ed.), *Models of Political Change in Latin American,* Praeger, N.Y., 1970, pp. 190-93.

Literature on the Latin American elites and oligarchies is relatively rare, especially if compared to information on the masses. Detailed studies on the connections of the Latin American elties to their metropolitan counterparts is at a minimum. Some studies which throw light on this area are: F. Goff and M. Locker, "The Violence of Domination: U.S. Power and the Dominican Republic," in Horowitz, *et al., op. cit.,** pp. 249-91; F. Bourricaud, "Structure and Function of the Peruvian Oligarchy," *Studies in Comparative International Development,* No. 2, Washington University, St. Louis, 1966; F. Borricaud, *Power and Society in Contemporary Peru,* Praeger, N.Y., 1970; Dean, *op. cit.;* J. Imaz, *Los que Mandan,* Editorial universitaria de Buenos Aires, Buenos Aires, 1964; J. Imaz, *La Alta Clase de Buenos Aires,* Investigaciones y Trabajos del Instituto de Sociología, Universidad de Buenos Aires, Buenos Aires, 1962; R. Blackburn, "Prologue to the Cuban Revolution,"* in *New Left Review,* Vol. 21, pp. 52-92.

The currents of revolution have been discussed in many of the anthologies listed at the beginning of this section. For Mexico, we found the following particularly useful: E. R. Wolf, *Peasant Wars of the Twentieth Century,* Chapter 1, Mexico, Harper & Row, 1969, pp. 3-50; J. Womack, Jr., *Zapata and the Mexican Revolution,* A. A. Knopf, N.Y., 1969; C. Fuentes, "Viva Zapata,"* *New York Review of Books,* March 13, 1969, pp. 5-11. For Cuba, insights came from J. Yglesias, *In the Fist of the Revolution,** Random House, N.Y., 1968; Blackburn, *op. cit.;* Wolf, *op. cit.,* 1969, pp. 251-75; K. S. Karol, *Guerrillas in Power,* Hill and Wang, 1970; E. Boorstein, *The Transformation of the Cuban Economy,* Monthly Review Press, N.Y., 1968; R. Debray, *Revolution within the Revolution,* Grove Press, N.Y., 1968.

Index

Valasco Ibarra, José Maria, 237
Vargas, Getulio, 246-60
Vekemans, Father Roger, 117
Veliz, Claudio, 198, 311
Vespucci, Americus, 3
Venezuela (origins of caudillo politics in), 216-23
Vientimilla, Mariano Suarez, 237
Villa, Pancho, 300, 302
Villarroel, President Gualberto, 234
violence (in politics), 225-42
Viqueira, Carmen, 95, 99

Wagley, Charles, 102, 126-27, 132
Wolf, Eric R., 113
Womack, John Jr., 296, 298-300, 303
Whyte, William F., 109, 110, 159

Yglesias, José, 338

Zapata, Emiliano, 297-98, 299-307
Zorita, Alfonso de, 40